Language, Communication, and Rhetoric in Black America

Under the Advisory Editorship of J. Jeffery Auer

Language, Communication, and Rhetoric in Black America

ARTHUR L. SMITH

University of California, Los Angeles

HARPER & ROW, Publishers

New York, Evanston, San Francisco, London

Contents

Preface

This is a book about the communicative experiences of black Americans. The articles included in it are extensive in scope, reflecting several disciplines, and representing nearly every aspect of the language behavior of blacks. Recognizing the need for an overview of the subject, the author examined every significant essay on black communication. From these has been chosen a wide range of investigative and critical essays that have informed the popular and academic discussions of language and communication in black America. The articles represented in this volume have been subjected to the critical eye of several speech scholars and have been reprinted here exactly as they appeared in the original unless otherwise indicated in the text.

Black Americans are essentially an oral people much like their African ancestors who found the expressive word to be the basis of society. In African society the alkali *or elder who kept the history and traditions in his head was among the most revered of the community. In black American communities the* alkali *could be anyone of several persons, from the preacher to the street-corner player of the dozens. What is important in this context is that orality has been preserved, and any real understanding of black history or sociology must begin with an examination of the place of language and commuincation in black society.*

Such an approach must begin with the questions of structure and grammar that relate to black dialect. The work of William Labov, Orlando Taylor, Joan Baratz, and William Stewart has greatly influenced the directions of research on black dialect. But we cannot stop with linguistic and grammatical analyses, which are physical, but must also consider black language as a social phenomenon. Pattern and structure say little about the function of language in a social context, and therefore we have chosen articles with linguistic and social content.

We have also wanted to know how black ethnic identity is used in black language. Inasmuch as language is culturally based, the use of language provides some understanding of the patterns of sociation among black Americans.

Communicologists and rhetoricians have recently begun to make careful study of the various language artifacts used by black Americans. But no systematic presentation of their endeavors has heretofore appeared. While the seminal work of Melville Herskovits and Lorenzo Turner suggested broad outlines in the realm of African survivals in Afro-American language, scholars have just now turned their attention to the intricacies of black rhetoric and communication. And with this interest has come a full investigation covering language acquisition, modes of persuasion, stylistic elaborations, and social and historical perspectives of black oratory. Emerging from this dialogue on language and communication in black America is a reconceptualization of the function of speech for blacks. In a larger sense, the research essays included in this volume have informed the field of speech itself. Thus a theory of language and rhetoric which does not take the uniqueness of black language behavior into consideration is hardly valid in the light of the work presented in this volume.

Several questions can be raised concerning the black communicative experience. How language comes to be used is one question, but another more basic consideration is how have blacks utilized whatever language they have acquired? An underlying premise is that blacks in America have developed peculiar modes of inventing and organizing language and communication. This book, recognizing the ubiquity of the word among blacks, addresses the whole expanse of language in the black experience covering the controversy over black and white dialect to critical and theoretical essays on the social significance of rhetoric. The structure of the book is based upon the ideas mentioned in this preface.

Acknowledgments are due to J. Jeffrey Auer, general editor of Harper's speech series for his support, encouragement and directions; and to Karen Borden, graduate student and research assistant at the University of California, Los Angeles, who read the manuscript and made valuable suggestions.

ARTHUR L. SMITH

PART 1
Black Language

This book begins with the provocative question raised by Joan C. Baratz "Should black children learn white dialect?" In recent times no controversy surrounding Afro-American behavior has raged more furiously than this issue. As it says something about the structure of society, and further still, the ultimate making of the black adult, it is a subject worthy of investigation. Whether the reader agrees or disagrees with Joan Baratz's conclusions, that her position is succinctly stated is irrefutable. Writing at a time when many Americans thought we were on the threshold of racial justice, Gordon C. Green argued that the so-called

"Negro Dialect" was the last barrier to integration. This controversial view has been questioned many times since, but Green's essay stands as one of the first ones on the social significance of black dialect. Frederick David Erickson tries to enlarge our perspective on black dialect by looking at its use in the elementary school. In the last article Walt Wolfram provides us with some basic viewpoints in the discussion on black language. His essay "Sociolinguistic Premises and the Nature of Nonstandard Dialects" is both provocative and highly informative. Thus this section includes a cross section of articles designed to provide the reader with a comprehensive view.

Joan C. Baratz

CHAPTER 1
Should Black Children
Learn White Dialect?

Should black children learn white dialect? No. Should black children be taught standard English? Yes.

Standardization is a socio-linguistic fact of life. Societies are socially stratified—be the organization by clan, tribe, or nation-state. We might wish for complex, socially stratified societies where the spectrum of standard language included under the heading of *standard* all the different grammars and usages of speakers of the many varieties of that language. Sad to say, human behavior

From *ASHA*, Vol. 12, No. 9 (September 1970), pp. 415–417. Reprinted by permission of the American Speech and Hearing Association and the author. Joan C. Baratz, Ph.D., is on the staff at the Education Study Center, 711 14th Street, N.W., Washington, D.C.

doesn't operate like that. To date, wherever research has been done—in Europe, Asia, and Africa—one variety of a language invariably becomes the standard. Grammar books are written in it; its orthography is established. It is studied by the populace in school. Language standardization is a universal aspect of language variation in a national context, particularly when literacy is involved. There is standard English, standard German, standard (literary) Arabic, standard Yoruba, and standard Hausa. Standardization is not a political invention of racist whites.

WHAT IS STANDARD ENGLISH?

Opponents of teaching standard English to black children do not understand language standardization. They falsely assume that the standardization of English in America is a white plot to exploit the Negro, rob him of his heritage, and deny his language.

Those who argue against teaching standard English dialect to black children confuse learning standard English with "talking like a honky." By standard English I mean that dialect which uses a set of grammatical patterns in oral production that are similar to those used in the written form of the language. A black child might be taught standard English from a frame of reference widespread in the black community of "talkin' proper." Talking proper refers to language usage that generally conforms to the rules of standard English grammar, but may or may not be ethnically marked in its phonology. For example, a black individual talking "proper" might say "He asked for something to write with" or "He aks fo' somethin' to wri' wif."

Within the black community, "talking proper" is contrasted with "talkin' country" or "talkin' bad," which refers to nonstandard varieties of black English (Mitchell, 1969). Although black speakers may use adjective reversal, e.g., "He a bad (usually drawn out vowel) cat," to mean on occasion the positive "He's a great guy," "talkin' bad" is not used in this way. In the black community "talkin' bad" means speaking a Negro nonstandard dialect. By Negro nonstandard dialect (sometimes referred to as black English) I mean the use of a set of distinctive grammar patterns that are not in conformity with the written forms of English (excluding such art forms as the use of Negro nonstandard dialect or other dialects in poetry and in dialogues) and which are used by a large portion of the black community.[1] Talking bad is important for in-group solidarity and, indeed, talking proper in an all black social group may be seen as "putting on airs." Nonetheless, the community has a concept of standard English that is carried in the notion "talking proper."

THE OPPOSITION

Those who oppose teaching standard English often claim that the parents don't want it. But most black parents insist that they want their children to learn to read and write and talk proper. Indeed, the problem is not so much that parents don't want their children to learn standard English; on the contrary, they are often so anxious to have their children learn "proper English" that they do not want Negro nonstandard dialect in the classroom —even if it is the best way to achieve competence in speaking, reading, and writing standard English.

Another frequent argument of those who object to teaching standard English to black children who speak only Negro nonstandard is that "the black man always is the one who has to change." Again, I submit that this admits to the erroneous notion that to learn another dialect or linguistic system means to change one's original system. I insist that teachers who wish to teach standard English to Negro nonstandard speakers learn their students' dialect. In the process the teacher sees that acquiring an additional linguistic system does not change the initial dialect system. The notion that learning an additional system means eradication and replacement of the existing system is completely false; just as one does not change or forget one's native language by learning a foreign language, he does not necessarily forget his first dialect when he learns a second.

Another argument presented by opponents of teaching standard English contends that Negro nonstandard dialect and standard English are mutually intelligible, therefore a nonstandard speaker need not learn standard English. I would submit that claim to empirical test. Mitchell's "unhesitating opinion" (1969) that the two systems are mutually intelligible is based on the scanty data of Labov (1968), Baratz (1969), and on her own data on sentence repetition. Such tests are hardly measures of mutual intelligibility except in the loosest sense. At present we do not know the extent of presumed mutual intelligibility, especially at the primary school level where reading and writing skills are introduced in standard English. Indeed, the failure of children in such programs to acquire reading and writing skills in standard English may in part be a testament to the lack of mutual intelligibility of the two systems for the young Negro nonstandard speaking child.

The final frequent argument against teaching standard English crassly dismisses the truism that economic ability is dependent upon acquisition of standard English skills. Thus, opponents of teaching standard English argue lack of economic mobility in the black community is the result of white oppression (failure to hire blacks)—not the result of blacks' ignorance of standard English. In addition, they argue, knowledge of standard English does not automatically grant black mobility within the white power structure. Knowledge of standard English is not a guarantee of job mobility, and discrimination has played a large role in the economic disadvantage of blacks; nevertheless, access to white collar and professional jobs is dependent upon knowledge of standard English both within and outside the black community.

EDUCATIONAL REALITY

The arguments against teaching standard English to black Negro nonstandard speakers cannot stand up to linguistic and social reality. The issue is not political; it is educational. Essentially our discussion asks: What is to be the language arts program in public education for black children who are monodialectal speakers of Negro nonstandard English? Whatever the political situation—separation or integration—we are ultimately faced with the question of language learning. Separatism in this country, if effected tomorrow, would do little to solve the language problems of black Negro nonstandard speaking children. What language would a black America use to sign a treaty with white America, and to conduct its other national and international affairs? Standard English? Negro nonstandard? Swahili? Whatever its language, this state would still confront the educational problems of teaching its citizens to read, write, and speak its national tongue. If the new nation chose standard English, as would be likely, the problems would remain unchanged. If Negro nonstandard were chosen, it would have the additional problems of producing an orthography for that language and developing grammar books and printing texts for reading, science, social studies, physics, etc., in Negro nonstandard. (In other words, it would have to "standardize" Negro nonstandard English.) It would also have to teach Negro nonstandard to all black speakers of standard English. Or if Swahili were chosen, the educators in the new state would be faced with the problem of teaching the entire nation to read, write, and speak Swahili. Whatever the politics, a language teaching problem remains—as can be seen by the language situation in newly independent African states.

We do not, however, at present have a separate state, and it is very unlikely that we ever will. What then are the language factors involved in educating black children in white America?

It is, I believe, the desire of black parents that their children learn standard English. A minority voice in the white liberal establishment and the middle class "militants" who already speak standard English argues against teaching standard English. But, the black parent wants "in" to the existing system and, therefore, wants his child to be educated to function in that system.

One can learn a second dialect without destroying one's culture and identity (e.g., witness experiences with Swiss-German dialect and standard German). Economic mobility is partially dependent on such knowledge. Yet, there is an even more important reason why children should be taught oral standard English: competence in reading and writing standard English (which everybody agrees is important) is highly dependent on oral language skills.

LINGUISTIC INTERFERENCE

One cannot overemphasize the relationship between the oral and the written language system. Although there are stylistic differences in standard speech as compared with the more formal written system, the grammar in both the written and oral forms of standard English is essentially the same. The black child who speaks Negro nonstandard English still must learn to read and write standard English. If he is not taught oral standard English, his difficulties with the written system are compounded by linguistic interference. His knowledge of Negro nonstandard will interfere with his written performance in standard English.

Linguistic interference—knowledge of one linguistic system interfering with performance in another linguistic system—is well documented. The development of the contrastive grammar technique in second language teaching is aimed precisely at eliminating the linguistic interference of the primary language system during the acquisition of a second system.

The educational literature on written skills of Negro children clearly illustrates the interference of black nonstandard English on performance in standard English. Contrary to the educational interpretation of that literature, their "mistakes" are not random errors but occur precisely at those points where standard English and Negro nonstandard English diverge. Thus, teachers make lists saying that their students overuse *be*, or overuse *do* (*be* takes *do* in the interrogative "He be working"—"Do he be working!"), use double negatives, fail to mark the plural, fail to use auxiliary verbs, fail to mark the possessive, use double subjects, and fail to mark the past (Loban, 1963).

Interference from black English on standard English is most evident in oral language performance, the predominant area of the language arts curriculum in which speech specialists have worked. An experiment with third and fifth grade inner city black children demonstrated that knowledge of one system (standard or black English) will invariably interfere with regenerating sentences in another system (black English or standard English). The children in this study were asked to render sentences in both standard and black English. The city children were predominantly black English speakers whereas the suburban children were all monodialectal standard English speakers. When asked to repeat the standard English utterance, "I asked Tom if he wanted to go to the picture at the Howard," 97% of the black children responded with "I aks Tom did he wanna go to the picture at the Howard." In response to "Does Deborah like to play with the girl that sits next to her in school?" 60% of the black children responded "Do Deborah like to play with the girl what sit next to her in school?" On the other hand, when white suburban children were asked to regenerate the black English sentence "I aks Tom do he wanna go to the picture that be playin' at the Howard," 78% said "I asked Tom if he wanted to go to the picture that was playing at the Howard." When asked to repeat "Do Deborah like to play wif the girl what sit next to her at school," 68% of the white suburbanites responded with "Does Deborah like to play with the girl that sits next to her at school?" (Baratz, 1969).

Linguistic interference becomes a major problem to the black child when he learns to read. Without knowledge of standard English, the black child, when confronted with the printed page, is actually given two jobs instead of one. He must not only decode the little black marks on the page but he must also translate them into black English as well. Only then can he make sense out of the material. But how can he translate if he hasn't been taught standard English? The enormous reading failure of low income black children (the overwhelming majority of whom speak Negro nonstandard English) is a testament to their quandary and their need to learn standard English. One can deal with the black child's lack of knowledge of standard English by teaching him first to read in his dialect and then, with the aid of transition texts that teach him the difference between his dialect and standard English, shift to standard English texts. We are doing just that at the Education Study Center. But, in the process of teaching him to read standard English, we are also teaching him to speak standard English.

Standard English is the *lingua franca* of the mainstream in America. If the black child is to participate and compete in that mainstream, he must be able to read, write, and speak standard English. If he wishes to opt out of the mainstream and not use these skills, that's his choice; he can make it. If, however, he does not learn these skills, he cannot "choose" to opt out. He is automatically excluded. We educators must provide the child with the tools of proficiency in reading, writing, and speaking standard English so that then he can choose to use or not use these tools.

NOTE

1 Although there are many features in black nonstandard English that are also present in other nonstandard dialects and in standard English, there are also many features that are not shared. The thing that makes black nonstandard English a distinct dialect is the sum total of its features, whether shared with other dialects or not.

SELECTED READINGS

Baratz, J. A bi-dialectal task for determining language proficiency in economically disadvantaged Negro children. *Child Development*, 40, 889–901 (1969).

Baratz, J. Teaching reading in an urban Negro school. In J. Baratz and R. Shuy. *Teaching Black Children to Read*, Center for Applied Linguistics, Washington, D.C. (1969).

Labov, W. A study of the nonstandard English of Negro and Puerto Rican speakers in New York City. Coop. Res. Proj. #3288, Vol. I, U.S. Office of Education (1968).

Loban, W. The language of elementary school children. *NCTE Res. Rep. 1*, Champaign, Ill.: NCTE (1963).

Mitchell, C. Language behavior in a black urban community. Doctoral dissertation, Univ. California, Berkeley (1969).

Gordon C. Green

CHAPTER 2
Section B: Negro Dialect,
the Last Barrier to Integration

Judging a man by the color of his skin has been, to put it mildly, démodé in this country for several years. The obvious barriers such as separate lunch counters and separate schools are disappearing. The segregation of people according to skin coloring is no longer valid according to Federal law. In theory as well as in practice, the position of the segregationist is untenable; the artificial social inclosures which he has traditionally maintained are collapsing everywhere. The American Negro's fight for equal

From *The Journal of Negro Education* Vol. XXXII (Winter 1963), pp. 81–83. Reprinted by permission of the publisher. Gordon C. Green was formerly a Teacher of Speech-Drama, Dillard University.

educational opportunity on all levels of education, elementary, secondary, and college, is encouraging. It means that the handicap of inferior education, particularly in the South, will begin to disappear noticeably even in the present generation.

After these obstacles have been overcome, the one prejudice of the educated white man toward the educated colored man which may remain in this country—certainly outside the backwashes of a few rural Southern areas and outside the minds of the fanatic minority of Southern traditionalists—will be based on the American Negro's dialect. This substandard speech has persisted for many generations in all segregated communities where the American colored population has been overwhelmingly in the majority; in the South and in the large industrial cities of the North, such as Harlem in New York and the South Side in Chicago. It is this corrupt and illiterate speech, not the skin coloring, which will be the chief reminder of the slave inheritance and the American ghettos, which are associated with the Negro and are responsible for the speech sounds he produces.

Just as no one can be held accountable for where and under what circumstances he is born, no one is responsible for the speech sounds he learns in childhood. Though speech can be changed in later years through conscious effort, it remains more commonly the unconscious imitation of sounds the person makes as a baby or young child. Parents and playmates are the chief speech teachers in any community.

Unfortunately, a speaker is not aware of the sounds he himself makes. For example, a colleague with a particularly noticeable illiterate speech approached me after a meeting we'd just attended and asked me if I didn't think that the speaker we had listened to had a dialect which was unnecessary and unforgivable for a man of his education and position. His comment is understandable. A speaker never hears his own voice as others hear it. This is proved over and over in making voice recordings; the speaker does not believe that his voice is truly recorded.

The problem of the American Negro who has been reared in a segregated community is that he has a dialect which constantly reminds his listener that he is a descendant of slaves; the sounds he imitates and repeats and passes on to his children are similar to the corrupt English used by his ancestors. Without formal education and with almost no contact with their white owners, save through an overseer whose speech was almost as illiterate as their own, the African slaves did the best they could to imitate and pass on to their children the new language they only occasionally heard in standard form. Except for the house servants, the vast majority worked in the fields and communicated with each other with a substandard form of English.

Regrettably this dialect has been popularized and stereotyped by the entertainment world through the old minstrel shows and such personalities as Step-an-fetch-it, Amos 'n' Andy, and Rochester; consequently, the dialect itself is considered a joke by most Americans and anyone using such a dialect is not easily taken seriously.

That Negroes are quite capable of speaking literate English is evident from listening to television to some of Africa's new university-trained political leaders. Here in the United States there are many examples of Negroes who speak without a dialect; often these are from families who have lived in an integrated society for more than one generation.

Most American Negroes, however, continue to live in segregated conditions, either because of local segregation laws, landlord and property-owner exclusion, or by their own choice. For an individual born in such an environment, there is little possibility that he will be able to break the speech chain which goes all the way back to the first slaves brought to this country. His parents speak with a dialect; his playmates use the same sounds; so do his teachers whom he hears during the week and his minister or preacher whom he listens to on Sunday; even his Negro radio station often promotes dialect and is a force working for segregation.

This special speech, filled with colloquial expressions which have meaning only for Negroes, promotes the concept of the in-group and gives the colored man a sense of belonging, which he does not feel among whites. Perhaps after the social barriers fall, there will be more effort on the part of Negroes to discard their dialect for the more standard Southern speech or the General American speech of the educated whites. (One should also add that there are millions of whites whose speech is substandard.)

The significant point, however, is that the Negro dialect is a major part of this social barrier—just as illiterate speech is a formidable barrier among white societies. A man's skin coloring is soon forgotten in a conversation between an educated white man and an educated colored man; particularly is this true between two men with common interests. All that remains, if the colored man comes from a segregated Negro community, is a difference in speech. For the white man listening to the exotic sounds of a dialect, it suggests that the colored man comes from a very different and often inferior background from his own and that the speech belongs to that of a minority group. If the white man thinks further about it, he may be reminded that the colored man in America has had to fight the white man for equal rights and that this man actually may feel antagonistic toward him because he is a white man. The Negro dialect is an anachronism hanging on from the segregated living conditions of plantation life in pre-Civil War days.

Much has been written lately about the segregation of the Negro and the white children in the schools of New Orleans. Something has been written about the segregation of the Negro and white populations in the lunchrooms and theatres of New Orleans. Nothing has been recorded concerning what will be the final barrier to integration in this city—long after the separate drinking fountain signs are taken down—the Negro dialect. As with the Cockney in London, the Negro in New Orleans will have to learn to eliminate his substandard speech sounds or be forever segregated in the lower economic and social levels of his city.

The following substandard speech sounds are among the most common errors made by Dillard University students, the great majority of whom are colored and from the New Orleans area. Using the International Phonetic Alphabet, I transcribed the sounds from students' speeches and oral drills in several speech classes. Many of these sounds also are heard among the lower economic and social levels of the white population of New Orleans. It should be stated that while a small minority of Dillard students are free of dialect, the majority of the students make one or more of 13 typical errors:

1. Such words as poem, oil, and soil become perm, erl, serl.
2. Such words as work and girl become woik and goil.
3. Such words as uncle, hungry, until become onkle, hongry, and ontil.
4. Words as read and bread become rayed and brayed.
5. Such words as metal, little, and treaty become medal, liddle, and tready.
6. The final *d* and *t* sounds are rarely pronounced as in the words past (pass), post (pos').
7. The *d* and *t* sounds also are dropped in such words as little (lil), medal (me-al), and industry (in-usry).
8. Such words as thrust, three, them become trust, tree, dem.
9. The final *th* becomes *f* or *t* in such words as oath (oaf), both (bof or boat).
10. Words as store and door become stow and dough.
11. Distortion of the final *l* to *o* in such words as little—little becomes lidow.
12. The substitution of *i* for *e* in such words as cent, sense, men—cint, since, min.
13. The substitution of *e* for *i* in such words as thing and mint—theng, meant.

Many hours were spent recording student voices on a tape recorder and listening to the tapes. Since speech is largely an unconscious act in which the speaker never hears himself—except when his voice is recorded and played back on tape—the student quickly learns to detect substandard sounds in others while continuing to make the same mistakes in his own speech. In one semester the speech teacher can do little more to help the student than to call his attention to the substandard sounds through continual use of the tape recorder. If the student can hear the speech sounds he makes, he will be taking the first step toward changing them.

By an enormous effort on the part of the American Negro, working with tape recorders and using phonetic principles under the direction of speech teachers who are themselves—and this is very important—free from any dialect, he can break down this last and most formidable barrier to integration. The idea is new.

George Bernard Shaw wrote a play to promote and publicize his belief: train the Cockney to speak as the upper classes speak and social barriers will disappear; the Cockney will no longer be a Cockney but an accepted member of the British society. Such things as clothes, diet, and address can be changed almost overnight; these are not the things which distinguish the Cockney and exclude him from being a first class citizen. Besides a few superficial and quickly learned rules of social behavior, the real thing which sets him apart is his speech. Because of this, those born within the sound of Bow Bells in London will live and die Cockneys. There is no escape, save for the one suggested by Shaw in *Pygmalion*. Change the speech sounds a Cockney makes, said Shaw, and you change his social status.

In this country there is much that the white citizenry can do to help the American Negro gain status as a fellow citizen with equal rights and responsibilities, but there is even more that the colored man can do for himself. Besides seeing to it that his civil rights are respected, that his vote is not wasted, and that he has an equal opportunity in obtaining the best possible education, he should take special pains to see that he and his children destroy this last chain that binds him to the past, the Negro dialect.

Frederick David Erickson

CHAPTER 3
"F'get You Honky!": A New Look at Black Dialect and the School

F'GET YOU (f'géchoo), *interjec.* Black dialect phrase. Many shades
   of meaning, from "Get out of here, stupid!" through "You're
   wrong!" to an affectionate form of banter, "Aw, go on."
HONKY, HONCKY (háwnkee), *n. sing.* A white man, more especially a stupid, racist white man. Black dialect equivalent of wh.
   dial. *nigger.* Poss. der. from wh. dial. *Hunky* (from wh. dial. *Bo-
   hunk,* from stan. Eng. *Bohemian*).

Last summer I was working with a discussion group at a human
relations workshop for teachers of ghetto Black children. The

From *Elementary English* (April 1969), pp. 495–499, 517. Copyright ©
1969 by the National Council of Teachers of English. Reprinted by permission of the publisher and Frederick David Erickson. Frederick David Erickson is Professor of Education, University of Illinois, Chicago Circle Campus.

group raised the question of what to do about children who spoke non-standard English in the elementary classroom. The response of one teacher was particularly interesting. She said, "I don't believe in making a child feel self-conscious by criticizing his language in front of the other children. So when a child says, 'Teacher I ain't got no pencil,' I say, 'What did you say?' If he says it again I say, 'What did you say?' and after a few times he realizes he made a mistake." Under such circumstances, one wonders how long it took for the child to get a pencil.

Such "I'm not prejudiced, but . . ." responses are common at workshops I attend. Listening to non-standard English in the classroom seems to make teachers very uncomfortable. They seem to feel a deep responsibility to say, "Don't say ain't." One reason for this may be the tradition of resistance to linguistic pluralism which characterizes the American public school. Until recently a major function of the public school was the Americanization of immigrants. Rigid adherence to standard English in the classroom was one of the school's defensive responses to its inundation by culturally different immigrant children.

"WE HAVE MET THE ENEMY AND HE IS US"

Unfortunately another reason for the resistance of inner city teachers to non-standard dialect may be a new tradition, fostered by workshops for teachers of the "disadvantaged." People like myself—white, professorial, and research-oriented—are responsible for this new tradition. Because of us, terms such as "cultural deprivation," "sensory deprivation," and "linguistic deprivation" have become part of the professional vocabulary of teachers, and part of their folklore as well. Ironically, what began in the university as an analytic term, after being transmitted through the journal and workshop, ends in the public school faculty lounge as a "neo-stereotype." Some teachers used to say that Black ghetto children were dirty, ignorant, came from immoral homes, and couldn't learn. Now those teachers can say "the children are culturally disadvantaged and *that* is why they can't learn."

One of the most persistent neo-stereotypes I have found in working with teachers is the concept of *linguistic deprivation*. In this instance, academic writing seems to have positively reinforced the values already present in the teacher "folk culture" regarding "bad language." Research on Black dialect (with a few exceptions; notably the work of William Stewart and his colleagues at the Center for Applied Linguistics) has been conducted from a perspective of "deprivation." Many of the research designs have been constructed around prior assumptions and hypotheses regarding the "pathology" of the dialect; its inhibiting effects upon cognitive development and its inadequacy in comparison with standard English. Few research propositions have been advanced regarding the adequacy of the dialect.

The setting for much of the research has been the school, or a "school-like" experimental situation. In these settings we can see how the dialect functions (or fails to function) in tasks that *we*, the scholars, define. We do not see the dialect used in tasks defined by the people who use the dialect well. Consequently we have little idea of the effectiveness of Black dialect as it is used on its own terms in congenial settings in which it is appropriate.

THE "BERNSTEIN HYPOTHESIS" AND RECENT RESEARCH

A frame of reference which has influenced many American research designs is the one developed by Basil Bernstein, a British sociolinguist. Briefly summarized, his position is that the social class dialects of the British upper, middle and lower classes differ not just in grammar and vocabulary, but in the way the dialects convey meaning. This difference, according to Bernstein, profoundly affects the cognitive development of children.

In the lower class English dialects, the meaning of a word or phrase is not specific. Meaning is determined by the social situation in which the word or phrase is used. Since meaning is dependent upon the social situation, Bernstein terms this type of dialect a *restricted linguistic code*, or *public language*.

In contrast to the restricted code of the lower classes, the British middle and upper class speak an *elaborated linguistic code* in which the meaning of a word or phrase is quite specific. The shadings of meaning conveyed depend on precise construction of language, not on social setting. For this reason an elaborated code can be described as a *private language*.

American Black dialect and standard American English fit quite well into Bernstein's schema. For example, the Black dialect phrase "F'get You" can be classified as a restricted code utterance which "translated" into elaborated code might be, "I disagree with you and wish that you would leave before I hit you."

It is easy to see how such language differences might find expression in child rearing. A mother in the Black ghetto might say, "Boy I ma whup you . . ." while her upper middle class white counterpart in suburbia might say, "Johnny, I'd rather you don't do that just now." The suburban mother would be teaching by example the ability to use spoken language very precisely and would be fostering the cognitive development of her child.

A critical issue in educational research is whether or not the lack of use of elaborated code in the home *necessarily* limits the cognitive development of lower class children, particularly lower class Black children. The literature on the "language of the disadvantaged" suggests that this is so. This is a reasonable conclusion, if based on the assumption that the vagueness of restricted code utterances *necessarily* limits the communication of abstractions or prevents a precise categorization of experience through language.

THE "CONTEXT PRINCIPLE"
AN ADDITION TO BERNSTEIN'S SCHEMA

Bernstein's schema implies a direct relationship between social class subculture and language style. My own research in a project titled "Sounds of Society" (conducted at Northwestern University with B. J. Chandler under a grant from USOE, Project No. 6-0244) suggests that an intervening factor may exist between social class and language style. Edward T. Hall and I developed a term for this intervening factor, the "shared context principle."

This principle was identified by Edward Sapir, the anthropological linguist, in 1931:

Generally speaking, the smaller the circle and the more complex the understandings already arrived at within it, the more economical can the acts of communication afford to become. A single word passed between members of an intimate group, in spite of its apparent vagueness and ambiguity, may constitute a far more precise communication than volumes of carefully prepared correspondence interchanged between two governments.

Sapir's statement can be paraphrased in Bernstein's terminology as, "When two communicators share considerable experience and point of view, restricted linguistic code can *function as precisely* as elaborated code." The paraphrase places the relationship between subculture, language style, and cognitive style in a new perspective. It provides a framework within which research on Black dialect takes on new meaning. It suggests that while Bernstein's original schema may have descriptive and classifactory value, it may not have analytic value unless altered to include the context principle.

We can think of *shared context* as a continuum, with "high shared context" at one end and "low shared context" at the other. High context communication (restricted code) is appropriate when there is considerable overlap of experience between communicators, and low context communication (elaborated code) is appropriate when little experience is shared. As context increases the volume of necessary communication signals decreases. This is illustrated in Figure 1:

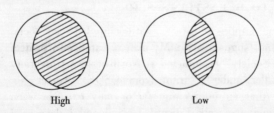

High   Low

Figure 1   Areas of High and Low Context Communication

An everyday high context communication situation would be two plumbers loosening a pipe. Plumber *A* could say to Plumber *B*, "Now!" (high context) and *B* would understand that *A* meant, "It is time for you to hand me the medium-sized pipe wrench" (low context). *A* could signal that he wanted a wrench, not a hammer, with a gesture or glance. He could even signal which wrench he wanted. The communication would be very precise, even though a restricted linguistic code was being used. Under conditions of even *higher* context (if *A* or *B* had worked together for some time) *B* would *already know* that a certain size wrench would be needed. *A* would not even need to use non-verbal signals. His "Now!" would be completely unambiguous and would communicate much faster than an elaborated code utterance.

Children in classrooms, of course, are not plumbers. In order to see the relevance of the context principle for the school it is necessary to examine a more "intellectual" setting for communication.

THE CONTEXT PRINCIPLE IN RESEARCH

This setting was provided in the "Sounds of Society" research project mentioned earlier. In the project informal discussion groups of young people were formed in various neighborhoods of the Chicago metropolitan area. Two types of neighborhoods were involved; lower class inner city Black neighborhoods and upper middle class suburban white neighborhoods. Inner city and suburban groups met separately and discussed the social significance of familiar popular song lyrics. The discussions were recorded and typescripts were prepared. A song was played at the beginning of each discussion to provide a discussion stimulus and a standardized "situation frame" which would permit comparative analysis. Adult leaders provided loose structure, but the discussions were extremely free flowing. They provided a congenial setting for informal language behavior.

When the discussions of the inner city groups and the suburban groups were compared, true to Bernstein's schema the language style of the suburban groups resembled elaborated code significantly $(P > .1)$ more than did the language style of the inner city groups (language style was operationally defined as the mean number of words per utterance in a given discussion typescript).

The data, however, showed a very wide variability of means. This suggested that major shifts in language style might be occurring within each group discussion. In a more detailed analysis, independent raters were asked to arbitrarily designate various sections of each discussion typescript as "high context" or "low context." A two-way analysis of variance was conducted in which the data were partitioned by both the context factor (high or low) and by the social class factor (inner city or suburban). A strong relationship between the context factor and language style was demonstrated (context factor $P > .01$, Social class factor $P > .05$, virtually no interaction effect).

The data suggest that both inner city and suburban groups

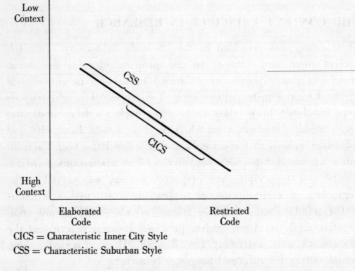

CICS = Characteristic Inner City Style
CSS = Characteristic Suburban Style

Figure 2   The Context Principle, Language Style, and Social Class

shifted back and forth between relatively restricted and relatively elaborated code, *depending on the context*. If the topic was familiar, high context communication tended to be used. As the discussion trailed off into the unfamiliar, low context communication predominated. Their "restricted code" and "elaborated code" did not seem to be discrete categories directly related to social class. They seemed to be relative categories closely related to shared context and also related to social class (see Figure 2).

Although inner city Black people may generally speak a more restricted linguistic code than suburbanites, neither group seems bound to one language style exclusively. Furthermore, analysis of the typescripts in my sample revealed extremely high context discussions by Black groups in which extremely abstract concepts were communicated (one example was a debate regarding free will and necessity which was conducted entirely in restricted code).

IMPLICATIONS FOR THE SCHOOL

Because "Sounds of Society" was an exploratory rather than experimental study, the findings presented here should be regarded as hypothesis rather than final conclusions. The study suggests a number of implications for research and teaching, however.

First, the concept of "linguistic deprivation" in the Black ghetto needs to be reviewed. It seems that, given a proper context, Black dialect can be used to communicate abstractions with considerable precision. But in order for the researcher to realize this *he must share the context of the speakers he observes*.

Second, teachers need to become sensitive to the context principle. The teaching act itself can be viewed as a continual process of shifting back and forth between high and low context situations. When the direct experience of ghetto children is involved in high context classroom discussions, restricted code may be a very effective model of discourse. In low context situations, restricted code may be inappropriate. The problem may not lie so much in the nature of the dialect as in the attitude of teachers toward allowing the experience and language of Black ghetto children a place in the classroom.

Third, considering "elaborated code" and "standard English" as synonymous may be misleading. I think that what most teachers teach as "standard English" is a *spoken* form of *written* English— a form that we read but don't often speak. The elaborateness of written language is functional in the most extreme of low context situations: the relationship between author and reader. Spoken language, however, is by definition more "low context" and less elaborate than "standard English." The suburban young people in my sample, who are very successful academically, did not speak "standard English." They did not even speak elaborated code all the time. They did use "standard grammar," which made their spoken language acceptable. (It may be useful to Black children to learn standard English as a second language because it is respectable and because it is occasionally functional in special situations. These, I think, are better reasons for teaching standard English than the assumption that one must learn to speak standard English before he can succeed in school.)

Fourth, high context communication can be very efficient when used in an appropriate setting. As I was discussing the context principle with a class of Black young people recently, one young man observed, "That elaborated code takes too long to get to the point." I know of few suburban mothers who invariably would say "Johnny, I'd rather you didn't do that just now." Many if not most would say, "Stop it!"

This is a time when increasing demands are being made for the inclusion of Black culture in the curriculum of the ghetto school. A hard look at the place of Black dialect in the ghetto classroom seems necessary (and a look at informal language in the suburban classroom as well). If well-meaning administrators and teachers in the ghetto resist the use of Black dialect on the ground that it is a source of cognitive deprivation, the schoolmen may find themselves resisted by the Black community.

Perhaps future research will show conclusively that Black dialect is pathological in the educative process. Perhaps not. But Black people will be very skeptical of school-people, white or Black, who tell them that the only way to learn is to "talk white." To this stance Black people today are saying, "F'get you, Honky!"

Walt Wolfram

CHAPTER 4
Sociolinguistic Premises and
the Nature of Nonstandard Dialects

During the last several years the speech of lower socio-economic
class blacks has been of interest to a number of different disciplines
including sociology, psychology, education, speech, and linguistics.
Correspondingly, we have heard varied proclamations about the
language behavior of this population. If all current views were
complementary, we could be comforted by the thought that we
were simply viewing the same phenomenon from several different
vantage points. Such is not the case, however. Views from different

From *The Speech Teacher* (September 1970), pp. 177–184. Reprinted by
permission of the publisher and the author. Walt Wolfram is at the Center
for Applied Linguistics, Washington, D.C.

disciplines and within different disciplines often come into sharp conflict with one another about the speech of lower socio-economic class blacks. Furthermore, some current views of this variety of English have challenged basic linguistic and sociolinguistic premises about the nature of language. Although it might be convenient to simply ignore some of these views, their current popularity and influence necessitates a more responsible evaluation. It is therefore the purpose of this paper to examine some basic premises about the nature of language which have a direct bearing on current viewpoints of nonstandard dialects in general and the nonstandard dialect spoken by lower socio-economic class blacks in particular.[1]

Although these premises are essential for any of the disciplines dealing with lower-class blacks, it is easy to see how they have special relevance for speech, because of the direct and pervading influence that this field has on the speech behavior of these children. For speech pathology, these premises give a perspective on the cruciality of distinguishing between authentic speech disorders and legitimate dialect differences. For speech arts and the speech teacher at any level, the sociolinguistic considerations have significant implications on the conventional criteria used in evaluating the speech behavior of these children. For example, they have much to say about the emphasis on the prescriptive norms for a "polished" speaker of standard English as compared with, say, the effectiveness of communication in an indigenous context. But more importantly, these considerations are essential for teachers' attitudes toward the speech behavior of the nonstandard-speaking children. These premises may serve as the basis for a nonpaternalistic respect for the speech patterns of these children.

One of the basic premises about the nature is that verbal systems are arbitrary, established only by convention.[2] Although one cannot deny a certain degree of consistency in the relation of language to the outside world, relationships between objects and linguistic signs are arbitrary. All languages are equally capable of conceptualization and expressing logical propositions, but the particular mode (i.e., grammar) for conceptualizing may differ drastically between language systems. The linguist, therefore, assumes that different surface forms for expression have nothing to do with the underlying logic of a sentence. There is nothing inherent in a given language variety which will interfere with the development of conceptualization. This is not to say that differences between the handling of logical operations may never correlate with different social classes; however, on the basis of this premise, it cannot be related to language differences, since all language varieties adequately provide for expression of syllogistic reasoning.

To those familiar with the current interest in nonstandard varieties of English, it should be apparent that this assumption does not coincide with the conclusions of some of the current projects in the area. To suggest, for example, that black English imposes certain cognitive limitations on the logical operations of the speaker and to reject it as "illogical" is not generally taken seriously by linguists. Yet, the work of Bereiter and Engelmann proposes such a view.[3] Ultimately, such notions seem to be derived from a prescriptive norm for language usage, although philosophical dictums about the logical nature of certain rules of a language add a ring of authority to such pronouncements.

To illustrate, one of the most cited examples of the inherent logical foundation of standard English is the use of negatives with indefinites. If a person uses a sentence such as *John didn't do anything*, it is understood negatively, but if a person should use the sentence, *John didn't do nothing*, it can only be meant as a positive statement since two negatives logically make a positive. In this view, if a person uses the construction in a sentence such as *John didn't do nothing because he was so lazy*, he is using English in an illogical way. Therefore the sentence does not mean what the speaker thought it meant. The speaker apparently means that *John* did not work, but by saying *John didn't do nothing* he affirms that *John* actually did something. Interpretations of this sort ignore a quite regular rule in black English (as well as in languages such as Spanish and Italian) which states that when you have a negative sentence with indefinites, you may add a negative element to every indefinite (e.g., *We ain't never had no trouble about none of us pullin' out no knife or nothin'*). In the underlying structure there is only one negative, which is simply realized on every indefinite.

Essential to understanding the underlying proposition of the above sentence is the distinction between "deep" and "surface" structure in language. Deep structure is basically a system of propositions which interrelate in such a way as to express the meaning of the sentence, while surface structure is realization of these propositions in terms of the particular grammatical devices (e.g., linear ordering, grammatical categories) of the language. The knowledge of language involves the ability to assign deep and surface structures to an infinite range of sentences, to relate these structures appropriately, and to assign a semantic interpretation and phonetic interpretation to the paired deep and surface structure. The failure to understand this relation is, no doubt, responsible for some of the misinterpretation of nonstandard varieties of language. We see, in the case of black English multiple negation, that the basis for arguing that it is not logical is found in the mistaken identity of a surface structure for a deep structure. The underlying structure of both the standard English and nonstandard English sentences are similar (i.e., Negative + *John* + *do* + Indefinite + *thing*) but the surface realizations are different.

Proclamations about the inadequacy of black English as a nonstandard language variety on logical bases, from a linguistic perspective, can be attributed to a naïve disregard for one of the primitive premises about the nature of language. Yet, Bereiter maintains that a difference between the negative patterns of black English and standard English is an indication that the black ghetto child is "deprived of one of the most powerful logical tools our language provides."[4] Bereiter claims that a black ghetto child "does not know the word *not*" since his subjects did not regularly give him the form in negating a sentence such as *This is not a book*. The assumptions of Bereiter, however, reveal two misconceptions. In the first place, he has confused the inability of the student to give him the word *not* in a specific elicitation task with the child's unfamiliarity with the lexical item. Labov observes that many of the formal elicitation procedures in the context of a classroom can be quite intimidating to the student and the best defense may be no verbal response at all.[5] Intensive research on the structure of black English in Washington, D.C., and Detroit clearly indicates that *not* is an integral part of black English. Secondly, Bereiter is apparently unaware that other negative patterns may serve the same purpose as *not*. Thus, a sentence such as *This ain't no book* may communicate the same negative pattern as *not* although the structure of the sentence is different. What is essential is *not* the occurrence of a particular lexical item, or a specific syntactical pattern, but the realization of a particular type of underlying structure involving negation. Whatever deficiencies in logical operations may or may not exist among black ghetto children, these have nothing to do with language.[6]

A second assumption of the linguist is the adequacy of all languages or dialects as communicative systems. It is accepted as a given that language is a human phenomenon which characterizes every social group, and that all language systems are perfectly adequate as communicative systems for the members of the social group. The social acceptability of a particular variety (considered the nonstandard variety because it is associated with a subordinate social group) is totally unrelated to its adequacy for communication. The question concerning different language varieties is not the *WHAT* but the *HOW* of communication. Thus, the consideration of the so-called disadvantaged child as "nonverbal," "verbally destitute," or at best, "drastically deficient" in his speech is diametrically opposed to this basic assumption. That there are typical situations in which young children do not respond because of the uncomfortableness of the social situation, or as a protective device against middle class meddling, should not be interpreted as meaning that the child lives in a verbally destitute environment, or even that the child does not emphasize the importance of verbal manipulation. For example, the staff of the Sociolinguistics Program at the Center for Applied Linguistics recently conducted interviews with forty-five Puerto Rican and Negro boys from Harlem, ranging in age from thirteen to seventeen. The school records of the boys in English would no doubt indicate that their writing and oral expression are far below the middle class standard. But consider their responses on a sentence completion drill designed to get at certain indigenous cultural values. As part of this drill they were asked to complete the sentence with what they considered the most appropriate reply—not in terms of school expectation, but with a culturally appropriate solution. Thus, given the sentence *"If you wanna be hip with the girls, you gotta _____,"* the vast majority of the respondents replied with hesitation, *"you gotta rap to her,"* or *"you gotta have a good rap." Rapping,* in black ghetto culture, refers to a distinctively fluent and lively way of talking, characterized by a high degree of personal style.[7] Linguists therefore assume that the label "verbal destitution" cannot refer to vernacular language patterns, but only to nonindigenous social situations which create such an impression.

The question of adequacy of nonstandard dialects as communicative systems brings out a very important matter on how one views a nonstandard language variety. In actuality, it is much broader than the linguistic situation, reverting back to the basic approach to different social groups. One can, for example, view black ghetto culture and language in terms of two basic models, which Baratz has called a *deficit* model or a *difference* model.[8] A deficit model treats speech difference in terms of a norm and deviation from that norm, the norm being middle class white behavior. From a sociological perspective, this means that much of black ghetto behavior, such as matrifocal homes, is viewed as a pathology. In terms of speech behavior, black English is considered, in the words of Hurst, "the pathology of nonorganic speech deficiencies."[9] On the other hand, a difference model, which seems to be much more common to anthropology than sociology and psychology, considers socially subordinate societies and language varieties as self-contained systems, inherently neither deficient nor superior.

Although this dichotomy between a deficit and difference model may be somewhat oversimplified, it sets a helpful framework for theoretical approaches to nonstandard dialects. But there is also a practical importance for such a distinction. If, for example, one

simply considers nonstandard dialects to be corrupt approximations of standard English, one may miss important structural facts
about the nature of these dialects. For example, consider the following interpretation of the finite use of the form *be*, a commonly
cited feature of black English. Ruth Golden, who views black
English in terms of a descending scale of deviation from standard
English states:

Individuals use different levels of language for different situations.
These levels vary from the illiterate to the formal and literary. For
instance, starting with the illiterate, *He don't be here*, we might progress to the colloquial, *He ain't here*, to the general and informal *He
isn't here* up to the formal and literary, *He is not present*.[10]

From the perspective of a deficit model, *be* is simply considered a
corrupt approximation of standard English. The possibility that
be may have a grammatically different function is precluded. Instead, it is only considered as a "substitution" for the finite forms
of standard English *am*, *is* and *are*. The linguist, however, looks at
this use of *be* descriptively; that is, he asks what the grammatical
function of this form is regardless of its social consequences.
When such an approach is taken, we find that the form *be* represents a grammatical category which seems to be unique to black
English. This, of course, is not to say that all linguists will
accept a given descriptive analysis of this form although a number
of analyses agree that it is used to represent an habitual action of
some type.[11] This type of disagreement is no more serious than
the disagreements that linguists may have over the function of the
have auxiliary in standard English. Common to each description
of *be*, however, is the rigorous method of linguistic analysis and
the assumption that this form has a linguistic function in its own
right. The insistence of language varieties as systems in their own
right (with both similarities and differences to related varieties)
is the reason that linguists look with suspicion when they see such
terms as "substitutions," "replacements," "omissions," "devia-
tions," etc. Such terms used with reference to nonstandard language varieties imply a value judgment about a given variety's

relation to the standard variety. Terms like "correspondence" and "alternation" do not have these same implications—they are statements of fact about language relations. While the terminology may seem to be a trivial matter for the linguist to pick on, the association of such terms with the deficit type of approach raises a danger signal to the linguist. To take the position that nonstandard constructions are simply inaccurate and unworthy approximations of standard English can only lead to an inaccurate description of what is assumed to be a self-contained system, which is perfectly adequate for communication.

In terms of sociolinguistic situations, it is quite common for a socially dominant culture to view a socially subordinate one as having an inadequate means of communication. This view is a common manifestation of linguistic ethnocentrism of the dominant classes. Thus, Spanish-speaking South Americans often consider the Indian peasants to have no valid language system—verbally destitute. The current treatment of nonstandard English varieties is no different, although it may be more subtle because Americans have sometimes denied the sociological facts concerning the subordinate role of some segments of the population in American society.

Our previous point concerning the adequacy of nonstandard varieties of English as a system of communication naturally leads us to our next premise concerning language, namely, that it is systematic and ordered. Any view of language differences which treats them as unsystematic and irregular will thus be categorically rejected by the linguist. It is assumed that descriptive data of related languages will always reveal regular and systematic correspondence between different types of constructions. One can readily see, then, why the linguist reacts negatively to a view of nonstandard language as that offered by Hurst, who subsumes differences between black English and standard English under the rubic "dialectolalia":

. . . dialectolalia involves such specific oral abberations as phonemic and subphonemic replacements, segmental phonemes, phonetic distortion, defective syntax, misarticulations, mispronunciations, limited or poor vocabulary, and faulty phonology. These variables exist most commonly in unsystematic, multifarious combinations.[12]

The above position unambiguously treats black English as an irregular, unsystematic and faulty rather than a different but equal system. Furthermore, such a position can only be taken when actual descriptive and sociolinguistic facts are ignored, for the linguist would claim that all evidence points to differences between standard English and black English which are systematic and regular. Take, for example, the case of word-final consonant clusters in such words as *test, ground,* and *cold.* In black English, the final consonant is regularly absent, the result of a systematic correspondence of a single consonant in black English where a cluster is found in standard English. Thus, we get *tes', groun',* and *col'* in black English. But these final consonants are not absent randomly or unsystematically. We observe that the correspondence of a single consonant for a word-final cluster only occurs when both members of a potential cluster are either voiced or voiceless, such as *st, nd,* and *ld.* But when one of the members is voiced and the other voiceless, as in the clusters *mp (jump), lt (colt),* and *nt (count),* this correspondence does not occur.[13] Instead, black English is like standard English in that both members of the cluster are present. The view that differences between related language varieties are random and haphazard is dangerous not only because it conflicts with a linguistic assumption but also from a practical viewpoint. It can lead to an unsystematic approach in teaching standard English and the teaching of points that may be irrelevant in terms of the systematic differences between the two language varieties.

As a final premise of the linguist, we must observe that language is learned in the context of the community. Linguists generally agree that children have a fairly complete language system by the age of five or six with minor adjustments in language competence occurring sometimes until eight or nine. This system is acquired from contact with individuals in their environment. Whether this is primarily the parent-child relationship (which some claim for the middle class white community) or from child peers (which is sometimes claimed for the Black ghetto community) their language is acquired through verbal interaction with individuals in the immediate context. The rate of development is parallel for children of different social groups, lower class children learning the nonstandard dialect at approximately the same rate as middle class children learning the standard variety of English. This assumption of the linguist concerning the rate of language development again comes into basic conflict with basic statements of educational psychologists as Engelmann, Bereiter and Deutsch, who speak of the communal "language retardation" of ghetto children. Bereiter concludes:

By the time they are five years old, disadvantaged children of almost every kind are typically one or two years retarded in language development. This is supported by virtually any index of language one cares to look at.[14]

Any linguist will look at such a conclusion with immediate suspicion. Closer investigation of this claim reveals that the fact that these children do not speak standard English is taken to mean that they are linguistically retarded, and, in many cases, that they are cognitively deficient. Thus, if a black lower class child says *He nice,* a correspondence of the present tense standard English *He's nice,* it is considered to be an underdeveloped standard English approximation and equivalent to the absence of copula at a particular stage of standard English development.[15] The fact that this form is used by adult speakers is irrelevant, only meaning that adults may have some stabilized form of language retardation. The linguist, however, suggests that black English is simply one of many languages and dialects, including Russian, which have a zero copula realization in the present tense. No meaning is lost; an "identity statement" is just as permissible in this dialect as any other language or dialect. This form has no relation to the ability or inability to conceptualize. Similarly, auditory discrimination tests which are designed on a standard English norm are *de facto* biased against the nonstandard system. For example, in the auditory discrimination test used by Deutsch, the failure to distinguish *wreath* from *reef* or *lave* from *lathe* may be considered to be indicative of underdeveloped auditory discrimination since these words are contrastive in standard English.[16] But we observe that such pairs are the result of a systemative pattern in which *th* and *v* or *f* are not distinguished at the end of a word in black English. Homophony is a widespread and common language phenomenon, and the above homophonous words should cause us no more concern than the homophony of *red*, the color and *read* [rɛd], the past tense of *read* [rid], or *roll*, the edible object and *role* relating to social behavior. What we observe, then, is that the black English speaker is penalized for the patterned homophony of his dialect, whereas a middle class New Englander is not penalized for the homophony between *caught*, the past tense of *catch*, and *cot*, the object for resting, or *taught*, the past tense of *teach*, and *torte*, the pastry. The learning of standard English must be clearly differentiated from language development of an indigenous dialect. Careful attention should be made, from the viewpoint of linguistic relativism, in order not to erroneously transfer legitimate dialect differences into matters of language acquisition.

The linguist, in support of the linguistic equality of nonstandard dialects, considers evidence on relative language proficiency as that recently provided by Baratz to be an empirical justification for his claims.[17] Baratz conducted a bidialectal test in which she has compared the proficiency of a group of black ghetto children in repeating standard English and black English sentences. As might be expected, the black children were considerably more proficient in repeating the black English sentences. When they repeated the standard English sentences, however, there were predictable differences in their repetitions based on interference from black English. The same test was then administered to a group of white middle class suburban children, who repeated the standard English sentences quite adequately, but had predictable differences in their repetition of the black English sentences based on interference from standard English. Which of these groups, then, was linguistically retarded? We must be careful not to confuse social acceptability, and no one would deny the social stigmatization of nonstandard dialects, with language acquisition.

In sum, the relativistic viewpoint of the sociolinguist emphasizes the fully systematic but different nature of nonstandard dialects. It would be nice if I had simply slain a dead dragon, but unfortunately, the views with which I have taken issue enjoy current popularity in a number of disciplines. What is more depressing, these views are often communicated to and adopted by those in a position which directly affects the lives of many ghetto children. Furthermore, these views have a direct bearing on the attitude of both white and black middle class teachers toward black English. The attitudinal problems towards this intricate and unique language system is probably the biggest problem we face. But there is also a practical reason for understanding some linguistic and sociolinguistic premises about the nature of language with reference to nonstandard dialects. An understanding of systematic differences between nonstandard dialects and standard English must serve as a basis for the most effective teaching of standard English. I am certainly not so naïve to suggest that standard English is not a prerequisite for making it in "whitey's world," and the child who desires to do so must be given that option. For the child who chooses this alternative, we must adopt an attitude and methodology which will take full advantage of what we know about the nature of language systems and language differences.

NOTES

[1] Several different terms have been used to describe this dialect, including "Black English," "Negro Dialect," and "Negro Nonstandard English." Unfortunately, there is no consensus about the use of one term to the exclusion of the others. For a technical description of the features of this dialect, see William Labov, et al., *A Study of the Non-Standard English of Negro and Puerto Rican Speakers in New York City: Phonological and Grammatical Analysis,* U.S. Office of Education Project No. 328 (New York, 1968) or Walter A. Wolfram, *A Sociolinguistic Description of Detroit Negro Speech* (Washington, D.C., 1969). For a nontechnical description, see Ralph W. Fasold and Walt Wolfram, "Some Linguistic Fea-

tures of Negro Dialect," eds. Ralph W. Fasold and Roger W. Shuy, *Teaching Standard English in the Inner City* (Washington, D.C., 1970).

2 Eugene A. Nida, *Toward a Science of Translating* (Leiden, 1964), p. 46. Nida notes that the arbitrary character of linguistic symbols refers to (1) the arbitrary relationship between the form of the symbol and the form of the referent, (2) the relationships between classes of symbols and classes of referents, and (3) the relationship between classes of symbols and classes of symbols.

3 Carl E. Bereiter and Sigmund E. Engelmann, *Teaching Disadvantaged Children in Preschool* (Englewood Cliffs, 1967).

4 Carl E. Bereiter, "Academic Instruction and Preschool Children," eds. Richard Corbin and Murial Crosby, *Language Programs for the Disadvantaged* (Champaign, 1965), p. 199.

5 William Labov, "The Logic of Non-Standard English," ed. James E. Alatis, *Georgetown University Monograph Series on Languages and Linguistics* (Washington, D.C., 1969).

6 It is interesting to note that a sample of language indices, Bereiter, pp. 199–200, cites as indicative of language competence have nothing to do with language. He consistently confuses the recognition of logical operations with language development.

7 Thomas Kochman, "Rapping in the Black Ghetto," *Trans-Action* (February 1969), pp. 26–34.

8 For a discussion, see Joan C. Baratz, "Language in the Economically Disadvantaged Child: A Perspective," ASHA (April 1968), pp. 143–145.

9 Charles G. Hurst, *Psychological Correlates in Dialectolalia* (Washington, D.C., 1965), p. 2.

10 Ruth I. Golden, "Effectiveness of Instructional Tapes for Changing Regional Speech" (Ed.D. diss., Wayne State University, 1963), p. 173.

11 See, e.g., Walter A. Wolfram, *A Sociolinguistic Description of Detroit Negro Speech* (Washington, D.C., 1969), pp. 188–196.

12 Hurst, p. 2.

13 Wolfram, pp. 50–51.

14 Bereiter, p. 196.

15 See, e.g., Bereiter and Engelmann, pp. 139–140.

16 Cynthia Deutsch, "Auditory Discrimination and Learning Social Factors," *Merrill Palmer Quarterly*, Vol. X (1964), pp. 277–296.

17 Joan C. Baratz, "Teaching Reading in a Negro School," eds. Joan C. Baratz and Roger W. Shuy, *Teaching Black Children to Read* (Washington, D.C., 1969), pp. 99–101.

PART 2
Language and Ethnicity

*Language is a manifestation of our cultural environment. In this
section several papers expand upon our understanding of language
and ethnicity. The first article, by Grace S. Holt, explores a
unique approach to speech-language learning. Professor Holt's
field work in the Chicago ghettos has verified that her
ethnolinguistic approach to speech-language learning significantly
increases a child's learning. She has worked with black and white
ethnics. The short essay by Ossie Davis "The English Language
Is My Enemy" points out the psychological implications in a black
man's use of the English langage. As a white language, English*

glorifies things white and uses black in a negative manner. The third article is by Thomas Kochman, who has done fieldwork in urban communities for his essay. The thrust of his article is to outline an ethnography of black American speech behavior. Concentrating on notes gathered from Chicago, he describes and analyzes urban black speech. Finally, Henry H. Mitchell presents a vivid account and example of black speech in his article "Black English." The black preacher has contributed immensely to black language behavior in tone and style, and Professor Mitchell's essay colorfully demonstrates the black style. The authors in Part 2 have closely observed the working of language and have captured the essence of an ethnography of black language.

Grace S. Holt

CHAPTER 5
The Ethno-linguistic Approach
to Speech-Language Learning

The current drive by black people to affirm their cultural identity
has important implications for theoretical bases of speech-language
teaching functions in relationship to the present quest for black
awareness. Blackness must be a recurring theme in a wide range
of expressions, celebrating black achievement with a view to serving the community's aspirations rather than someone else's idea
of content, emotional distance, and style. Traditional speech-
language teaching methodologies do not address themselves to this

From *The Speech Teacher* (March 1970), pp. 98–100. Reprinted by permission of the publisher and the author. Grace S. Holt is Associate Professor
of Speech, University of Illinois, Chicago Circle Campus.

problem; and the current trend in methodology based upon recent linguistic research in Black Speech seems destined to repeat the tragedy.

Most black inner-city children enter school inquisitive, curious, eager to know about the world surrounding them, and utilizing to varying degrees speech-language competencies different in many ways from the textbook variety of Standard English used in schools. Assuming that these black children have a passive knowledge of Standard English and are making errors in their attempts to produce it, teachers proceed to teach with little or no regard for the children's own language competencies. In fact, few teachers realize the necessity for taking the children step-by-step, from the levels of the taxonomic categories of his cultural group, to the taxonomic categories of the dominant group in equivalent stimuli, distinctive labeling, and discrimination between items and concepts. Thus speech-language programs have generally responded to black children's differences with a systematic process of destruction. Anyone familiar with black inner city schools recognizes the characteristics of the language destruction process:

1. The omission of Black Speech and black bi-dialectal *models,* i.e., black people who speak both English and a regional Standard.
2. Denial of the validity of Black English usage even in interpersonal communication.
3. Failure to recognize the denial of opportunity to black children to demonstrate their knowledge, and speech-language competencies developed around objects, experiences, and the language norms of black communities as valid indices of abilities.
4. Failure to base teaching content and methodology on speech-language similarities and differences between black culture and the dominant culture.

In order to lift the burden of accountability from the shoulders of the children some basic objectives which will require the re-education and acculturation of teachers must be accomplished.

Non-productive, "corrective" approaches which imply that teachers are continuously doing something which needs correcting must be replaced with approaches and methodologies based on interdisciplinary knowledge related to speech-language learning. Research into Black English, until recently, has been neglected by linguists, and their findings remain fragmentary and incomplete. Final agreement on what Black English is, based on intensive research, seems far away. Moreover, there is the accelerating movement, understandable and regretable, to close the doors of black communities to researchers. Yet these facts in no way relieve the teacher of the responsibility for proceeding on the basis of what socio-linguistic research has made available to date. Amelioration of institutionalized child destruction and the maximizing of academic success are dictated by the social dynamite present within all black communities. Society cannot afford less, and speech-language teachers have a vital role to play.

The Ethno-Linguistic Approach was developed with the cooperation of black inner city parents, teachers, and children in Chicago on the assumption that viable, effective, speech-language programs for culturally different, encapsulated children would accomplish the following objectives:

1. Actively involve parents, teachers, and students in curricular changes.
2. Maintain and enhance the self identity and cultural heritage of the black child.
3. Tap into the child's culture, providing the child opportunities to use the range and variety of language he already possesses so that teachers can realistically assess the linguistic competencies of their students.
4. Serve as a vehicle for acculturation of the teacher, sensitizing her to the difficulties experienced by the children in bi-cultural learning.
5. Contribute to significant positive attitudinal changes of teachers affecting speech-language content and objectives in classroom practice.

Furthermore, the model provides frameworks for language learning designated as (1) Language Elicitation Approach, (2) The Self-Identity Approach, (3) The Modified Bi-dialectal Approach, and (4) The Modified Audio-Lingual Approach.

Language Elicitation provides that the children will express what they know in the only way they know. As a method of deriving language lesson content from language elicitation episodes the children tell all they can about an object. Objects are multi-sensory, self-contained, self-demonstrating, and self-motivating. Utilizing objects from the child's own culture provides the teacher with means of assessing the concepts, knowledge, lexicon, linguistic system and style normally employed by the child relative to the referent.

When the child is called upon to make a comment or formulate a reply about an object, the function of language is immediately supplied. The referent object provides a central continuing experience, and represents concepts which engender various forms of speech operating within that experience, i.e., grammatical, lexical, and phonological items. The purpose of the language elicitation lesson, therefore, is to make the child a contributing participant in decision making related to acquiring a stock of culturally relevant linguistic items on which the practice-learning can be based. All the skills and concepts that will operate within that experimental lesson may be incorporated for multiple learning purposes.

In terms of procedure, the teacher initially solicits parental help in assembling a collection of objects from the children's culture. The objects are sorted out to elicit the desired concepts and language. For the language lesson each child is given an object and asked to talk about it. In addition, each elicitation lesson is taped for the teacher's use. Using the elicited language the teacher writes the audio-lingual practice lessons; the referent object is subsequently always used for the practice lessons until the children are able to manipulate (adapt and vary) all the desired linguistic features demonstrating the desired concepts.

Self-identity lessons provide the child with self-enhancing

models correlated with practice in manipulation of structure and vocabulary. Again the teacher with parental help assembles a picture collection of black model identity figures, would-be well-known live models to increase the student's believability in, and acceptance of, the socio-linguistic context. The teacher may begin with an elicitation lesson of the kind previously described. However, if the teacher prefers initiating practice lessons in controlled language structures which will operate on the pictures chosen, then the teacher presents the basic patterns and models the patterns for each language practice lesson. Alternating lessons provide manipulation of the practice structures through adaptation, variation, and expansion when the children are expressing themselves about the pictures. Sufficient practice in continuing lessons provides sufficient linguistic independence for the child to state that he knows in the syntax and lexicon of the classroom.

To provide the child with a means of developing an awareness of the similarities and differences between Black and Standard English, the Modified Audio-lingual lessons are used. Black English speakers and Standard English speakers are mutually intelligible to each other in varying degrees, and points of differences and mutual unintelligibility are not always apparent to the child. Further, a great deal of dialect blend exists in the speech of black children which the approach recognizes by greatly modifying the phonological aspect. The speech-language learning lessons are limited to drill in phonological features closely related to syntax, such as consonant clusters in reduced verb forms, presentatives, etc. In addition, lessons of "free conversation" alternate with drill lessons, providing opportunities for immediate application of practiced materials in a "live" communication situation using the referent objects and pictures.

In the Modified Bi-dialectal lessons the child is unburdened of the difficult and unrealistic goal of avoiding dialect blends, and of keeping the two systems *rigidly* separated. The approach provides for practice in standard syntax, but dialect blends are permitted, and even encouraged, when they seem appropriate to the black model and situation. Language learning lessons are limited to the Standard verb system, Standard expansion pattern systems, and items for which the child does not really understand the Standard equivalent. The teacher uses objects, pictures, bi-dialectal people from the community (contrary to myth, they do exist), and audio-lingual techniques in the lessons. Structured drills, expansion drills, semi-structured drills developed from the elicited language, and free creative conversation are practiced in lessons according to need.

In conclusion, the Ethno-linguistic Model, incorporating Black Culture as a meaningful basis for speech-language implementation, utilizing realistic contexts, modified techniques, and emphasizing functional meaning, offers much needed flexibility in the teaching-learning process for black children.

Ossie Davis

CHAPTER 6
The English Language
Is My Enemy

I stand before you, a little nervous, afflicted to some degree with stage fright. Not because I fear you, but because I fear the subject.

The title of my address is, "Racism in American Life—Broad Perspectives of the Problem," or "The English Language Is My Enemy."

In my speech I will define culture as the sum total of ways of living built up by a group of human beings and transmitted by one generation to another. I will define education as the act or process of imparting and communicating a culture, developing

Reprinted from the April, 1967, issue of the *American Teacher*, official publication of the American Federation of Teachers.

the powers of reasoning and judgment and generally preparing oneself and others intellectually for a mature life.

AN EDUCATION IN WORDS

I will define communication as the primary means by which the process of education is carried out.

I will say that language is the primary medium of communication in the educational process and, in this case, the English language. I will indict the English language as one of the prime carriers of racism from one person to another in our society and discuss how the teacher and the student, especially the Negro student, are affected by this fact.

The English language is my enemy.

Racism is a belief that human races have distinctive characteristics, usually involving the idea that one's own race is superior and has a right to rule others. Racism.

The English language is my enemy.

But that was not my original topic—I said that English was my goddamn enemy. Now why do I use "goddamn" to illustrate this aspect of the English language? Because I want to illustrate the sheer gut power of words. Words which control our action. Words like "nigger," "kike," "sheeny," "Dago," "black power"—words like this. Words we don't use in ordinary decent conversation, one to the other. I choose these words deliberately, not to flaunt my freedom before you. If you are a normal human being, these words will have assaulted your senses, may even have done you physical harm, and if you so choose, you could have me arrested.

Those words are attacks upon your physical and emotional well-being; your pulse rate is possibly higher, your breath quicker; there is perhaps a tremor along the nerves of your arms and your legs; sweat begins in the palms of your hands, perhaps. With these few words I have assaulted you. I have damaged you, and there is nothing you can possibly, possibly do to control your reactions—to defend yourself against the brute force of these words.

These words have a power over us; a power that we cannot resist. For a moment you and I have had our deepest physical reactions controlled, not by our own wills, but by words in the English language.

WHAT ROGET REVEALS

A superficial examination of Roget's *Thesaurus of the English Language* reveals the following facts: The word "whiteness" has 134 synonyms, 44 of which are favorable and pleasing to contemplate. For example: "purity," "cleanness," "immaculateness," "bright," "shiny," "ivory," "fair," "blonde," "stainless," "clean," "clear," "chaste," "unblemished," "unsullied," "innocent," "honorable," "upright," "just," "straightforward," "fair," "genuine," "trustworthy,"—and only 10 synonyms which I feel to have been negative and then only in the mildest sense, such as "glossover," "whitewash," "gray," "wan," "pale," "ashen," etc.

The word "blackness" has 120 synonyms, 60 of which are distinctly unfavorable, and none of them even mildly positive. Among the offending 60 were such words as "blot," "blotch," "smut," "smudge," "sullied," "begrime," "soot," "becloud," "obscure," "dingy," "murky," "low-toned," "threatening," "frowning," "foreboding," "forbidding," "sinister," "baneful," "dismal," "thundery," "wicked," "malignant," "deadly," "unclean," "dirty," "unwashed," "foul," etc. In addition, and this is what really hurts, 20 of those words—and I exclude the villainous 60 above—are related directly to race, such as "Negro," "Negress," "nigger," "darkey," "blackamoor," etc.

THINKING IS SUBVOCAL SPEECH

If you consider the fact that thinking itself is subvocal speech (in other words, one must use words in order to think at all), you will appreciate the enormous trap of racial prejudgment that works on any child who is born into the English language.

Any creature, good or bad, white or black, Jew or Gentile, who uses the English language for the purposes of communication is willing to force the Negro child into 60 ways to despise himself, and the white child, 60 ways to aid and abet him in the crime.

Language is a means of communication. This corruption, this evil of racism, doesn't affect only one group. It doesn't take white to make a person a racist. Blacks also become inverted racists in the process.

A part of our function, therefore, as teachers, will be to reconstruct the English language. A sizeable undertaking, but one which we must undertake if we are to cure the problems of racism in our society.

DEMOCRATIZING ENGLISH

The English language must become democratic. It must become respectful of the possibilities of the human spirit. Racism is not only reflected in words relating to the color of Negroes. If you will examine some of the synonyms for the word "Jew," you will find that the adjectives and the verb of the word "Jew" are offensive. However, if you look at the word "Hebrew," you will see that there are no offensive connotations to the word.

When you understand and contemplate the small difference between the meaning of one word supposedly representing one fact, you will understand the power, good or evil, associated with the English language. You will understand also why there is a tremendous fight among the Negro people to stop using the word "Negro" altogether and substitute "Afro-American."

You will understand, even further, how men like Stokely Carmichael and Floyd McKissick can get us in such serious trouble by using two words together: Black Power. If Mr. McKissick and Mr. Carmichael had thought a moment and said Colored Power, there would have been no problem.

We come today to talk about education. Education is the only valid transmitter of American values from one generation to another. Churches have been used from time immemorial to teach certain values to certain people, but in America, as in no other country, it is the school that bears the burden of teaching young Americans to be Americans.

Schools define the meaning of such concepts as success. And education is a way out of the heritage of poverty for Negro people. It's the way we can get jobs.

THE ONE-BY-ONE ROUTE

Education is that which opens that golden door that was so precious to Emma Lazarus. But education in the past has basically been built on the theory that we could find those gifted individuals among the Negro people and educate them out of their poverty, out of their restricted conditions, and then they would in turn serve to represent the best interests of the race; and if we concentrated on educating Negroes as individuals, we would solve the problem of discrimination by educating individual Negroes out of the problem. But I submit that that is a false and erroneous function and definition of education. We can no longer, as teachers, concentrate on finding the gifted black child in the slums or in the middle-class areas and giving him the best that we have. This no longer serves the true function of education if education indeed is to fulfill its mission to assist and perpetuate the drive of the Negro community to come into the larger American society on the same terms as all other communities have come.

Let us look for a brief moment at an article appearing in *Commentary* in February, 1964, written by the associate director of the American Jewish Committee. "What is now perceived as the revolt of the Negro amounts to this," he says.

The solitary Negro seeking admission into the white world through unusual achievement has been replaced by the organized Negro insisting upon a legitimate share for his group of the goods of American society. The white liberal, in turn, who, whether or not he is fully conscious of it, has generally conceived of progress in race relations as the one-by-one assimilation of deserving Negroes into the larger society, now finds himself confused and threatened by suddenly having to come to terms with an aggressive Negro community that wishes to enter en masse.

Accordingly, in the arena of civil rights, the Negro revolution has tended to take the struggle out of the courts and bring it to the streets and the negotiating tables. Granting the potential for unprecedented violence that exists here, it must also be borne in mind that what the Negro people are now beginning to do, other ethnic minorities who brought to America their strong traditions of communal solidarity did before them. With this powerful asset, the Irish rapidly acquired political strength and the Jews succeeded in raising virtually an entire immigrant population into the middle class within a span of two generations. Viewed in this perspective, the Negroes are merely the last of America's significant ethnic minorities to achieve communal solidarity and to grasp the role of the informal group power structure in protecting the rights and advancing the opportunities of the individual members of the community.

LIBERAL GRADUALISM

Teachers have a very important function. They have before them the raw materials of the future. And if we were satisfied by the job that was being done in our country and in our culture, it would not be necessary to call a protest conference. It would be necessary only to call a conference to celebrate.

I submit that racism is inherent in the English language because the language is an historic expression of the experience of a people; that racism, which is the belief that one group is superior to the other and has the right to set the standards for the other, is still one of the main spiritual policies of our country as expressed in the educational process.

Those of us who are concerned, those of us who are caught up, those of us who really want to be involved must be prepared at this conference to tear aside our most private thoughts and prejudices remembering that we have been taught them because we are all born to the English language.

Let us not feel personally guilty or personally responsible for the fact that we may not like Negroes. Let us remember that we are participating in the culture which has taught us not to like them, so that, when we are tempted to teach a child from above his position, or to say that "I represent white Anglo-Saxon gentility and culture, and out of the gratitude and graciousness of my heart I am going to reach down and lift you up to my level," we know that is the incorrect attitude.

We cannot reach down and lift up anymore, we must all get down together and reciprocate one to the other and come up together.

Let us, above all, be honest one to the other. Let us pursue truth though it hurts, though it makes us bleed. I said in the beginning that my purpose in using those lacerating words was to expose our innermost feeling. We must dig even deeper for the roots in our own consciousness, black and white, of the real fact of racism in our culture, and having faced that in ourselves, go back to the various schools from which we came and look upon the children before us as an opportunity, not only to practice the craft of teaching and the imparting of knowledge but, equally important, as an opportunity to learn from a subjugated people what its value, its history, its culture, its wealth as an independent people are. Let there be in our classrooms a sharing of the wealth of American democracy.

WHY TEACHERS FAIL

Liberal opinion in the North and in the South thus continues to stand upon its traditions of gradualism—that of one-by-one admission of deserving Negroes into the larger society and rejection of the idea that to help the Negro it must help first the Negro community.

Today in America, as elsewhere, the Negro has made us forcefully aware of the fact that the rights and privileges of an individual rest upon the status obtained by the group to which he belongs.

In the American pattern, where social power is distributed by groups, the Negro has come to recognize that he can achieve equal opportunities only through concerted action of the Negro community. We can't do it one by one anymore, we must do it as a group.

Now, how is education related to the process not of lifting individuals but of lifting a whole group by its bootstraps and helping it climb to its rightful place in American society?

One of the ways is by calling such meetings as this to discuss Negro history—to discuss those aspects of Negro culture which are important for the survival of the Negro people as a community. There is nothing in the survival of the Negro people as a community that is inherently hostile to the survival of the interests of any other group.

So when we say Black Power and Black Nationalism we do not mean that that is the only nationalism that we are concerned about or that it is to predominate above all others. We merely mean that it should have the right of all other groups and be respected as such in the American way of life.

A BOOTLEG TEACHER

I have had occasion (and with this I'll come to a close) to function as a teacher—I'm a bootleg teacher, I teach Sunday school, it's the closest I can get to the process—I teach boys from nine to twelve, and I have the same problem with getting them to appreciate the spoken and written word, as you do, in your daily classrooms. Most of them can't read. I don't see how they're going to get, not only to Heaven—I don't see how they're going to get to the next grade unless they can command some of these problems that we have.

But, more importantly, I am also involved in the educational process. And those of us who are involved in culture and cultural activities do ourselves and our country and our cause a great injustice not to recognize that we, too, are communicators and have therefore a responsibility in the process of communication. I could be hired today to communicate to the great American public my great delight in smoking a cigarette, but I know that a cigarette would cause you cancer and I could be paid for that. I could be used to do many other things in the process of communications from the top to the bottom.

I have a responsibility to show that what I do, what is translated through me, is measured by the best interest of my country and my people and my profession. And in that I think we are all together.

Thomas Kochman

CHAPTER 7
Toward an Ethnography
of Black American Speech Behavior

In the black idiom of Chicago and elsewhere, there are several words that refer to talking: *rapping, shucking, jiving, running it down, gripping, copping a plea, signifying,* and *sounding.* Led by the assumption that these terms, as used by the speakers, referred to different kinds of verbal behavior, this writer has attempted to discover which features of form, style, and function distinguish one type of talk from the other. In this pursuit, we would hope to be able to identify the variable threads of the com-

Reprinted with permission of The Macmillan Company from *Afro-American Anthropology,* by Normal E. Whitten, Jr., and John F. Szwed (eds.). Copyright © 1970 by The Free Press, a division of The Macmillan Company.

munication situation: speaker, setting and audience, and how they influence the use of language within the social context of the black community. We also expect that some light would be shed on the black perspective behind a speech event, on those orientating values and attitudes of the speaker that cause him to behave or perform in one way as opposed to another.

The guidelines and descriptive framework for the type of approach used here have been articulated most ably by Hymes in his introduction to the publication, *The Ethnography of Communication* (Gumperz and Hymes, 1964:2ff.), from which I quote:

In short, "ethnography of communication" implies two characteristics that an adequate approach to the problems of language which engage anthropologists must have. Firstly, such an approach cannot simply take results from linguistics, psychology, sociology, ethnology, as given, and seek to correlate them, however partially useful such work is. It must call attention to the need for fresh kinds of data, to the need to investigate directly the use of language in contexts of situation so as to discern patterns proper to speech activity, patterns which escape separate studies of grammar, of personality, of religion, of kinship and the like, each abstracting from the patterning of speech activity as such into some other frame of reference. Secondly, such an approach cannot take linguistic form, a given code, or speech itself, as frame of reference. It must take as context a community, investigating its communicative habits as a whole, so that any given use of channel and code takes its place as but part of the resources upon which the members of the community draw.

It is not that linguistics does not have a vital role. Well analyzed linguistic materials are indispensable, and the logic of linguistic methodology is a principal influence in the ethnographic perspective of the approach. It is rather that it is not linguistics, but ethnography —not language, but communication—which must provide the frame of reference within which the place of language in culture and society is to be described.

The following description and analysis is developed from information supplied mainly by blacks living within the inner city of Chicago. Their knowledge of the above terms, their ability to recognize and categorize the language behavior of others (e.g., "Man, stop shucking!"), and on occasion, to give examples themselves, established them as reliable informants. Although a general attempt has been made here to illustrate the different types of language behavior from field sources, I have had, on occasion, to rely on published material to provide better examples, such as the writings of Malcolm X, Robert Conot, Iceberg Slim, and others. Each example cited from these authors, however, is regarded as authentic by my informants. In my own attempts at classification and analysis I have sought confirmation from the same group.

Rapping, while used synonymously to mean ordinary conversation, is distinctively a fluent and lively way of talking which is always characterized by a high degree of personal narration, a colorful rundown of some past event. A recorded example of this type of rap follows, an answer from a Chicago gang member to a youth worker who asked how his group became organized.

Now I'm goin tell you how the jive really started. I'm goin tell you how the club got this big. 'Bout 1956 there used to be a time when the Jackson Park show was open and the Stony show was open. Sixty-six street, Jeff, Gene, all of 'em, little bitty dudes, little bitty. . . . Gene wasn't with 'em then. Gene was cribbin (living) over here. Jeff, all of 'em, real little bitty dudes, you dig? All of us were little.

Sixty-six (the gang on sixty sixth street), they wouldn't allow us in the Jackson Park show. That was when the parky (?) was headin it. Everybody say, If we want to go to the show, we go! One day, who was it? Carl Robinson. He went up to the show . . . and Jeff fired on him. He came back and all this was swelled up 'bout yay big, you know. He come back over to the hood (neighbourhood). He told (name unclear) and them dudes went up there. That was when mostly all the main sixty-six boys was over here like Bett Riley. All of 'em was over here. People that quit gang-bangin [fighting, especially as a group], Marvin Gates, people like that.

They went on up there, John, Roy and Skeeter went in there. And they start humbuggin (fighting) in there. That's how it all started. Sixty-six found out they couldn't beat us, at *that* time. They couldn't *whup* seven-o (70). Am I right Leroy? You was cribbin over here then. Am I right? We were dynamite! Used to be a time, you ain't have a passport, Man, you couldn't walk through here. And if didn't nobody know you it was worse than that. . . .

Rapping to a woman is a colorful way of "asking for some pussy." "One needs to throw a lively rap when he is 'putting the make' on a broad" (Horton, 1967:6).

According to one informant the woman is usually someone he had seen or just met, looks good, and might be willing to have sexual intercourse with him. My informant remarked that the term would not be descriptive of talk between a couple "who have had a relationship over any length of time." Rapping, then, is used by the speaker at the beginning of a relationship to create a favorable impression and be persuasive at the same time. The man who has the reputation for excelling at this is the pimp, or mack man. Both terms describe a person of considerable status in the street hierarchy, who, by his lively and persuasive rapping (*macking* is also used in this context), has acquired a stable of girls to hustle for him and give him money. For most street men and many teen-agers he is the model whom they try to emulate. Thus, within the community you have a pimp walk, pimp style boots and clothes, and perhaps most of all "pimp talk." A colorful literary example of telephone rap, which one of my informants regards as extreme, but agrees that it illustrates the language, style, and technique of rapping, is set forth in Iceberg Slim's book *Pimp: The Story of My Life* (© 1967 Holloway House, Los Angeles; used by permission), p. 179. "Blood" is rapping to an ex-whore named Christine in an effort to trap her into his stable.

Now try to control yourself baby. I'm the tall stud with the dreamy bedroom eyes across the hall in four-twenty. I'm the guy with the pretty towel wrapped around his sexy hips. I got the same hips on now that you x-rayed. Remember that hump of sugar your peepers feasted on?

She said, "Maybe, but you shouldn't call me. I don't want an incident. What do you want? A lady doesn't accept phone calls from strangers."

I said, "A million dollars and a trip to the moon with a bored, trapped, beautiful bitch, you dig? I'm no stranger. I've been popping the elastic in your panties ever since you saw me in the hall. . . ."

Field examples of this kind of rapping were difficult to obtain primarily because talk of this nature generally occurs in private, and when occurring in public places such as parties and taverns, it is carried on in an undertone. However, the first line of a rap, which might be regarded as introductory, is often overheard.

What follows are several such lines collected by two of my students in and around the south and west side of Chicago:

Say pretty, I kin tell you need lovin' by the way you wiggle your ass when you walk—and I'm jus' the guy what' kin put out yo' fire.

Let me rock you mamma, I kin satisfy your soul.

Say, baby, give me the key to your pad. I want to play with your cat.

Baby, you're fine enough to make me spend my rent money.

Baby, I sho' dig your mellow action.

Rapping between men and women often is competitive and leads to a lively repartee, with the women becoming as adept as the men. An example follows:

A man coming from the bathroom forgot to zip his pants. An unescorted party of women kept watching him and laughing among themselves. The man's friends "hip" [inform] him to what's going on. He approaches one woman—"Hey baby, did you see the big black Cadillac with the full tires ready to roll in action just for you?" She answers—"No mother-fucker, but I saw a little gray Volkswagen with two flat tires."

Everybody laughs. His rap was *capped* (excelled, topped).

When "whupping the game" on a "trick" or "lame" (trying to get goods or services from someone who looks like he can be swindled), rapping is often descriptive of the highly stylized verbal part of the maneuver. In well established "con games" the verbal component is carefully prepared and used with great skill in directing the course of the transaction. An excellent illustration of this kind of "rap" came from an adept hustler who was playing the "murphy" game on a white trick. The maneuvers in the "murphy" game are designed to get the *trick* to give his money to the hustler, who in this instance poses as a "steerer" (one who directs or steers customers to a brothel), to keep the whore from stealing it. The hustler then skips with the money (Iceberg Slim 1967:38).

Look Buddy, I know a fabulous house not more than two blocks away. Brother you ain't never seen more beautiful, freakier broads than are in that house. One of them, the prettiest one, can do more with a swipe than a monkey can with a banana. She's like a rubber doll; she can take a hundred positions.

At this point the sucker is wild to get to this place of pure joy. He entreats the con player to take him there, not just direct him to it.

The "murphy" player will prat him (pretend rejection) to enhance his desire. He will say, "Man, don't be offended, but Aunt Kate, that runs the house don't have nothing but highclass white men coming to her place. . . . you know, doctors, lawyers, big-shot politicians. You look like a clean-cut white man, but you ain't in that league are you?"

After a few more exchanges of the "murphy" dialogue, "the mark is separated from his scratch."

An analysis of rapping indicates a number of things. For instance, it is revealing that one raps *to* rather than *with* a person, supporting the impression that rapping is to be regarded more as a performance than a verbal exchange. As with other performances, rapping projects the personality, physical appearance, and style of the performer. In each of the examples given above, in greater or lesser degree, the intrusive "I" of the speaker was instrumental in contributing to the total impression of the rap.

The relative degree of the personality-style component of rapping is generally highest when "asking for some pussy" (rapping 2) and lower when "whupping the game" on someone (rapping 3) or "running something down" (rapping 1). In each instance, however, the personality style component is higher than any other in producing the total effect on the listener.

In asking "for some pussy," for example, where personality and style might be projected through non-verbal means (stance, clothing, walking, looking), one can speak of a "silent rap" where the woman is won without the use of words, or rather, with the words being implied that would generally accompany the non-verbal components.

As a lively way of "running it down" the verbal element consists of two parts: the personality-style component and the information component. Someone *reading* my example of the gang member's narration might get the impression that the information component would be more influential in directing the audience response—that the youth worker would say "So that's how the gang got so big," in which case he would be responding to the information component, instead of saying "Man, that gang member is *bad* (strong, brave)," in which instance he would be responding to the personality-style component of the rap. However, if the reader would *listen* to the gang member on tape or could have been present (*watching-listening*) when the gang member spoke, he more likely would have reacted more to the personality-style component, as my informants did.

Supporting this hypothesis is the fact that in attendance with the youth worker were members of the gang who *already knew* how the gang got started (e.g., "Am I right, Leroy? You was cribbin over there then"), and for whom the information component by itself would have little interest. Their attention was held by the *way* the information was presented—i.e., directed toward the personality-style component.

The verbal element in "whupping the game" on someone, in the above illustration, was an integral part of an overall deception in which the information component and the personality-style component were skillfully manipulated to control the "trick's" response. But again, greater weight must be given to the personality-style component. In the "murphy game," for example, it was this element which got the trick to *trust* the hustler and to leave his money with him for "safekeeping."

The function of rapping in each of the forms discussed above is *expressive*. By this I mean that the speaker raps to project his personality onto the scene or to evoke a generally favorable response from another person or group. In addition, when rapping is used to "ask for some pussy" (rapping 2) or to "whup the game" on someone (rapping 3), its function is *directive*. By this I mean that rapping here becomes the instrument used to manipulate and control people to get them to give up or do something. The difference between rapping to a *fox* (pretty girl) for the purpose of "getting inside her pants" and rapping to a *lame* to get something from him is operational rather than functional. The latter rap contains a concealed motivation whereas the former does not. A statement made by one of my high school informants illustrates this distinction. "If I wanted something from a guy I would try to *trick* him out of it. If I wanted something from a girl I would try to *talk* her out of it (emphasis mine).

Shucking, shucking it, shucking and jiving, S-ing and J-ing or just *jiving* are terms that refer to one form of language behavior practiced by the black when interacting with "the Man" (the white man, the establishment, or *any* authority figure), and to another form of language behavior practiced by blacks when interacting with each other on the peer group level.

When referring to the black's dealings with the white man and the power structure, the above terms are descriptive of the talk and accompanying physical movements of the black that are appropriate to some momentary guise, posture, or facade.

Originally in the South, and later in the North, the black learned that American society had assigned to him a restrictive role and status. Among whites his behavior had to conform to this imposed station and he was constantly reminded to "keep his place." He learned that before white people it was not acceptable to show feelings of indignation, frustration, discontent, pride, ambition, or desire; that real feelings had to be concealed behind a mask of innocence, ignorance, childishness, obedience, humility, and deference. The terms used by the black to describe the role he played before white folks in the South was "tomming" or "jeffing." Failure to accommodate the white southerner in this respect was almost certain to invite psychological and often physical brutality. The following description by black psychiatrist Alvin F. Poussaint (1967:53) is typical and revealing:

Once last year as I was leaving my office in Jackson, Miss., with my Negro secretary, a white policeman yelled, "Hey, boy! Come here!" Somewhat bothered, I retorted: "I'm no boy!" He then rushed at me, inflamed and stood towering over me, snorting, "What d'ja say, boy?" Quickly he frisked me and demanded "What's your name, boy?" Frightened, I replied, "Dr. Poussaint, I'm a physician." He angrily chuckled and hissed, "What's your first name, boy?" When I hesitated he assumed a threatening stance and clenched his fists. As my heart palpitated, I muttered in profound humiliation, "Alvin."

He continued his psychological brutality, bellowing, "Alvin, the next time I call you, you come right away, you hear? You hear?" I hesitated. "You hear me, boy?" My voice trembling with helplessness, but *following my instincts of self-preservation,* I murmured, "Yes, sir." *Now fully satisfied that I had performed and acquiesced to my "boy" status,* he dismissed me with, "Now boy, go on and get out of here or next time we'll take you for a little ride down to the station house! (emphasis mine)."

In northern cities the black encountered authority figures equivalent to the southern "crackers": policemen, judges, probation officers, truant officers, teachers, and "Mr. Charlies" (bosses), and soon learned that the way to get by and avoid difficulty was to *shuck.* Thus, he learned to accommodate "the Man," to use the total orchestration of speech, intonation, gesture, and facial expression to produce whatever appearance would be acceptable. It was a technique and ability that was delivered from fear, and a respect for power, and a will to survive. This type of accommodation is exemplified by the "Yes, sir, Mr. Charlie," or "Anything you say, Mr. Charlie," "Uncle Tom" type of "Negro" of the North. The language and behavior of accommodation was the prototype out of which other slightly modified forms of shucking evolved.

Through accommodation, many blacks became adept at concealing and controlling their emotions and at assuming a variety of postures. They became competent actors in the process. Many developed a keen perception of what affected, motivated, appeased, or satisfied the authority figures with whom they came into contact. What became an accomplished and effective coping mechanism for many blacks to "stay out of trouble" became for others a useful artifice for avoiding arrest or "getting out of trouble" when apprehended. *Shucking it* with a judge, for example, would be to feign repentance in the hope of receiving a lighter or suspended sentence, with a probation officer to give the impression of being serious and responsible so that if you violate probation, you would not be sent back to jail. Robert Conot reports an example of the latter in his book (1967:333):

Joe was found guilty of possession of narcotics. But he did an excellent job of shucking it with the probation officer.

The probation officer interceded for Joe with the judge as follows:

His own attitude toward the present offense appears to be serious and responsible and it is believed that the defendant is an excellent subject for probation.

Some field illustrations of *shucking* to get out of trouble after having been caught come from some seventh grade children from an inner city school in Chicago. The children were asked to "talk their way out of" a troublesome situation. Examples of the situation and their impromptu responses follow:

Situation: You're cursing at this old man and your mother comes walking down the stairs. She hears you. Response to "talk your way out of this," "I'd tell her that I was studying a scene in school for a play."

Situation: What if you were in a store and were stealing something and the manager caught you. Responses: "I would tell him that I was used to putting things in my pocket and then going to pay for them and show the cashier."

"I'd tell him that some of my friends was outside and they wanted some candy so I was goin to put it in my pocket to see if it would fit before I bought it."

"I would start stuttering. Then I would say, 'Oh, Oh, I forgot. Here the money is.' "

Situation: What do you do when you ditch school and you go to the beach and a truant officer walks up and says, "Are you having fun?" and you say, "Yeah," and you don't know he is a truant officer and then he says, "I'm a truant officer, what are you doing out of school?" Responses: "I'd tell him that I had been expelled from school, that I wasn't supposed to go back for seven days."

"I'd tell him that I had to go to the doctor to get a checkup and that my mother said I might as well stay out of school the whole day and so I came over here."

Situation: You're at the beach and they've got posted signs all over the beach and floating on the water and you go past the swimming mark and the sign says "Don't go past the mark!" How do you talk your way out of this to the lifeguard? Responses: "I'd tell him that I was having so much fun in the water that I didn't pay attention to the sign."

"I'd say that I was swimming under water and when I came back up I was behind the sign."

One literary and one field example of shucking to avoid arrest follow. The literary example of shucking comes from Iceberg

Slim's autobiography, already cited above (1967:294). Iceberg, a pimp, shucks before "two red-faced Swede rollers (detectives)" who catch him in a motel room with his whore. My [italicizing] identifies which elements of the passage constitute the shuck.

I put my shaking hands into the pajama pockets. . . . *I hoped I was keeping the fear out of my face. I gave them a wide toothy smile.* They came in and stood in the middle of the room. Their eyes were racing about the room. Stacy was open mouthed in the bed.

I said, *"Yes gentlemen, what can I do for you?"* Lanky said, "We wanta see your I.D."

I went to the closet and got the phony John Cato Fredrickson I.D. I put it in his palm. I felt cold sweat running down my back. They looked at it, then looked at each other.

Lanky said, "You are in violation of the law. You signed the motel register improperly. Why didn't you sign your full name? What are you trying to hide? What are you doing here in town? It says here you're a dancer. We don't have a club in town that books entertainers."

I said, *"Officers, my professional name is Johnny Cato. I've got nothing to hide. My full name had always been too long for the marquees. I've fallen into the habit of using the shorter version. My legs went out last year. I don't dance anymore. My wife and I decided to go into business. We are making a tour of this part of the country. We think that in your town we've found the ideal site for a southern fried chicken shack. My wife has a secret recipe that should make us rich here."*

The following example from the field was related to me by one of my colleagues. One Negro gang member was coming down the stairway from the club room with seven guns on him and encountered some policemen coming up the same stairs. If they stopped and frisked him, he and others would have been arrested. A paraphrase of his shuck follows: "Man, I gotta get away from up there. There's gonna be some trouble and I don't want no part of it." This shuck worked on the minds of the policemen. It anticipated their questions as to why he was leaving the club room, and why he would be in a hurry. He also gave *them* a reason for wanting to get up to the room fast.

It ought to be mentioned at this point that there was not uniform agreement among my informants in characterizing the above examples as shucking. One informant used shucking only in the sense in which it is used among the black peer group—viz., bull-shitting—and characterized the above examples as *jiving or whupping game*. Others, however, identified the above examples as shucking and reserved *jiving and whupping game* for more offensive maneuvers. In fact, one of the apparent critical features of shucking is that the posture of the black when interacting with members of the establishment be a *defensive* one. Some of my informants, for example, regarded the example of a domestic who changed into older clothing than she could afford before going to work in a white household as shucking, provided that she were doing it to keep her job. On the other hand, if she would be doing it to get a raise in pay, they regarded the example as *whupping the game*. Since the game guise and set of maneuvers are brought into play in working on the mind and feeling of the domestic's boss, the difference would seem to be whether the reason behind the pose were to protect oneself or to gain some advantage. Since this distinction is not always so clearly drawn, opinions are often divided. The following example is clearly ambiguous in this respect. Frederick Douglass (1968:57), in telling of how he taught himself to read, would challenge a white boy with whom he was playing by saying that he could write as well as the white boy, whereupon he would write down all the letters he knew. The white boy would then write down more letters than Douglass did. In this way, Douglass eventually learned all the letters of the alphabet. Some of my informants regarded the example as whupping game. Others regarded it as shucking. The former were perhaps focusing on the maneuver rather than the language used. The latter may have felt that any maneuvers designed to learn to read were justifiably defensive. One of my informants said Douglass was "shucking *in order to* whup the game." This latter response seems to be the most revealing. Just as one can *rap* to whup the game on someone, so one can *shuck* or *jive* for the same purpose—i.e., assume a guise or posture or perform some action in a certain way that is designed to work on someone's mind to get him to give up something. The following examples from Malcolm X (1965:87) illustrate the use of *shucking* and *jiving* in this context, though *jive* is the term used. Today, *whupping game* might also be the term used to describe the operation.

Whites who came at night got a better reception; the several Harlem nightclubs they patronized were geared to entertain and *jive* (flatter, cajole) the night white crowd to get their money.

The maneuvers involved here are clearly designed to obtain some benefit or advantage.

Freddie got on the stand and went to work on his own shoes. Brush, liquid polish, brush, paste wax, shine rag, lacquer sole dressing . . . step by step, Freddie showed me what to do.
"But you got to get a whole lot faster. You can't waste time!" Freddie showed me how fast on my own shoes. Then because business was tapering off, he had time to give me a demonstration of how to make the shine rag pop like a firecracker. "Dig the action?" he asked. He did it in slow motion. I got down and tried it on his shoes. I had the principle of it. "Just got to do it faster," Freddie said. *"It's a jive noise, that's all. Cats tip better, they figure you're knocking yourself out!"* (Malcolm X 1965:48, emphasis mine).

I was involved in a field example in which an eight-year-old boy whupped the game on me as follows:

My colleague and I were sitting in a room listening to a tape. The door to the room was open and outside was a soda machine. Two boys came up in the elevator, stopped at the soda machine, and then came into the room and asked: "Do you have a dime for two nickels?" Presumably, the soda machine would not accept nickels. I took out the change in my pocket, found a dime and gave it to the boy for two nickels. After accepting the dime, he looked at the change in my hand and asked, "Can I have two cents? I need carfare to get home." I gave him the two cents.

At first I assumed the verbal component of the maneuver was the rather weak, transparently false reason for wanting the two cents. Actually, as was pointed out to me later, the maneuver began with the first question, which was designed to get me to show my money. He could then ask me for something that he knew I had, making my refusal more difficult. He apparently felt that the reason need not be more than plausible because the amount he wanted was small. Were the amount larger, he would no doubt have elaborated on the verbal element of the game. The form of the verbal element could be directed toward *rapping* or *shucking and jiving*. If he were to rap, the eight-year-old might say, "Man, you know a cat needs to have a little bread to keep the girls in line." Were he to shuck and jive he might make the reason for needing the money more compelling: look hungry, or something similar.

The function of shucking and jiving as it refers to transactions involving confrontation between blacks and "the Man" is both expressive and directive. It is language behavior designed to work on the mind and emotions of the authority figure to get him to feel a certain way or give up something that will be to the other's advantage. When viewed in its entirety, shucking must be regarded as a performance. Words and gestures become the instruments for promoting a certain image, or posture. In the absence of words, shucking would be descriptive of the *actions* which constitute the deception, as in the above example from Malcolm X, where the movement of the shine rag in creating the "jive noise" was the deceptive element. Similarly, in another example, a seventh grade boy recognized the value of stuttering before saying, "Oh, I forgot. Here the money is," knowing that stuttering would be an invaluable aid in presenting a picture of innocent intent. Iceberg showed a "toothy smile" which said to the detective, "I'm glad to see you" and "Would I be glad to see you if I had something to hide?" When the maneuvers seem to be defensive, most of my informants regarded the language behavior as shucking. When the maneuvers were offensive, my informants tended to regard the behavior as "whupping the game." The difference in perception is culturally significant.

Also significant is the fact that the first form of shucking which I have described above, which developed out of accommodation, is becoming less frequently used today by many blacks, as a result of a new found self-assertiveness and pride, challenging the system "that is brutally and unstintingly suppressive of self-assertion" (Poussaint 1967:52). The willingness on the part of many blacks to accept the psychological and physical brutality and general social consequences of not "keeping one's place" is indicative of the changing self-concept of the black man. Ironically, the shocked reaction of the white power structure to the present militancy of the black is partly due to the fact that the black has been so successful at "putting whitey on" via shucking in the past—i.e., compelling a belief in whatever posture the black chose to assume. The extent to which this attitude has penetrated the black community can be seen from a conversation I recently had with a shoe shine attendant at O'Hare airport in Chicago.

I was having my shoes shined and the black attendant was using a polishing machine instead of the rag that was generally used in the past. I asked whether the machine made his work any easier. He did not answer me until about ten seconds had passed and then responded in a loud voice that he "never had a job that was easy, that he would give me one hundred dollars for any *easy* job I could offer him, that the machine made his job 'faster' but not 'easier.' " I was startled at the response because it was so unexpected and I realized that here was a new "breed of cat" who was not going to *shuck* for a big tip or ingratiate himself with "whitey" anymore. A few years ago his response would have been different.

The contrast between this "shoe-shine" scene and the one illustrated earlier from Malcolm X's autobiography, when "shucking whitey" was the common practice, is striking.

Shucking, jiving, shucking and jiving, or *S-ing and J-ing,* when referring to language behavior practiced by blacks when interacting with one another on the peer group level, is descriptive of the talk and gestures that are appropriate to "putting someone on" by creating a false impression, conveying false information, and the like. The terms seem to cover a range from simply telling a lie, to bull-shitting, to subtly playing with someone's mind. An important difference between this form of shucking and that described earlier is that the same talk and gestures that are deceptive to "the Man" are often transparent to those members of one's own group who are able practitioners at shucking themselves. As Robert Conot has pointed out (1967:161), "The Negro who often fools the white officer by 'shucking it' is much less likely to be successful with another Negro. . . ." Also, S-ing and J-ing within the group often has play overtones in which the person being "put on" is aware of the attempts being made and goes along with it for the enjoyment of it or in appreciation of the style involved. An example from Iceberg Slim illustrates this latter point (1967:162):

He said, "Ain't you the little shit ball I chased outta the Roost?"
I said, "Yeah, I'm one and the same. I want to beg your pardon for making you salty (angry) that night. Maybe I coulda gotten a pass if I had told you I'm your pal's nephew. I ain't got no sense, Mr. Jones. I took after my idiot father."

Mr. Jones, perceiving Iceberg's shuck, says,

"Top, this punk ain't hopeless. He's silly as a bitch grinning all the time, but dig how he butters the con to keep his balls outta the fire."

Other citations showing the use of *shucking* and *jiving* to mean simply *lying* follow:

It was a *jive* (false) tip but there were a lot of cats up there on humbles (framed up charges) (Brown 1965:142).
How would you like to have half a "G" ($500) in your slide (pocket)?
I said, "All right, give me the poison and take me to the baby."
He said, "I ain't *shucking* (lying). It's cream-puff work" (Iceberg Slim 1967:68).

Running it down is the term used by ghetto dwellers when they intend to communicate information, either in the form of an explanation, narrative, giving advice, and the like. The information component in the field example cited under rapping (1) would constitute the "run down." In the following literary example, Sweet Mac is "running this Edith broad down" to his friends (King 1965:24):

Edith is the "saved" broad who can't marry out of her religion . . . or do anything else out of her religion for that matter, especially what I wanted her to do. A bogue religion, man! So dig, for the last couple weeks I been quoting the Good Book and all that stuff to her; telling her I am now saved myself, you dig.

The following citation from Claude Brown (1965:390) uses the term with the additional sense of giving advice:

If I saw him (Claude's brother) hanging out with cats I knew were weak, who might be using drugs sooner or later, I'd *run it down* to him.

Iceberg Slim (1967:79) asks a bartender regarding a prospective whore:

Sugar, *run her down* to me. Is the bitch qualified? Is she a whore? Does she have a man?

It seems clear that running it down has simply an informative function, telling somebody something that he doesn't already know.

Gripping is of fairly recent vintage, used by black high school students in Chicago to refer to the talk and facial expression that accompanies a *partial* loss of face or self-possession, or displaying of fear. Its appearance alongside *copping a plea*, which refers to a total loss of face, in which one begs one's adversary for mercy, is a significant new perception. Linking it with the street code which acclaims the ability to "look tough and inviolate, fearless, secure, 'cool,' " (Horton 1967:11) suggests that even the slightest weakening of this posture will be held up to ridicule and contempt. There are always contemptuous overtones attached to the use of the term when applied to others' behavior. One is tempted to link it further with the degree of violence and level of toughness that is required to survive on the street. The intensity of both seems to be increasing. As one of my informants noted, "Today, you're *lucky* if you end up in the hospital" (i.e., are not killed).

Both *gripping* and *copping a plea* refer to behavior that stems from fear and a respect for superior power. An example of gripping comes from the record *Street and Gangland Rhythms* (Band 4, Dumb boy). Lennie meets Calvin and asks him what happened to his lip. Calvin tells Lennie that a boy named Pierre hit him for copying off him in school. Lennie, pretending to be Calvin's brother, goes to confront Pierre. Their dialogue follows:

LENNIE: "Hey you! What you hit my little brother for?"
PIERRE: "Did he tell you what happen man?"

LENNIE: "Yeah, he told me what happen."

PIERRE: "But you . . . but you . . . but you should tell your people to teach him to go to school, man. (Pause) I . . . I know . . . I know I didn't have a right to hit him."

Pierre, anticipating a fight with Lennie if he continued to justify his hitting of Calvin, tried to avoid it by "gripping" with the last line.

Copping a plea, originally used to mean "to plead guilty to a lesser charge to save the state the cost of a trial" (Wentworth and Flexner 1960:123) (with the hope of receiving a lesser or suspended sentence), but is now generally used to mean "to beg, plead for mercy," as in the example "Please cop, don't hit me. I give" (*Street and Gangland Rhythms*, Band 1, Gang fight). This change of meaning can be seen from its use by Piri Thomas (1967:316) in *Down These Mean Streets*.

The night before my hearing, I decided to make a prayer. It had to be on my knees, cause if I was gonna *cop a plea* to God, I couldn't play it cheap.

For the original meaning, Thomas (1967:245) uses "deal for a lower plea."

I was three or four months in the Tombs, waiting for a trial, going to court, waiting for adjournments, trying to *deal for a lower plea*, and what not.

The function of gripping and copping a plea is obviously expressive. One evinces noticeable feelings of fear and insecurity which result in a loss of status among one's peers. At the same time one may arouse in one's adversary feelings of contempt.

An interesting point to consider with respect to copping a plea is whether the superficial features of the form may be borrowed to mitigate one's punishment, in which case it would have the same directive function as shucking, and would be used to arouse feelings of pity, mercy, and the like. The question whether one can arouse such feelings among one's street peers by copping a plea is unclear. In the example cited above from the record *Street and Gangland Rhythms*, which records the improvisations of eleven- and twelve-year-old boys, one of the boys convincingly *acts out* the form of language behavior, which was identified by all my informants as "copping a plea" with the police officer: "Please cop, don't hit me. I give." In this example it was clearly an artifice with a directive function and here we have the familiar dynamic opposition of black vs. authority figure discussed under shucking.

"Signifying" is the term used to describe the language behavior that, as Abrahams has defined it, attempts to "imply, goad, beg, boast by indirect verbal or gestural means" (1964:267). In Chicago it is also used as a synonym to describe a form of language behavior which is more generally known as "sounding" elsewhere and will be discussed under the latter heading below.

Some excellent examples of signifying as well as of other forms of language behavior discussed above come from the well known "toast" (narrative form) "The signifying monkey and the lion" which was collected by Abrahams from black street corner bards in Philadelphia. In the above toast the monkey is trying to get the lion involved in a fight with the elephant (Abrahams 1964:150ff.):

Now the lion came through the jungle one peaceful day,
When the signifying monkey stopped him, and that is what he
started to say:
He said, "Mr. Lion," he said, "A bad-assed motherfucker
down your way,"
He said, "Yeah! The way he talks about your folks is a
certain shame.
"I've even heard him curse when he mentioned your grandmother's
name."
The lion's tail shot back like a forty-four
When he went down that jungle in all uproar.

Thus the monkey has goaded the lion into a fight with the elephant by "signifying," indicating that the elephant has been "sounding on" (insulting) the lion. When the lion comes back, thoroughly beaten up, the monkey again "signifies" by making fun of the lion:

. . . a lion came back through the jungle more dead than alive,
When the monkey started some more of that signifying jive.

He said, "Damn, Mr. Lion, you went through here yesterday,
the jungle rung. . . .
"Now you come back today, damn near hung."

The monkey, of course, is delivering this taunt from a safe distance away on the limb of a tree when his foot slips and he falls to the ground, at which point

Like a bolt of lightning, a stripe of white heat,
The lion was on the monkey with all four feet.

In desperation the monkey quickly resorts to "copping a plea":

The monkey looked up with a tear in his eyes.
He said, "Please, Mr. Lion, I apologize."

His "plea," however, fails to move the lion to any show of pity or mercy so the monkey tries another verbal ruse: "shucking":

He said, "You lemme get my head out of the sand
Ass out of the grass, I'll fight you like a natural man."

In this he is more successful as

The lion jumped back and squared for a fight.
The motherfucking monkey jumped clear out of sight.

A safe distance away again, the monkey returns to "signifying":

He said, "Yeah, you had me down, you had me at last.
"But you left me free, now you can still kiss my ass."

The above example illustrates the methods of provocation, goading, and taunting as artfully practiced by the signifier. Interestingly, when the *function* of signifying is *directive*, the *tactic* which is employed is one of *indirection*—i.e., the signifier reports or repeats what someone else has said about the listener; the "report" is couched in plausible language designed to compel belief and arouse feelings of anger and hostility. There is also the implication that if the listener fails to do anything about it—what has to be "done" is usually quite clear—his status will be seriously compromised. Thus the lion is compelled to vindicate the honor of his family by fighting or else leave the impression that he is afraid, and that he is not "king" of the jungle. When used to direct action, "signifying" is like "shucking" in also being deceptive and subtle in approach and depending for success on the naïveté or gullibility of the person being "put on."

When the function of signifying is only expressive (i.e., to arouse feelings of embarrassment, shame, frustration or futility, for the purpose of diminishing someone's status, but without directive implication), the tactic employed is direct in the form of a taunt, as in the above example where the monkey is making fun of the lion. Signifying frequently occurs when things are dull and someone wishes to generate some excitement and interest within the group. This is shown in another version of the above toast:

There hadn't been no disturbin in the jungle for quite a bit,
For up jumped the monkey in the tree one day and laughed, "I guess I'll start some shit."

Sounding is the term which is today most widely known for the game of verbal insult known in the past as "playing the dozens," "the dirty dozens," or just "the dozens." Other current names for the game have regional distribution: *signifying* or "sigging" (Chicago), *joning* (Washington, D.C.), *screaming* (Harrisburg), and so on. In Chicago, the term "sounding" would be descriptive of the initial remarks which are designed to "sound" out the other person to see whether he will play the game. The verbal insult is also subdivided, the term "signifying" applying to insults which are hurled directly at the person and the "dozens" applying to insults hurled at your opponent's family, especially, the mother.

Sounding is often catalyzed by "signifying" remarks referred to earlier, such as "Are you going to let him say that about your mama?" in order to spur on an exchange between two (or more) other members of the group. It is begun on a relatively low key and built up by means of verbal exchanges.

Abrahams (1962b:209–10) describes the game:

One insults a member of another's family; others in the group make disapproving sounds to spur on the coming exchange. The one who has been insulted feels at this point that he must reply with a slur on the protagonist's family which is clever enough to defend his honor (and therefore that of his family). This, of course, leads the other (once again, more due to pressure from the crowd than actual insult) to make further jabs. This can proceed until everyone is bored with the whole affair, until one hits the other (fairly rare), or until some other subject comes up that interrupts the proceedings (the usual state of affairs).

McCormick (1960:8) describes the dozens as a verbal contest

. . . in which the players strive to bury one another with vituperation. In the play, the opponent's mother is especially slandered . . . then, in turn fathers are identified as queer and syphilitic. Sisters are whores, brothers are defective, cousins are "funny" and the opponent is himself diseased.

An example of the "game" collected by one of my students goes as follows:

Frank looked up and saw Leroy enter the Outpost. Leroy walked past the room where Quinton, "Nap," "Pretty Black," "Cunny," Richard, Haywood, "Bull," and Reese sat playing cards. As Leroy neared the T.V. room, Frank shouted to him.

FRANK: "Hey, Leroy, your mama—calling you man."

Leroy turned and walked toward the room where the sound came from. He stood in the door and looked at Frank.

LEROY: "Look motherfuckers, I don't play that shit."

FRANK, signifying: "Man, I told you cats 'bout that mama jive" (as if he were concerned about how Leroy felt).

LEROY: "That's all right Frank; you don't have to tell those funky motherfuckers nothing; I'll fuck me up somebody yet."

Frank's face lit up as if he were ready to burst his side laughing. "Cunny" became pissed at Leroy.

"CUNNY": "Leroy, you stupid bastard, you let Frank make a fool of you. *He* said that 'bout your mamma."

"PRETTY BLACK": "Aw, fat ass head, 'Cunny' shut up."

"CUNNY": "Ain't that some shit. This black slick head motor flicker got 'nough to call somebody 'fathead.' Boy, you so black, you sweat super Permalube Oil."

This eased the tension of the group as they burst into loud laughter.

"PRETTY BLACK": "What 'chu laughing 'bout 'Nap,' with your funky mouth smelling like dog shit."

Even Leroy laughed at this.

"NAP": "Your mama motherfucker."

"PRETTY BLACK": "Your funky mama too."

"NAP" strongly: "It takes twelve barrels of water to make a steamboat run; it takes an elephant's dick to make your Grandmammy come; she been elephant fucked, camel fucked and hit side the head with your Grandpappy's nuts."

REESE: "Goddor damn; go on and rap motherfucker."

Reese began slapping each boy in his hand, giving his positive approval of "Nap's" comment. "Pretty Black," in an effort not to be outdone but directing his verbal play elsewhere, stated:

"PRETTY BLACK": "Reese, what you laughing 'bout? You so square you shit bricked shit."

FRANK: "Whoooowee!"

REESE sounded back: "Square huh, what about your nappy ass hair before it was stewed; that shit was so bad till, when you went to bed at night, it would leave your head and go on the corner and meddle."

The boys slapped each other in the hand and cracked up.

"PRETTY BLACK": "On the streets meddling, bet Dinky didn't offer me no pussy and I turned it down."

FRANK: "Reese scared of pussy."

"PRETTY BLACK": "Hell yeah; the greasy mother rather fuck old, ugly funky cock Sue Willie than get a piece of ass from a decent broad."

FRANK: "Goddor damn! Not Sue Willie."

"PRETTY BLACK": "Yeah ol' meat beating Reese rather screw that cross-eyed, clappy bitch, who when she cry, tears drip down her ass."

HAYWOOD: "Don't be so mean, Black."

REESE: "Aw shut up, you half-white bastard."

FRANK: "Wait man, Haywood ain't gonna hear much more of that half-white shit; he's a brother too."

REESE: "Brother, my black ass; that white ass landlord gotta be this motherfucker's paw."

"CUNNY": "Man, you better stop foolin with Haywood; he's turning red."

HAYWOOD: "Fuck yall" (as he withdrew from the "sig" game).

FRANK: "Yeah, fuck yall; let's go to the stick hall."

The above example of "sounding" is an excellent illustration of the "game" as played by fifteen-, sixteen-, and seventeen-year-old Negro boys, some of whom have already acquired the verbal skill which for them is often the basis for having a high "rep." Abrahams (1964:62) observed that ". . . the ability with words is as highly valued as physical strength." In the sense that the status of one of the participants in the game is diminished if he has to resort to fighting to answer a verbal attack, verbal ability may be even more highly regarded than physical ability. However, age within the peer group may be a factor in determining the relative value placed on verbal vis-à-vis physical ability.

Nevertheless, the relatively high value placed on verbal ability must be clear to most black boys at an early age in their cognitive development. Abrahams (1964:53) is probably correct in linking "sounding" to the taunt which is learned and practiced as a child and is part of "signifying," which has its origins in childlike behavior. The taunts of the "Signifying Monkey," illustrated above, are good examples of this.

Most boys begin their activity in "sounding" by compiling a repertoire of "one liners." When the game is played among this age group, the one who has the greatest number of such remarks wins. Here are some examples of "one liners" collected from fifth and sixth grade black boys in Chicago:

Yo mama is so bowlegged, she looks like the bite out of a donut.
You mama sent her picture to the lonely hearts club, and they sent it back and said "We ain't that lonely"!
Your family is so poor the rats and roaches eat lunch out.
Your house is so small the roaches walk single file.

I walked in your house and your family was running around the table. I said, "Why you doin that?" Your mama say, "First one drops, we eat."

Real proficiency in the game comes to only a small percentage of those who play it, as might be expected. These players have the special skill in being able to turn what their opponents have said and attack them with it. Thus, when someone indifferently said "fuck you" to Concho, his retort was immediate and devastating: "Man, you haven't even kissed me yet."

The "best talkers" from this group often become the successful street-corner, barber shop, and pool hall story tellers who deliver the long rhymed, witty narrative stories called "toasts." A portion of the toast "The Signifying Monkey and the Lion" was given above. However, it has also produced entertainers, such as Dick Gregory and Redd Foxx, who are virtuosos at repartee, and preachers, whose verbal power has been traditionally esteemed.

The function of the "dozens" or "sounding" is invariably self-assertive. The speaker borrows status from his opponent through an exercise of verbal power. The opponent feels compelled to regain his status by "sounding" back on the speaker or some other member of the group whom he regards as more vulnerable. The social interaction of the group at the Outpost, for example, demonstrated less an extended verbal barrage between two people than a "pecking order." Frank "sounds" on Leroy; "Cunny" "signifies" on Leroy; "Pretty Black" "sounds" on "Cunny"; "Cunny" "sounds" back on "Pretty Black" who (losing) turns on "Nap"; "Nap" "sounds" (winning back on "Pretty Black"; "Pretty Black" finally borrows back his status by "sounding" on Reese. Reese "sounds" back on "Pretty Black" but gets the worst of the exchange and so borrows back his status from Haywood. "Cunny" also "sounds" on Haywood. Haywood defaults. Perhaps by being "half-white," Haywood feels himself to be the most vulnerable.

The presence of a group seems to be especially important in controlling the game. First of all, one does not "play" with just anyone since the subject matter is concerned with things that in reality one is quite sensitive about. It is precisely *because* "Pretty

Black" has a "black slick head" that makes him vulnerable to "Cunny's" barb, especially now when the Afro-American "natural" hair style is in vogue. It is precisely *because* Reese's girl-friend *is* ugly that makes him vulnerable to "Pretty Black's" jibe that Reese can't get a "piece of ass from a decent broad." It is *because* the living conditions are so poor and intolerable that they can be used as subject matter for "sounding." Without the control of the group "sounding" will frequently lead to a fight. This was illustrated by a tragic epilogue concerning Haywood; when Haywood was being "sounded" on in the presence of two girls by his best friend (other members of the group were absent), he refused to tolerate it. He went home, got a rifle, came back, and shot and killed his friend. In the classroom from about the fourth grade on fights among black boys invariably are caused by someone "sounding" on the other person's mother.

Significantly, the subject matter of "sounding" is changing with the changing self-concept of the black with regard to those physical characteristics that are characteristically "Negro," and which in the past were vulnerable points in the black psyche: blackness and "nappy" hair.

They still occur, as in the above example: from the Outpost, and the change in the above illustration is notably more by what has been added than subtracted—viz., the attack on black *slick* hair and half-white color. With regard to the latter, however, it ought to be said that for many blacks, blackness was always highly esteemed and it might be more accurate to regard the present sentiment of the black community toward skin color as reflecting a shifted attitude for only a *portion* of black community. This suggests that "sounding" on someone's light skin color is not new. Nevertheless, one can regard the previously favorable attitude toward light skin color and "good hair" as the prevailing one. "Other things being equal, the more closely a woman approached her white counterpart, the more attractive she was considered to be, by both men and women alike. 'Good hair' (hair that is long and soft) and light skin were the chief criteria" (Liebow 1966: 138). Also, children's rhymes which before "black power" were

If you like black
Keep your black ass back

and

If you like white
You're all right

have respectively changed to

If you like black
You have a Cadillac

and

If you like white
You're looking for a fight.

Both Abrahams and McCormick link the "dozens" to the over-all psychosocial growth of the black male. McCormick has stated that a "single round of a dozen or so exchanges frees more pent-up aggressions than will a dose of sodium pentothal." The fact that one permits a kind of abuse within the rules of the game and within the confines of the group which would otherwise not be tolerated is filled with psychological importance, and this aspect is rather fully discussed by Abrahams. It also seems important, however, to view its function from the perspective of the non-participating members of the group. Its function for them may be directive: i.e., they incite and prod individual members of the group to combat for the purpose of energizing the elements, of simply relieving the boredom of just "hanging around" and the malaise of living in a static restrictive environment. One of my informants remarked that he and other members of the group used to feed insults to one member to hurl back at another if they felt that the contest was too uneven, "to keep the game going." In my above illustration from the Outpost, for example, Frank seemed to be the precipitating agent as well as chorus for what was going on and "Bull" did not directly participate at all. For them the "dozens" may have had the social function of "having a little fun," or as Loubee said to Josh of just "passing the time" (Shorris 1966:65).

A summary analysis of the different forms of language behavior which have been discussed permits the following generalizations.

The prestige norms which influence black speech behavior are those which have been successful in manipulating and controlling people and situations. The function of all the forms of language behavior discussed above, with the exception of "running it down," was either expressive or expressive-directive. Specifically, this means that language was used to project personality, assert oneself, or arouse emotion, frequently with the additional purpose of getting the person to give up or do something which will be of some benefit to the speaker. Only "running it down" has as its primary function to communicate information and often here, too, the personality and style of the speaker in the form of "rapping" is projected along with the information.

The purpose for which language is used suggests that the speaker views the social situations into which he moves as essentially agonistic, by which I mean that he sees his environment as consisting of a series of transactions which require that he be continually ready to take advantage of a person or situation or defend himself against being victimized. He has absorbed what Horton (1967:8) has called "street rationality." As one of Horton's respondents put it: "The good hustler . . . conditions his mind and must never put his guard down too far, to relax, or he'll be taken."

I have carefully avoided, throughout this paper, delimiting the group within the black community of whom the language behavior and perspective of their environment is characteristic. While I have no doubt that it is true of those who are generally called "street people" I am not certain of the extent to which it is also true of a much larger portion of the black community, especially the male segment. My informants consisted of street people, high school students, and blacks, who by their occupation as community and youth workers possess what has been described as a "sharp sense of the streets." Yet it is difficult to find a black male in the community who has *not* witnessed or participated in the "dozens" or heard of "signifying," or "rapping," or "shucking and jiving" at some time while he was growing up. It would be equally difficult to imagine a high school student in a Chicago inner city school not being touched by what is generally regarded a "street culture" in some way.

In conclusion, by blending style and verbal power, through "rapping," "sounding," and "running it down," the black in the ghetto establishes his personality; through "shucking," "gripping," and "copping a plea" he shows his respect for power; through "jiving" and "signifying" he stirs up excitement. With all of the above, he hopes to manipulate and control people and situations to give himself a winning edge.

SELECTED READINGS

Roger D. Abrahams, 1962 b. Playing the dozens. *Journal of American Folklore*, 75: 209–220.

———, 1964. *Deep Down in the Jungle—Negro Narrative Folklore in the Streets of Philadelphia*. Hatboro, Pennsylvania: Folklore Associates.

Claude Brown, 1965. *Manchild in the Promised Land*. New York: Macmillan.

Robert Conot, 1967. *Rivers of Blood, Years of Darkness*. New York: Bantam.

Frederick Douglass, 1968. *Narrative of the Life of an American Slave*. New York: New American Library.

John Gumperz and Dale Hymes, eds., 1964. The ethnography of communication. *American Anthropologist*, 66: No. 6, pt. 2.

John Horton, 1967. Time and cool people. *Trans-Action*, 4: 5–12.

Woody King, Jr., 1965. The game. *Liberator*, 5: 20–25.

Elliot Liebow, 1967. *Kally's Corner: A Study of Negro Street-Corner Men*. Boston: Little, Brown.

Mack McCormick, 1960. *The Dirty Dozens. The Unexpurgated Folksongs of Men*. Arhoolie Record Album.

Malcolm X, 1965. *The Autobiography of Malcolm X*. New York: Grove Press.

Alvin Poussaint, 1967. A Negro psychiatrist explains the Negro psyche. *New York Times*, August 20, Section 6: 52 ff.

Earl Shorris, 1966. *Ofay*. New York: Dell.

Piri Thomas, 1967. *Down These Mean Streets*. New York: Knopf.

Harold Wentworth and Stuart Berg Flexner, 1960. *Dictionary of American Slang*. New York: Crowell.

Henry H. Mitchell

CHAPTER 8
Black English

Black preaching requires the use of Black language—the rich rendition of English spoken in the Black ghetto. To many Americans, of whatever color, such an assertion may cause some consternation. People will ask, "Do you want me to say 'dis and dat'?" or "Must I unlearn all my learning and talk 'flat'?" This raises three important questions: 1.) Why Black English in the first place? 2.) How is it learned? 3.) And what is Black English anyway? I shall try to resolve them in the order given.

The not-very-well-known fact about all spoken English is that there is no one universally accepted or "proper" version. "Standard" American English, to the extent that there is a version more generally accepted than others, is probably a North-Midland white, middle-class variety of English. Every other region of the U.S.A. will have its own variant of this speech standard, even within the same middle-class white majority. Every ethnic group or regional subculture will have its variants, each peculiarly conditioned by the influences of history, geography, social class, and the like.

Such groups are sometimes referred to as speech communities. Within such a speech community it is easiest to communicate by using the language of that group. The subtle meaning and shades of meaning, the particular pronunciation and accent, the intonation and total signal system of any given group are altogether "proper" to that group. In fact, no language is improper among its own users, since it alone is most capable of the task for which all language exists: communication.

This rule is especially meaningful to missionaries in foreign lands. They take great care to learn the communication system of the people among whom they are to work. However, in America, a diabolical combination of racism, class snobbery, and naïveté has caused Blacks as well as whites to assume, consciously or unconsciously, that there is a single proper American English, and that the language spoken by most Black people is a crude distortion of it. In religious circles, standard white middle-class English is assumed to be the only vehicle for the preaching of the gospel and the praising of the Lord in public. The results have been rather disastrous for the church of the Black masses, because the vast majority of Black-culture churches have found it difficult to understand or relate to trained Black clergymen preaching whiteese to them. Consequently, those trained Blacks who are also fluent in Black English—the language of their people—are conspicuously effective and in great demand.

It is true that Black clergymen have had to be, for the most part, white-culture proficient in order to satisfy college and seminary requirements. But then American colleges and seminaries are heavily conditioned by the not-so-subtle assumption that "white is right," especially the white, middle-class culture and its language.

The result is that, when a substantial number of Black-culture churches have been faced with the choice between a pastor who could communicate with them or a man who was merely educated, they have chosen communication over education. In fact, it has often been argued by the faithful that those preachers who deliberately tried to preach white to their Black congregations were possibly not even "saved." The sincerest efforts of trained men to relate themselves to the Black-ghetto church have accordingly been misunderstood at times. Their efforts have been tainted by their unconscious lack of the cultural integrity which is crucial to Black identity. To lose one's language is to lose one's identity. To refuse to learn and use the people's language is an affront to the people one presumes to serve. The new breed of truly educated Black clergymen has been lately awakened to the subtleties of this impasse, and they are doing something about it. While it may still be embarrassing to the educated Black seminarian, who is still conditioned by the presumptions of the white middle class, it is rewarding for others who have learned to come to terms with their heritage to have it whispered around the churches that "the pastor's finally got religion!"

On the other hand, some Black churches have pastors whose fluency is limited to the Black idiom. Because they feel themselves limited, such pastors often avoid contact beyond their home churches and their own culture. As a result, their churches may forfeit involvement in issues or programs which are relevant to many needs of the Black man today. Their limited effectiveness creates a vacuum or a distortion in ghetto leadership, and the Black community may be divorced from the larger influence of the church.

One answer to this problem lies in teaching pastors who are already fluent in Black exposition to be at home in standard English, so that they can increase their capacities to deal with issues. Another answer lies in the teaching of Black language and religious culture to the professionally trained Black clergy, who may then make more effective use of their training and deal more effectively with the needs of the Black masses and the issues affecting their well-being. Still a third answer lies in the recruitment of able Black-culture-oriented candidates for training in the seminaries, carefully avoiding brainwashing them or stripping them of their original culture. All too many theological seminaries have been in the habit of molding Blacks into a white image and sending them out to serve Black people in Black churches. And this unfortunate practice is not limited to seminaries that are white. But the rigidity of these white-oriented seminaries is diminishing somewhat, and a new generation of Blacks is being permitted to discover the beauty of being what they are—Black.

The question will no doubt arise as to why the church is not used to convey standard culture and "lift" the Black masses into the mainstream of the American culture and its benefits. The answer is very simple: no free Black-culture church will ever call a pastor who cannot speak the language of its people. To expect them to learn their cultural duality from a Black white man is absurd. Neither faith nor culture will be communicated by a preacher whose language sounds to the ghetto resident as if he is putting on airs, for implicit in his posturing is a deprecation of the people he wants to serve. His rejection will be summary if it is sensed that his fundamental loyalties are to his white reference group rather than to the religious culture of his own people.

The seminary-trained Black must be a model of all things to all men, helping the cultures to come closer together by being an instrument of translation of each to the other. He must be fluent in Black language, for this is fundamental to his calling, and yet he must also be fluent in standard English, because he must communicate beyond his congregation. His language must be Black enough to generate confidence in an identity which is clearly Black. He must be able to reach the souls of Black folk with Soul language, putting them at ease and gaining maximum access by avoiding all the linguistic signals of social distance from his congregation. Yet he must also be able to reinforce and keep alive the language learnings of the young people of his congregation which link them to the larger community. He must assure his congregation that he doesn't talk flat all the time, so that they will have confidence that he can adequately represent their interests outside the ghetto.

This type of bilingual skill has been resisted by middle-class teachers in the Black ghetto, on the grounds that it is phony and seems to make fun of the ghetto culture as a setting for an Amos-and-Andy set of mannerisms. If Black language were suggested as the sole vehicle of spoken communication, then of course the protesting teachers would seem to have a point. Even so, Black language is far more than an ignorant jumble of unaspirated mumbling. It is the lingua franca of the Black ghetto, full of subtle shadings of sound and significance, cadences and color. It beguiles the hearer because it is familiar. It establishes rapport with him and influences him, without his being conscious of the fact that the preacher has deliberately chosen the language most appropriate to his task of meaningful communication. This is one of the chief skills of the Black preacher who is effective and charismatic despite his white-oriented professional training. The cadences of the late Dr. Martin Luther King, Jr., were unashamedly Black. His learning could be used to lead the Black masses because he was always heard as a Soul Brother.

Before offering some technical description and analysis of the Black language presently in wide use, I should perhaps explain, as far as possible, how this language is learned. All languages are learned best by living and identifying with the people who speak them. In a sense, one must for a time burn his bridges and identify solely with the target culture group. When this is done, the language will be learned subconsciously. Thus children reproduce the speech of those socially closest to them (family and peer group) rather than those whom they may hear most—e.g., teacher or television. Should the family change neighborhoods and encounter a difference between their speech and the speech of the child's new playmates, the child's choice of identity will be subconsciously decided, but that choice will become evident through his choice of speech patterns. The preacher who grew up with white speech will best learn Black speech after he has overcome the subtle vestiges of the white self-identity that went with his white tongue. To be sure, he may need to retain some whiteness in order to be truly bicultural and bilingual. But if he is to talk Black, and if he hopes to reach Blacks effectively, he will have to become a person of primarily Black identity. Given an acceptance and appreciation of Black identity, one's ear is attuned to the sounds of one's folks, and one's tongue consciously and subconsciously shapes its own sounds to avoid contrast with those to whom one feels closest. The more unconscious and therefore not self-conscious the Black utterance is, the better the possibilities of perfect communication.

The Black preacher might well develop a range of situations in which he employs degrees of Blackness in utterance. For example, a sermon or conversation might include a quote of extremely Black speech in such a way as not to ridicule the original speaker and, in fact, to interpret that person more accurately. In another situation, one might deal rather analytically with a matter in the pure standard dialect. In still another situation, one might paraphrase a verse of scripture. For instance, a Black preacher might render God's speech to Peter in the text against racism (Acts 10:14–15): "Looka here, Peter, don't you be callin' *nothin'* I made common or dirty!"

This, of course, requires the Black intonation and accent so necessary to the complete Black signal system, but the Blackness of such a translation must, in some measure, come through on even the black and white of this paper. It has several important advantages. In the first place it presents the message in a familiar and authentic folk-art form, and attracts attention by giving pleasure and making folks at home more comfortable. Secondly, it reinforces and supports Black identity by putting in the mouth of God the language of the people. In white-language preaching this highly important emotional support is reserved for members of the white-speech community. No Black man can truly identify with a God who speaks only the language of the white oppressor. A Black rendition of scripture does in language what a Black Christ or a Black Madonna does in art. God is divested of his "proper," white, socially distant role, a personification of deity completely outside Black culture and life. Just how great is this need for re-identification of God with Black people can be seen in the words of a prayer by a faithful Black deacon: "If your blue eyes in glory find anything wrong in this place . . ."

Finally, the message is made much more understandable by the use of familiar language. The lesson of the message is better learned because the scene is experienced in the worship rather than simply heard in theory. The experience factor is greatly reduced when the message is offered in a foreign tongue.

The progress here discussed is parallel to the changes of language and image now being developed in textbooks for Black ghetto schools across the country. Just as the language of the "Dick and Jane" readers gets minimal response from the Black-ghetto child (and has therefore to be discarded), so must total dependence on white middle-class language be translated for effective Black-ghetto preaching, and for the same reasons. In fact, if a preacher uses standard English exclusively with no Black sounds and shadings, the chances of his being asked back to a Black-culture church are not great. It goes without saying that his chances of receiving a call to pastor such a church are virtually nil. The rejection of the preacher will not be a rejection of his education per se, but a resistance to the imposition of a different culture on an institution that is Black owned and Black controlled, and can therefore insist on being led by a Black pastor.

What then are the contrasting features which distinguish Black English from standard English? One is the slower rate of delivery. Another is Black sentence structure, which on the average is simpler than white middle-class sentence structure. Still other differences range all the way from highly technical and subtle usages down to the peculiar tonal inflections characteristic of Southern Blacks. As I have said, no book about these speech features could teach one to use them effectively. The best that can be done in a book is to describe them. Only a healthily Black identity, born of acute exposure to the Black experience and of complete Black self-acceptance, can complete the process of lingual identification and implant Black language naturally on one's tongue.

Perhaps the commonest feature stereotypically associated with Black speech is the "down home" drawl, which must not be confused with the white Southern drawl from the same region. The Black drawl is accompanied by "flatness," a word denoting lazily articulated vowels and consonants, and imprecise closure or dropped word endings. This description must not be taken as a white-standard judgment against Black language or culture. It is simply a fact that the word "lazy" applies to both Black and white Southern pronunciation of the long vowel "I." It is composed of "ah" and "ee," and both give only the first part. But the whites probably drop it more than Blacks, either North or South. In fact, the first Black President of the United States will probably have to sound much more standard on his long "I" vowels than did the first President from Texas, who was white.

If one can forget the negative connotations of lazy speech, one can sense that soft velvet sounds have a much greater capacity to communicate warmth and avoid harsh overtones. Few can deny the charm of a drawl. Many Southern whites go so far as to consider it an identity signal of Southern aristocracy. Whatever fear Blacks have of a drawl, as used by whites, has been conditioned not by the sound itself but by the racist treatment that has all too often gone with it. In a word, the softened consonants have universal advantage and signal value in the Black speech community. The degree of softening may vary greatly, but Blackese is surely not characterized by crisp consonants.

A full-fledged drawl, however, is obviously not by any means a universal characteristic of Black speech. Neither is another feature: unmatched subjects and verbs. This failure of agreement between subjects and verbs is called bad grammar, and it may be so within the white middle-class communication system. But the word "bad" must never be used by one culture regarding another. No language is bad which conveys adequately the intended meaning to the intended audience. "Ungrammatical" is a less judgmental term, but it still implies that there is one form which is standard, by which all others are judged. Among Blacks of the ghetto, the speaker does not have to say "You is" to be accepted, but he is certainly permitted to say it if he wishes, and many will not hear anything wrong about it. "You is" *and* "You are" are permitted in the Black mother tongue.

Much good communication takes place in Black culture without such extreme contrasts with white language as "You is." One can be quite Black and still use neither a drawl nor such bad grammar as "He play the piano." Perhaps the most important thing is that a Black hears departures from white standard English and has no urge to correct them, because he has lost all desire to please the white man with his own speech.

Another interesting contrast between Blackese and standard speech is in the different uses to which Blacks put function words or prepositions. When one says in Blackese "I got sick behind it," he means after it in time and not behind it in space. Blacks sang "Freedom over Me" in slavery days, and young Blacks popularized the slave song in the sit-in era, but the word "over" designated no relationship normally associated with the preposition "over" in white speech. Then there is the common Black statement "I'm gonna go up side your head." It means, "I'm going to hit you on the head." It implies two prepositions, "up" and "beside," but here again is a wide and common departure from standard usage. A final illustration is the word "around." To "mess around" is colloquial for aimless or nonproductive activity. But in Blackese the usage is altered to give the verb "mess" a direct object. It is common to hear a Black complain, "You messed me around."

It is not mandatory that a Black use this language, but it never hurts. A Black English teacher in a high school told me recently of a noisy back row of Blacks who simply would not join the class. When she departed from the script and sternly declared, "Y'all ain't talkin' 'bout nothin'!" they sat up and took notice. This was her opening wedge of communication.

Another common contrast with standard English involves archaic English and logical but ungrammatical constructions. One of these is quoted above in God's response to Peter. "Don't you be callin' . . ." is a logical combination, but the grammatical or accepted way to say it in whitese is "Don't you dare call . . ." This same irregular verb "to be" is treated by Blacks as a regular verb and a report on a person's condition may be rendered "He be's all right." An archaic pronunciation of the auxiliary verb "might" survives in a common response in Black lodge ritual as they intone: "So mote it be." And it survives as "mought" (rhymes with "out") in the conversation of Blacks from Virginia and North Carolina. Blacks also use words like "fetch," "tote," "holp" (for "help"), and "yonder," to a greater extent than other groups. But all these usages can be found among whites, particularly Appalachian whites.

It may be argued on the basis of this shared vocabulary that language differences are regional rather than racial. But, as has been pointed out already, there is a considerable difference between white Southern dialect and Blackese. Regional influences will indeed be shared between Black and white, but the major influence on Black culture and language is the Black experience, and this is not shared with whites. The Black man lives in another world from the white man of the same Southern city. And the racial aspect of cultural difference only increases in the North, where white Southerners are assimilated or at least distributed, and Blacks from the South are huddled together to cling to their beleaguered dignity and their mother tongue. Blackese will mean far more to a Northern-born resident of the ghetto than Southernese would mean to an ex-Southern white, simply because the white man can literally be assimilated and the Black cannot.

However, even with the easy adjustment of whites among whites, the rule that all men love to hear their mother tongue is illustrated by the popularity among whites of Hillbilly or Country and Western music, a part of whose charm is the dialect. Affluent whites, as well as deprived white migrants, like to hear the way people spoke "when I was a kid." Blacks whose natural inclinations have not been destroyed will follow the rule also. The native language is comforting to all who have not denied their roots and dignity.

This indicates something very significant to the educated Black clergyman, about how he must be linguistically flexible in order to communicate with all of his congregation at all times and in all circumstances. In times of crisis especially, no man hears well the words of a stranger spoken in a foreign tongue. To communicate effectively the Black preacher has to adjust his language to a variety of contexts and many shadings within the two basic cultures, Black and white. The most crucial of his contexts is the Black pulpit, and the most demanding culture for his purposes is Blackamerican, in contrast with what is considered standard or white middle class.

PART 3
Rhetorical Case Studies

The seven articles in this section provide us with representative analyses of the rhetoric of a range of black communicators, from Henry Highland Garnet to Martin Luther King, Jr. In the first article Arthur L. Smith analyzes Garnet's rhetorical position as a preacher and a revolutionary. This discussion is followed by Robert C. Dick's interpretative essay "Negro Oratory in the Anti-Slavery Societies: 1830–1860." Thomas E. Harris and Patrick C. Kennicott explain Booker T. Washington's stance as conciliatory rhetoric. In a fourth article, Finley C. Campbell sees Malcolm X's "Message to the Grass Roots" as symbolically

*significant for the black movement. Following Campbell's article,
John Illo adds to an understanding of the prophetic vision
and radical departure of Malcolm's rhetoric. A thorough, critical
examination by Wayne Brockriede and Robert L. Scott puts the
rhetorical tactics of Stokely Carmichael into focus. A final
essay by Haig A. Bosmajian analyzes the rhetorical dimensions
of Martin Luther King's "Letter from Birmingham Jail."*

*These rhetorical case studies illustrate that discourse, historical
and contemporary, among black Americans has been concerned
with the making and sustaining of a viable protest against
injustice. Each author tries to lay bare the essential structure
of a given black communicative experience by making analyses
and critical judgments according to a rhetorical methodology.
In the end these scholars give us a varied but coherent look at
black rhetoric through their investigations.*

Arthur L. Smith

CHAPTER 9
Henry Highland Garnet:
Black Revolutionary in Sheep's Vestments

In the nineteenth century no social movement captured the imaginations and commanded the minds of intellectuals, black and
white, more than the antislavery effort. Numerous speeches were
made by black and white abolitionists bent on the death of slavery,
and some rhetorical studies have been made of the significant
white abolitionists.[1] On the other hand, black spokesmen for abolition have seemed to be invisible men, not so much because they

From *Central States Speech Journal*, Vol. XXI, No. 2 (Summer 1970), pp.
5–14. Reprinted by permission of the author and the Central States Speech
Association. Arthur L. Smith (Ph.D., UCLA, 1968) is Associate Professor of
Speech and Director, Center for Afro-American Studies, University of California, Los Angeles.

were, but more because rhetorical critics have tended to look through a glass whitely.[2] During the entire course of antislavery agitation such men as Charles Remond, Frederick Douglass, and Henry Highland Garnet were in the front ranks of the movement. Their voices, stronger than most, and their messages, keener than most, were the whips and lashes of an abominable system. But like the ranks of the white abolitionists, the black crusaders were badly split on the issue of means.[3]

Among the black abolitionists Henry Highland Garnet was the leader of the discordant voices; the majority wanted moral suasion; but he demanded violent insurrection. During a time when few black abolitionists yet envisioned the need for violence, Garnet spoke before the 1843 convention of blacks pleading for insurrection. To what influence was he responding in this speech? How did he attempt to persuade the convention?

Already in 1843 Garnet was considered an outstanding public speaker, brilliant, articulate, certain to have a verbal key to every political house in the antislavery campaign. Of the chief black abolitionists Garnet was the most generously endowed with a combination of intellectual discipline and rhetorical talents; an intensely emotional man, inspirational and eager, liking to have his voice heard on significant matters, Garnet was always ready with a speech or a resolution. A militant preacher, he justified violence to his religious conscience by keeping the end, abolition, larger than the means. An activist, he conquered his fear by remembering his slave childhood and found the memory sufficient to neutralize cowardice. He opened the windows of his imagination to every conceivable solution for abolition of slavery, and concluded that violent resolution was both practical and essential.

As a public speaker, Garnet was of the lineage of Patrick Henry rather than John Adams. Like Henry he was an eloquent crier though never quite as inconsistent, and always more troubled by the honesty of his speech, than the effect. All his public life, his rhetorical emotionalism was constrained by his sincerity and ministerial loyalties. The pulpit was a hard taskmaster. As a child of the congregation, certain to be damned for militant behavior, his public speeches attested to great skill as he maneuvered to be true to himself and to his church. As one of the leading sons of the church, made so by his powerful declamations against injustice and slavery, it pained him to denounce the church's hypocrisy. To repudiate the church for its duplicity and to damn the Christian religion for its conformity to slavery while remaining honest to himself was perhaps one of Garnet's greatest rhetorical accomplishments. Having been shaped in the fluted mold of Presbyterianism, religion was the very blood of his antislavery activities, and repudiation of religion would have taken the sting out of his rhetoric. The material of which he was fashioned would neither allow him to be dishonest to himself nor the church; thus Garnet's speeches are masterpieces, not of audience adaptation, but unblemished sincerity. Indeed his impassioned rhetoric, mental acumen, and concentrated militancy made him the outstanding revolutionary of his day, although for quiet rhetorical artistry he was not worthy to untie Douglass' shoestrings.

Unlike the black preachers who grew from Baptist or Methodist soil, Garnet's mental bent was less keen to subliminal fantasies and vivid images due to his Presbyterian training.[4] Instead, the language of his speeches and sermons was simple and concrete, employing common figures and illustrations. But the humble trope or figure became highly exalted in his dynamic delivery.

No black antislavery speaker was by temperament and training better suited to embrace militancy than Garnet. Born a slave in New Market, Maryland, in 1815, he escaped with his parents to New York at the age of nine.[5] Garnet received his basic education at a private school in New York operated by free blacks. As a young man of twenty, he organized a hundred and fifty youths into the Garrison Literary and Benevolent Association, a group more interested in revolution than literature. The same year he was invited to attend an academy at Canaan, New Hampshire, but the attempt was foiled when certain of Canaan's population dispelled any notion that it was the Promised Land.[6] A mob of irate residents marched onto the campus and destroyed the school building. However, Garnet was befriended by a minister, Beriah Green, who encouraged him to continue ministerial training at Oneida Institute in Whitestown, New York.[7] Although the Oneida experience served to increase his ministerial desires it did not lessen the bitterness developed from the Canaan experience. Turning his natural gift for the platform to persistent agitation against slavery was an exceedingly simple task made easier by the harshness of his childhood, his status as a fugitive slave, and his religious fervor.

After graduation in 1840 Garnet held numerous ministerial posts from Kingston, Jamaica, to New York City, simultaneously developing his speaking skills and popularizing his reputation as a fervent antislavery spokesman.[8] During the Civil War he was an active supporter of the Union, exhorting blacks to join the ranks of the Union Army and strike blows for the freedom of their brothers. His eloquent speeches prompted the House of Representatives to secure him to give a speech in Congress celebrating the thirteenth amendment to the Constitution.[9]

Following his speech to Congress he served as president of Avery College in Pittsburgh, Pennsylvania, and had a successful career as an educator. When he died in 1882 he was serving as United States Minister to Liberia.

The occasion of Henry Highland Garnet's most militant, and most famous, speech was the National Convention of Colored Citizens held in Buffalo, New York, August 21–24, 1843. Seventy outstanding delegates from Northern states assembled to assess the race's progress, chart strategy, and appeal for total black unity. In attendance among the delegates were such notable orators as Charles Lenox Remond, Frederick Douglass, and William Wells Brown.

Undaunted by this august array of eloquent campaigners, the twenty-eight-year-old Garnet gave his "Address to the Slaves of the United States of America" to a startled audience. The speech provoked considerable debate among men whose antislavery credentials were beyond question, and when the vote was taken on the controversial address as the resolution of the group, it was rejected by one vote. The free blacks, beguiled by caution, took the moderate path of urging moral suasion rather than violent insurrection. A few years later John Brown, convinced that violence was the road to liberty, had the speech published at his own expense. Thus despite the thin margin by which the address was rejected at the assembly in 1843, by 1848 Garnet had developed into a leading revolutionary.

What did Garnet say that sent tremors through his audience? Why did his speech set off such vehement controversy among men joined in the antislavery fight? Was he a demagogue, or a political realist? The answers to these and similar questions are best found in the speech itself, the volatile context of antislavery agitation, and the influence upon the speaker.

Let it be noted that Garnet, immediately after a terse introduction: "Brethren and Fellow Citizens" (which reminds one of Malcolm X's equally acid openings with the exception that in Garnet's day women did not attend public meetings), charged that the delegates had been accustomed "to meet together in National Conventions, to sympathize with each other . . ."[10] over the conditions of the slaves. Indeed talk had proved extremely cheap since the initial meetings of the Colored Citizens when the price of political involvement was paid with expensive actions. Garnet's indictment was not a foul; he had scored a direct hit. In 1827 the First General Assembly of Colored Citizens met in Boston, the womb of radicalism, to seek black unity and to discuss ways to help the slaves. Meetings of one kind or another had been held annually or semiannually on the slavery issue ever since, and no one had introduced resolutions of action. Speeches proliferated like so much fallout but were certain not to have any immediate effect on the slaves' liberation. Thus Garnet's opening statement served vivid notice that he had little sympathy with the past actions of the conventions. Speaking as to the slaves, he said, "We have been contented in sitting still and mourning over your sorrows, earnestly hoping that before this day your sacred liberties would have been restored."[11] Again Garnet accused the antislavery giants of do-nothingness in the liberation of the slaves. In fact, the introduction threw a good deal of light on Garnet's rhetorical strategy in the remainder of the speech: He lashed the free blacks as he whipped up the emotions of the enslaved, both because of their inaction in the face of oppression.

In developing his speech Garnet utilized the theory-practice vulnerability pattern to establish the cruelty and villainy of Christians. He contended that "the first dealings they (Africans) had with men calling themselves Christians exhibited to them the worst features of corrupt and sordid hearts."[12] Inconsistency between ideal and reality, between theory and practice has always been the classic chasm giving aggressive rhetoric its energy. And in the case of Christians and slavery the gulf was not bridgeable in the mind or rhetoric of Henry Highland Garnet. A stout supporter of the Christian's God, loyal to the church, even at the risk of being unloyal to his brethren, Garnet saw the Christian's complicity in slavery as godless and unspeakable. The sacred documents and preachers say one thing and the pews do another wholly different thing. Furthermore, what is done is harmful to black people. Consider Garnet's disdain that "Slavery had stretched its dark wings of death over the land, the church stood silently by—the priests prophesied falsely, and the people loved to have it so."[13] Echoing his rhetorical master, David Walker, who had written in 1829 that the "Christian Americans were the most cruel people on earth,"[14] Garnet saw the church as distorting the image of Christianity. Christian Americans were hypocritical; they blamed England for the horrible system of slavery, but once the colonies were free they added new links to the slaves' chains.

With the stage set to highlight the inexcusable apathy of his brethren, free and enslaved, and the cruel villainy of the Christians, Garnet had one more prop to put into place. He must hammer his own theology into the religious molds of his brethren. They must be convinced that his theological position is justified and in keeping with their own religious beliefs. It is on this point that Garnet demonstrated his rhetorical genius. In view of the extreme suffering of the slaves, he urged upon them two major considerations on slavery: (1) "to such degradation it is *sinful* (italics mine) in the extreme for you to make voluntary submission, and (2) neither God nor Angels, or just men, command you to suffer for a single moment. Therefore it is your solemn and imperative duty to use every means, both moral, intellectual, and physical, that promises success."[15]

Such a strong argument for insurrection based upon morality is meant to overpower whatever religious objections the free and enslaved blacks might have. It is not simply wrong, but sinful in the extreme to submit voluntarily to slavery. A crucial moral issue has been inserted into the political and social predicament of the religiously motivated slave. Rebellion is given a moral sanction and if not directly authorized by God, certainly not condemned by him. Furthermore, Garnet argued that slaves had a "solemn and imperative duty" to use every means whether moral, intellectual, or physical. For the nineteenth century slave the word "duty" had a familiar ring to it, and Garnet wisely chose to employ it in the same context with resistance and insurrection. For the Garrisonians, such as Remond and Douglass, not yet ready for other than moral and intellectual means, this must have been an uneasy moment in Garnet's speech. But to Garnet slavery was not merely distasteful, it was abominable, and as such demanded a drastic response: "He counsels insurrection motivated by moral commitment. Look around you, and behold the bosoms of your loving wives heaving with untold agonies! Hear the cries of your poor children! Remember the stripes your fathers bear. Think of your wretched sisters, loving virtue and purity, as they are driven into concubinage and are exposed to unbridled lusts of incarnate devils."[16] Thus the slaves must tell their owners plainly that they are "determined to be free." As words alone may evoke no reaction or an adverse reaction from the slave owners, Garnet proposed a contingency plan. "You had far better all die—die immediately, than live as slaves, and entail your wretchedness upon your posterity."[17] At this point in the speech heroic examples trod upon each other's heels as Garnet praises Denmark Vesey, Nathaniel Turner, Joseph Cinque and Madison Washington. In passing he invokes the names of Moses, Hampden, Tell, Bruce, Wallace, L'Ouverture, Lafayette, and George Washington. Appealing to pride as well as shame, Garnet urges the slaves to follow the path of "those who have fallen in freedom's conflict."[18]

Although the tone of the discourse had been established early, it was the peroration which clearly marked Garnet as a militant advocate bent on insurrection. Witness the call to arms: "Brethren, arise, arise! Strike for your lives and liberties, now is the day and the hour. Let every slave throughout the land do this, and the days of slavery are numbered. You cannot be more oppressed than you have been—you cannot suffer greater cruelties than you are already. Rather die freemen than live to be slaves. Remember that you are four millions."[19] Furthermore, he concluded "Let your motto be resistance! resistance! Resistance!"[20] Such was the language of Henry Highland Garnet before the star-studded audience at Buffalo. However, while the arguments were clear and sharp vis-à-vis the slaves' obligations, nothing was required of the free blacks. If Garnet's message could have been disseminated to four million slaves, most of whom could not read, it would have been a singular achievement. If four million slaves had somehow read and been persuaded to participate in an insurrection, it would have been a miracle. Had Garnet counseled the free black to infiltrate the South in efforts to organize the slaves, his plan may have appeared more practicable. But even that kind of plan for insurrection would not have moved the Garrisonians.

When Garnet finished speaking, a vigorous debate ensued which divided the conference into two philosophical camps. The Garrisonians were not about to relinquish antislavery leadership to militants whom they feared would disrupt the cooperation between blacks and whites in the abolition movement. When the din of debate ended and a single voice called for the question, the resolution had failed as the sentiments of the delegates by one vote. The vote, like the polarization during the debates, reflected a fundamental cleavage in the black antislavery movement. Rejecting Garnet's resolution, by even so slight a margin, the delegates had voted to remain unprovocative.

Five years later Garnet produced a volume which contained David Walker's *Appeal to the Colored Citizens of the World* and his *Address to the Slaves of the United States.*[21] In 1849 the Ohio State Convention of Colored Citizens authorized the purchase and distribution of five hundred copies of the work.[22] Thus the circulation of Garnet's radical ideas continued despite his rebuffs by the National Convention of Colored Citizens in 1843.

NOTES

[1] See particularly Marie Hochmuth and Normal Mattis, "Phillips Brooks," and Willard Hayes Yeager, "Wendell Phillips," both in William Norwood Brigance, ed. *A History and Criticism of American Public Address* (New York: Russell and Russell, 1960), Volume I, 294–328 and 329–362, respectively.

[2] Indeed the stage of rhetoric and public address has been set without due consideration to minority public speakers. What has often appeared is a sort of institutional racism in criticism, a "house criticism" limited to white politicians' rhetoric. This means, of course, that Prince Saunders, John Langston, George White, and Henry Garnet among numerous other black speakers have seldom been scrutinized. While it is possible for a critic to comment on the rhetorical skills and talents of a Webster, Phillips, or Sumner, theoretically he can never be sure that his criticism has taken into consideration all the possibilities within a given rhetorical situation. One gets a certain *déjà vu* that the problem of frame of reference so often discussed in other disciplines in recent years has found its expression in speech communication.

[3] Lerone Bennett, *Before the Mayflower* (Baltimore: Penguin Books, 1966), pp. 141–152.

[4] Unlike many black preachers of his day Garnet had the benefit of seminary training in homiletics. For the role of the seminary in training black preachers, see W. E. B. DuBois, *The Negro Church* (Atlanta: Atlanta University Press, 1903); Benjamin Mays, *The Negro Church* (New York: Russell and Russell, 1969); and E. Franklin Frazier, *The Negro Church in America* (New York: Schocken Books, 1963).

[5] Herbert Aptheker, *One Continual Cry* (New York: Humanities Press, 1965), p. 38.

[6] *Ibid.*

[7] *Ibid.*

[8] *Ibid.*

[9] Carter G. Woodson, *Negro Orators and Their Orations* (Washington: Associated Publishers, 1925), p. 312.

[10] Thomas Frazier, ed., *Afro-American Primary Sources* (New York: Harcourt Brace Jovanovich, 1970), p. 114.
[11] *Ibid.*
[12] *Ibid.*
[13] *Ibid.*, p. 115.
[14] Aptheker, p. 69.
[15] Frazier, p. 116.
[16] Woodson, p. 312.
[17] *Ibid.*, p. 117.
[18] *Ibid.*, p. 118.
[19] *Ibid.*, p. 119.
[20] *Ibid.*
[21] Aptheker, p. 39.
[22] *Ibid.*, p. 40.

Robert C. Dick

CHAPTER 10
Negro Oratory in the Anti-Slavery
Societies: 1830–1860

The current racial revolution in America has drawn attention to
the key Negro spokesmen of our times, and perhaps has made us
more aware of the role which the Negro himself is playing in his
struggle for equality. Accordingly, students of rhetoric and public address are prompted to take a second look at Negro speakers
in earlier periods of American history, particularly in the era of
anti-slavery and disunion. Although isolated speeches of such
orators as H. Ford Douglass and Frederick Douglass have been

From *Western Speech Journal* (Winter 1964), pp. 5–14. Reprinted by permission of the publisher and the author. Robert C. Dick is Instructor in
Speech, Stanford University.

studied, the subject of *black abolitionism* in the ante-bellum period remains to be investigated. This is a brief exploration of the role of Negro oratory in the anti-slavery societies from 1830–1860.

Historians have observed that the Negro began protesting against slavery long before the year 1830. Indeed, it was the Negro who initiated the long vocal struggle for his freedom. Carter Woodson, Herbert Aptheker, and John Hope Franklin, among others, have noted that in the United States the first abolitionists, individually or in groups, were the Negroes themselves. Franklin wrote: "The whites were not alone in their opposition to slavery. From the beginning the Negro, who suffered most from the subjugation of his race, gave enthusiastic support to abolition. Indeed, strong abolitionist doctrine was preached by Negroes long before Garrison was born."[1] Even before the Revolutionary War the slaves in Massachusetts brought actions against their masters because they considered freedom their inalienable right. During and after the war, Negroes had petitioned state and federal governments to abolish the slave trade and establish a program of general emancipation.[2] In the late Eighteenth Century, Negroes such as Prince Hall, Benjamin Banneker, Absolom Jones, and Richard Allen issued strong denunciations of slavery. There are few extant texts of the earliest Negro abolition speeches, since the freedom of speech was not afforded those who arose in protest. One of the first recorded Negro speeches of protest was written in 1789 by Banneker under the pseudonym of "Othello." The speech was written in essay form by the aggrieved Negro because he sought a larger audience.[3] In addition to individual efforts there were abolitionist organizations, such as the Free African Society of Philadelphia, formed by Negroes before the year 1800.

During the period prior to 1830 many of the white people had approached the slavery problem with considerable caution, since efforts were being made to alleviate the problem by means of colonization. The American free Negroes rose in opposition to colonization as well as to slavery itself. The Negroes recognized that the leaders of the American Colonization Society were not interested in freeing slaves but in shipping troublesome blacks out of the country, thereby tightening their control over those who remained in bondage. In 1817, less than a month after the American Colonization Society was established, the free Negro speakers of Richmond and Philadelphia militantly expressed their opposition. By the year 1830, the Negroes had 50 groups, including the several active ones in Boston, New York, and Philadelphia. It is evident, therefore, that black abolitionists were active prior to the period from 1830–1860. As Philip Foner put it, "during the years when many white anti-slavery men were growing more cautious, the cause did not lack for militant fighters. The Negro people battled both slavery and the colonization movement and spoke out sharply on these issues."[4]

The period from 1830 to the Civil War has been generally conceded to be that of the anti-slavery movement: "Beginning with 1830 the anti-slavery crusade burst forth with a new intensity and within a few years was to establish itself as one of the most profound revolutionary movements in the world's history."[5] Three events mark the upsurge of militant abolitionism in the early 1830's. The first was the publication, in the nation's first Negro periodical, of Negro David Walker's "Appeal . . . to the Coloured Citizens of the World, but in Particular and Very Expressly to Those of the United States." Walker's "Appeal," a fiery indictment of slavery, called for revolution by those persons held in bondage. The second event which enhanced the struggle was the publication of *The Liberator* by William Lloyd Garrison, and the third was the great slave insurrection led by Nat Turner in Southhampton County, Virginia. The period was a significant one for the American Negro speaker. More Negro orators appeared on the American scene than ever before and they initiated widescale protest with a dedication not unlike that being witnessed in the United States today. Earl E. Thorpe describes the emergence of the Negro advocate:

The period from 1830–1860 is one of the most stirring in the history of Negro thought and action. Through the black abolitionists, this era also saw the underground railroad shift into high gear and spread, the emergence of Negro oratory, journalism, and organized protest. The mass meeting, used so fittingly in this period by the black abolitionists, has been a constant weapon used by the Negro in his fight for equality of citizenship.[6]

With this understanding of the abolition activities leading to the upsurge of the movement in the 1830's, a closer perspective can be drawn on the specific role of the Negro speaker in both the colored and white abolition societies of the ante-bellum period.

The first of the annual Conventions of the Afro-Americans was held September 20, 1830, in Philadelphia. The meeting was regarded as successful and similar conventions were held annually for the next five years. The purpose of the conventions was to devise ways and means for bettering the condition of American Negroes. A number of important projects evolved from the meetings including the raising of money for refugees in Canada, formation of temperance societies, boycotting of slave-made products, and the submission of numerous petitions against slavery and discrimination to the state and national legislatures. But the significant factor to be emphasized is the role of public speaking in the strategy of the convention movement. From the outset, the Afro-American Conventions laid considerable stress on the importance of moral suasion. In the second annual convention address, the speaker impressed his listeners with the idea that they would some day become a body "not inferior in numbers to our State Legislatures, and the phenomenon of an oppressed people, deprived of the rights of citizenship in the midst of an enlightened nation, devising plans and measures for their personal and mental evaluation by moral suasion alone."[7] Incidentally, the annual convention addresses were not written by the speakers who were to give them, but by committees which had been chosen to study the public sentiment of America on the subject of race prejudice. In addition to encouraging their people to speak out on the racial problem, the second convention determined to "employ a Negro lecturer on the question of Negro rights."[8] This was especially important since a number of anti-slavery societies did not allow Negroes in their organizations. The job of the hired lecturer was to break down the barrier of prejudice which existed within the very societies dedicated to freeing Negroes.

After the Convention of 1835, the National Negro Convention movement temporarily dissolved because of dissension among the leaders. The split in the ranks of national Negro leaders centered around the choice of the approach to abolitionism which should be espoused in their campaign efforts. Some of the chief Negro spokesmen were in favor of colonization while others were convinced that they should stress the need for social equality within the United States itself. Some wanted to urge segregation of schools and churches, while others wanted immediate and complete integration into American life. Also, there was a dispute as to whether they should use the political approach to the problem or stay exclusively with the Garrisonian doctrine of moral suasion. The key issue which the Negroes debated during the entire movement centered about the choice between the use of moral suasion and the use of violence or insurrection. It was primarily due to key speakers and leaders such as Frederick Douglass that the Negroes, as a group, steered away from violence as a weapon. Douglass's choice of moral suasion appears similar to the choice of Martin Luther King and certain other Negro leaders of today.

Although the National Colored Conventions had created a strong impression on the people of the North by the "intelligence, order, and excellent judgment which prevailed,"[9] they had created counter-propaganda material for the Southerners. The conventions appeared inconsistent in that the very organizations which were seeking freedom for the Negro were segregated, and completely separate efforts were being exerted by the black and white anti-slavery people of the North.

In late 1835, the national colored organizations were gone, and their members integrated into the national white societies. There were still some societies which rejected colored members, but they became fewer in number. George W. Williams pointed out that in the following year "every barrier was . . . broken down inside of anti-slavery organizations; and having conquered the prejudice that crippled their work, they enjoyed greater freedom in prosecution of their labors."[10] What were the labors of the white organizations? Primarily, they involved the dissemination of propaganda through speeches and the press. It was admittedly not the purpose of these societies to be objective reporters of the slave situation in the South. The abolitionists believed that the institution of slavery was wrong in itself, and should thus be depicted at its worst. Therefore, they dramatized the issues of human freedom and equality, still central problems of our revolutionary age.

The propaganda activities promoted by the societies were many and varied. Among other things, they circulated petitions by the thousands which were sent to Congressmen and state legislators; appeared before legislative committees; slipped printed handkerchiefs bearing anti-slavery slogans into bales designed for Southern markets; and mailed pictures depicting the cruelties of slavery. Most significantly, they held anti-slavery meetings everywhere they could, including barns, taverns, schools, and Negro churches. There were annual meetings of the various local organizations as well as the regional and national ones. There were also anti-slavery bazaars, anti-slavery soirees, and anti-slavery festivals. Resolutions were passed, ardent speeches were made and hymns were sung.[11]

The key features of the agitation were the lecturers or "travel agents," and the various forms of printed propaganda materials. Although Negroes held positions in various organizations and had a hand in nearly all of the propaganda activities, their most active work was as lecturers or "traveling agents." The traveling agents went throughout the country delivering speeches at the various meetings which were being held at the time.

It must be remembered that during this same period the South was producing considerable counter-propaganda concerning the justification of slavery. Southern propagandists depicted the slave as a relatively happy, secure person who was perhaps better off than the free Northern laborers. Abolitionists, therefore, needed something powerful and irrefutable with which to offset the effects of the Southern agents. It was primarily for this purpose that the white abolition societies turned to the Negro orator. It was observed that: "Obviously the need could best be filled by the Negro himself. Who else could refute so effectively the testimony of those who upheld slavery and argued that the slaves actually benefited from their bondage? Small wonder that after 1840 the number of Negroes employed as Abolitionist agents grew in leaps and bounds."[12]

A number of the Negro speakers were ex-slaves who were used to present a vivid oral picture of the atrocities which they had experienced and witnessed in bondage. Some whites thought that such a simple expository role should be the extent of the oratory performed by Negroes. "Many middle and upper-class white abolitionists could not see the former Negro slave as anything but an exhibit. The white anti-slavery leaders would be the main actors; the Negroes would be the extras or only part of the stage props."[13] It was as a "stage prop" relating his experiences as a slave that Frederick Douglass began his career as an abolitionist speaker. In fact, when he started developing his own reasoned discourses, he was met with the advice to "give us the facts, we will take of the philosophy."[14]

There were numerous Negro orators with refined skills in public speaking who were prominent in the abolition movement. These well-trained speakers had a most challenging responsibility in their performances. During this period of history there were people throughout the country who believed that the Negroes were inferior beings, and undeserving of the rights of equality and citizenship. These Negro orators were living examples of what members of their race were capable of doing. The societies became increasingly aware of the capabilities of the Negro speakers and eagerly introduced them to doubting audiences in order to demonstrate what Negroes could do if given the opportunity. Among the better known Negro orators were Frederick Douglass, Theodore S. Wright, William Jones, Charles Lenox Remond, Henry Foster, Lunsford Lane, Henry H. Garnet, Charles Gardner, Andrew Harris, Abraham Shadd, David Nickens, James Bradley, and Sojourner Truth. There were numerous other full-time and part-time speakers for both the national and local societies. Many, of course, worked and lectured on the local level without fee. Franklin wrote that "to the local and regional anti-slavery organizations, which carried the burden of work, Negroes gave their time, energy, and money."[15]

In addition to their local and national speaking efforts, the Negro agents were also sent to Europe in order to gain monetary support for the anti-slavery cause. The societies subsidized the speaking tours of a select number of colored lecturers. Although the exact number of speakers sent abroad cannot be ascertained, it has been noted that more than a score of the black abolitionists went to England, Scotland, France, and Germany.[16] Among those who are known to have made European tours were Douglass, Brown, Remond, Pennington, Garnet, Nathaniel Paul, Ellen and William Craft, Samuel Ringgold Ward, Sarah Parker Remond, and Alexander Crummell. The orators raised considerable funds for the anti-slavery cause while they were in Europe. "Almost everywhere they were received with enthusiasm and were instrumental in linking up the humanitarian movement in Europe with various reform movements on this side of the Atlantic."[17]

The American Anti-Slavery Society had a well organized group of agents who traveled across the country and world, speaking on abolitionism and forming local societies. The agents operated under the direction of Theodore Weld, a master at all forms of agitation, and Elizur Wright, organizational genius of the American Society. Speakers were required to have good moral character, sincerity, and trustworthiness; and they had to be thoroughly informed on the subject. Prospective agents were sometimes investigated for more than a month in order to determine their qualifications for the work.[18] Only after approval could the agent begin his travels.

The influence of the society upon the Negro orators who were schooled therein was apparently strong. A number of the black abolitionists had little, if any, formal education, so were able to take on the "polish of Anglo-Saxon scholarship" by their association in the society. Marie Weston Chapman commented as follows on the society's influence on its colored members:

It is the church and university, high school and common school, to all who need real instruction and true religion. At it what a throng of authors, editors, lawyers, orators, and accomplished gentlemen of color have taken their degree! . . . He has a place at their firesides, a place in their hearts—the man whom they once cruelly hated for his color. So feeling, they cannot send him to a Coventry with a hornbook in his hand, and call it instruction! They inspire him to climb to their side by a visible, acted gospel of freedom.[19]

In 1837, just after the Negroes started integrating on a large scale into the white societies, a special convention was held in New York City for the traveling agents. Some seventy agents were selected to attend. At that convention "Theodore Weld as their central luminary, held forth for a fortnight at the three daily sessions."[20] The subject matter discussed at the sessions focused upon such questions as: "What is slavery? What is immediate emancipation? Why don't you go to the South? Will the slaves overrun the North if they are emancipated?" Other subjects discussed included Hebrew servitude, colonization, prejudice, treatment and condition of our free colored population, and gradualism. The speakers were also given preparation in refuting the arguments of their opponents. Garrison wrote that "all the prominent objections to our cause were ingeniously presented, and as conclusively shown to be futile."[21]

The local abolition societies flourished in conjunction with, and often as a result of, the national organizations. The campaign to "reach all" of the listeners through societal meetings reached its peak around the year 1840 when there were over 2,000 societies with a membership of 200,000.[22] In fact, even after the national all-colored organization dissolved there were still local societies composed entirely, or almost entirely, of Negro membership. Negro organizations sprang up throughout New England and the Middle States. Free Negro societies appeared in the larger cities of the West such as Detroit, Chicago, and Cincinnati. Annual State conventions of Negro societies were held in the Western States of Michigan, Indiana, Illinois, and Ohio. Although it would be impossible to list all of the Negro orators in the local societies,

George Williams gives us a brief account of the more outstanding Negroes of the bigger states: "Such Colored men as John B. Vashon and Robert Purvis, of Pennsylvania; David Ruggles and Philip Bell, of New York; and Charles Lenox Remond and William Wells Brown, of Massachusetts, were soon seen as orators and presiding officers in the different anti-slavery societies of the free states."[23]

After an eight-year's lapse, the National Negro Convention convened at Buffalo in 1843, and was again marked by conflict among the Negro speakers who attended. The debate was over the old issue of force vs. moral suasion. A key spokesman, Henry H. Garnet challenged the Negro: "Brethren, arise, arise! Strike for your lives and liberties. Now is the day and the hour. Let every slave throughout the land do this, and the days of slavery are numbered. You cannot be more oppressed than you have been— you cannot suffer greater cruelties than you have already. Rather die free men than live to be slaves. Remember that you are four millions."[24]

Frederick Douglass took issue with Garnet and proposed a policy of moral suasion to encourage slave owners to release their slaves from bondage. Thanks to Douglass's persuasive abilities the convention decided to take the public speaking route to abolitionism; "They voted to send capable Negro speakers into northern communities to inform whites and Negroes about claims, disabilities, sentiments, and wishes of the colored people."[25]

The National Convention met again in 1847 and formed a committee to explore the best means of abolishing slavery. The committee, with Douglass as its chairman, condemned any attempt to lead the Negro people to trust in brute force as an instrument of reform. They endorsed moral suasion as "the only means within our reach to overthrow this foul system of blood and ruin."[26] A similar meeting, held in Cleveland in 1848, also met with strife and confusion in the Negro ranks. The Compromise of 1850 intensified the struggle and the Negroes held a National Convention in Rochester in 1853, and a final one in Philadelphia in 1855.

Although the National Negro Convention movement was disrupted by non-cooperation, it is evident that it provided a significant opportunity for Negro oratory. Not only was there an emphasis placed upon public speaking within the meetings themselves, but Negro speakers were urged to carry the racial cause to the people of the country through speeches. As Foner put it, "Sponsoring itinerant speakers, the National Convention emphasized the importance of rudimentary education and advanced study in arts and sciences even where public education facilities were restricted. Particularly did the Convention address itself to the courage, the self-reliance of the Negro people to counteract the propaganda of white newspapers and speakers."[27]

It has been shown here that the Negro people played an active part in the work of the anti-slavery societies before and during the period from 1830–1860. They emerged as orators and assumed the responsibility of not only countering Southern propaganda and denouncing the institution of slavery, but also of speaking out against the prejudice of many Northerners and even abolitionists. These orators, due to their own experience as people of color, had a feeling and understanding of the problem which could not be fully acquired by their white colleagues. They initiated the movement and gave strength to it. Williams wrote: "So it was meet that Negro orators of refinement should go from town to town. The North needed arousing and educating on the anti-slavery question, and no class did more practical work in this direction than the little company of orators, with the peerless Douglass at its head, that pleaded the cause of their brethren in the flesh. . . ."[28]

There are many questions to be answered concerning the Negro orators themselves and what their relationship was to the over-all movement. For instance, what were the ideas of the key Negro orators? How did their philosophies relate to those of other Negroes and to the various points of view espoused by their white colleagues? Where did the Negro orators come from, and how did they emerge onto the American scene? What was the specific content of their speeches, and how were their speeches received? Numerous sources can give the rhetorician answers to these questions. Texts of the more significant black abolition speeches are printed in Garrison's *Liberator*, and in anthologies such as Carter Woodson's *Negro Orators and Their Orations*, or Alice M. D. Nelson's *Masterpieces of Negro Eloquence*. Other sources replete with documentary materials include *The Journal of Negro History*, Herbert Aptheker's *Documentary History of the American Negro*, Fisk University's Social Science Documents on *Unwritten History of Slavery*, *The National Anti-Slavery Standard*, and *The North Star*. An extensive bibliography can be compiled on the subject from Dorothy B. Porter's "Early American Negro Writings: A Bibliographical Study," *Papers of the Bibliographical Society of America*, 21:191–268. Yet with all the materials available for study, it appears that little has been done to investigate the place of the Negro in the early history of American public address. Studies in this area should prove both useful and rewarding.

NOTES

[1] John Hope Franklin, *From Slavery to Freedom* (New York, 1948), p. 246.
[2] *Ibid.*, p. 246.
[3] Carter G. Woodson, ed., *Negro Orators and Their Orations* (Washington, D.C., 1925), p. 14.
[4] Philip S. Foner, *The Life and Writings of Frederick Douglass*, I (New York, 1950), p. 31.
[5] *Ibid.*, p. 31.
[6] Earl E. Thorpe, *The Mind of the Negro* (Baton Rouge, 1961), p. 179.
[7] George W. Williams, *History of the Negro Race in America*, II (New York, 1883), p. 78.
[8] Thorpe, p. 28.
[9] Williams, p. 63.
[10] *Ibid.*, p. 81.
[11] Foner, p. 35.
[12] *Ibid.*, p. 46.
[13] *Ibid.*, p. 59.
[14] *Ibid.*, p. 59.
[15] Franklin, p. 248.
[16] *Ibid.*, p. 249.
[17] *Ibid.*, p. 249.
[18] Foner, p. 35.
[19] Williams, p. 80.

[20] Foner, p. 36.
[21] *Ibid.*, p. 36.
[22] *Ibid.*, p. 38.
[23] Williams, p. 79.
[24] Philip S. Foner, *The Life and Writings of Frederick Douglass*, II (New York, 1950), p. 22.
[25] *Ibid.*, p. 23.
[26] *Ibid.*, p. 23.
[27] *Ibid.*, p. 37.
[28] Williams, p. 81.

Thomas E. Harris

Patrick C. Kennicott

CHAPTER 11
Booker T. Washington:
A Study of Conciliatory Rhetoric

*The philosophy and methods of Booker T. Washington have re-
mained controversial since his ascendance in 1895. Rhetorical
strategies reflected in his speaking confirm charges that as leader
of American Negroes he was a pacifier and conciliator rather than
a promoter of aggressive action.*

From *Southern Speech Journal* (Fall 1971). Reprinted by permission of
the publisher and the authors. Thomas E. Harris (M.A. in Speech Communication, 1971, University of Maryland) is Instructor in Speech, Rutgers University, New Brunswick, New Jersey. Patrick C. Kennicott (Ph.D. in Speech
Communication, 1967, Florida State University) is Assistant Professor and
Director, Speech Communication Division, Department of Speech and Dramatic Art, University of Maryland.

W. E. Burghardt Du Bois, the most famous and influential critic of Booker T. Washington, began his classic critique of Washington by admitting "the most striking thing in the history of the American Negro since 1876 is the ascendancy of Mr. Booker T. Washington."[1] Many years later he affirmed "there was no question of . . . Washington's undisputed leadership of the ten million Negroes in America, a leadership recognized gladly by the whites and conceded by most of the Negroes."[2]

Washington's leadership of American blacks was a subject of controversy from the beginning.[3] Early critics accused him of extending a "palm branch" of peace to white America that aided the South in securing black disenfranchisement, civil inferiority, and economic peonage.[4] Modern critics of Washington have perpetuated such criticism, suggesting that at best his leadership was a futile attempt "to deal with the present in terms of the past,"[5] and at its worst subjected American blacks to the curse of "Uncle Tomism" for two crucial decades of history.[6]

On the other side of the coin, Washington was staunchly defended by many of his contemporaries. Ray Stannard Baker wrote:

I have found the mark of him everywhere in happier human lives. . . . Measured by any standard, white or black, Washington must be regarded today as one of the great men of this country. . . .[7]

And a few present-day scholars have commended Washington. Samuel R. Spencer, Jr., for instance, defended his program of modest objectives by asserting:

To criticize his methods is to make the facile assumption that he had some choice in the matter. He did what was possible given the time and place in which he lived, and did it to the utmost.[8]

The heart of the Washington controversy is his philosophy concerning the means for black progress and the methods he employed to implement that philosophy. Stated briefly, he believed that black Americans should work toward equal status in American society by gaining economic power through vocational training and diligent vocational pursuits and by working within the system rather than challenging or attempting to change that system.[9] In order to win acceptance of that philosophy, he launched a national program of *personal persuasive diplomacy* designed to win support for his Tuskegee program of black vocational education. His diplomacy brought angry protests from liberals such as Du Bois who considered his methods a sellout to America's white power structure.[10]

Although he preferred action to talk, Washington relied heavily on the medium of public address to disseminate his views and perpetuate his influence. He spoke constantly throughout America and in Europe as well; he addressed audiences that were all black, all white, and many that were mixed; he spoke to conventions of businessmen, religious workers, educators, and politicians.[11] One scholar estimated that he delivered from two to four thousand speeches during his public career.[12] While his power was partly realized through his role as chief black adviser to national white political leaders and philanthropists and his substantial influence on the American press, it would be difficult to underestimate the importance of Washington's speechmaking—his oral persuasion—in building and maintaining his fame and power.

The extensive record of Washington's speechmaking raises several questions relevant to the Washington controversy: What inferences can be made concerning Washington's persuasive strategy by examining representative speeches? Could Washington's speaking be reasonably judged astute persuasion, or was it, as hostile critics suggest, cowardly cowtowing to the white power structure of America? Were there covert elements in Washington's speeches that might have suggested to discriminating listeners a more militant stance toward black social, economic and political progress than has been traditionally associated with Washington, or does his speaking indeed reflect a clear application of carefully limited procedures to the accomplishment of limited goals?

The following rhetorical investigation will attempt to provide tentative answers to these questions by examining the circumstances under which Washington spoke, identifying major themes that appeared in his speeches, and assessing the persuasive strategies reflected in those speeches.

HISTORICAL SITUATION

In order to understand the persuasive strategy of Booker T. Washington, it is necessary to consider the general historical context in which he functioned. At the turn of the century, ninety percent of America's ten million Negroes remained in the South.[13] The people of the North, many of whom had never entertained the notion of social equality, were "for the most part in substantial agreement that the South should be allowed to deal with the [Negro] problem in its own way."[14] In fact, public opinion in the North had become increasingly anti-black during the post-reconstruction era; the majority believing "that Negroes were an inferior race, unfit for the franchize, and that white domination was justified."[15]

In the South, the status of black people was in a state of rapid deterioration that began with the election of 1876. Politically, "through violence, fraud, and complicated registration and voting procedures, Negro political influence was effectively curtailed. . . ."[16] Socially, "the walls of segregation and caste were raised higher and higher by law and custom."[17] Economically, blacks were "relegated almost entirely to menial occupations and unskilled labor. . . . In some instances, their condition descended almost to a state of peonage."[18]

THE SPEAKER

Born a slave and raised in the South, Booker T. Washington was accustomed to the atmosphere of suspicion, hostility, and sometimes overt repression that partially enveloped the building of Tuskegee Normal and Industrial Institute.[19] Assuming the presidency of Tuskegee in 1881, Washington brought with him a strong belief in the virtue of cleanliness, godliness, and hard work nurtured by childhood labors in West Virginia's salt mines and sustained by diligent efforts to work his way through the vocational program at Hampton Institute and graduate studies at Wayland Seminary in Washington, D.C. He tirelessly guided Tuskegee in a developing program of practical vocational training and promoted it with zest, speaking every chance he could get. His early rhetorical efforts were so favorably received that he was invited to address the Cotton States Exposition in Atlanta on September 18, 1895; a gesture of confidence in a black man unprecedented in the reconstructed South. His "Atlanta Exposition Address" was received with "hysterical enthusiasm" in Atlanta[20] and favorably in most of America's newspapers.[21] As he walked off the Exposition platform he was generally recognized "as the leader of his race, the Moses of his people, and one of America's great men."[22]

THEMES

Our analysis of Washington's speaking will be based on three of his speeches identified as representative and chosen because each was delivered to one of the three kinds of audiences—Northern white, Southern white, and black—Washington regularly addressed.[23] Fortunately, the determination of "representativeness" was simplified by the fact that the bulk of Washington's speeches are available at the Library of Congress and also by the fact that "Washington's expressed ideology remained remarkably consistent throughout his public life."[24]

The first of the speeches to be examined, "The Educational and Industrial Emancipation of the Afro-American,"[25] was delivered to a largely white audience of approximately 4,000 heartily clapping listeners in the Brooklyn Academy of Music.[26] The second speech, untitled, was delivered to a largely black audience in the packed auditorium of Zion Church, San Francisco.[27] Many of his words to the Zion congregation were greeted with deafening applause. "Men rose in their seats and cheered while women waved their arms."[28] The third speech, "How the White Man Can Best Help the Negro to a Higher Moral and Social Life,"[29] was delivered to an audience of Southern white students and faculty at Vanderbilt University, Nashville, Tennessee. His words at Vanderbilt were "accorded the strictest attention" and drew an enthusiastic response.[30]

The themes appearing in these speeches generally reflect Washington's message to America. To the white Northern audience at Brooklyn Academy, Washington opened in the classical rhetorical tradition of modestly disclaiming the ability to do justice to the worthy audience or high occasion and then developed the following five themes: 1) The spirit of freedom upon which America was founded should be extended to *all* of her citizens; 2) Since the Negro is a permanent part of America, a means for his advancement must be found and implemented; 3) In the light of his accomplishments, the Negro deserves a better image and higher status in the United States; 4) The North and South share responsibility for the moral and economic progress of the Negro; and 5) Progress toward a resolution of America's race problem is predicated on calm, rational, and determined deliberation by members of both races.[31]

Washington's address to the predominantly black audience at Zion Church was unusually brief and to the point. In an almost paternalistic tone,[32] he advanced three themes: 1) The Negro in America should be cohesive in pride and dignity; 2) The key to black progress in America is the willingness of black people to start at the bottom and work up; and 3) Negroes must wisely invest their energies and talents in productive occupations.[33]

In his address to the white Southern audience at Vanderbilt, the most demanding kind of rhetorical situation he regularly encountered, Washington advanced five themes: 1) Since the Negro is a permanent part of the South, it is imperative that a resolution of the race problem be found; 2) Involvement in the education of the Negro would produce substantial economic and political advantages for the South; 3) Both whites and blacks should work to reduce mutually degrading interracial immorality; 4) Lynching is morally and politically degrading to the South and should be eliminated; and 5) Southern Negroes do not seek social equality or political dominance and therefore pose no threat to the white people of the South.[34]

STRATEGIES

More illuminating than a summary of the themes that appeared in Washington's speeches is an assessment of the persuasive strategies that were reflected in those speeches. While elements of strategy varied from audience to audience, five fundamental persuasive strategies characterized Washington's public address: the strategies of self-interest, moral principle, flattery, concession, and exclusion.

Appeal to self-interest was the most predominant persuasive strategy that Washington employed. He consistently linked his philosophy and program to the immediate and long-range gratification of listeners' interests. His appeal to white New Yorkers divorced geographically from America's black population was general but firm. He suggested that America's indifference to the race problem was unjust and in the end the nation would pay a penalty in "hardening and blunting of the conscience . . . sapping of the growth of human beings in the direction of kindness, justice, and all the higher, purer and sweeter things in life." He reminded his white listeners that no race "can oppress another without that race being degraded." Inversely he assured the Northern whites that their constructive efforts to uplift the black man would result in their acquiring a more Christ-like personality.

Washington appealed to the self-interest of his black audience at Zion Church pointedly affirming "We must begin at the bottom and put our best efforts into the practical things about us, or they are taken from us." He complained that blacks were losing their entrée into such "life-blood" vocations as barbering and cooking because they scorn to put their education to "humble pursuits," and he told them the key to black economic progress was recognizing the dignity of common labor and getting to work:

> When a black man receives an education he looks for a position ready-made for him. I want to see him make his own position. I want to see a man go out in the field and dig a furrow, stand in that furrow and wrest success from that soil.

Diligent vocational pursuits, he affirmed, would enable black people "to put money in the bank and in homes for ourselves." In short, the Washington program served best the interests of the American Negro.

Washington was particularly deliberate in appealing to the Southern white in the spirit of self-interest. At Vanderbilt he contended that black vocational education and the overall advancement of black people would be economically advantageous to the South. He observed that the Negro race in Virginia "has gotten to the point where it pays taxes upon one twenty-sixth of the land in the state," and he suggested

that it will pay every white man in the South who operates a large plantation to see to it that on that plantation . . . there is a school that is comfortable . . . In proportion as that is done, what will be the result? Instead of the owner having to seek labor, labor will seek him. . . . There are those in this room who remember that during the days of slavery . . . the master who was most kind and considerate was in most cases the individual who, from a money point of view, made his plantation pay; while the master who was careless in those respects, in many cases, ended his industrial or business career in bankruptcy.

Washington continued by using a wide variety of examples to show that educated blacks, who "have learned the disgrace of idleness and the dignity of labor," become better, more dependable workers, socially responsible taxpayers, and reliable contributors to community welfare. He even dared launch into the foreboding waters of law and politics with a strategy of self-interest. Addressing himself to the sensitive subject of lynching, he insisted that *all* men were threatened by that lawless institution:

I believe that there is only one safety for all of us, one safety for your race, for my race, and that is the absolute enforcement of the law. When we go outside the law we are treading upon dangerous ground.

Since black people were the victims of lynching, he deemed it necessary to show his white listeners that its prevalence threatened the "image" of the South:

In nine-tenths of our Southern communities there is peace and harmony, good will and friendship; but when one goes outside of the Southern States . . . and reads the dispatches that come from the South, it is always one thing—lynching. And you never hear of any other news from the South except of lynchings. Those people naturally get the idea . . . that we are living in a state of turmoil, at daggers-points, throughout the South. . . . And for that reason alone, my friends, if for no other higher consideration, I believe we owe it to ourselves to bring about such a public sentiment as will get rid of this unusual and barbarous method of punishing criminals.

Using an inverse appeal to self-interest, Washington ended his Vanderbilt address by assuring his listeners that black progress involved no threat to white social standing or political power. Referring to the Southern "bug-bear" of social equality, Washington asserted:

There is not a white man in the city of Nashville today, my friends, however high he may stand in social or business circles, who is afraid that my friend . . . Mr. J. C. Napier will ever intrude himself into your social circles where he is not asked or where he is not wanted. What is true of him, my friends, is true of the average, educated, sensible colored man.

He also categorically stated:

It is not the ambition or the desire of the Negro in this country to intermingle socially with the white people. Neither is it his ambition or his desire to domineer the white man in matters of politics.

Black progress, according to Washington, could only serve, never threaten, the interests of the South.

A second persuasive strategy that appeared in Washington's speeches was the appeal from moral principle. He attempted to link his philosophy and program to the dominant values motivating the behavior of his listeners. Consequently, his speech to Eastern whites was richly amplified with references to cherished historical traditions and historically based values such as:

It was the desire for liberty, ever burning in the hearts of the Pilgrim Fathers and the Quakers, that led them to cut loose from kindred and native land and risk the perils and hardships of an almost unsailed and unknown sea.

After a series of complex allusions to historical figures and events reflecting his reverence for the values and traditions embodying American society, he expressed the hunger of black people for the liberty promised by America: "It is impossible that the passionate plea of Patrick Henry, 'give me liberty or give me death,' should have no influence upon our black citizens," and he charged white Americans, North and South, with a place of responsibility in the cause of black progress:

It should always be borne in mind that, unlike other races, we not only were forced to come into this country against our will, but were brought here in the face of our most earnest protest. Both as slaves and as freemen, we have striven to serve the interests of this country as best we could. . . .

In the face of all this I cannot believe, I will not believe, that a country that invited into its midst every type of European, from the highest to the very dregs of the earth, and gives these comers shelter, protection, and the highest encouragement, will refuse to accord the same protection and encouragement to her black citizens.

The heart of Washington's appeal to white Northerners was the assurance that his program of vocational education was an implementation of the belief that blacks will make enduring progress "by laying the foundations carefully, patiently, in ownership of the soil, the exercise of habits of economy, the saving of money . . . and the cultivation of Christian virtues," in short, the embodiment of those values ensconced in the traditions and life-style of white, middle-class America.

Washington's speech at Zion Church did not directly reflect the strategy of moral principle, although Washington frequently addressed black audiences on such matters, particularly during his Sunday evening talks to Tuskegee students.[35]

At Vanderbilt, although he spent more time on the practical matters of economics and political image, Washington did appeal from moral principle. His address communicated the assumption that the audience, the "Christian men of the South," was interested in the race question for constructive moral reasons. He asked his white listeners to help dispel the popular notion that education degraded Negro moral and spiritual life. Referring to the problem of inter-racial sexual promiscuity, he claimed that "whenever you find a low state of morals existing among my people . . . you will find that in some degree that condition extends to the members of your race," and he boldly asserted that "the degradation of the Negro woman will, in many cases, prove the damnation of many of your best Southern white men." The solution to the promiscuity problem, he said, is a joint effort to "Christianize members of both races."

Washington concluded his address to white Southerners with the moral suggestion "If you want to know how to solve the race problem, place your hands upon your hearts and then with a prayer to God, ask Him how you today, were you placed in the position that the black man occupies, how you would desire the white man to treat you, and whenever you have answered that question in the sight of God and man, this problem in a large degree will have been solved."

The strategies of self-interest and moral principle grew out of the substance of Washington's persuasive position and were designed to increase the acceptability of that position with a given audience. The other three basic strategies reflected in Washington's speeches were related less closely to the substance of his case and more closely to the enhancement of his audience credibility of ethos.

Probably least important of the credibility-building devices he employed was the rhetorical strategy of flattery. He told his New York audience "I cannot bring myself to feel that I am worthy of speaking to the members of Brooklyn Institute. . . ." He complimented his black audience at Zion Church by saying, "From the time I came to California, I have been investigating the condition of my race in this state, and it has been most gratifying to note the progress made, the high esteem in which you are held." And he congratulated the white Vanderbilt audience on the interest they were "constantly manifesting in the education of the colored people. . . ." By reflecting such positive regard for his listeners, Washington was, of course, aiming at enhancing his personal credibility and thereby winning a more serious hearing for his case.

Washington's strategy of concession was, perhaps, of weightier significance to his immediate and long-range response. The speaker was clearly willing to acknowledge weaknesses that were attributed to his own race. In doing so before white audiences he probably confirmed some of the very prejudices he sought to eliminate; before black audiences he probably reinforced insecurities he sought to dispel.[36]

His use of concession may be seen at the Zion Church where, in spite of the fact that he affirmed the desirability of racial pride by proclaiming "We should feel honored that we are permitted to belong to the colored race," he admitted that Negroes have yet to realize the kinds of accomplishments that would make them "the greatest people on earth." While he acknowledged "tremendous progress" on the part of black people, he counseled his audience to "start at the bottom" and thereby put them in what he believed—and many no doubt perceived—to be their place.

Washington's strategy of concession, apparent to a minimal degree in his New York speech, was most clearly apparent when he addressed the white men of the South. To them he conceded boldly, "In material, industrial and economic directions, I fully realize all the shortcomings of my race; I never attempt to hide them, never attempt to minimize them. . . ." Although he warned against the tendency to over-generalize by accusing *all* Negroes of the faults of a few, he conceded

that there is criticism, and true, a just criticism, in regard to the Negro as a laborer, in regard to his unreliability, whether it is on the farm or in the shop or in the kitchen or in the dining room or in the laundry or elsewhere. But we must remember that . . . in a state of freedom, along with the elements of industry there has got to be one other element, and that is the element of intelligence, the element of education.

Moreover, he acknowledged the existence of promiscuity among Negro women (although he also clearly implicated whites in the problem) and disavowed Negro pretensions to "social equality" or "political domination." In an attempt to minimize his listeners' fear of the "bug-bear of what is called 'social equality,'" he said:

Robert E. Lee and his family, Stonewall Jackson and his family, and men of that stamp, in the old state of Virginia, used to go into the

Negro Sunday School every Sunday and teach Negro classes. They were not afraid of their standing being affected by helping to lift up and Christianize the *lowly who were right about them.* [Emphasis mine.]

While there was, in this statement and others, no direct suggestion that Washington had conceded the innate, as opposed to relative, inferiority of the Negro race, it is clear that he readily acknowledged the cultural inferiority of the American Negro and *allowed a larger latitude of interpretation for the prejudiced beholder.*

This brings us to a final and critical persuasive strategy reflected by Washington, that of exclusion. The key to understanding his strategy is to consider not so much what he said, but what he did not say; the issues he avoided rather than the issues he discussed.

At the Brooklyn Academy, Washington expended considerable effort reviewing the historical development of American democratic ideals and institutions, but instead of forcefully showing his white listeners how their nation's practices were not consistent with revered traditions, he counseled blacks, few of whom were present, that "freedom comes through seeming restriction," and must be sought "patiently, quietly, doggedly, persistently, through summer and winter, sunshine and shadow. . . ." Instead of denouncing the pernicious and lasting evils of the institution of American slavery, he dismissed the subject by saying:

It is interesting, and perhaps instructive, to note that during the greater part of the period in which agitation and struggle were kept up for the most complete freedom for the white race, another and growing race was being held in servitude by the very people seeking liberty for themselves.

Then he attempted to show his audience that the black man entered slavery as a savage and emerged a civilized man:

I confine myself to a statement of cold, bare facts when I say that when the Negro went into slavery, he was a pagan; when he ended his period of bondage he had a religion. When he went into slavery he was without anything which might properly be called a language;

when he came out of slavery he was able to speak the English tongue with force and intelligence.

Here, his strategy apparently was to exclude discussion of slavery's lasting evils thereby implicating members of his audience in the degradation of the Negro[37] and, instead, consider slavery's supposed advantages.

Washington's strategy at Zion Church was also notable for its avoidance of topics that could produce a spirit of resentment, bitterness, or militancy in black listeners. Sidestepping the controversial, Washington restricted himself to "acceptable" topics and concluded asserting "If we have the force [he did not define "force"] we cannot be kept down on account of our color."

At Nashville, Washington's remarks were particularly notable for the issues he apparently sidestepped. He never asked the "Christian men of the South" to bring their practices regarding the Negro to the level of their principles, at least not directly. He never challenged the popular assumptions of Negro racial inferiority and the justice of racial discrimination apparent everywhere in the South. He was quick to acknowledge prevalence of substandard behavior among blacks but overlooked it among whites. He did not mention the causes or historical antecedents of black degradation but chose, instead, to claim that the two dominant races in the South shared interdependence and mutual affection:

We don't want to part from you and you don't want to part from us. If you want to see a real lonesome Southern white man, meet him in Europe or somewhere in a portion of the world where he can't see any colored people; he is the most lonesome creature you ever saw.

Washington excluded demands for social, economic and political liberation from his Vanderbilt address and from similar addresses to other white Southern audiences. Instead he called upon his white listeners to "call attention more often . . . to the general progress that our people are making," and he assured them "you have a right to be proud of this progress."

CONCLUSIONS

If we are to judge the persuasive strategy of Booker T. Washington exclusively in terms of his role as an educational promoter, it seems fair to credit him with strategic wisdom and tangible effectiveness. He considered it expedient to ask his people to cast down their buckets where they were, and equally expedient not to muddy the waters below. He told the majority what they wanted to hear, nothing more, and he was rewarded for it. For himself, he probably won more political influence than had ever been accorded a black American, and his personal following was immense. His endeavors on behalf of Negro education were generally tolerated and sometimes respected and rewarded in the South—a substantial accomplishment—and he succeeded in winning considerable philanthropic support for many of the programs he sponsored. If strategic wisdom and effectiveness are to be measured in terms of dollars raised and buildings built, then Washington was, indeed, a wise strategist and successful persuader.[38]

But Booker T. Washington's public career extended beyond the confines of educational promotion. He was the recognized leader of black Americans for twenty years. He not only assumed that role, he welcomed it and guarded it jealously.[39] Considering his persuasive posture in this context, a posture characterized not only by the strategies of self-interest and moral principle, but also by flattery, concession, and particularly exclusion, a posture that shunned suggestions of militancy for the soothing tones of conciliation, one is forced to conclude that his persuasion, successful in the arena of immediate and favorable response, was carefully limited to produce goals determined by a pragmatism that disregarded many of the immediate needs of the people for whom Washington spoke.

NOTES

1 W. E. Burghardt Du Bois, *The Souls of Black Folk: Essays and Sketches* (Greenwich: Fawcett Publications, 1903), p. 42.
2 W. E. Burghardt Du Bois, *Dusk at Dawn: An Essay Toward an Autobiog-*

raphy of a Race Concept (New York: Harcourt Brace Jovanovich, 1940), p. 72.

3 Hugh Hawkins, ed., *Booker T. Washington and His Critics: The Problem of Negro Leadership* (Lexington: D. C. Heath, 1962), pp. vi–ix.

4 Du Bois, *Souls*, pp. 42–54.

5 C. Vann Woodward, *Origins of the New South, 1877–1913* (Baton Rouge: Louisiana State University Press, 1951), IX, p. 367.

6 Charles E. Silberman, *Crisis in Black and White* (New York: Random House, 1964), pp. 125, 131.

7 Ray Stannard Baker, *Following the Color Line* (New York: Harper & Row, 1964), p. 222.

8 Samuel R. Spencer, Jr., *Booker T. Washington and the Negro's Place in American Life* (Boston: Little, Brown, 1955), p. 200.

9 Booker T. Washington, *The Negro Problem* (New York: James Pott, 1903), p. 10.

10 August Meier, *Negro Thought in America 1880–1915, Racial Ideologies in the Age of Booker T. Washington* (Ann Arbor: University of Michigan Press, 1966), pp. 190–206.

11 Emmett J. Scott and Lyman Beecher Stowe, *Booker T. Washington: Builder of a Civilization* (Garden City, N.Y.: Doubleday, 1966), pp. 36–37.

12 Karl R. Wallace, "Booker T. Washington," *History and Criticism of American Public Address*, ed. William Norwood Brigance (New York: McGraw-Hill, 1943), I, p. 407.

13 Henry Allan Bullock, *A History of Negro Education in the South: From 1916 to the Present* (Cambridge, Mass.: Harvard University Press, 1967), p. 149.

14 Paul H. Buck, *The Road to Reunion, 1865–1900* (Boston: Little, Brown, 1937), p. 168.

15 Meier, *op. cit.*, p. 21.

16 *Ibid.*, p. 19.

17 Woodward, p. 355.

18 Meier, *op. cit.*, pp. 20–21.

19 Biographical data is based on Washington's autobiography, *Up From Slavery* (Garden City, N.Y.: Doubleday, 1901) and on the following selected biographies: Spencer, Scott and Stowe, and Basil Mathews, *Booker T. Washington: Educator and Interracial Interpreter* (Cambridge, Mass.: Harvard University Press, 1948).

20 Scott and Stowe, p. 19.

21 Rayford W. Logan, *The Negro in American Life and Thought: The Nadir, 1877–1901* (New York: Dial Press, 1954), pp. 80–86.

22 Scott and Stowe, p. 19.

23 Scores of Washington's speeches spanning his entire public career were used to determine the general kinds of audiences he addressed and to

determine representativeness. The personal papers of Mr. Washington located in the Manuscript Division of the Library of Congress, though disorganized, contain hundreds of speech manuscripts that were of primary service. Also of value was E. Davidson Washington's *Selected Speeches of Booker T. Washington* (Garden City, N.Y.: Doubleday, 1932). Only those speeches designed for special occasions and his moral lectures to Tuskegee students were eliminated from consideration.

24 Meier, p. 103.

25 *Brooklyn Times-Herald*, February 23, 1903, p. 1.

26 *New York Times*, February 23, 1903, p. 1. Similar reports were carried in the *New York Tribune, New York Herald*, and *Brooklyn Times-Herald*, February 23, 1903.

27 *San Francisco Bulletin*, January 12, 1903, p. 1.

28 *Ibid.*

29 *Memphis Appeal*, March 30, 1907, p. 1.

30 *Knoxville Statement*, March 30, 1907, p. 1.

31 Booker T. Washington Papers, Manuscript Division, Library of Congress, "Speeches," 1903. All subsequent references to this speech were taken from this source and will not be noted further.

32 In his opening remarks, for instance, he said, "It is a constant source of regret that I cannot spend more time among the people of my own race— to talk with you and take you by the hand."

33 Booker T. Washington Papers, Manuscript Division, Library of Congress, "Speeches," 1903. All subsequent references to this speech were taken from this source and will not be noted further.

34 Booker T. Washington Papers, Manuscript Division, Library of Congress, stenographic report. All subsequent references to this speech were taken from this source and will not be noted further.

35 Spencer, pp. 80–81.

36 Critics of Washington generally confirm this judgment. See, for instance, Rayford W. Logan, "The Atlanta Compromise," in Hawkins, pp. 21–26.

37 They helped to sustain a culture that has perpetuated slavery-born prejudices, social codes, and institutions that discriminate against the black man.

38 Horace Mann Bond, *Negro Education in Alabama: A Study in Cotton and Steel* (Washington: Associated Publishers, 1939), pp. 224–225. See also Kelly Miller, "Washington's Policy," *The Making of Black America: Essays on Negro Life and History*, eds. August Meier and Elliot Rudwick (New York: Athenaeum, 1969), II, pp. 119–124.

39 Francis L. Broderick, *W. E. B. Du Bois: Negro Leader in a Time of Crisis* (Palo Alto: Stanford University Press, 1959), pp. 62ff.

Finley C. Campbell

CHAPTER 12
Voices of Thunder, Voices of Rage:
A Symbolic Analysis of a Selection from
Malcolm X's Speech, "Message to the Grass Roots"

There are several ways that one can approach a speech, particularly as a form of communication. It can be conceived of as a form of monodrama or as the structured oral form of that broad field called rhetoric. From the perspective of literature, the speech can be approached as an aesthetic product, open to the kinds of critical analysis applicable to literature in general, such as, for example symbolic action analysis.[1] The general aim of this paper is to apply such an analysis to a contemporary speech, Malcolm

From *The Speech Teacher* (March 1970), pp. 101–110. Reprinted by permission of the publisher and the author. Finley C. Campbell is Assistant Professor of English, Wabash College. He formerly headed the Communication Division at Morehouse College.

X's "Message to the Grass Roots."[2] The essential point will be that only such an analysis can reveal the complex richness which characterizes the power of this speech.

Such a discussion involves three main points: the nature of symbolic action, Malcolm's speech as an example of such action, and the use of symbolic action analysis to reveal that "multi-dramatic ambience" characteristic of black oratory in general and Malcolm's power in particular. A full explication of these factors should reveal to the reader both the thunder and the rage inhering not only in this particular speech but all those speeches which form the substance of the oral-aural tradition in Afro-American rhetoric and literature.

Literature in all of its genres must be seen as a field of imaginative force, of creative energy, connecting the author to the reader through an interlock of aesthetic factors, called literary elements. When taken together or separately, they form a work's purely literary or textural nature. Within this field of force, these elements are, psychologically speaking, in a constant state of "action" and that *action*, the interpenetration and interdependence of literary qualities, "acts out," "dramatizes," *symbolizes* the sets of meaning which form a work's structure of themes, a structure which exists in addition to and often regardless of a writer's stated or intended meaning. Because of the constancy and continuation of this dynamism, the key theme, or more precisely, the central idea, can be an infinite number of possible meanings. And, the imaginative critics can constantly uncover new and even contradictory central ideas in the same work. For, at any one moment in "critical" time, the analyst can only have an interpretational hypothesis about the ontological meaning of a work and that hypothesis becomes, for him, the central idea. This process creates a seemingly inexhaustible spiral of meaning and permits a startling variety of major and minor ideas to be uncovered within the same work, each valid so long as the critic has carefully and imaginatively examined the texture either *in toto* or in part and has not violated the objective data of the texture by misreadings, distortions, and omissions. In other words, the meaning or theme is organically related to the literary work in its totality, not as a static body of ideas in a fixed relation, but as a dynamic interplay of the texture and the thematic structure.

When seen together, the aesthetic aspects of literature may be said to form "texture," that is, figuratively speaking, a mix of elements comparable to the blending of different threads to form a fabric. There is a special texture for poetry, drama, prose fiction, and literary non-fiction. However, the threads or elements remain fairly constant: plot, character, language, setting, tone, and form. The thematic structure, symbolized by this interaction of elements, consists of a central idea which holds together a set of major and minor themes.

It is the capacity for any element (or part of that element) and any idea to act as the synecdoche for the entire thematic structure (and especially for the central idea) which is the immediate constituent for symbolic action.[3] Up a ladder of increasing complexity, then, we arrive at that supreme moment when all the elements operating separately, concurrently, and/or simultaneously "act out" the meaning, creating what Burke also calls "the dancing of an attitude." At this imaginary moment, who can tell the dancer from the dance? They are at once the same and different, bringing into view a dramatization of the writer's psychological state and philosophic attitudes.

This rather complex analytical paradigm can best be applied to written works, especially those of obvious genius, although it has applicability to any form of aesthetic discourse, no matter how inferior. Since in this article I am discussing the symbographic transcript of Malcolm's speech and since he represents such genius, a symbolic action analysis can be fruitfully applied. I have chosen "The Message to the Grass Roots" because the rhetorical intensity of his denunciations allows that special quality of the black orator, what I have called the multidramatic ambience, to shine through without the moderating ambiguities of his later, more statesmanlike speeches.

Earlier in this essay, I referred to six literary elements. In analyzing Malcolm's speech, I shall only use three, because of space limitations: language, setting, and character.

When the term language is used, the reference is not to words *per se;* the reference is to the way those words have been shaped into aesthetic patterns, i.e., figurative and imagistic language, and phonetic, syntactical, and rhythmic structures, in order to create a style. Of these components, figures and images are the most salient characteristic of Malcolm's speech in its written form. The speech abounds in powerful, judicious similes, metaphors, and analogies which enrich the total texture of his presentation. They do not occur haphazardly; there is a discernible pattern revealing the brilliant play of Malcolm's wit and rhetorical talent. The key pattern is polarity: the Grass Roots versus Grass Leaves, colonialized peoples versus the colonializing people, "landless against the landlord," violence versus non-violence, "swinging" versus "singing," field niggers against house niggers, the Patient versus the Dentist, pain versus novacain, Martin Luther King against Malcolm X, the Black March on Washington versus the Negro March on Washington, coffee versus cream, Burt Lancaster against James Baldwin, the explicit unreality of Hollywood against the implicit reality of Harlem.

Then each polarized image-figure can be further broken down to reveal the highly charged power [with] which Malcolm imbues his language. Take, for example, this key conceit:

It's just like when you've got some coffee that's too black, which means it's too strong. What do you do? You integrate it with cream, you make it weak. But if you pour too much cream in it, you don't even know you ever had coffee.

Black coffee becomes a tasteless liquid with the addition of too much cream. "It used to be hot, it becomes cool. It used to be strong, it becomes weak. It used to wake you, it puts you to sleep. This is what (the whites) did with the march on Washington."

The setting of the speech, the next element, is both complex and simple. The external is given by the editor: the King Solomon

Baptist Church (place), in Detroit, Michigan (geo-political area), in 1963 (time), at the Grass Roots Conference (the rationale of the setting). The internal or suggestive context is more interesting, based initially on Malcolm's ability to play with the sub-elements of time and place. Now it is 1963 in Detroit, now 1954 at Bandung; now the time and places of the great Western revolutions: America 1776, France 1784, Russia 1917. We are in Africa; then in China, but most of all in America, the America of slaves in the nineteenth century and ex-slaves in the twentieth. And then more specifically we are simultaneously in Washington in August, 1963, watching the March and in the Carlyle Hotel in New York much earlier watching the march being betrayed. Malcolm manipulates history to make it render up individual settings which emphasizes points in his speech. But more important, he uses history to supply a dramatic context *for his audience,* to place the audience in the shoes of revolutionary and counter-revolutionary personae, transforming his audience into Bandung delegates, French revolutionaries, Russian peasants, field niggers, and betrayed black men.

But there is another internal setting, here, less visible than the historical ones, constructed, as it were, by the very passion of the speech. As we see Malcolm there above that crowd at King Solomon, a metamorphosis takes place; the time is all ages of struggle, the place is the citadel of man, the geo-political area is Troy, not as a historical city but as the image of all besieged peoples everywhere, and the rationale for the setting a coming struggle against the conditions of oppression.

Thus we have a tri-leveled overlay of the factual, the rhetorical, and the archetypal settings. Together, they shape the environment of the hero of the people who stands amidst his followers haranguing them in a fierce and uncompromising call for action, against besieging Greeks outside the walls.

Hero of the People: this brings us to the element of character. When symbolic action critics insist that all literary discourse, including non-fiction and personal lyrics, has characters and characterization, traditionalists, who have associated characters only with certain literary forms, believe that the nature of literature has been distorted to fit a critical theory. Yet, all literary works do in fact have two fundamental characters: the author and the reader, or in the case of a speech, the speaker and the auditor. From this obvious fact come all the other kinds of personae. In "Message to the Grass Roots," the two major characters, at this level, are Malcolm X and the audience, which is both the auditor and a participant in the plot like a Greek chorus. The audience complements Malcolm and yet is also an antagonist at certain moments, signaled by reiterative variations on the theme of "I know you don't like what I'm saying but I'm going to tell you anyway!"

Beyond this level, there is another character set, also linked in the same polarized pattern which defined the figures and images: an antagonist, the leader of the Negro revolution, Martin Luther King, Jr., and a protagonist, the leader of the Black revolution, Malcolm X. This antithesis provides us with the personality traits shaping these figures into their roles of villain and hero.[4]

Martin Luther King, Jr., appears in Malcolm's speech as the villain, primarily as a compound figure. On the surface he is "compound" because he is a composite of several Negro leaders: Wilkins, Young, Randolph, Rustin, etc. In other words, Malcolm *invents* a Martin Luther King, Jr., made up of people whom Malcolm felt had betrayed the Washington March and who had, at the personal level, denied him attendance to the Detroit conference.

More complicatedly, King is a compound character in that all the personality traits which Malcolm gives him complement each other. In the first place, the King-Villain is pro-white and hence a part of the disruptive force which keeps black people divided. The King-Villain's insistence on white participation reveals a basic sycophancy toward the oppressor which in Malcolm's uncompromising spirit prevents unity. Second, the King-Villain insists on bringing quarrels out into the open, in publicly announcing disagreement with a rejection of the black nationalists. Such indiscretion relates directly to such sycophantic behavior as the Negro leaders' continual disassociation of themselves from the black militants, a trait which, alas, still persists.

Third, the King-Villain advocates, on the one hand, that the black man kill the enemies of the white man (North Koreans, Japs, Nazis) and, on the other, rejects violence against the enemies of the black man (white genocidal maniacs). Moreover, the King-Villain's rejection even of self-defense for the Negro while accepting self-defense for the United States becomes the clearest indication of a basic hypocrisy, a hypocrisy ultimately resulting from his inability to support the kind of black nationalist zeal necessary to irrigate the droughted lives of the grass roots people. Since King is a house-niggering Tom in Malcolm's eyes, whose ultimate loyalty is to the White Master's oppression not to the oppressed field-niggers he emerges as a "singer" when what is needed is a "swinger." Malcolm's description of the life-style, psychology, and existential debasement of the house nigger's voluntary servitude prepares us for the ultimate indictment of the Negro revolutionist.

Despite his seeming identification with oppressed blacks, he is, in fact, being used to keep the masses "in check, to keep us under control, keep us passive and peaceful and non-violent" for status and money. Indeed, the Negro revolution is supported by whites so long as it does not touch the basic nature of the system which sustains them and oppresses the black masses. The King-Villain joins with the Dentist (referred to earlier) as the novacain which enables him to strip the black man of those teeth which indicate his potentiality to change, let us say, into a panther. And because of the novacain the Patient submits without the normal reactions to anguish, dread, and anger.

Now the point here is quite complex in terms of the characterization through which Malcolm portrays his antagonist. The twentieth century Uncle Tom is no passive servant of the Dentist. On the contrary, he is seemingly battling against him. For, the King-Villain has in fact mobilized a vast array of power against the Dentist. The grass roots people do support the Negro revolution. And for a while the antagonist is successful in seeming to fight against white power (a fact which Malcolm deliberately suppresses). Then come two major defeats: one non-violent (the Albany fiasco) and one violent (the Birmingham riots). As the result of the house Negro's failures, the field Negroes erupt on their own and begin to take to the streets, begin to mobilize for a march on Washington which will bring full rights or close the city down.

To combat this uncontrollable revolution, the Masters consult with the grass leaves rulers (or Leaves of Grass) who for a million and a half dollars are brought over to the side of the master, not so much for the money but for the power which the money enables them to have as Negro revolutionists. Their job is to change a black revolutionary move into a Negro one, to give the semblance of militancy without its substance. The plan works. The thunder and the rage of the angry black masses are muted. The March on Washington becomes "a picnic, a circus" led by "white clowns and black clowns." It becomes something worse.

a performance that beat anything Hollywood could ever do, the performance of the year. Reuther and those other three devils should get an Academy Award for the best actors because *they acted like they really loved Negroes and fooled a whole lot of Negroes.* (italic ours) And the six Negro leaders should get an award too, for the best supporting cast.

Thus the King-Villain emerges as a race traitor, who transforms the anguish of the Grass Roots into a Hollywood spectacle. The King-Villain's treachery, his final character trait, is worst because it is masked by seeming virtue. In his hands, the march becomes a simulated revolutionary gesture, since all the while the Kennedys

controlled it so tight, they told those Negroes what time to hit town, how to come, where to stop, what signs to carry, what songs to sing, what speech they could make, and what speech they couldn't make; and then told them to get out of town by sundown. And every one of those Toms was out of town by sundown.

Thus the Negro revolutionary emerges as a hypocritical, treacherous showman whose essential function is not to challenge the oppressor but to dissipate the anger of the oppressed with cathartic rituals.

In X's speech, then, the authentic antagonist is not the white man but the Negro traitor. It is he who is the target for Malcolm's angry contempt.

(Let me hasten to emphasize that the villain and hero terms used here are to designate the nature of the symbolic activity created by Malcolm in this particular speech. It does not designate Malcolm's ultimate feelings about Dr. King as a person or himself as a leader. The evidence is clear that after he left the Muslims, Malcolm was more statesmanlike in his attitude toward Dr. King, although he disagreed with him about the validity of absolute non-violence as a revolutionary tactic.)

Malcolm X is, of course, the protagonist, but not as himself, rather as a character in an aesthetic discourse. He is the Malcolm-Hero who stands in clear opposition to the villain within the speech. The implied contrast is clear. The Malcolm-Hero is the black nationalist revolutionary who accepts unhesitatingly the conceptual meaning of revolution: "Revolution is bloody, revolution is hostile, revolution knows no compromise, revolution overturns and destroys everything that gets in its way." From this acceptance follow his compound character traits.

He is black-minded and rejects out of hand white participation in his movement. Whites are the enemy, directly and indirectly, because they oppress the field niggers. In his description of the life-style, feelings, and desires of the field workers, X describes the attitude of the Malcolm-Hero toward white power: a violent rejection of white institutions—government, astronauts, or Navy— which stand in the way of getting "land." Yet, in terms of the survival of the Grass Roots, the Malcolm-Hero counsels discretion: the enemy must never know of any major disagreement among Negroes and blacks. Having family squabbles on the sidewalk is "uncouth, unrefined, uncivilized, savage." An image of unity must be maintained at all cost against the powerful institutions of Diablo Blanco.[5]

Third, Malcolm rejects any double standard of modern violence. If white America has the right to defend itself in Korea, black America has the right to defend itself in Mississippi. The Hero is willing to "off" his own father if his father would betray the revolution. The Malcolm-Hero wished to build a nation, violently if necessary. Hence to be a black nationalist revolutionary becomes his highest goal. The Malcolm-Hero understands what the King-Villain cannot or will not: that it is the diabolic Dentist who is the essential cause of violence through his attempts to defang the Patient. And the Patient must endure this violence because someone "has taught [him] to suffer—peacefully." The protagonist will endure no such suffering. He will be "peaceful . . . courteous, obey the law, respect everyone; but if someone puts his hand on [him, he will] send him to the cemetery." Further, he will not counsel the sheep to submit peacefully to wolves hungry for their blood. "Any time a shepherd, a pastor, teaches us and me not to run from the white man and, at the same time, teaches us not to fight the white man, he's a traitor to you and me."

The Hero, because of his awareness of the function of violence as an essential sign of the black nationalist impulse in the Grass Roots and because of his identity with it, feels no need to calm the masses down. Instead he works with them in harmony, no matter what their strategy. He trusts the new leaders and unlike the King-Villain feels no necessity to control them; instead he seeks to incite and excite them. He commends their violence during the Birmingham uprising, their stabbing of Crackers in the back, and their "busting them up side the head." He embraces wholeheartedly their "black" march on Washington; their bold strategy of using any means necessary to dramatize the desperate anguish of the masses:

to march on the Senate, march on the White House, march on the Congress, and tie it up, bring it to a halt, not let the government proceed. They even said they were going out to the airport and lay down on the runway and not let any planes land. . . . That was revolution. . . . That was the black revolution.[6]

Such identification of hero and people defines the final and perhaps the salient trait of the black nationalist as protagonist: an unqualified loyalty to the Roots of Grass. How could there be a sellout with him? He has no time to get embroiled in the money-matters which corrupt the Villain. He is not interested in palliating the fears of the Kennedy family and its allies because he does not need their media and their influence. In his hand, the coffee would have remained coffee; the desperate courage of the march would have been triumphant or tragic, but it would not have been a Hollywood spectacle; he and his cohorts would have not left by sundown. And whether it would have come white violence, resistance, or acquiescence, he would not have been afraid to challenge fundamentally the "same white element that put Kennedy into power." Thus Malcolm's loyalty to the cause of the Grass Roots, within this speech at least, shapes him into that figure of populist history: the uncompromising hero of the people.

There is a more archetypal characterization, which emerges out of this last epithet, within the symbolic action of the speech. If the whites are demons, then the blacks are angels in terms of the polarization structure. If the King-Villain is a representative of the whites, he becomes identified as the Negro Beelzebub to a white Satan. The opposing parallel is to see the Malcolm-Hero as the Michael to a black Allah, as one sent from God to enlighten the benighted and to rescue a buried people from the tombs of delusion, betrayal, and fear through the gospel of black nationalism. Thus, within the characterization symbolism one can discern a struggle between the forces of Whiteness (the Dark) and the forces of blackness (the light) acted out in the dialectic polarity of antagonist and protagonist.[7]

So far the textural aspect of symbolic action has been examined in and of itself, with only a hint here and an explanation there of the thematic structure acted out by the elements of language, setting and character. Let us now examine this structure in more detail.

The thematic structure of a work consists of the minor themes, the major themes, the central idea, and their logical relation to each other. I call it a structure in order to metaphor the way in which the major and minor ideas relate to the central concept. Visually this structure may be seen as an open or schematic cube. At each corner are located the major ideas linked together by schematic lines representing their logical relation. The whole "structure" is then connected by lines angling out at 45° from the central idea to each corner of the cube, lines representing the logical relation between this center and the major themes. The minor ideas are represented visually as smaller nodes on the various lines. For those of you familiar with the schematic model of a cesium chloride crystal, this description should be much clearer.

The main point is that no matter how many ideas a work may yield through symbolic action analysis, it is necessary for the critic to separate major from minor, and then separate the central idea from the major themes. The differentiating characteristics of major and minor ideas depend on the critic's emphasis. The differentiating characteristic of the major theme and the central idea is more easily determined. The central idea must be a truly universal statement about the nature of mankind and it must be able to incorporate logically all the other ideas in the work, no matter how contradictory they may seem on the surface. Thus, the ultimate function of symbolic action criticism is to arrive at a convincing interpretational hypothesis about the central idea, or what we also call the universal imperative.[8]

The essential method for this involves the following steps: an analysis and synthesis of these ideas to some paraphrastic meaning; the conversion of this meaning into major themes, or what we also call the categorical imperatives;[9] and then the conversion of the most important of these categorical insights into a universal statement.

On the paraphrastic level, "Message to the Grass Roots," begins with Malcolm describing white America's most serious problem: the presence of the black aliens and the white Americans' intense dislike of black people and people of color around the world. He then discusses the necessity of identifying this American enemy and the absolute need for Afro-Americans to submerge their differences in order to deal with him. Next Malcolm distinguishes between the black and Negro revolutions, defining the former as a violent struggle for land and the latter as a trick to pacify the Grass Roots. Finally, he applies his analysis to contemporary problems: the failure of the Albany and Birmingham movements as Negro revolutions, the rise of the Grass Roots' or black revolution, and the betrayal of that revolution by the subversion of the Grass Roots' March on Washington. The excerpt ends with a denunciation of the hypocrisy and treachery of those Negro revolutionists who participated in the subversion.

This paraphrastic meaning can be converted into a myriad of major themes or categorical imperatives. Simply defined in this critical system, a categorical imperative refers to a truth which has general and absolutely necessary applicability only to *a* certain category of human experience. In "Message to the Grass Roots" there are several such ideas: the white racist can never be trusted to deal fairly with black people; Uncle Toms always betray the Grass Roots; and integrated black revolution is impossible; avaricious leaders can be bought off; and the black revolution seeks the violent destruction of oppressive white institutions. Of these possible choices the one which seems to dominate and which emerges as a key idea is the nature of revolution.

The very nature of a black revolutionary encounter, Malcolm insists, involves the need for polarization. The white enemy must be clearly delineated and opposed; the black friends must be clearly known and supported. The essential problems of the black masses is to achieve unity around common goals and to eliminate or convert those who have the color of the oppressed but who are not really prepared to unite with them in a struggle, using any means necessary, to end white oppression. In this light, the imperative for the category, black revolution, is that the absolute and necessary prerequisite for a successful revolution in America is the unity of all Negroes around the principles of black nationalism.[10]

Unlike the categorical imperative the universal must relate to all experience everywhere; it must have general and absolutely necessary applicability to mankind as envisioned by the critic. The word "unity" offers a clue to an interpretational hypothesis which will satisfy the above definition. The unity of the black nationalist is for a purpose: the impending conflict with what we have symbolically called, the Dentist. He not only wants to inflict the most sadistic kind of mutilation on his Negro Patient, but he wants the Patient to suffer this mutilation, peacefully. For if the Patient really knew the extent of the horror being done to him, he would have to, if need be, kill the Dentist, but it is precisely the function of the Uncle Toms to act as novacain, to convince the Patient that his suffering is, in fact, painless. Their essential power is that they seem to be identified with the interests of the Patient. Thus, he is caught in a deadly trap: those whom he trusts the most are in fact delivering him into the hands of horror and degradation. It is the ignorance of the Grass Roots which permits this perfidy. But it is the treachery of the Grass Leaves, whose loyalty is ultimately with the Masters and not the masses, which for Malcolm, is the true horror. Therefore, how can there be a unified effort when such traitors abound.

The divisive Tom now emerges in his true colors: the hypocrite, the false-illusive "Hollywood" star who generates the disunity plaguing the struggle. This aspect of the categorical imperative is now ready for conversion into a universal imperative. In the age-long struggle between good and evil (or in the existential struggle between opposing viewpoints) it is the hypocrite who debilitates and destroys the power of the good to eventually and finally overcome evil; it is hypocrisy which emerges as the enemy in polarized situations. The hypocritical Christian, Communist, or revolutionary has done more to destroy the essential validity of Christianity, Communism, and revolution than their antitheses. Those who appear to be loyal to a cause but who, in reality, are agents of the opposition emerge as the true enemies of that cause, as the dissimulators whose essential aim is to mislead and betray those who most believe in them. And as Milton states,

For neither man nor angel can discern
Hypocrisy, the only evil that walks
Invisible, except to God alone,
By his permissive will . . .
And oft though wisdom wake, suspicion sleeps

At wisdom's gate . . . while goodness thinks no ill
where no ill seems . . .

And ain't nothing more universal than that.

This, therefore, is the thematic center lying in the midst of Malcolm's powerful work, "The Message to the Grass Roots."

With the discovery of the universal imperative, the dance of Malcolm's attitude—that interpenetration of his texture and his themes which shapes his power—can now be appreciated and understood. The language with its emphasis on polarized figures and images, the three levels of the setting, and the characters themselves all "act out" separately and together the centralizing idea of the hypocrite's corrupting nature in the clash of opposing forces, his danger both to those who support the Pearl against the Pig and to the black revolution in its competition with the Negro one.

The image, for example, of the dilution of the coffee concretizes the debilitating results of both white and Negro hypocrisy. The rhetorical settings with their emphasis on revolutionary times and beseiged citadels contrast the clear demand for action in the black revolution with the more dissembled pantomimes of action in the Negro one. The conflict between the Malcolm-Hero and the King-Villain, is, in fact, a conflict between the authentic hero of the Grass Roots and a seeming hero. All the major and minor ideas, and especially the key categorical imperative, the need for black nationalist unity, receive a relation-contrastual bonding with the universal imperative. And these ideas in turn are also together and separately symbolized in the dynamics of the texture. This then is the literary richness which a symbolic action analysis permits the imaginative critic to uncover in works of such genius.

The relation of this critical technique to speech *per se* should be quite clear. For, through this kind of analysis, with its emphasis on the written speech as a dynamic field of creative energy, with its awareness of Malcolm as a character and without the written speech, the words come alive and bring to the fore the multi-dramatic audience of black militant oratory. For, as Burke insists, the final result of the dance of the attitude is the creation of the ritual drama, defined as a psychological phenomenon projected by the writer toward the reader through his work in order to dramatize the writer's conscious and subconscious feelings, attitudes, and beliefs.[11]

This dramatic quality is revealed in the mere process of the dancing attitude. The language used to incarnate the imperatives is theatrical and perhaps even melodramatic with its reiterated antithetical comparisons and sensory images. Certainly Malcolm's handling of phonetic, syntactical, and rhythmic structures in the written speech parallels the dramatic power of the spoken one. The setting itself emerges in the symbolic action analysis as both a physical and imagined "set," creating a proscenium in which literally Malcolm is one-center stage as the star of a monodrama, while his audience acts as a chorus, as both participant and auditor. Malcolm's use of polarized characters fulfills the demands of the old Aristotelian doctrine of theater in which the *agon* between a protagonist and an antagonist forms the ontological structure of dramatic action. All these kinds of theatrical imputs render up in written form a reflection of those elements which in the spoken form create the multidramatic ambience permeating the oratory of the black speaker.

It is the disciplined though imaginative freeing of the critic's fancy permitted by symbolic action analysis which returns us through lifeless words to the interest vitality of Malcolm as a black orator. It is such analysis which shows us his grounding in the main stream of the black American's oral-aural tradition and his peculiar use of that ambience which gives to the black speakers their special authority and charisma. Power to the People.

NOTES

[1] The term was developed by Kenneth Burke in his *Philosophy of Literary Form*. However, the definition which will operate in this discussion combines a variety of sources derived mainly from a judicious blend of my own insights and those of the now defunct "New Criticism."

2 *Malcolm X Speaks*, ed. George Breitman, paperback edition (New York, 1966), 4–17. This is a thirty minute excerpt from the much longer speech, but it is complete in itself to justify our analysis of it.

3 My use of the term "synecdoche" (i.e., the metaphor in which the part stands for the whole) also conforms with Burke's usage.

4 Here we must make clear the fact that symbolic analysis allows us to uncover relevant patterns of interpretations via element investigation which need not be consciously intended by the artist. Thus such an analysis assumes the *a priori* importance of the finished work rather than the *a priori* importance of the artist's intention.

5 We wonder here if Malcolm is not breaking his own rule. But the word is that at this particular meeting no whites, reporters included, were allowed to attend.

6 It is interesting to note that Malcolm does not reject non-violence out of hand here. He seems willing to use it as one of the means necessary to accomplish revolutionary ends.

7 This last point is open to all kinds of attack. But it does illustrate the kind of freewheeling interpretation which has been both the bane and power of symbolic action analysis.

8 Here we borrow the term but not the definition from Immanuel Kant.

9 Also a term borrowed from Kant, but not his definition.

10 Notice how this categorical imperative sums up the meaning of the paraphrase and how it logically relates to the other major themes.

11 In *The Philosophy of Literary Form*, Kenneth Burke uses a symbolic action analysis to show that Samuel Coleridge's *The Rime of the Ancient Mariner* is a ritual drama. It is not our function here to describe Burke's brilliant exigesis of this rather complex idea. We simply take off from his insights toward another, though similar, kind of analysis.

John Illo

CHAPTER 13
The Rhetoric
of Malcolm X

In a nation of images without substances, of rehearsed emotions, in a politic of consensus where platitude replaces belief or belief is fashioned by consensus, genuine rhetoric, like authentic prose, must be rare. For rhetoric, like any verbal art, is correlative with the pristine idea of reason and justice which, if it decays with the growth of every state and jurisprudence, now has developed

Reprinted from *The Columbia University Forum*, IX (Spring 1966), pp. 5–12, by permission of the author. John Illo teaches English at Monmouth College and received the M.A. degree from Columbia University in 1955. His critical essays have appeared in several literary journals. This is his second contribution to *The Forum*.

into an unreason that aggressively claims the allegiance of the national mind.

Jurisprudence is the prudent justification of an absurd society, of institutionalized inequity and internal contradiction. Law, and juridical logic, and grammar conspire to frustrate the original idea of a just and good society, in which all men may freely become the best that they may be. Rhetoric, like the Shelleyan poetic, returns us to primal intelligence, to the golden idea and the godly nature whose mirror is unspoiled reason. The critical and reformist function of rhetoric, apparent in processes like irony and paradox, is perceptible in the whole range of tropes and syntactic and tonal devices. Repetitions and transposals of syntax recall the emphases of nature, before civil logic; and metaphor recalls the true relations, resemblances, predications, that we have been trained to forget. Love is not a fixation but a fire, for it consumes and cleanses; and man is not a rational animal so essentially as he is dust and breath, crumbling, evanescent, and mysterious because moved invisibly.

To use schemes, figures, tropes, in a plan or plot that corresponds with the broad proceeding of the juridically logical mind, is to make an oration. Within the grammatical frame of his society, the orator, using the language of primordial reason and symbol, restores to his audience the ideas that have been obscured by imposed categories that may correspond to institution but not to reality. Rhetoric, Aristotle taught, is analogous to logic because enthymeme is related to syllogism; but, more significantly, rhetoric is related to logic as logic is related to reality. And rhetoric is also related to poetry, as Cicero observed, his prosaic Roman mind reducing poetry to ornamented language, as the lyric mind of Plato had reduced rhetoric to "cookery." Cicero and Aristotle were each half right. Rhetoric is in fact poeticized logic, logic revised by the creative and critical imagination recalling original ideas. Rhetoric, the art that could grow only in a *polis* and a system of judicature, is the art that restores the primitive value of the mystical word and the human voice. With a matured craft and a legalist's acuteness, orators contrive the free language of childlike reason, innocently reproving the unnatural and perverse, which institution, custom, law, and policy ask us to accept as the way of the world.

And so great orators, when great, have spoken for absolute justice and reason as they perceived it, in defiance of their governments or societies, accusing tyrants, protesting vicious state policies that seduced the general will, execrating the deformation of popular morality. We think of an Isaiah prophesying against the corruption of ancestral religion, of a Demosthenes against Philip, a Cicero against Antony, a Burke against a colonial war, a Garrison against slavery. At the summit of their art they recalled the language of primal intelligence and passion in defense of elemental truth; and their symbols and transposed syntax, though deliberated, were no more spurious or obtrusive than in poetry. But unlike the pure poet, the orator always holds near enough to the juridical logic, grammar, and semantic of the institution to be able to attack the institution. He never yields his reformist responsibility for the private vision that may be illusive, and may be incommunicable. The orator unlinks the mind-forged manacles, but refashions them into an armor for the innocent intelligence, the naked right.

Lesser oratory, venal, hypocritical, in defense of the indefensible, is patently factitious, its free language a cosmetic, a youthful roseate complexion arranged on an old, shrewd and degenerated visage, as in the forced prosopopoeias of Cicero appealing for a criminal Milo, or in the tedious predictable alliterated triads of Everett McKinley Dirksen. Bad morals usually produce bad rhetoric, and such is the dureful weight of institutions and their parties that *rhetoric* had been pejorated, generally, into *bad rhetoric*. Even Henry Steele Commager can regard oratory like Senator Long's as "eloquent but shameless," attributes ideally exclusive. The swelling anaphoras of a Southern Congressman are not eloquent but ludicrous, raising irrepressible images of toads and swine. Little else but bad rhetoric is possible to those within the establishment, so far from original reason, so committed to the apologetics of unreason. And those outside are conditioned by established styles, or are graceless, or are misdirected in eccentric contrariety. The poetry of Bob Dylan veers in its metaphoric texture between the more lyrical ads and the *Daily News* editorials; the new left sniffles and stumbles into the unwitting anacolutha of *uh* and *you-know*; the old left tends to rant and cant, persuasive only to the persuaded. There are clear teachers like Allen Krebs and Staughton Lynd, but as good teachers they are probably not orators.

The achievement of Malcolm X, then, though inevitable, seems marvelous. Someone had to rise and speak the fearful reality, to throw the light of reason into the hallucinatory world of the capitalist and biracial society that thinks itself egalitarian, that thinks itself humanitarian and pacific. But it was unexpected that the speaking should be done with such power and precision by a russet-haired field Negro translated from conventional thief to zealot and at the end nearly to Marxist and humanist.

For the rhetoric of the American black outsider in this age has seldom been promising; this is not the century of Toussaint L'Ouverture or the nation of Frederick Douglass. The charismatic strength of Father Divine, or of Elijah Muhammad, did not derive from rhetoric. The language of one was hypnotically abstruse, if not perfectly unintelligible, related not to oratory or to religion but to New Thought. The oratory of the other is diffusing and halting, unornamented, solecistic, provincial, its development over-deliberate, its elocution low-keyed though rising to an affecting earnestness. Robert Williams has force but not majesty or art. Men like James Baldwin and LeRoi Jones are primarily writers, and each is deficient in the verbal and vocal size and action required in oratory, which is neither writing nor talking. The young Negro radicals are beyond criticism, the gloomy product not so much of the ghetto as of TV and the American high school. The Nobel Laureate and the Harlem Congressman have different oratorical talents, but neither is an outsider.

The rhetoric of Malcolm X was in the perennial traditions of the art, but appropriate to his audiences and purpose—perennial because appropriate. A Harlem rally is not the Senate of the Roman Republic, but Cicero would have approved Malcolm's discourse as *accommodatus, aptus, congruens,* suitable to his circumstances and subject. His exordia were properly brief, familiar, sometimes acidly realistic (". . . brothers and sisters, friends and enemies: I just can't believe everyone in here is a friend and I don't want to leave anybody out."), and he moved to his proposition within the first minute, for his audience needed relevant ideas and theses, not dignity and amplitude. His perorations were similarly succinct, sometimes entirely absorbed into the confirmations. His personal apologiae, negative or self-depreciatory, contrary to those of a Cicero or a Burke, assured his hearers that he was on the outside, like them: "I'm not a politician, not even a student of politics; in fact, I'm not a student of much of anything. I'm not a Democrat, I'm not a Republican, and I don't even consider myself an American," an ironic gradation or augmentative climax that was, in the world of Malcolm and his people, really a kind of declination or reversed climax.

His narration and confirmation were densely analytical, but perspicuous because of their familiar diction and analogies, and their catechetical repetitions: "And to show you what his [Tshombe's] thinking is—a hired killer—what's the first thing he did? He hired more killers. He went out and got the mercenaries from South Africa. And what is a mercenary? A hired killer. That's all a mercenary is. The anti-Castro Cuban pilots, what are they? Mercenaries, hired killers. Who hired them? The United States. Who hired the killers from South Africa? The United States; they just used Tshombe to do it."

Instruction was the usual purpose of Malcolm's oratory; he was primarily a teacher, his oratory of the demonstrative kind, and his speeches filled with significant matter. It was the substantive fullness and penetration, the honesty and closeness to reality of Malcolm's matter that imparted much of the force to his oratory.

A representative political speech in the United States is empty of content. What did President Kennedy's Inaugural Address contain that a commencement address does not? Indeed, the Inaugural displayed the meaningless chiasmus, the fatuous or sentimental metaphor, the callow hyperbaton of a valedictory. President Johnson's speeches on foreign affairs vitiate reason and intelligence as his foreign policy violates international morality: temporarily not to attack a neutral nation is a positive beneficence that should evoke gratitude and concessions, and one is ready to negotiate with any party under any conditions except the party and conditions that are relevant. But such is the tradition of vacant and meaningless political oratory in America, and such the profusion of the universally accepted and discredited rhetoric of advertising, that the public nods and acquiesces, not believes. We expect truth and substance not in open oration, but in secret conference or in caucus, "on the inside"—where we can't hear it. We assume that rhetoric is a futile and deceptive or self-deceived art, because rhetoric should persuade through rational conviction, but business and government are ruled by power and interest. And perhaps Congressional or party oratory is a facade, the votes having been decided not by analogies and metonymies but by the Dow-Jones averages.

Yet the people, closer to reason than their legislators, may still be moved by rhetoric, and popular oratory may still be a political force. We wonder how a crowd in Havana can listen to the Premier for three hours. A revolution needs people, and to explain a revolution needs time, and three hours is little enough. To explain a self-maintaining American polity and economy while evading its real problems needs very little time, and three hours of Hubert Humphrey would be unconscionable.

Malcolm's speeches, if not so complex, not so informed or copious as those of an accomplished revolutionary, were not vacuous. The man whose secondary education began painstakingly and privately in the Norfolk Prison Colony was able to analyze for his people their immediate burden, its maintenance in a system of domestic power and its relation to colonialism, more acutely than the white and black Ph.D's with whom he debated. A man about whose life it is difficult not to sentimentalize was seldom sentimental in his oratory, and though he simplified he did not platitudinize.

Malcolm's simplifications, sometimes dangerous, though commonplace in popular oratory and less sophistic than those in establishment rhetoric, derived from the simplicity of his central message: that colored people have been oppressed by white people whenever white people have been able to oppress them, that because immediate justice is not likely ("Give it to us yesterday, and that's not fast enough"), the safest thing for all is to separate, that the liberty to "sit down next to white folks—on the toilet" is not adequate recompense for the past 400 years. Like Robert Owen or John Brown or William Lloyd Garrison, Malcolm spent the good years of his life asserting one idea and its myriad implications and its involved strategies in a society in which the black is often a noncitizen even *de jure*. And because what he said was as intelligible and obvious as a lynching, his rhetorical content was not embarrassed by the tergiversations, the sophisms, the labored evasions, the empty grandiloquence of American political oratory.

The American press attributed the preaching of violence to a man who was no political activist, who moved in the arena of words and ideas, and who usually described a condition of violence rather than urged a justifiably violent response. The *New York Times* obituary editorial, magisterially obtuse, was representative. At worst, Malcolm X, like St. Alphonsus Liguori, taught the ethic of self-defense. *Méchant animal!* The weakness of Malcolm, in fact, and of Elijah Muhammad, is that they were not activists; unlike Martin Luther King, neither had a "movement," for neither went anywhere. Malcolm's success in enlarging the Nation of Islam from 400 to 40,000 and in drawing "well-wishers" by the hundreds of thousands was from the ideas and the words, not from an appeal to action, and not from an appeal to license: the call to moral responsibility and the perpetual Lent of the Muslims repelled most Negroes as it would repel most whites.

But Malcolm's essential content was so simple and elemental, his arguments, like Thoreau's, so unanswerable, that the American press, even when not covertly racist, could not understand him, accustomed as it is to the settled contradictions of civil logic in a biracial country.

What answer is there to the accusations that in a large part of America, a century after the 14th Amendment, some kinds of murderers cannot be punished by law, that the law is the murderer? Is it an answer that we must tolerate injustice so that we may enjoy justice? Condemning such deformed logic, and adhering to obvious moral truths, Malcolm, like the Bogalusa Deacons, had little difficulty in understanding and explaining to his audiences the Thomistic concept of law better than the Attorney General of the United States understands it. Malcolm was always disconcerted when the powers that be and their exponents refused to recognize the legality of humanity. His strongest vocal emphases were on words like law and right: "They don't use *law*," he exclaimed of the United States Government, which directed the Central Congolese Government, and the lawfulness of the Eastern Government was more valid, he thought, because it was of its own people.

Justice and equality and emancipation, not violence, not hatred, not retribution, and not the theology of the Muslims were the central matter of Malcolm's oratory, though that theology was useful as a repudiation of American white Christianity. He had entered the stream of sane and moral social teaching before his parting from Elijah Muhammad, and was deepening his knowledge and expression of it at the moment of the death he expected each day.

If his theses were terrible, it was because they were asserted without compromise or palliation, and because the institutional reality they challenged was terrible. How else to indicate reality and truth if not by direct challenge? Indirection is not workable, for the state has stolen irony; satire is futile, its only resource to repeat the language of the Administration. To say that the American tradition beckons us onward to the work of peace in Vietnam, or that they who reject peace overtures are great servants of peace, is to speak out ironically but authoritatively. The critical efficacy even of absurd literature is threatened by real reductions toward the absurd and beyond, and when usable, absurd statement cannot be at once terse, clear, complex, and unequivocal. The only useful attack is directness, which, opposed to outrage, is outraged and, to apologists of outrage, outrageous.

Malcolm's challenge soon implied anticolonialism, in which was implied anticapitalism. Not a doctrinal Marxist when he died, Malcolm had begun to learn a relation between racism and capitalism during his first African journey, and a relation between socialism and national liberation. Rising above the ethical limitations of many civil rights leaders, he rejected a black symbiosis in the warfare state. The black housewife may collect Green Stamps or dividends, the black paterfamilias may possess an Impala and a hi-fi, the black student an unimpeachable graduate degree and a professorship, but what moral black or white could be happy in the world of color TV and Metrecal and napalm? If a rising Negro class could be contented by such hopes and acquirements, if it yearned for the glittering felicities of the American dream, for the Eden of *Life* and *Ebony*, Malcolm had finer longings, and so his following was small: his vision was more intense, more forbidding than that of King or Wilkins or Farmer. They preached integrated Americanism; Malcolm taught separation for goodness, the co-existence of morally contrary cultures in a geographic unit, in "America."

Because the black had been always alien in America, had been always taught to hate himself in America ("We hated our heads . . . the shape of our nose . . . the color of our skin. . . ."), he now had the freedom to despise, not embrace, a society that had grown alien to humanity, and whose profound alienation had been intimated for the black first in slavery, then in racism. Separation promised not the means to make a black image of Beverly Hills or Westchester, but the liberty to build a new Jerusalem. How might such an evangel be grasped by a social worker or a Baptist minister?

Malcolm's earlier expressions of racism, sometimes augmented or distorted in the misreporting, were a means or an error that receded after his Islamic-African pilgrimage, qualified into renouncement. Their white counterparts have been the political hardware of thousands of local American statesmen and scores of United States Congressmen, and how many have not outgrown them, are legislators because of them? An American President can admit to prior racism with little embarrassment, with becoming repentance.

It is the growth and maturing that matter, and Malcolm's ideological journey, truncated after beginning late, was leftward, enlightened, and opening toward humanitarianism and unsentimental fraternalism, contrary to that of some British lords and some Yale graduates, contrary to that of the young American Marxists of the 1930s, now darkening into polarized anticommunism. There were no saner, more honest and perspicuous analyses of the racial problem than Malcolm's last speeches and statements, beside which the pronouncements of most administrations and civil officials are calculated nonsense. Only from the outside can some truths be told.

In the rhetoric of Malcolm X, as in all genuine rhetoric, figures correspond to the critical imagination restoring the original idea and to the conscience protesting the desecration of the idea. Tropes and schemes of syntax are departures from literal meaning, *abusiones*, "abuses" of a grammar and semantic that have themselves grown into abuses of original reason. As Shelley saw, the abusion, or trope, like revolutionism, destroys conventional definitions to restore original wholeness and reality. Rhetoric, like revolution, is "a way of redefining reality."

The frequent repetitions in Malcolm's rhetoric, like those of Cicero or St. Paul, are communications of the passion that is not satisfied by single statement, but that beats through the pulses. Good rhetorical repetition is viscerally didactic.

But it is an especially dangerous device, its potential of fraudulence proportionate to its elemental power to persuade. It may reinforce truths, it may add stones to build great lies. The anaphoras of Administration rhetoric lead successive clauses each further from reality. Abstractions in repetitions, like the "peace" and "freedom" of the Presidential addresses, are usually doubtful, because ambiguous and inaccessible to testing. War may very well be peace, and slavery freedom, if the predications are repeated often enough.

The substantives and verbs in Malcolm's repetitions were usually concrete, exposing themselves to empirical judgment:

As long as the white man sent you to Korea, you bled. He sent you to Germany, you bled. He sent you to the South Pacific to fight the Japanese, you bled. You bleed for white people, but when it comes to seeing your own church being bombed and little black girls murdered, you haven't got any blood. You bleed when the white man says bleed; you bite when the white man says bite; and you bark when the white man says bark.

Malcolm here began with epistrophe for reinforcement of a repeated reality, combined it with anaphora to shift focus to "the man," moved to epanastrophe in the third and fourth sentences, in which "the man" and the black man share the repeating emphasis, and to epanadiplosis in the fourth for a doubled emphasis on *bleed*, while a tolling alliteration of labials and liquids instructs the outer ear, while asyndeton accelerates a tautness and indignation, and while the fullness of emotion evokes a pathetic-sardonic syllepsis on *blood*.

His rhetorical questions and percunctations with repetition, here anaphora and epistrophe, have the urgency of a Massillon convincing a noble audience of the probability of their damnation:

Why should white people be running all the stores in our community? Why should white people be running the banks of our community? Why should the economy of our community be in the hands of the white man? Why?

The orator may redirect as well as repeat his syntactic units. Malcolm used chiasmus, or crossing of antithetic sets, not deceptively, not to confound realities, but to explore the calculated fantasies of the American press, to untangle the crossing of image and reality:

. . . you end up hating your friends and loving your enemies. . . . The press is so powerful in its image-making role, it can make a criminal look like he's the victim and make the victim look like he's the criminal. . . . If you aren't careful, the newspapers will have you hating the people who are being oppressed and loving the people who are doing the oppressing.

Malcolm was attracted to chiasmus as an economy in dialectic. In the Oxford Union Society debate of December 1964, he explicated and defended Senator Goldwater's chiasmus of *extremism* and *moderation*, converting the memorable assault upon radical reform into an apology for black militancy.

As the strict clausal scheme may be varied to represent emotional thought, strict demonstration may be relieved by paradox and analogy. Paradox, here climactic and with repetitions, writes itself into any narrative of American Negro history since 1863:

How can you thank a man for giving you what's already yours? How then can you thank him for giving you only part of what's already yours?

With an analogy Malcolm dismissed Roy Wilkins' quaver that though the black may be a second-class American, he is yet an American, with his little part of the affluent dream:

I'm not going to sit at your table and watch you eat, with nothing on my plate, and call myself a diner. Sitting at the table doesn't make you a diner, unless you eat some of what's on that plate. Being here in America doesn't make you an American. Being born here in America doesn't make you an American.

We see a black man with half the income of a white, and think of other hungers, and the analogy works as symbol and image, like Bacon's winding stair to a great place or Demosthenes' Athenian boxer defending himself from multiple blows.

Metaphor and metonymy are the symbolic image condensed and made freer from customary logic than the more explicit analogy. Like repetitions and analogies they may be recognizably fraudulent, for symbolic language is not dissociated from truth. We must know or imagine the referent before we can judge and be moved by the symbol. When an American President now says, "The door of peace must be kept wide open for all who wish to avoid the scourge of war, but the door of aggression must be closed and bolted if man himself is to survive," he is disquieting tame, weary metaphors, long since grown insipid and moribund, into a defiance of meaning, and the very antithesis emphasizes the inanity of the ghostwritten rhetoric in a linguistic culture that has not finally adopted Newspeak. If the figures are initially suspect because of the designed, limitless ambiguity and abstractness of the referents, they are contemptible when related to the realities they profess to clarify. Such metaphor is not the discovery of truth but its concealment. "When I can't talk sense," said the eighteenth-century Irish orator, John Curran, "I talk metaphor."

The metaphors of Malcolm X, sometimes ethnically conventional, sometimes original, sometimes inevitable ("I don't see an American dream. I see an American nightmare."), were rarely ambiguous in the abstract member, and were often concrete in both, lending themselves to the touch of common experience. They were infrequent, less frequent than in the elevated tradition of Pitt and Burke and Webster. Malcolm's oratory resembled rather that of the self-educated reformer Cobden in its simple, unornamented vigor, in its reduction to essential questions, in its analytic directness and clarity. In Malcolm's oratory as in Cobden's, metaphor was exceptional in a pattern of exposition by argumentation in abstract and literal diction.

And because Malcolm wished to demonstrate rather than suggest, he preferred the more fully ratiocinative structure, the analogy, to the more condensed and poetic metaphor: he had wished to be not a poet but a lawyer when his elementary school English teacher advised him to turn to carpentry. So also, Malcolm composed in the larger grammatical unit, the paragraph, which corresponds to analogy, rather than in the sentence, which corresponds to metaphor. In answering questions he often prefaced his extended expositions with the request not for one more word or one more sentence, but for "one more paragraph"—and a paragraph indeed was what he usually produced, extemporaneous and complete with counterthesis, thesis, development, synthesis and summary.

The metaphors and metonymies, restricted in number, often suggested truth, like the analogies, by fusing image and symbol, as in poetry: Blake's little black thing amid the snow is sensuously and spiritually black, the snow sensuously and spiritually white. Malcolm used the same deliberate indetermination of perception in the image by which he characterized white immigrants in America:

Everything that came out of Europe, every blue-eyed thing is already an American.

Synechdoche and tmesis combine to refocus on generic essentials for a black audience.

In quick answer to an immoderating Stan Bernard and an uncivil Gordon Hall, and trying to defend the thesis that the Muslims were a force in the Negro movement though numerically insignificant, Malcolm compared them with the Mau Mau, then condensed an implicit analogy to a metaphor and, with characteristically temerarious simplification, expanded and explicated the metaphor into analogy:

The Mau Mau was also a minority, a microscopic minority, but it was the Mau Mau who not only brought independence to Kenya, but ... but it brought it—that wick. The powder keg is always larger than the wick. . . . It's the wick that you touch that sets the powder off.

By a folk metonymy in one pronoun, more convincing than the usual rhetorical patriotic genealogies, Malcolm enlarged to their dimension the time and space of the Negro's misfortune:

many of us probably passed through [Zanzibar] on our way to America 400 years ago.

The identification of Malcolm with his audience, not merely through the plural pronoun, was so thorough that he effected the desired harmony or union in which the speaker can disregard his audience as an object and speak his own passion and reason, when between himself and his hearers there is no spiritual division. The great orator does not play upon his audience as upon a musical instrument; his verbal structures are artful but urged from within.

Malcolm's composition and elocution were remarkable in their assimilative variety. Before the mixed or white audiences, as at college forums, the composition was more abstract and literal, austerely figured, grammatically pure, and the elocution sharper, somewhat rapid and high-pitched, near his speaking voice, enunciated precisely but not mimetic or over-articulated. Before the great black audiences Malcolm adopted a tone and ornament that were his and his audience's but that he relinquished before the white or the academic. The composition of the black speeches was rich in ethnic figuration and humor, in paronomasia, alliteration, and rhyme (the novocained patient, blood running down his jaw, suffers "peacefully"; if you are a true revolutionary "You don't do any singing, you're too busy swinging"; the Negroes who crave acceptance in white America "aren't asking for any nation—they're trying to crawl back on the plantation"). The elocution of this, Malcolm's grand style, was deeper, slower, falling into a tonal weighting and meiosis, wider in its range of pitch, dynamics, emphasis.

Always exhibiting a force of moral reason, never hectic or mainly emotional, Malcolm changed from *homo afer* to *homo europaeus* as the ambience and occasion required. In the mosques he employed the heavy vocal power of impassioned Negro discourse; in academic dialogue and rebuttal his voice sometimes resembled that of Adlai Stevenson in its east-north-central nasality, and in its hurried, thoughtful pauses, its wry humor, its rational rather than emotional emphases.

It is understandable that he was correct, intelligible, lucid, rational, for few public orators in our time have been as free as Malcolm from the need to betray their own intelligence. John Kennedy, who in January pledged a quest for peace and a revulsion from colonialism, in one week of the following April repudiated the Cuban invasion he was then assisting, in another week of the same April pugnaciously justified the intervention, and, having been rebuked by reality, reproached reality with a dialectic from the Mad Tea-Party. His audience was appropriate: American newspaper editors. Later, waving a flag in the Orange Bowl, he would promise the émigré landlords warfare and their restored rents with melodramatic and puerile metonymy. Adlai Stevenson, who twice had talked sense to the American people, denied his government's aggression in Cuba with juridical solemnity, with the noble anaphoras, the poignant metaphors, the sensitive ironies of the campaign speeches, and, fatally drawn to display *expertise*, derisively censured the oratory of Raul Roa. His indignant exposure of revolutionaries was submerged in the laughter of the black galleries of the world; he indulged himself, during the Congo debates, in the pointless metonymies of Independence Day addresses; and his recurrent denunciations of colonialism were freaks of unintended irony.

"Who would not weep, if Atticus were he?" Malcolm, more fortunate than these, was not ordained by history to be the spokesman or the apologist of violence and unthinkable power, and so was not forced to violate reason. In his last years he was in the great tradition of rational and moral speech, consanguineous with Isaiah, with Demosthenes and Cicero, with Paine and Henry, Lincoln and Douglass, as they were allied to the primitive idea of goodness. He was not an emotionalist or a demagogue, but an orator who combined familiarity with passion, with compelling ideas and analytic clarity, and with sober force of utterance, and with a sense, now usually deficient except when depraved, of rhetoric as an art and a genre.

His feeling for the art was probably the benefit of his old-fashioned verbal and literary education in prison. As the rhetoric of Frederick Douglass, then a young slave, originated in his readings of Sheridan's oratory, so Malcolm's alma mater, he said, was "books." The methodical longhand copying of thousands of logical definitions, his nightly labor with the dictionary in prison, left an impress of precision in diction and syntax, later tested and hardened in hostile debate. As he learned the science and the habits of grammar, Malcolm learned the unfamiliar subtleties of the art of rhetoric within a few years. As late as 1961 he prevailed in debate more by conviction than by linguistic accuracy, and the solecisms were embarrassing to his literate admirers and probably to himself, as were the parochial pronunciations, atavistic traces of which could be heard very rarely in the last year ("in*flu*ence"). But this sense of rhetoric derived also from his perception of the ideas that antedate rhetoric and that inform all moral language. His teaching, because elemental and unsophisticated in its morality, was more sane, more philosophic than the wisdom of many an academician who, detached from the facts of human pain, has the institutionalized intelligence to devise a morality to fit his institution, who can make policy his morality: Arthur Schlesinger, Jr., can regard the genocidal war in Vietnam as "an experiment . . . something you have to try."

In his maturity, Malcolm was always aware of the centrally ethical and honest enough not to elude it, and so he soon outgrew what was doctrinally grotesque in the Nation of Islam (what native American religious movement is without such grotesqueness?). But he retained the religious commitment and the wholesome ascesis of the Muslims, and thus was helped in the exhausting work of the last years, the weeks of eighteen-hour days. A mixed seed fell in good soil.

He emerged from dope, prostitution, burglary, prison, and a fanciful sectarianism to enter a perennial humanist art, to achieve a brilliant facility in oratory and debate, in less time than many of us consume in ambling through graduate school. His developing accomplishment in the last year was, as a *New York Times* reporter exclaimed but could not write, "incredible." The Oxford Union Society, venerable, perceptive, and disinterested because un-American, adjudged him among the best of living orators after his debate there months before his death, a pleasant triumph ignored by the American press. Though he may be diluted, or obliterated, or forgotten by the established civil rights movement, which is built into the consensus, Malcolm was for all time an artist and thinker. In the full Aristotelean meaning he was a rhetorician, who, to be such, knew more than rhetoric: ethics, logic, grammar, psychology, law, history, politics; and his best speeches might be texts for students of that comprehensive science and art.

His controlled art, his tone of pride without arrogance, have followers if not a school, in his own Muslim Mosque and among the Nation of Islam, audible in the rational and disdainful replies of Norman 3X in the murder trial. But Malcolm is distinct rhetorically from his admirers among the surly school of Negro speakers, the oratorical equivalent of *Liberator*, who have little to offer their mixed auditory but insolence and commonplaces in broken and frenetic, in monotonous or ill-accented language. And he was remote from the misanthropic and negativist among the alienated. Malcolm, a religionist, could not be "bitter," or descend to scatology in expressing moral outrage. The laughter or chuckling, in his several oratorical styles, was, in motive and in sound, not embittered, or malicious, or frustrated, but apodictic; it was the laughter of assured rectitude, and amusement at the radical unreason of the opposition. For not he but the established structures were the opposition, dissentient to godly reason and justice, which were the authority for his teaching. Hearing Malcolm was an experience not morbid or frightening, but joyous, as Mark Van Doren said of reading *Hamlet*. Though the drama and the man were tragic, in each the confident and varied movement of language and moral ideas told us something superb about our humanity. Malcolm combined magnificence and ethnic familiarity to demonstrate what he asserted: the potential majesty of the black man even in America, a majesty idiosyncratic but related to all human greatness. And so his last ten years tell us that a man can be more fully human serving a belief, even if to serve it requires that he borrow from the society that his service and belief affront. If he and his people illustrate that the grand primal ideas and their grand expression can be spoiled for men by institutions, the whole work and life of Malcolm X declare that the good man, if he has the soul to resist the state and its courts and senates, can restore the ideal world of art and justice.

Wayne Brockriede
Robert L. Scott

CHAPTER 14
Stokely Carmichael:
Two Speeches on Black Power

When during the Meredith march in Mississippi in June, 1966,
Stokely Carmichael thrust himself and the phrase Black Power
into public controversy, students of rhetoric might have asked
themselves two questions. In the inevitable interchange which
would filter through the mass media to the public at large, what
meaning would emerge as dominant for a phrase obviously ambiguous enough to generate many interpretations? What principal
image would people develop of Stokely Carmichael, a man capable
of evoking many attitudes toward himself?

From *Central States Speech Journal*, Vol. XIX, No. 1 (Spring 1968), pp.
3–13. Reprinted by permission of the authors and the Central States Speech
Association.

On July 6, 1966, the Vice-President of the United States spoke to the convention of the NAACP in Los Angeles. In an analysis of that speech we argued that the term Black Power permitted a pacific interpretation and that Hubert Humphrey was in an excellent position to take the lead in defusing the explosive content of the term while expediting its constructive potential.[1] The Vice-President chose, rather, to follow the lead of Roy Wilkins in emphasizing the belligerently divisive thrust of the term by suggesting adroitly that it was simply "black racism."

The month following Humphrey's speech, a member of the federal administration did say that "it is hard to know yet what the term means to the average Negro. . . . But if it means assertive action by the various splinter groups to achieve full political, economic, and social equality, then good will come of it."[2] But Assistant United States Attorney General for civil rights John M. Doar did not hold the position to command widespread national attention, nor was a speech before the convention of the National Bar Association, "a largely negro group," as the *Detroit News* put it, an important occasion compared with the NAACP Convention.

The immediate response saw few probing to locate a basis for making the term constructive; indicative is Martin Luther King's statement on July 9, 1966, that Black Power threatened to split the civil rights movement permanently.[3] The next month, however, Rev. Andrew J. Young, the executive director of King's Southern Leadership Conference, conceded that SNCC's position on Black Power "isn't too far from ours except in style and semantics."[4]

Just as the phrase Black Power permits several interpretations, the man Stokely Carmichael generates several images. Relatively few, however, now see Carmichael as Robert Lewis Shayon did when he wrote, after hearing him interviewed on WBAI-FM, that he discerned "a plausible human being firm in conviction and purpose, but quietly rational."[5]

Within a few months of the advent of Carmichael and Black Power and continuing to this moment, one meaning and one image thoroughly has engulfed the public mind and has dominated the attitudes of most white liberals: Black Power is violent racism in reverse, and Stokely Carmichael is a monster. Late last year, an Associated Press dispatch pictured Carmichael taking his place on "Bertrand Russell's tribunal deliberating alleged U.S. war crimes in Vietnam" and being "welcomed by the first 'witness' on the stand . . . (that day) Pham Ngoc Thach, North Vietnam's health minister."[6] Carmichael's odyssey from August to December, 1967, occasioned anti-American propaganda from Havana to Hanoi and across North Africa. His actions are taken, of course, as verification of the quick negative response to Carmichael and to Black Power. Yet this response seems lamentably to miss an opportunity to respond to a plausible challenge, not a demonic threat, and to reconcile views which were far from irreconcilable. Eric Hoffer's "a bishopric conferred on Luther at the right moment might have cooled his ardor for a Reformation"[7] is far too strong to be applied wistfully to Carmichael. But he and his slogan deserved to be taken seriously.

The purpose of this essay is to examine the rhetoric of Stokely Carmichael and to try to answer two questions: (1) What were the rhetorical strategies? (2) What accounted for the predominantly negative response to the man and his message? We shall focus on two speeches which seem to illustrate well the characteristic strategies. One was made to a predominantly Negro audience in Detroit on July 30, 1966.[8] The other was delivered to a predominantly white audience in Whitewater, Wisconsin, February 6, 1967. Actually, the substance of the latter speech is an essay published in the autumn, 1966, issue of the *Massachusetts Review*.[9] The two speeches, therefore, are in a sense nearly simultaneous efforts to express Carmichael's views on Black Power to markedly different audiences.

Before examining the strategies, we should make explicit our assumption that Stokely Carmichael is decidedly a rhetorician. The two speeches we are analyzing are outstanding examples of audience adaptation. Carmichael's fundamental thought is highly consistent in both speeches—he makes many of the same points and strikes essentially the same posture in making them. The two speeches differ distinctly in style and in persuasive appeals, however; in each instance style and appeals are appropriate to the audience addressed. Carmichael seemed to repeat one or the other of these two speeches on other occasions, varying each "with the audience, the area, the news that day, [and] his mood."[10] Carmichael himself seems to recognize, and worry about, his rhetorical tendencies. He reveals his recognition and anxiety in an interview with Robert Penn Warren, conducted more than a year before Carmichael became well known:

You've got to think about whether or not you're opportunistic. It bothers me a lot. If I see my name in the paper, I'm not sorry it's there. When you write and say you want to interview me, I'm not sorry, I feel sort of good. That's one of the things you have to be worried about. The trouble is that you get an opportunist, and he becomes a rhetorician, he says things that are going to appease people, he's not going to really look for solutions.[11]

A year later few people would accuse him of a rhetoric of appeasement, but his advocacy of Black Power was very much the action of a rhetorician.

I

What were Carmichael's rhetorical decisions?

First, he decided to address himself primarily to a black audience. *Newsweek* reports that Carmichael charged white audiences $1000.00 for "a rather tame exposition of black power" and Negro colleges $500.00 for "the gloves-off treatment."[12] More significantly, when speaking to mixed audiences or through the mass media to the general public, he aims his appeals at black people. Bruce Detweiler explained the rationale for this decision:

In the early days of the movement, when organizations were appealing to whites, SNCC gave the word "Freedom" its magical ring. Now the appeal is to disenfranchise Negroes, and now the cry is "Black Power." For political reasons, and for their own dignity, Negroes must learn to do their own bidding politically and economically.[13]

In following the strategy of aiming primarily at Negroes, Carmichael personified the ideology he was advancing and aimed at identification with his chosen primary audience.

Second, he decided to compress his ideology into the ambiguous slogan Black Power. For Carmichael the slogan seems to carry three major implications: personal pride in being black, responsibility to other blacks, and power as a group to deal with outsiders.

Foremost among the implications of his ideology is his insistence that black people, as a matter of personal pride, must assume the right to define their own identity, their relation to to the total society, and the meaning of such important terms as Black Power. He explained the significance of this right to his predominantly white audience at Whitewater:

> Our concern for Black Power addresses itself directly to this problem, the necessity to reclaim our history and our identity from the cultural terrorism and depredation of self-justifying white guilt.
>
> To do this we shall have to struggle for the right to create our own terms through which to define ourselves and our relationship to the society, and to have these terms recognized. This is the first necessity of a free people, and the first right that any oppressor must suspend.[14]

Carmichael urged that black people must define "what freedom is, what a white liberal is, what black nationalism is, what power is."[15] He insisted that at this point in the struggle only Negroes "can preach to other Negroes in the fight for identity and power."[16] Although responsibility and independence are reflected in these statements, unquestionably one of his major motives is to stress black pride. He underscored this concern in the Detroit speech:

> I'm disturbed by a lot of black people running around saying, "Oh, man, anything all black, it ain't no good." I want to talk to that man. . . . You ain't never heard no white people say anything all white is bad. You ain't never heard them say it.

Carmichael views power as a "black declaration of independence. It is a turn inward, a rallying cry for a people in the sudden labor of self-discovery, self-naming, and self-legitimization."[17]

Black identity and black pride must be mobilized into a group effort to improve the black community. This second implication of Carmichael's ideology is sharply pragmatic. Clearly it has evolved out of his observation of the effects of the black-white coalition to integrate individual Negroes. To the Whitewater audience, he said:

Also the program that evolved out of this coalition was really limited and inadequate in the long term and one which affected only a small select group of Negroes. Its goal was to make the white community accessible to "qualified" Negroes and presumably each year a few more Negroes armed with their passports—a couple of university degrees—would escape into middle-class America and adopt the attitudes and life-styles of that group; and one day the Harlems and the Watts would stand empty, a tribute to the success of integration.[18]

To Carmichael the assumptions behind integration are highly suspect: At best, the Negro abolished himself; more realistically, a few integrate while conditions in the ghettos grow steadily worse. Carmichael is more concerned with institutionalized racism, the systematic oppression of a whole race, than with individualized racism. His goal is to improve the lot of black people *as a group*, rather than to have a few educated black people absorbed into white society each year. He told his Whitewater audience, "You can integrate communities, but you assimilate individuals."[19]

Carmichael's objection to individualized integration, apart from its slow futility, is that it weakens the black community as a whole. Of the integration of schools and housing, he told his black audience in Detroit:

Baby, they ain't doing nothing but absorbing the best that we have. It's time that we bring them back into our community (applause). You need to tell Lyndon Baines Johnson and all them white folk that we don't have to move into white schools to get a better education. We don't have to move into white suburbs to get a better house. All they need to do is stop exploiting and oppressing our communities and we going to take care of our communities.

To realize this brave assertion means keeping the best-educated, most able Negroes working for the community interest. Carmichael concludes:

We have to begin to define success. . . . It's time for us to say to our black brothers that success is going to mean coming back into your community and using your skills to help develop your people.

Carmichael was trying to build a sense of community among black people.

The most difficult ideological question relates to the meaning of "power." The issue is this: Where on the continuum between non-violent political, economic, social, and cultural influence and violent rebellion does Carmichael's Black Power belong? The only certain conclusion is that no one can be certain. The WKNR announcer who introduced Carmichael's Detroit speech on the "Project Detroit" radio broadcast said:

Black power has been damned by most; praised by few, if any. . . . Most have interpreted Carmichael's phrase (as) . . . "the greatest setback for the cause of the Negro and civil rights in this century." Others, and they have been few, argue that all Carmichael means is political and economic power—the Negro population uniting.

But the minority version is plausible. Carmichael has often argued that black votes have too often benefited others and that black politicians are apt to be the puppets of white-dominated major parties. In an interview with Gordon Parks, he stressed Black Power as a political and economic bloc which would serve its own purposes first.

We pick the brother and make sure he fulfills *our* needs. Black Power doesn't mean anti-white, violence, separatism or any other racist thing the press says it means. It's saying, "Look, buddy, we're not laying a vote on you unless you lay so many schools, hospitals, playgrounds and jobs on us."[20]

To his Wisconsin audience Carmichael put his interpretation in the mainstream of American ideals: "Traditionally, for each new ethnic group, the route to social and political integration into America's pluralistic society has been through the organization of their own institutions with which to represent their communal needs within the larger society."[21] Yet in the same speech the overtones of violence also appear, as in this passage referring to the ghettos:

These areas can become either concentration camps with a bitter and volatile population whose only power is the power to destroy, or organized and powerful communities able to make constructive contributions to the total society. Without the power to control their lives and their communities, without effective political institutions through which to relate to the total society, these communities will exist in a constant state of insurrection.[22]

The suggestion of violent resistance is even stronger in the Detroit speech:

I'm no Negro leader, so I don't ever apologize for any black person. And don't you ever apologize for any black person who throws a Molotov cocktail (applause). Don't you ever apologize (continued applause). And don't you ever call those things riots, because they are rebellions, that's what they are (applause). That's what they are (continued applause).[23]

In his speeches before predominantly white audiences, the hints of rebellion and support for violence in self-defense are undeniable in Carmichael's amplification of the meaning of power. Yet even in his speeches before predominantly black audiences, one finds nowhere in his rhetoric an espousal of violence for the sake of violence. The stress throughout is on improving the black community through a call for group pride and support for *"independent* political, social, economic, and cultural institutions that . . . [Black Power] can control and use as instruments of social change."[24]

In addition to his decision to concentrate his rhetoric on the black audience and to present an ideology appropriate primarily for that audience, Stokely Carmichael seems to have made a third rhetorical decision—the choice to project an image and to utilize a style which would reinforce the ideology by a personal identification with his chosen audience.

The quotations already cited from his Detroit speech reflect his attempt to identify stylistically. A contrast of these with the quotations from his Whitewater speech suggests that Carmichael's attempt to adjust his style to his audience is a conscious choice. He shows his awareness of his urge to identify in answering a question after a speech in the fall of 1966 at an interracial camp at Glen Falls, Vermont: "As a person oppressed because of my

blackness, I have common cause with other blacks who are oppressed because of *their* blackness."[25] Bernard Weinraub describes
Carmichael's delivery when speaking to black audiences:

> He shakes his head as he begins speaking and his body appears to
> tremble. His voice, at least in the North, is lilting and Jamaican. His
> hands move effortlessly. His tone—and the audience loves it—is cool
> and very hip. . . . No preacher harangue. No screaming. He speaks
> one tone above a whisper, but a very taut, suppressed whisper.[26]

The desire, obviously, is to be perceived not as a pedestaled
"Negro leader," but as a peer.

The answer to our first major question, then, is that Stokely
Carmichael formed an ideology for a black audience with whom
he identifies stylistically. We turn now to a second question: Why
did the selection of these rhetorical strategies result in such an
overwhelmingly negative reaction from the public at large and
especially from many white liberals who had long supported
strenuously the civil rights movement?

II

The most important response to this question is that the white
audience received a distorted version of the message and the
image. In commenting on Vice-President Humphrey's speech to
the NAACP Convention, we noted the role of the press in reporting to the "second audience," to the general public, emphasizing
that the passage labeling Black Power as "racist" was consistently
reported and that nothing else in the speech was.[27] The role of
the press in transmitting the rhetoric of Stokely Carmichael, with
a vigorous reinforcement from the power structure, was to dis-
ambiguate the Black Power message into violent racism and to
filter a complex and ambivalent Carmichael into a simple and
satanic Stokely.

Carmichael is aware, of course, of the role of the press in his
Black Power campaign. In his Whitewater speech, he argued that
Negroes have suffered continually from press distortion:

> One of the most pointed illustrations of the need for Black Power,
> as a positive and redemptive force in a society degenerating into a

form of totalitarianism, is to be made by examining the history of distortion that the concept has received in national media of publicity. In this "debate," as in everything else that affects our lives, Negroes are dependent on, and at the discretion of, forces and institutions within the white society which have little interest in representing us honestly.[28]

He makes a similar point with bitter humor in the Detroit speech:

Not these guys. Those guys over there. They're called the press. I got up one morning and read a story. The were talking about a cat named Stokely Carmichael. I say he must be a bad nigger (laughter). For he's raising a whole lot of sand! I had to get up and look in the mirror and make sure it was me.

Although most Americans are apt to shrug off such complaints as simply to be expected of those they perceive as radicals, Carmichael's claim that he and Black Power were not represented fairly can be supported. How did the press distort the message and filter the image?

Selective reporting is heavily accountable. Seldom did the mass media report anything designed to develop a constructive interpretation of Black Power. A long story in the *Detroit News*, for example, reported Carmichael's visit and the speech analyzed in this essay, but it contained little more than a count of the audience at the Cobo Auditorium and at various rallies, emphasizing with unmistakable satisfaction that Carmichael was not drawing well in the Negro community.[29] A dozen column inches include no reference to any of the ideas he articulated so challengingly. Furthermore, when Lyndon Johnson, Hubert Humphrey, and Roy Wilkins repudiated Black Power, they got front-page coverage. For the most part, reports of support for the concept were buried in the back pages.

Perhaps even more damaging was the way the broadcasting media sharpened a single, simple, unambiguous caricature of Carmichael. T. George Harris describes the treatment:

White ears discriminate. The public hears Negroes best when they sound wild . . . or beg for welfare. . . . [When Stokely Carmichael] tries to define his Black Power motto in terms of economic and political development, he finds himself shouting into deaf ears. But when, pacing like a panther, he twists himself into a trance, snarling terror, he makes the evening TV news for millions of very alert people, both races. . . . Carmichael mutters at the invincible stupidity of reporters —but cannot resist performing in their spotlight.[30]

Robert Lewis Shayon lamented the "monster treatment" by two major TV newscasts which gave Carmichael the "air of militancy. . . . That's all there was to the portrait—short, sharp, demagogic." After commenting on a more sympathetic treatment on WBAI-FM, Shayon drew this incisive conclusion:

Now you may argue that the civil rights leader, speaking in a white man's studio, was making white man's talk in sweet reasonableness, but that the television cameras saw more truly when he was pep-talking people down South. You may be right. It is also possible that the real Stokely Carmichael embraces both images (which of us talks singly in all roles?). The fact remains that people fortunate enough to [hear the] . . . broadcast have a great deal more evidence before them to account for this man and his meaning to the present struggle for human rights than is available to the viewers who saw only the monster-half of the story on television.[31]

Given the message and the image most people received, could they not be expected to reject them? The interesting question for students of rhetoric is the speculation about what might have been. Had the mass media presented more shades of meaning in Black Power and a fuller portrait of Carmichael, how then would white liberals have responded?

Carmichael's strategies relating to his choice of audiences, of ideology, and of modes of identification might have caused most white liberals to reject Black Power even had they received a more complete version. They might have been antagonized by the stress he put on talking to black listeners. Although he often made his choice on the rational basis of redressing a past imbalance ("Black leaders have been running across town so long worrying about what white people are saying that they don't know what it means to stay at home and worry about what black people are saying"[32]), often he seemed simply, irrationally to deny interest in communicating to white audiences ("We don't have to explain anything to anybody. . . . Your job is to understand us"[33]). Furthermore, when Carmichael did speak to white audiences, he sometimes wearied in the struggle to communicate to them. When a white girl in the Wisconsin audience asked him to define Black Power after he had dealt with the term explicitly in his speech, he shrugged her off and missed an opportunity to underscore his claim that whites must pay serious attention. At other times he seems to close the possibility of dialogue with white men altogether. For example, he told his Detroit audience, "When I talk about Black Power, it is presumptuous for any white man to talk about it, because I'm talking to black people." He recognized what he was doing and also a possible consequence of the strategy: "Whites get nervous when we don't keep talking about brotherly love. They need reassurance. But we're not about to divert our energies to give it to them."[34]

However, in spite of Carmichael's disclaimers, he did try to communicate with white audiences as well as black. As early as the Meredith march in June, 1966, at the beginning of the public controversy over Black Power, Bruce Detweiler reports that he was particularly impressed with Carmichael's "eagerness to communicate his ideas to the whites who would listen to him."[35] After a militant speech, according to Gene Roberts, "White liberals or newsmen will draw Carmichael aside and ask if 'black power' is really an antiwhite philosophy, and often Mr. Carmichael will say, 'Of course not' . . . Carmichael is so sincere and convincing during these private explanations that many of his questioners come away believing that they completely missed the point of his public utterances."[36]

Clearly, Carmichael seems to have put different constructions on Black Power for different groups of listeners. But the potentiality for strengthening the pacific interpretation was present for some white listeners to capitalize on. Carmichael was intent on this interpretation when speaking before audiences like that at Whitewater, and in writing for publications like the *Massachusetts Review* and the *New York Review of Books*. He wrote a letter to the *New York Times Magazine* in which he disputed statements in Gene Roberts' article (cited above) concerning SNCC's promotion of Ivanhoe Donaldson and his own arrest in Atlanta.[37] Carmichael wanted to talk to both black and white people. He wanted to challenge white audiences to a new relationship with blacks. On the balance, he was more concerned with the latter than with the former; he may have been at fault in often suggesting a violent specter. Regardless, had the press contributed to the potential dialogue by presenting a fuller view of Carmichael and Black Power, white liberals might have been less threatened and more able to respond constructively to what they were too prone to take as a wholly hostile ideology from a satanic spokesman.

How might they have responded to the three ideological implications of Black Power had they perceived them as challenges rather than threats? White liberals might have recognized, first of all, the need for black people to assume pridefully the leadership in defining the term and goals of the struggle for black justice and equality. They might have recognized that their own leadership and that of such moderates as Martin Luther King and Roy Wilkins no longer appeared meaningful and effective to many Negroes in the ghettos to whom the gains of civil rights legislation had not gone. A new leadership had emerged, and the old coalition had disintegrated. The civil rights movement, which, in the words of David Danzig, "originated with whites and at its height became a nationwide coalition of whites and blacks, now faces the prospect of becoming an all-black movement."[38] Danzig argues that such a change was inevitable:

The dilemma is real and cannot be escaped by blaming the Negro militants for alienating white supporters by their anti-white rhetoric: even if every Negro in America daily professed his great love for the whites, the coalition would still be breaking up for having fulfilled so much of the civil-rights program which brought it together, and for having no program on which it can agree to deal with the economic plight of the Negro masses.[39]

In part because white liberals did not hear Carmichael's full message and in part because they seemed not to listen carefully to what they did hear, they inferred that Carmichael was saying that black people had no further need for them in any way. A more accurate inference is that black people wanted to control the definition and direction of their own independent movement, but that Black Power does not necessarily imply that whites may not cooperate with that movement in the formation of a new coalition. Perhaps Carmichael might have increased the likelihood of a coalition of equals had he stressed more the constructive challenge implicit in the message. Instead, perhaps because another emphasis was attractive to his primary audience, Carmichael hammered at the failure of the old coalition and his dogged determination to reject it. "We got to examine our white liberal friends," he told his Detroit audience. No doubt many of those who so counted themselves were deeply wounded by the accusations that they were serving their own interests and using Negroes to their own ends. Carmichael was fond of citing the failure of the 1964 Democratic Convention to seat the Mississippi Freedom delegates and of the House of Representatives to "unseat the Mississippi Delegation to the House which has been elected through a process which methodically and systematically excluded over 450,000 voting-age Negroes."[40] White freedom marchers, again, might be inclined to mark both the ingratitude and inaccuracy of Carmichael's charge that they could afford to march because colored maids were taking care of things back home.[41]

No one can doubt that Carmichael failed to solve the dilemma of facing two audiences. Totally ignoring white listeners would have been a serious error (given the nature of the root problem) and in the end impossible (given the mass media). Perhaps had Carmichael been less extreme in speaking to Negroes he would have been less inclined to alienate non-blacks, but he would have paid dearly in his effort to develop pride in a black movement. Nonetheless, had a more complete picture of the ambiguous, ambivalent Carmichael enabled more listeners to perceive the rhetorical dilemmas he faced and the priority of his intentions, the overall liberal response might have been more constructive.

What about the response to the second ideological implication of Black Power—the need to improve the conditions of the entire group? Again, perhaps Carmichael's emphasis unfortunately may have reinforced the simplified message common to the mass media's treatment—unalterable opposition to integration. He did often attack the consequences of integration; he told his Detroit audience, "I'm going to talk tonight about integration. About what it means. About who it's for. About who it benefits. And what it does to black people. I want to talk about integration tonight (shouts and applause)." Even as sympathetic an observer as Bayard Rustin concluded that Black Power is a "slogan directed primarily against liberals by those who once counted liberals among their closest friends."[42] Those who had long regarded "integration" as a god-word predictably resented the attack on their concept.

Yet if liberals had listened carefully to Carmichael's position on integration, they might have realized that his opposition was to *individualized* integration which, he argued convincingly, was not an effective antidote to *institutionalized* racism. They might have accepted Carmichael's shift from a goal of integrating "qualified" individuals to the goal of integrating the black community as a whole into a society. This ambitious goal may well have entailed changes in society that many liberals would approve on quite different grounds. Again, of course, the mass media did not channel the subtleties of Carmichael's distinctions, and by the time white liberals had access to the full message they may have conceived so rigidly Carmichael's position as being anti-integration and anti-white that they could not hear the position as pro-integration of the black *community*.

Finally, had the press channeled Carmichael's full ideology, white liberals might have been challenged to search for new ways of achieving power rather than being threatened to fear riots. They might have seen as compatible with their own values such statements as occurred in the Whitewater speech:

We must organize black community power to end these abuses, and to give the Negro community a chance to have its needs expressed. A leadership which is truly "responsible"—not to the white press and power structure, but to the community—must be developed. Such leadership will recognize that its power lies in the unified and collective strength of that community. This will make it difficult for the white leadership group to conduct its dialogue with individuals in terms of patronage and prestige, and will force them to talk to the community's representatives in terms of real power.[43]

They might have heard Carmichael claim, as he did several times during the question period at Whitewater, that Negroes are acting in self-defense. They might, at least, have recognized the ambiguity of "power" and sought to develop relatively peaceful meanings for the term rather than to assume, with the press and Establishment spokesmen, that power means violence. They might have recognized, with Bayard Rustin, the tragedy that would follow if "white liberals allowed verbal hostility on the part of Negroes to drive them out of the movement or to curtail their support for civil rights. The issue was injustice before 'black power' became popular, and the issue is still injustice."[44]

Carmichael's ability to identify stylistically with his audience was both an asset and a liability. When speaking to black or mixed audiences, he identified with Negroes. His rhetorical decisions left him no other choice. But the tendency of the mass media to present predominantly this image to the general public undercut the potential effect of his ability to speak the language of the white audience. He did not, of course, take the position of subservient supplicant—his message and his character precluded that choice; but his style did reflect a man genuinely interested in interacting with white audiences and being not only recognized as an equal but also as a representative of a distinct community. Had more liberal leaders been fully exposed to the sort of speaking Carmichael did at Whitewater, a constructive interpersonal dialogue would have been much more likely.

In this essay we have examined Stokely Carmichael's strategies in choosing an audience, an ideology, and a mode of identification. The general public reacted negatively to his rhetoric; most tragic is that most liberals apparently failed to react differently. At this writing, Carmichael seems to be removed effectively, both physically and figuratively, from any position to be an active voice for change *within* our society. Black Power is virtually a synonym for threatened violence; it has the slenderest possibility of being transformed to a constructive rallying cry.

Since Carmichael's image and his slogan will continue to haunt our hopes and fears in the days ahead, we ought to ask how we can account for the initial failures. The reasons seem to be three-fold.

First, the mass media conveyed only part of the man and his message to the mass audience. Students of contemporary rhetoric must re-examine the role of media specialists. The presumption that a journalist functions only to channel passively a rhetorician's message to a mass audience seems altogether unwarranted. Rather, a journalist is himself an active agent who makes rhetorical decisions of his own which may or may not be compatible with those of the rhetorician he reports. Press Power seems to have defeated Black Power in a battle of unequals.

Second, Carmichael himself might have increased his chances of persuading white liberals by making clearer to them how they could become involved in a new coalition dedicated to new goals which were compatible with their own values and motives. Perhaps he reasoned, however, that to go very far in communicating this message might have jeopardized his primary message to his primary audience. Perhaps to carry both rhetorical burdens demanded more ability than Carmichael has. To do both adequately would be truly remarkable.

Third, white liberals must bear a substantial share of responsibility for reacting so quickly and so thoughtlessly to the distorted image and partial message and for having failed to have caught the total thrust of the rhetoric of Stokely Carmichael and Black Power.

NOTES

1 Robert L. Scott and Wayne Brockriede, "Hubert Humphrey Faces the Black Power Issue," *Speaker and Gavel*, 4, 1 (November 1966), pp. 11–17.
2 *Detroit News*, August 4, 1966, p. 8D.

3 *The New York Times*, July 9, 1966, p. 1.

4 Quoted in Paul Good, "A White Look at Black Power," *The Nation*, August 8, 1966, p. 115; see also Frank Millspaugh, "Black Power," *Commonweal*, August 5, 1966, pp. 500–503.

5 Robert Lewis Shayon, "The Real Stokely Carmichael," *Saturday Review*, July 9, 1966, p. 42; see also Robert Penn Warren, "Two for SNCC," *Commentary*, April, 1965, pp. 38–48, and T. George Harris, "Negroes Have Found a Jolting New Answer," *Look*, June 27, 1967, pp. 30–31.

6 *Minneapolis Star*, November 29, 1967, p. 17A.

7 *The True Believer* (New York, Harper & Row, 1951), p. 132.

8 The speech was delivered in Cobo Auditorium (*Detroit News*, July 31, 1966, p. 8A). A tape recording was broadcast by radio station WKNR on August 7, 1966. The speech was edited somewhat to fit the time allotted the half-hour program "Project Detroit." Quotations from the speech come from our transcription of the broadcast.

9 After a brief extemporaneous introduction, Carmichael announced to his Whitewater audience that he would read either an article he had written for the *New York Review of Books* (see Sept. 22, 1966, pp. 5–8) or an article from the "Massachusetts Quarterly." He chose the latter saying that it was "tighter" and read with some extemporaneous comments, an article from the *Massachusetts Review* (Stokely Carmichael, "Toward Black Liberation," 7, 4 (Autumn 1966), pp. 639–651). Quotations will be from the article except for extemporaneous remarks which are transcribed from a complete tape recording of the speech and question period.

10 Bernard Weinraub, "The Brilliancy of Black," *Esquire*, January 1967, p. 132.

11 Warren, *op. cit.*, pp. 47–48.

12 "Which Way for the Negro?" *Newsweek*, May 15, 1967, p. 28.

13 Bruce Detweiler, "A Time to Be Black," *New Republic*, Sept. 17, 1966, p. 22.

14 Carmichael, *op. cit.*, pp. 639–640.

15 Quoted in Lerone Bennett, Jr., "Stokely Carmichael: Architect of Black Power," *Ebony*, September 1966, p. 28.

16 Quoted in "Marching Where?" *Reporter*, July 14, 1966, p. 16.

17 Quoted in Bennett, *loc. cit.*

18 Carmichael, *op. cit.*, p. 647.

19 *Ibid.*

20 *Life*, May 19, 1967, p. 82.

21 Carmichael, *op. cit.*, p. 642. For a further discussion of this interpretation, see Millspaugh, *op. cit.*, p. 500.

22 Carmichael, *op. cit.*, p. 651.

23 In the extemporaneous asides and, especially, in the question period of the Whitewater speech, Carmichael's tone is closer to that in the Detroit

speech than it is in the article he is reading; but even so, the threatening temper never reaches the pitch of the Detroit speech.

24 Quoted in Bennett, *loc. cit.*

25 Quoted in Weinraub, *op. cit.*, p. 134.

26 *Ibid.*, p. 132.

27 Scott and Brockriede, *op. cit.*, p. 14.

28 Carmichael, *op. cit.*, p. 639; see also Carmichael's statement quoted in Millspaugh, *op. cit.*, p. 500, and in Good, *op. cit.*, p. 114.

29 *Detroit News*, July 31, 1966, p. 8A.

30 Harris, *loc. cit.*

31 Shayon, *loc. cit.*

32 Quoted in Bennett, *loc. cit.*

33 Quoted in Gene Roberts, "The Story of Snick: From 'Freedom High' to 'Black Power,'" *The New York Times Magazine*, September 25, 1966, p. 120.

34 Quoted in Good, *op. cit.*, p. 114; for similar statements by Carmichael concerning the importance of concentrating primarily on black audiences, see Weinraub, *op. cit.*, p. 134. Detweiler, *loc. cit.*; and *Life*, May 19, 1967, p. 82.

35 Detweiler, *op. cit.*, p. 20.

36 Roberts, *op. cit.*, p. 128.

37 *The New York Times Magazine*, October 16, 1966, pp. 98–100.

38 "In Defense of Black Power," *Commentary*, September 1966, p. 43.

39 *Ibid.*, p. 46.

40 Carmichael, *op. cit.*, p. 640.

41 Detroit Speech.

42 Bayard Rustin, "'Black Power' and Coalition Politics," *Commentary*, September 1966, p. 40.

43 Carmichael, *op. cit.*, p. 650.

44 Rustin, *op. cit.*, p. 39.

Haig A. Bosmajian

CHAPTER 15
The Letter
from Birmingham Jail

The public letter, in the tradition of Emile Zola's 1898 letter to the President of the French Republic denouncing the Dreyfus decision and Thomas Mann's 1937 public letter to the Dean of the Philosophical Faculty of the University of Bonn, has long been a means of persuasion used by reformers and politicians, writers, and prisoners. We can now place among the lists of great public letters Martin Luther King's "Letter from the Birmingham Jail,"

From "Rhetoric of Martin Luther King's Letter From Birmingham Jail" in *The Midwest Quarterly*, 1967, pp. 127–143. Reprinted by permission of the publisher.

dated April 16, 1963. On Good Friday of that year, the Reverend Dr. King, participating in a civil rights march in Birmingham, Alabama, was arrested, held incommunicado for twenty-four hours in solitary confinement, and not allowed to see his lawyers during that time. After eight days of imprisonment, Dr. King accepted bond and was released. While he was imprisoned, there appeared in the newspapers a plea signed by eight Alabama priests, rabbis, and ministers urging the Negro community in Birmingham to withdraw support from the civil rights demonstrations being conducted there. These eight clergymen said they were "convinced that these demonstrations are unwise and untimely." Dr. King's now famous "Letter from the Birmingham Jail" was his answer to them.

The letter, as King had observed, was written "under somewhat constricting circumstances. Begun on the margins of the newspaper in which the statement [of the eight clergymen] appeared while I was in jail, the letter continued on scraps of writing paper supplied by a friendly Negro trusty, and concluded on a pad my attorneys were eventually permitted to leave me." It was not long before the letter was reprinted in several national periodicals and distributed across the nation in single reprints.

"Letter from the Birmingham Jail" was obviously not directed only to the eight clergymen critical of King's civil disobedience in Birmingham and laudatory of the Birmingham police force for keeping "order" and "preventing violence." The letter was not directed only to the Negroes of the community who were being asked by the clergymen to withdraw support from the civil rights demonstrations. "Letter from the Birmingham Jail" was addressed primarily to the moderate clergymen and laymen, black and white, in both the North and the South; King's appeals, however, turned out to be relevant to all Americans. Just as King was speaking to clergymen and laymen alike, so too did he himself speak as a Christian and as an American.

Essentially the letter is a confirmation by King of his own case; the letter, however, must also be, and is, a refutation. It is refutative in the sense that King attempts to deal with the accusations and arguments presented by the eight clergymen. Apparently King felt that their attacks might have significant consequences, for he does not delay at all in his refutation. The eight clergymen had stated in their letter that the people of Birmingham were "now confronted by a series of demonstrations by some of our Negro citizens, directed and led in part by outsiders." From the outset of his public letter, King turns his attention to this worn-out "outsider" charge. That he found it necessary to justify his involvement in the civil rights activities in Birmingham is in itself a commentary on his audience, the eight clergymen, the "moderates," the Church in particular, Americans in general. He was, of course, dealing with an area of the nation where the "outsider" was especially suspect; he was in Birmingham, Alabama, where the "outsider" meant the Northerner, the carpetbagger, the "foreign" element.

King asserts that he is not an "outsider" on three counts: First, because of his organizational ties; second, because of his Christianity; third, because he is an American. At the outset, King makes the point that the Southern Christian Leadership Conference is an organization operating in every Southern state with headquarters in Atlanta, Georgia; further, the organization has eighty-five affiliates all across the South. He reminds his readers that he has come to Birmingham by invitation and that he has come to fulfill a promise. As a Christian he comes to Birmingham to speak and demonstrate because "injustice is here." He compares his situation with that of the early Christian prophets and thus not only argues by analogy, but also enhances his *ethos:* "Just as the eighth-century prophets left their little villages and carried their 'thus saith the Lord' far beyond the boundaries of their home town, and just as the Apostle Paul left his little village of Tarsus and carried the gospel of Jesus Christ to practically every hamlet and city of the Graeco-Roman world, I too am compelled to carry the gospel of freedom beyond my particular town. Like Paul, I must constantly respond to the Macedonian call for aid." Then King asserts that since he is an American he cannot be an outsider:

I cannot sit idly by in Atlanta and not be concerned about what happens in Birmingham. Injustice anywhere is a threat to justice everywhere. We are caught in an inescapable network of mutuality tied in a single garment of destiny. Whatever affects one directly affects all indirectly. Never again can we afford to live with the narrow, provincial, "outside agitator" idea. Anyone who lives inside the United States can never be considered an outsider anywhere in this country.

King's refutation takes into account the criticism by the eight clergymen of the civil rights demonstrations and of King's participation in them. "I would not hesitate to say that it is unfortunate that so-called demonstrations are taking place in Birmingham at this time," writes King, "but I would say in more emphatic terms that it is even more unfortunate that the white power structure of this city left the Negro community with no other alternative." Using a form of refutation known as the Method of Residues, King points out that of the various possible avenues of action which could be used to help solve the problem, the Negro community was deprived of them all, *except* demonstrations. The Negro was left with no alternative except to demonstrate, said King, because (1) the political leaders of the city "consistently refused to engage in good faith negotiations"; (2) leaders of the economic community in Birmingham had made promises, such as removing the humiliating racial signs from the stores, and these promises were never kept; (3) Birmingham was a community which "has constantly refused to negotiate." At the same time he was doing this, King portrayed the dismal Birmingham situation: "Birmingham is probably the most thoroughly segregated city in the United States. Its ugly record of police brutality is known in every section of this country. Its unjust treatment of Negroes in the courts is a notorious reality. There have been more unsolved bombings of Negro homes and churches in Birmingham than any other city in this nation. There are the hard, brutal, and unbelievable facts." The authenticity of these "facts" was not to be challenged by King's audience, for the police brutality, the mockery of justice, and the bombings had been exhibited by various news media for all America to see.

Since the clergymen had claimed in their letter that the Birmingham demonstrations were "unwise and untimely," King turned to explaining the necessity for nonviolent direct action. "You may well ask," he writes, "Why direct action? Why sit-ins, marches, etc.? Isn't negotiation a better path?" He considers similar questions later in the letter and he thus demonstrates his awareness of what is in the minds of many Americans. Some have asked, he writes, "Why didn't you give the new [city] administration time to act?" By airing such questions, King ackowledges his familiarity with the questions that might be asked by his critics. And by considering these questions, King demonstrates a certain amount of honesty and fairness. He asserts again and again his advocacy of negotiation; but the avenues of negotiation have been closed to the civil rights leaders, he says. Hence the turn to nonviolent direct action. He tells the eight clergymen: "You are exactly right in your call for negotiation." As King explains it, "Nonviolent direct action seeks to create such a crisis and establish such creative tension that a community that has constantly refused to negotiate is forced to confront the issue. It seeks so to dramatize the issue that it can no longer be ignored."

To justify nonviolent direct action King turns to a persuasion which combines the various means available to the advocate. All through the letter, of course, he identifies the actions and principles of the civil rights movement with various men of renown, philosophers, theologians, and other historical figures; on the other hand, he identifies his adversaries' cause and principles with all that is evil. The creative tension which he hopes to stimulate through nonviolent direct action he compares to Socrates' attempts: "Just as Socrates felt that it was necessary to create tension in the mind so that individuals could rise from the bondage of myths and half-truths to the unfettered realm of creative analysis and objective appraisal, we must see the need of having nonviolent gadflies to create the kind of tension in society that will help men rise from the dark depths of prejudice and racism to the majestic heights of understanding and brotherhood." Two paragraphs later, King turns to Reinhold Niebuhr to support the contention that the segregationists and Southern privileged groups are not about to voluntarily give up their privileges. King writes: "Individuals may see the moral light and voluntarily give up their unjust posture; but as Reinhold Niebuhr has reminded us, groups are more immoral than individuals." A few paragraphs later, in a discussion of the differences between just and unjust laws, King turns to St. Thomas Aquinas, Martin Buber, and Paul Tillich to support his position. For those who might not be impressed with the arguments of these Catholic, Jewish, and Protestant theologians, King turns again to the name of Socrates: "To a degree academic freedom is a reality today because Socrates practiced civil disobedience." A clergyman attempting to persuade other clergymen could hardly amass a more formidable and respectable group of philosophers and theologians.

All through his letter King has developed his ethos by demonstrating his intelligence, good will, and high purpose. His character is enhanced by his identification with men like Socrates, St. Paul, Niebuhr, Buber, and Tillich. His very familiarity with these great men reflects his intelligence. A feeling of good will pervades the entire letter. It is at times very emotional, yet never does King turn to the use of such emotions as hate, anger, envy, and fear, except in one or two instances. His good will is reflected in the continued call for negotiation and in the reflective, non-belligerent tone of his entire argument.

Dr. King handles the emotional aspects of the letter just as competently as he does his ethical proof. As he advocates non-violent direct action and criticizes those people who ask the Negro "to wait," as he reproves those people who denounce the Birmingham demonstrations as "untimely," King reminds them that he has never "yet engaged in a direct action movement that was 'well timed,' according to the timetable of those who have not suffered unduly from the disease of segregation." One of the most emotional passages in the letter comes at that point when King explains why the Negro can no longer "wait." In this passage he piles one upon another the injustices, insults, and indignities suffered by the Negroes:

I guess it is easy for those who have never felt the stinging darts of segregation to say wait. But when you have seen vicious mobs lynch your mothers and fathers at will and drown your sisters and brothers at whim; when you have seen hate-filled policemen curse, kick, brutalize, and even kill your black brothers and sisters with impunity; when you see that vast majority of your twenty million Negro brothers smothering in an air-tight cage of poverty in the midst of an affluent society; when you suddenly find your tongue twisted and your speech stammering as you seek to explain to your six-year-old daughter why she can't go to the public amusement park that has just been advertised on television, and see tears welling up in her little eyes when she is told that Funtown is closed to colored children, and see the depressing clouds of inferiority begin to form in her little mental sky, and see her begin to distort her little personality by unconsciously developing a bitterness toward white people; when you have to concoct an answer for a five-year-old son asking in agonizing pathos: "Daddy, why do white people treat colored people so mean?" when you take a cross country drive and find it necessary to sleep night after night in the uncomfortable corners of your automobile because no motel will accept you; when you are humiliated day in and day out by nagging signs reading "white" men and "colored"; when your first name becomes "nigger" and your middle name becomes "boy" (however old you are) and your last name becomes "John," and when your wife and mother are never given the respected title "Mrs."; when you are harried by day and haunted by night by the fact that you are a Negro, living constantly at tip-toe stance never quite knowing what to expect next, and plagued with inner fears and outer resentments; when you are forever fighting a degenerating sense of "nobodiness"—then you will understand why we find it difficult to wait.

King follows this emotional passage with a sentence which carries the emotional impact even further: "There comes a time when the cup of endurance runs over, and men are no longer willing to be plunged into an abyss of injustice where they experience the bleakness of corroding despair." After these highly moving passages, King turns to his critics and says with a smack of irony: "I hope, sirs, you can understand our legitimate and unavoidable impatience."

King handles the emotional passages very well; where other writers might have become saccharine, he maintains balance and dignity. He never permits the highly emotional portions of the letter to run on too long; the moving, specific pictures he creates for the reader are preceded or followed by serious, philosophical thought. On the one hand, we see "tears welling up" in the eyes of the six-year-old girl because she cannot go to the for-whites-only Funland and we can hear the five-year-old son asking "in agonizing pathos: "Daddy, why do white people treat colored people so mean?"" The innocence of children and the hurt they feel are universal experiences, in the worlds of both black and white. Parents, black and white, know the difficulty of answering such questions posed by the child. On the other hand, King does not dwell long on what might become overly sentimental; he quickly takes the reader back to the philosophical, back to concepts of good and bad laws, back to Socrates, Jesus, Aquinas, Jefferson, Buber, Tillich, and Niebuhr.

King ties the civil rights movement and demonstrations to the American dream, and more than once do the actions of Negroes demonstrating for their rights appear next to the political and social concepts and dreams of the American people. In well chosen language, King pictures the individualism and dignity of the civil rights heroes: "One day the South will recognize its real heroes. They will be the James Merediths, courageously and with a majestic sense of purpose, facing jeering and hostile mobs and the agonizing loneliness that characterizes the life of the pioneer. They will be old, oppressed, battered Negro women, symbolized in a seventy-two-year-old woman of Montgomery, Alabama, who rose up with a sense of dignity and with her people decided not to ride the segregated buses, and responded to one who inquired about her tiredness with ungrammatical profundity: 'My feets is tired, but my soul is rested.'" Here is the pioneering American, the one-time oppressed American struggling for freedom and dignity. As in the rest of the letter, the American is linked to the religious values of the Judeo-Christian heritage: "One day the South will know that when these disinherited children of God sat down at lunch counters they were in reality standing up for the best in the American dream and the most sacred values in our Judeo-Christian heritage, and thus carrying our whole nation back to great wells of democracy which were dug deep by the founding fathers in the formulation of the Constitution and the Declaration of Independence." King makes it clear, again and again, that what happens to the Negro in America is tied directly to the destiny of America: "We will reach the goal of freedom in Birmingham and all over the nation, because the goal of America is freedom. Abused and scorned though we may be, our destiny is tied up with the destiny of America."

In his reasoned, nonbelligerent manner, King goes about the business of answering a question implied in the letter of the eight clergymen, and a question also in the minds of many Americans: "How can you advocate breaking some laws and obeying others?" Recognizing what may appear to some people a contradiction, he devotes a significant portion of his letter to coping with this problem; his willingness to discuss the matter fairly is exemplified in his remarks at the beginning of the section on obeying just laws and disobeying unjust ones: "You express a great deal of anxiety over our willingness to break laws. This is certainly a legitimate concern. Since we do diligently urge people to obey the Supreme Court's decision of 1954 outlawing segregation in the public schools, it is rather strange and paradoxical to find us consciously breaking laws." Here King again draws upon the names of Augustine, Thomas Aquinas, Martin Buber, and Paul Tillich. It is King's contention that one "has not only a legal but a moral responsibility to obey just laws. Conversely, one has a moral responsibility to disobey unjust ones." Like Augustine, King contends that "an unjust law is no law at all." In distinguishing between the just law and the unjust law, King turns to Aquinas for support. "To put it in the terms of Saint Thomas Aquinas, an unjust law is a human law that is not rooted in eternal and natural law. Any law that uplifts human personality is just. Any law that degrades human personality is unjust." King's deductive argument is clearly developed; if one accepts the premises, then one must necessarily accept his conclusion. He argues logically: All laws which degrade human personality are unjust. Segregation distorts the soul and damages the personality (in effect, degrades human personality). Therefore, all segregation statutes are unjust.

Turning from Catholic to Jewish support, King puts the second premise of his deductive argument: "Segregation, to use the terminology of the Jewish philosopher Martin Buber, substitutes an 'I-it' relationship for an 'I-thou' relationship and ends up relegating persons to the status of things. Hence segregation is not only politically, economically, and sociologically unsound, it is sinful." The second premise: Segregation relegates the person to the status of things. Conclusion is sinful. Again, King has constructed a logically developed argument.

Using a Protestant theologian as his source for a first premise in the development of another argument, King writes: "Paul Tillich has said that sin is separation." The second premise: Segregation is "an existential expression of man's tragic separation." Therefore, segregation is sin. The validity of King's reasoning here is dependent on the interpretation of the first premise. If "Sin is separation" is to be taken in the "Men are mortal" sense, then the argument is invalid. If, however, "Sin is separation" is to be taken to mean that "Separation is sin," then King's argument is a valid one.

After presenting these arguments and after dealing with the abstract, King turns to the specific. He distinguishes between the evasion of the law by the civil rights demonstrators and the evasion of the law by the segregationists. The latter evasion he sees as leading to anarchy. But, he argues, "one who breaks an unjust law must do so openly, lovingly, and with a willingness to accept the penalty. I submit that an individual who breaks a law that conscience tells him is unjust and who willingly accepts the penalty of imprisonment in order to arouse the conscience of the community over its injustice is in reality expressing the highest respect for law." Then King demonstrates further *ethos* for his cause by declaring that there "is nothing new about this kind of civil disobedience," which was practiced, he writes, by Shadrach, Meshac, and Abednego in their refusal to obey the laws of Nebuchadnezzar and by the early Christians who "were willing to face hungry lions rather than submit to certain unjust laws of the Roman empire." By piling one example upon another, King demonstrates that the history of civil disobedience goes back many years and that it has been practiced by respected and revered individuals.

King devotes a large part of the letter to his disappointment with the "white moderates" and the Church. Essentially, he is disappointed in both for the same reason. In his consideration of the white moderate who is more devoted to "order" than to justice, King writes: "We will have to repent in this generation not merely for the vitriolic words and actions of the bad people, but for the appalling silence of the good people." Similarly, he says of the Church: "The contemporary Church is so often a weak, ineffectual voice with an uncertain sound. It is so often the arch-supporter of the *status quo*. Far from being disturbed by the presence of the Church, the power structure of the average community is consoled by the Church's silent and often vocal sanction of things as they are."

In answer to those moderate whites who charge that the civil rights demonstrations, "even though peaceful, must be condemned because they precipitate violence," King again turns to Jesus and Socrates for support. He answers the charge with a series of rhetorical questions which force his audience to indict themselves through their answers: "But can this assertion [that even though peaceful, the demonstrations must be condemned because they lead to violence] be logically made? Isn't this like condemning the robbed man because his possession of money precipitated the evil act of robbery? Isn't this like condemning Socrates because his unswerving commitment to truth and his philosophical delvings precipitated the misguided popular mind to make him drink the hemlock? Isn't this like condemning Jesus because His unique God-consciousness and never-ceasing devotion to His will precipitated the evil act of crucifixion?" King's disappointment in the moderate white is expressed in the bitter realization of a harsh sociological fact; he is at the same time expressing disapproval and an understanding when he states the following: "Maybe I was too optimistic. Maybe I expected too much. I guess I should have realized that few members of a race that has oppressed another race can understand or appreciate the deep groans and passionate yearnings of those that have been oppressed, and still fewer have the vision to see that injustice must be rooted out by strong, persistent, and determined action."

King's disappointment in the Church is no less than his disappointment in the moderate whites and is, in fact, deeper, for he is in "the rather unique position of being the son, the grandson, and the great grandson, of preachers." As with his estimate of the moderate white, King confesses the possibility that he has been too optimistic regarding the church. The questioning of his optimism turns to self-searching: "Maybe I must turn my faith to the inner spiritual church, the church within the church, as the true *ecclesia* and the hope of the world. But again, I am thankful to God that some noble souls from the ranks of organized religion have broken loose from the paralyzing chains of conformity and joined us as active partners in the struggle for freedom." King sees an inevitability in the goal of freedom and justice for the Negro and he has "no despair for the future," for if the church fails, King puts his hopes in God and America: "We will win our freedom because the sacred heritage of our nation and the eternal will of God are embodied in our echoing demands." King makes a good case against the church with its adjustment to the *status quo* and its clergymen who "have been more cautious than courageous and have remained silent behind the anesthetizing security of stained glass windows." He has amassed enough evidence to warrant his indictment which he phrases, in part, in the following manner: "So here we are moving toward the exit of the twentieth century with a religious community largely adjusted to the *status quo* standing as a tail light behind other community agencies rather than a headlight leading men to higher levels of justice."

King warns the moderates who see his nonviolent direct action as excessively extremist that his movement has acted as an outlet to the pent-up resentments and latent frustrations experienced by the Negro. So let the Negro march sometimes, says King; "let him have his prayer pilgrimages to the city hall; understand why he must have sit-ins and freedom rides. If his repressed emotions do not come out in these nonviolent ways, they will come out in ominous expressions of violence. This is not a threat; it is a fact of history." And, of course, King is right, as any elementary text on psychology will explain. Those people who reject his nonviolent direct action cannot ignore the ominous threat of reality when he writes: "If this philosophy had not emerged I am convinced that by now many streets of the South would be flowing with floods of blood. And I am further convinced that if our white brothers dismiss us as 'rabble rousers' and 'outside agitators'—those of us who are working through the channels of nonviolent direct action —and refuse to support our nonviolent efforts, millions of Negroes, out of frustration and despair, will seek solace and security in black nationalist ideologies, a development that will lead inevitably to a frightening racial nightmare." King's reference to black nationalism and the Muslim movement with their racist implications is the closest he ever gets to using the emotion of fear to persuade his audience. And even here, he asserts that this is not a threat on his part, "it is a fact of history."

Towards the end of the letter, King turns his attention to the praise which the eight clergymen had in their letter for the Birmingham police department. The clergymen had written: "We commend the community as a whole, and the local news media and law enforcement officials in particular, on the calm manner in which these demonstrations have been handled." King amasses several telling specifics to challenge this evaluation of police conduct by the clergymen. The misconduct of the police which King described had already been seen by millions of Americans over television and in the newspapers and magazines; the eight clergymen were obviously in error in their evaluation. With his comments directed to the clergymen, King said: "I don't believe you would have so warmly commended the police force if you had seen its angry violent dogs literally biting six unarmed nonviolent Negroes. I don't believe you would so quickly commend the policemen if you would observe their ugly and inhuman treatment of Negroes here in the city jail; if you would watch them push and curse old Negro women and young Negro girls; if you would see them slap and kick old Negro men and young Negro boys; if you will observe them, as they did on two occasions, refuse to give us food because we wanted to sing our grace together." Unarmed, nonviolent Negroes being attacked by the police dogs, small groups of unarmed, nonviolent girls and women being beaten by the police, individual Northern clergymen taking part in the demonstrations being abused—all this was part of the public record, yet the eight clergymen from Alabama saw fit to denounce the demonstrators and to praise the police. Then with a touch of irony, King says: "I'm sorry that I can't join you in your praise for the police department."

"Letter from the Birmingham Jail" ends with a mixture of irony and conciliation. Although he seems to be speaking directly to the eight clergymen, King concludes his letter with comments relevant to all Americans. He describes the circumstances under which he writes the letter and remarks on the length of the letter: "I'm afraid that it is much too long to take your precious time. I can assure you that it would have been much shorter if I had been writing from a comfortable desk, but what else is there to do when you are alone for days in the dull monotony of a narrow jail cell other than write long letters, think strange thoughts, and pray long prayers?" Of course, King's time is just as precious as the "precious time" of the eight clergymen. It is implied earlier in the letter that the "precious time" of the eight clergymen is being used for nothing more than to maintain the *status quo*. Further, there is a reprimand, implied criticism in his reference to sitting in the narrow cell while the eight clergymen sit at their "comfortable desks." Although King cannot resist the irony, his letter seemingly ends on a note of conciliation when he asks to be forgiven if he has overstated the truth and when he writes that he hopes "this letter finds you strong in the faith."

At the end of the letter King once more returns to the dichotomy between earthly and divine law when he says: "If I have said anything in this letter that is an overstatement of the truth and is indicative of an unreasonable impatience, I beg you to forgive me.

If I have said anything in this letter that is an understatement of the truth and is indicative of my having a patience that makes me patient with anything less than brotherhood, I beg God to forgive me." Once more it is more important to do that which pleases God than man: Understatement would please man, but overstatement of the situation would please God. Under the guise of humility King makes another ironic thrust at the eight clergymen.

Even in his final good wishes to his fellow clergymen, King cannot resist indirectly pleading his cause. For when he says in his final paragraph that he wishes to meet the clergymen not as an integrationist, but as a Christian brother, he is asserting one of the primary aims of his struggle: A true Christian brotherhood of white and Negro.

Considering the time, the place, the audience, the speaker, and the form, "Letter from the Birmingham Jail" can stand side by side with the great public letters of the past. Dr. King has chosen premises, upon which he builds his arguments, that are acceptable to almost all Americans and more particularly to the eight clergymen; he has identified his premises with respected, revered men, from Socrates to Tillich, from Aquinas to Buber. His premises come from laymen and clergymen, Protestant, Jew, and Catholic. There is nothing mean, low, or hateful in his premises. The validity of his arguments stands up to examination. He has amassed more than enough specifics and examples to make his inductive arguments acceptable. King's use of emotional proofs and his style are not only appropriate for his audience but are also consistent with the man, his philosophy, and his movement. He has reasoned with the audience; he has not insulted them by speaking down to them nor has he taken the pose of the intellectual superior. While he has aroused the emotions, he has not turned to exciting anger or hate, fear or envy. Martin Luther King's letter is rhetorically superior to any specific persuasive discourse which his critics and adversaries have produced. He has remained on a high plane; his goal for the brotherhood of man is thus exemplified in the word and in the spirit of his "Letter from the Birmingham Jail."

PART 4
Criticism and Social Change

The following articles represent initial and theoretical examinations of contemporary black protest rhetoric. In this section the authors are in search of norms, definitions, and recurring themes. In the first article Arthur L. Smith examines some common topics in black protest rhetoric. Examining Malcolm X's speeches at Harvard, Archie Epps sees the theme of exile as a constant notion. Parke G. Burgess presents his view of the black power rhetoric in a provocative essay. The fourth article, by Richard B. Gregg, A. Jackson McCormack, and Douglas J. Pedersen, is based upon field work in an urban setting and attempts to provide a street-level interpretation of black power. The articles in this section represent a vigorous attempt at criticism and explication of the rhetorical behavior of blacks as it relates to social change.

Arthur L. Smith

CHAPTER 16
Topics of
Revolutionary Rhetoric

In part, many rhetorical themes propagated by the contemporary black revolutionists have their source in the religious traditions of the slaves.[1] White justification for the importation of slaves during the era of black slavery often took the form of religious sanction. Self-congratulatory whites told themselves that by introducing Christianity to the slaves, they were civilizing the African savages. Many blacks, seeking a heavenly solace, believed and accepted the white man's religion with passionate zeal and accompanying emotionalism. When the social demands of slavery caused

From *Rhetoric of Black Revolution* (Boston: Allyn & Bacon, 1970), Ch. 3, pp. 4–361. Reprinted by permission of the publisher.

the black converts who had worshipped in their masters' churches to be segregated, small meeting places were built on the plantation for the slaves. These church houses, usually located on the edge of the plantation, were the centers of social and religious gatherings for blacks. During slavery, black preachers galvanized the members of the plantation churches with long moanful intonations of the sufferings of the children of Israel. The slave preachers exercised considerable influence over their congregations because of their positions of leadership, which suggested superior abilities and gifts. It is little wonder that Denmark Vesey and Nat Turner could command followers when it is revealed that they were both preachers. Thus, the black preacher was in a unique position that could be used either to compromise the longings of his congregation or to lead the revolt.

Realizing the power of the black preacher over his congregation, the slave owners often rewarded with household goods the preachers who performed well. In many instances, the black preachers became informers, pimps, and justifiers of slavery. Using the material gifts to the preacher, the white slave owner continued his domination of his slaves and put the minister in debt to the master.

The unique position of the black preacher also gave him the opportunity to organize and incite rebellions. Because the preacher had a direct path to the master and a direct path to God, he became the leader of the black community. Black preachers were reserved a special place in the community because they were 'in with the man.' In this position, the black preacher could get favors that other slaves could not acquire in their non-ministerial capacities. There might be a connection between the preacher's ability to secure special privileges from 'the man' and the fact that in many small Southern communities there is still an abundance of preachers. By allowing the master an opportunity to control the masses through the preacher, Christianity proved to be a powerful force; but it was later to figure in the black man's liberation and continuing struggle against discrimination and prejudice. This became inevitable when black preachers who were 'in with the man' used their knowledge to aid their congregations. They developed a thematic emphasis that indicated their concern about their parishioners.

It was not enough for the black preacher to bring gifts from the master to the slaves; he had to comfort them in their destitution by pointing to a heavenly reward for good living. In this role, the black preacher perfected the art of inducing cathartic experiences for his members. Indeed after some sermons, members of the audience were prostrate on the floor with foam running out of their mouths. The business of the black preacher during slavery was the business of consolation. He consoled in life as well as in death, for life was often a living death. He also developed a strong imagination to go with his ministerial functions. It is from this imagination that the black preacher received his special 'revelations' on certain scriptural themes.

As with the spirituals, the black preacher's sermons were often cryptic, suggesting more than they purported to say on the surface, thereby providing a deeper temporal meaning for the audience. In some church circles within the black community even now when a preacher touches on a theme with ambiguous meaning, church members might respond, "that's deep." Often when the slaves sang as they worked in the fields, "Swing Low, Sweet Chariot, Coming for to Take me Home," they were sending messages to one another; for example, "If you Get there Before I do, Tell All My Friends I'm Coming too," suggested that their escape was being planned. Other spirituals contained similar messages. The black preacher, similarly, gave out texts from the pulpit that contained dual meanings, "one for the spirit, and one for the body." In many places in the South today, some sermons with dual meanings are still heard. A favorite among black preachers during slavery, and still preached in the deep South is, "The Eagle Stirreth Her Nest," which suggested that the slaves were restive and ready for an uprising. The black preacher was the instrument through whom the "message" of the Lord came to bring consolation and advice to the slaves.

Out of this context came the black rhetors' basic reliance on Biblical concepts for the black man's liberation. Observing in the

Old Testament the dramatic pronouncements made by the prophets Amos, Micah, and Jeremiah, the black preacher became a prophet. Among the themes that permeated the sermons were the broad concepts of justice, righteousness, and truth. Black preachers used these religious abstractions in much the same way as politicians employ the political abstractions. Justice, in the Old Testament, seems to be a major concern of the Israelitic prophets, and black preachers have traditionally found their texts in the prophets. The early Christian writers have had less influence on the black church, because the sufferings of the early Christians were not perceived as being parallel to that of black people. In Israel's deliverance from bondage and subsequent struggle to remain free, the black preacher found reason to moralize and counsel. It is the justice of God working its way out for an eternal good, according to the black preacher who explained the distress of black people whose parents were tortured and whose own lives were wretched with misery. Often in describing the aspirations of the black masses, the preachers would suggest that our way is "the way of righteousness,"[2] and thus another theme emerges in the rhetoric.

The plan of deliverance, as seen by the black rhetors, was not immoral, unjust, or ungodly but rather only the 'righteous strivings' of a persecuted people. Truth was used to sanction the hope of the oppressed. In this case, using the Old Testament text as a foundation, the preachers would proceed to the New Testament's "Ye shall know the truth, and the truth shall make you free."[3] Freedom was taken to mean much more than spiritual freedom, and often the audience only received the meaning that provided them with immediate reality—freedom from economic and social oppression. The truth was often no more than the preacher's latest interpretation of a passage or impression of the white race. Somehow the truth was to make the black masses free, and it is perhaps true to say that many were deceived when their preacher's vague truth effected little or no change in their oppressive situations. Even though the use of these concepts to galvanize the black masses failed to deliver them from their social degradation, it was an attempt on the part of the preachers to bring consolation.

Beyond and occasionally within the basic themes of justice, righteousness, and truth, the black preacher appropriated key expressions to his messages. Some of the common images used appear below:

> 'suffering children of Israel'
> 'written in God's Law'
> 'down in the valley of oppression'
> 'been to the mountain top'
> 'way down in Egypt's land'
> 'eternal ruin of devils'
> 'God will fight our battle'
> 'Let justice roll down like water'

Using these and other religious expressions, the black rhetors motivated the black masses to have hope, patience, and faith in the ultimate victory of right over wrong, of good over evil. Some saw the eventual downfall of a corrupt system as early as the first part of the nineteenth century. Although David Walker was not a preacher, his language shows a strong religious emphasis. In 1829 he wrote, "O Americans! Americans!! I call God—I call angels— I call men, to witness, that your *DESTRUCTION* is at hand, and will be speedily consummated unless you repent."[4]

The foregoing discussion considered the major religious themes of black rhetors. While these themes are still used in some quarters of the black community, they have been replaced by secular themes proclaimed by more militant rhetors.

William E. B. Du Bois, who was like a voice crying in the wilderness during his lifetime, has become the most productive source for the secular themes in the rhetoric of the black revolution. Throughout his career, Du Bois tried to appeal to the intellect of white America. He employed the themes of power, democracy, brotherhood, humanity, and justice. Unlike the justice of the religious images, Du Bois' justice was not a supra-rational concept signifying God's intervention in human history, but rather equal justice under the law. He spoke in concrete terms concerning the needs and aspirations of the black masses.

In recent years, power as a theme in the secular rhetoric of the black rhetors has superseded brotherhood. The emergence of Malcolm X as a charismatic spokesman for black nationalism is responsible for a new look at the American situation. Coinciding with the dethroning of religious solutions was the emphasis on secular answers to the black man's problems. In 1965, a black leader, speaking to a college group in Los Angeles said, "moral suasion has seldom changed the minds of those in power."[5] Probably echoing the sentiments expressed a thousand times in as many different ways by oppressed people, this black rhetor indicated the public shift from religious images to secular concepts. In the same year, Malcolm X's proclamation to "let the Klan know that we can do it [use violence] tit for tat"[6] was a further signal of the changing emphasis of the rhetoric to a more aggressive stance.

Yet it is only a reaction to the position of the white society. Consequently, as a recourse to evade the constant denial of full brotherhood by the society, the black rhetors suggest the possibility of seizing power for themselves. However, the black revolutionists have yet to articulate a plan for the organization and manipulation of power outside the white system.[7] Indeed, the black masses can only discover the strength of collective power within the total American society because of their intimate history within this national context. While power outside this frame of reference is not unthinkable, it is highly unlikely for some of the same reasons that the rhetoric of black separation soon exhausts itself.

Having witnessed the death of brotherhood through moral suasion as a rhetorical theme, the contemporary rhetor of black revolutions suggests that morality might be encouraged by the wielding of power by blacks. According to the rhetoric of the black secular leaders, power allows the blacks to exhibit, in truth, a sense of worth. The reasoning behind this emphasis seems to be that no one can claim brotherhood with one who is not his equal. As long as the whites have economic, political, and military power exclusively, then it is impossible to consider the blacks equal; at most, they are the recipients of benevolent paternalism. In Malcolm X's manhood speeches, the intense interest in the black man helping himself and doing his own thing is a reason for a black writer to say of Malcolm X, "he was our manhood."[8] Following Malcolm X's lead, power as a major theme pervades the rhetoric of the black secular rhetors such as Stokely Carmichael, Maulana Karenga, H. Rap Brown, LeRoy Jones, and Huey P. Newton. Their belief, shared by some of the black preachers, is that the respect of the black man will come when he has something with which to bargain.

Although the use of the power theme in speeches and essays suggests an inward turn (the black man to his own potentials and abilities), the concept is militant to the extent that the acquisition of power always presupposes the relinquishing of power by another. If Karenga says "we will control South Central Los Angeles,"[9] he means that someone will have to give up control of that area.

Earlier we saw that the rhetoric of black militancy is aggressive. Inasmuch as the rhetors do not allow their positions to be defensive, they refuse to be placed on the defensive when speaking of power. Utilizing the emotional reactions produced by the term black power, the black rhetor accomplishes terror without the accompanying physical violence. Unquestionably, however, the recent uprisings in the major cities of the nation do give those whites who are frightened by the terms a referent. While the referent is inadequate and perhaps distorted by looters and the holiday spirit, it nevertheless suggests to many white Americans the explosive potential within the society.

Even the names of various organizations in the black community emphasize power; for example, consider FIGHT, US, Black Panthers, Bootstrap, Afro-American, Action Committee. Reflecting in their names the newness as well as the vitality of power as a concept, these organizations are peopled with blacks who consider the traditional civil rights groups such as Urban League, National Association for the Advancement of Colored People and even Congress of Racial Equality, to be archaic and conservative. Even though CORE's emphasis did change when Floyd McKissick embraced black power, it is still considered one of the old line groups by many black revolutionists.

In pursuing the concept of power, the black revolutionist uses other themes to establish his rhetorical aim. He is concerned with attacking the opposition and supporting his own position. Thus, the rhetor employs language that serves these dual purposes.

An analysis of the speeches and writings of the black secular rhetors reveals that there are four major recurring themes, insofar as prevalent topics are concerned. The black rhetors are convinced that all black people face a common enemy, that there is a conspiracy to violate black manhood, that America is a hypocritical country, and that unity among blacks must be achieved for liberation.

In research for this study, I heard and read speeches by many black militants, including Malcolm X, H. Rap Brown, Maulana Karenga, Bobby Seale, and Stokely Carmichael. The essential differences between these speakers were determined by temperament, intellectual vigor, stylistic expression, and manner of delivery, not by the basic content of their messages. Perceiving the same society, these black rhetors see similar obstacles to black liberation, and sanction almost identical action for the removal of those obstacles. Universally, the black militants see themselves as victims of the society, and agree with Malcolm X who said in his famous speech "The Ballot or the Bullet," "I do not speak as an American, but as a victim of this American system."[10]

Every speech I examined referred in some way or another to the common enemy. Some speakers used the term 'common enemy' within their speeches; others used such epithets as 'the man,' 'the white man,' 'Mr. Charlie,' and 'the one who's keeping you down.' The prevalence of this theme reminds one of how deeply imbedded in the black revolutionist's psyche is his anger. For in all things, the white man becomes the accursed symbol of corruption, race debasement, self-hatred, discrimination, white racism, and more than is admitted, the slavemaster. Just as the master was considered the enemy of the field Negro who had to be broken, so the common enemy today remains the same.

One method used by black organizers of rebellions and escape during slavery was to convince the reluctant blacks that 'we all got the same enemy.' Although it is true that some slaves had masters more sympathetic than others, the black organizers saw all slave-owners as the enemy. It is this vision that has come down to the militant blacks as they look on white America as the enemy bent on breaking the black man's will and spirit.

No aspect of black life is completely free of the enemy, according to the rhetors of black revolution. Malcolm X saw the common enemy in the ghetto shops, in the furniture stores, downtown, uptown, on the Southern plantations, and as employer in the factories. Calling for black self-help, Malcolm X declared, "any time you have to rely on your *enemy* for a job, you're in bad shape."[11] There is seldom any doubt in the minds of the audients of the black revolutionists about the referent for the enemy. Stokely Carmichael contends that "the man"[12] controls black neighborhoods, although he does not live in those neighborhoods. Black people have come to distrust the man who pervades their economic and political life. Using this basic distrust of white America, the rhetors of black revolution have shown the man to be the source and origin of the black man's fundamental problems in American society. In this way, it is clear that the man is used as an objectification technique for channeling the grievances of the black masses.

Another major theme expressed in the rhetoric of revolution is America's hypocrisy. The rhetor usually starts with the American Constitution as he demonstrates that the Constitution was not intended to include black people. Some rhetors, however, begin their arguments at the Declaration of Independence. They contend that the founding fathers had no intentions of bringing the blacks into the American society, and therefore the society was formed with a basic flaw, the inherent superiority of the white race.[13] To correct this flaw, many black rhetors contend that the present system must be replaced.

The hypocrisy theme also is seen when the black rhetors accuse whites of holding American democracy up to the world as the most humanitarian government. While white America extols the virtues of Americanism, black people curse their American predicament. Malcolm X shouts to a black audience, "You and I haven't benefited from America's Democracy; we've only suffered from America's hypocrisy."[14] Carmichael draws thunderous applause when he indicts, "this country is too hypocritical."[15] He contends that if polarization of the races occurs, it is because the white Americans are too hypocritical to accept their "responsibility as the majority power to make the democratic process work."[16]

The black revolutionists have no illusions about America's willingness to eradicate its double standard in racial matters. They profess no faith in America's benevolent intentions toward black people in this nation, or any other nation. Indeed, the black rhetors of revolution believe that survival depends on the cooperation of all black peoples. They see the American Dream leading large American corporations to South Africa to partake in the exploitation of black labor; they see America's economic control of large portions of South America; and they know that this is a white man's government.

Eldridge Cleaver suggests in a speech that black people should follow Malcolm X's suggestion to involve the United Nations in the liberation of blacks in this country.[17] According to the black rhetors of revolution, if blacks had anything to do with the nation's policies then it would not be involved in Vietnam and in South Africa exploiting the colored peoples of the world. So the black revolutionist is certain that America is a hypocritical nation that bases its decisions on race. Some even give as proof America's political flirtations with Russia in an effort to link up white power against the colored peoples. The black revolutionists are saying that racism is America's basic hypocrisy, because it contradicts all of the myths handed down from the founding fathers.

Because of the racism ingrained in the American soul, black rhetors have often suggested that a new American Constitution should be written, one that would give the people a more favorable basis for developing a great society. Inasmuch as this rhetoric addresses the primary foundations of national origin, it is akin to the rhetoric of David Walker and William Lloyd Garrison, who called for a new compact of government. If the nation cannot deliver the rewards of democracy to all of its people on the basis of the present political contract, then blacks have reason to seek another solution.

In 1923, Marcus Garvey, convinced that America would never grant freedom and equality to black men, declared, "we are determined that we shall have a flag; we are determined that we shall have a government second to none in the world,"[18] as he encouraged blacks to join his back to Africa movement. In 1968, Professor Vincent Harding wrote that black power advocates shout, "Go to hell, you whited sepulchers, hypocrites. All you want is to cripple our will and prolong our agony. . . ."[19]

America's failure to deliver the fruits of democracy to the black masses has produced a colossal distrust of white America's intentions. Building on the reservoir of frustration that long years of dreams and promises deferred has created, the black revolutionists possess enormous rhetorical credibility. As Nathan Wright, Jr., puts it, "In all fairness, black Americans cannot be asked to make emotional commitments to white friendships into which white people have historically built a guarantee of soon or late frustration."[20] He continues that here is often a "black time-ingrained cynicism at the systematic way in which cards are stacked against black people."[21] In a recent essay, a black militant revealed that she came to understand that "there wasn't room enough in the society for the mass of black people, that the majority of Americans are acting in unbearably bad faith or in tragic ignorance when they project to their children the image of an American society where all men are free and equal."[22]

The more significant fact is that when the rhetors of black revolution speak of American hypocrisy, they are able to support their assertions with clearcut examples of the society's failure to deliver the promise. In fact, the black rhetors often know that many of their followers have never been visited by the American dream; they have only known "the American nightmare," as Malcolm X put it.[23] One cannot forget that Stokely Carmichael and H. Rap Brown were two of the leading black youths in the nonviolent movement just a few years ago. Actually, they were engaged in teaching other civil rights workers the techniques of nonviolent resistance; but the vision of black and white together was shattered too many times by the American society.

The distance between the American ideal and the black man's reality is the area of the black revolutionist's most effective grievances. Using the revealing dichotomies of America, the black rhetors rally their audiences. For example, the fact that blacks fight for democracy for the Vietnamese but are not granted full equality in America often is cited as proof of American hypocrisy. The black rhetors also point out that black children in America have a higher mortality rate than do Vietnamese children; that black soldiers from the South cannot even be buried in some city cemeteries; and that the Vietnamese could come to this country and receive greater acceptance than blacks. American hypocrisy then is used as an issue to influence blacks to seek redress by any means necessary.

Convinced that America will not make any significant efforts to correct the situation by vigorously attacking racism, the black revolutionist contends that his actions cannot be defined by the criminal who concocted black people's sufferings in the first place. Indeed, one tenet of the Black Panthers is that all black men held in Federal, state, county, and city prisons and jails should be released.[24] The Black Panthers contend that a racist system is responsible for the brothers being in prison because they are not tried by a jury of their peers.

Even though rhetoric employing the hypocrisy theme has been heard more vigorously lately, it has been around for many years. It also should be noted that there are still some blacks who believe that redress can occur within the present system even as they admit American hypocrisy. The black rhetor uses the black masses' unique position to know that the American pretense to humanitarian qualities is, in fact, only make-believe.

Somewhat related to the hypocrisy theme that pervades the black revolutionist's rhetoric is the conspiracy theme. The black rhetor attempts to demonstrate that America deliberately designs to deny the black man his full share in the society. Before the conspiracy theme is developed in some speeches, the rhetor cites many examples of hypocrisy, then he may cite instances where blacks had their homes invaded or were brutalized by police or store keepers. Everything done by the white society is held in suspect by the black rhetors.

In a speech or an essay, the rhetor might encourage his audience to deal cautiously with, say, the Kerner Report,[25] because the man is not going to indict himself. In the rhetoric, the black revolutionist tries to convince his audience that they have no reason to trust the white man. Nathan Hare says, "I have no faith that—given the nature of its existing institutions, belief systems and practices—white America can fully rectify the situation."[26] Although this is not a statement suggesting a conspiracy, it does indicate the utter distrust many black rhetors have in America's present institutions; from this position, the conspiracy theme is easily drawn. Now we can understand the nature of a black revolutionist's rhetoric when he says, "the government is against you —that is, the White House, the Court and the Congress—they've got Negroes in a trick bag."[27]

Having no faith in the government, the black revolutionist is capable of contending that the government has a conspiracy against black people. Every action by the government becomes suspect in the black revolutionist's rhetoric. The white man is not to be trusted with anything or at any time because he "has fooled us too long and too much."[28] Examples of this monumental distrust can be found in almost any major American city where there is a planned parenthood organization in the ghetto. Black revolutionists claim that the centers are a part of the American conspiracy to eliminate the black people in this nation. They warn black mothers against taking the birth control pills because it will mean a reduction in the number of black babies born.

An argument often heard in support of the conspiracy theme is developed from the number of accidental and justifiable homicides committed in the black communities by the police. In 1966, the Progressive Labor Party came out with a broadside that purported to show "The Plot Against Black America."[29] It contended that

under direct orders from Johnson and the White House racist cops
and soldiers carried out vicious campaigns of terror against Black
America. Throughout the essay, there are allusions to "well-
planned and systematic" provocations on the part of the police.
The killing of fifteen-year-old James Powell in New York by a
policeman became identified with the police war against blacks in
the rhetoric of the black revolutionists. Blacks in the ghetto are
told by the black rhetors that every time a black person is killed
by a policeman is simply the brutal expression of racism. This
rhetoric is especially careful to mention that what the coroner's
office rules as a justifiable homicide is nothing but cold murder.

Distrust in white America is also seen when the black rhetors
tell their followers that white politicians are all playing a game
to suppress blacks. The rhetors explain to their audiences that
one white politician will say one thing and another will say something else, but in fact both are in agreement about black people.
The technique of one man playing your friend while another poses
as your enemy is called trickery by the black rhetors. Malcolm X
suggested in a speech in Detroit that LBJ's best friend was Richard
Russell, an arch racist.[30] He says in the speech that when LBJ
deplaned after taking the oath of office for President, the first
thing he wanted to know was "Where is Dickie?"[31] The speaker
concluded that they must have been working in concert, if so, how
could Johnson be the best friend of Russell's and the black man's
friend at the same time? According to Malcolm X, they were in
cahoots to deny the black man his liberation.

Even though most black revolutionists see some kind of conspiracy against America's black population, only a few have taken
the extreme position that America plans to commit genocide. These
few revolutionists insist that America is as racist and therefore as
susceptible to genocide as Germany was during the Third Reich.
Thus, they articulate their fears to their audiences in an effort to
plant still more distrust of white America.

When one considers the daily examples of police over-reaction
in the black ghetto, the constant poverty of many black families,
and the rabid prejudice that betrays many white Americans, it

becomes clear how the rhetoric of black revolution can be made to appeal to the black community by the rhetor's skillful use of the conspiracy theme.

A fourth theme permeating the rhetoric of black revolution is unity of the black community. It is something of a cliché with Black Power advocates to accuse 'the man' of trying to keep blacks from organizing.

The rhetors tell their audiences that it has always been the strategy of the white man to divide and conquer. Seizing on historical examples of the white man's use of this strategy to overcome other peoples, the black revolutionist calls attention to the political unions that emerged in Africa after the intervention of colonial forces. Furthermore the slavery experience is cited to give additional support to the contention that whites have used the technique of divide and conquer whenever they were faced with threatening situations. During slavery, the black revolutionist contends, the slaves from different tribes were placed together while slaves with the same culture background, heritage, and language were separated to keep them weak and powerless. The black revolutionist goes further to suggest that after slavery some blacks were made the Uncle Toms of the white man and were constantly running to the man with information from the black community. This situation occurred when the white man made certain 'Negroes' feel that they had an inside track to his ear, while others were not so fortunate. But the black revolutionist insists that the white man was using these house Negroes against one another.

Inasmuch as that was the white man's method of rule and control in the past, that will probably be his method for the future, the masses are told by the black revolutionist.

To avoid oppression, then, the black masses must get themselves together so that they can speak with one voice and move with one spirit. In 1968 at an organizational meeting of black faculty in California, Walter Bremond revealed that "the only way we can hope to obtain true freedom is through getting together. Even the black pimps are getting together now. They are organizing. You must organize."[32] In a speech at UCLA, Adam Clayton

Powell argued that if other ethnic groups can have their organizations, then the blacks must have theirs.[33]

While there have been a number of traditional civil rights groups working in the black community, they have usually been shunned by the black revolutionists because of too much white control. Consequently, there has been a proliferation of black organizations in the last few years. Operating outside the influence of groups like the NAACP and the Urban League, these newly formed organizations seek to represent the lowest man on the totem pole. Preaching unity based on blackness, the black revolutionist apparently hopes to create a massive base from which to deal with the problems of black people in the American society.

Malcolm X was the great evangelist of black unity, especially as he saw it manifested in black nationalism. He argued that one could "stay right in his own church and believe in black nationalism."[34] Black nationalism was more essential to survival than the sect of a man's church, according to Malcolm X. In his famous retort of those who questioned the basis of his unity he said, "They don't hang you because you are a Baptist or a Methodist, they hang you because you're black."[35] In this statement, he defined the basis and the limits of black nationalism. In other words, these black rhetors say to the oppressed masses, 'take what you have and use it to your advantage.' Thus, the people are encouraged to rally around one thing that keeps them down—their blackness. And in finding strength in their blackness, they become like the Jews who have been persecuted for their religion yet find much of their unity in their religious heritage. Once unity is accomplished, the rhetors of revolution contend that nothing will be denied the black people because of the significant power base that their unity commands.

Unity, therefore, is a prevalent theme in the rhetoric of black revolution. Taken together with the themes of a common enemy, conspiracy, and a hypocritical nation, it becomes acceptable doctrine for the black masses who are eloquent proofs of so much of the rhetoric.

NOTES

Editor's Note: This article is the third chapter in the book, *Rhetoric of Black Revolution*. Previously the author discussed revolutionists' situations and strategies; this chapter is an exposition of the rhetorical topics and themes.

1 For a more comprehensive view of Afro-American religion, see William E. B. Du Bois, *The Negro Church*, Atlanta, 1903; Mark Fisher, *Negro Slave Songs in the United States*, Ithaca, 1953; and Carter G. Woodson, *The History of the Negro Church*, Washington, 1921.

2 Proverbs 12:28.

3 John 8:32.

4 Herbert Aptheker, *One Continual Cry*, New York, Humanities Press, 1965, p. 108. All quotations from Walker's *Appeal* reprinted by permission of Humanities Press.

5 Speech given by William Green to the Human Relations Club, Pepperdine College, Los Angeles, California, September, 1965.

6 Malcolm X, *Malcolm X Speaks*, edited by George Breitman, New York, 1965, p. 113.

7 The Nation of Islam is an obvious exception. Based on metaphysical and social concepts, the Black Muslim's separation policy is relatively well articulated. For an in-depth study of Black Muslims, see C. Eric Lincoln, *The Black Muslims in America*, Boston, 1961.

8 See Malcolm X and Alex Haley, *The Autobiography of Malcolm X*, New York, 1964, p. 454. The expression cited was used by actor Ossie Davis at Malcolm X's funeral.

9 Speech given by Maulana Karenga at Purdue University, December 12, 1968.

10 *Malcolm X Speaks*, p. 26.

11 Malcolm X, "The Ballot or the Bullet," long-playing record published by the Afro-American Broadcasting and Recording Company, Detroit, 1965.

12 See Robert L. Scott and Wayne Brockriede, *The Rhetoric of Black Power*, New York, 1969, p. 87.

13 This sentence was incorrectly printed. It should read, ". . . and therefore the society was formed with a basic flaw, the *assumed* inherent superiority of the white race."

14 Malcolm X, "The Ballot or the Bullet."

15 See Charles Lomas, *The Agitator in American Society*, Englewood, New Jersey, 1968, p. 149.

16 *Ibid.*, p. 139.

17 Eldridge Cleaver, "Political Struggle in America—1968," Peace and Free-

dom Party Forum, Oakland, California, February 11, 1968. This speech appears in Chapter 6 of *Rhetoric of Black Revolution*.

18 Marcus Garvey, "Deceiving the People," in *The Black Power Revolt*, ed. Floyd B. Barbour (Boston: Porter Sargent, 1968), p. 57.

19 Vincent Harding, "Black Power and the American Christ," in *The Black Power Revolt*, ed. Floyd B. Barbour (Boston: Porter Sargent, 1968), p. 91.

20 Nathan Wright, Jr., "The Crisis Which Bred Black Power," in *The Black Power Revolt*, ed. Floyd B. Barbour (Boston: Porter Sargent, 1968), p. 117.

21 *Ibid.*, p. 118.

22 Jean Smith, "I Learned to Feel Black," in *The Black Power Revolt*, ed. Floyd B. Barbour (Boston: Porter Sargent, 1968), p. 209.

23 *Malcolm X Speaks*, p. 26.

24 *The Black Panther*, January 25, 1969.

25 *Report of the National Advisory Commission on Civil Disorders*. This report was a response to President Lyndon B. Johnson's executive order of July 29, 1967. A series of black uprisings that began in 1965 in Los Angeles, California, had spread quickly across the nation. The National Advisory Commission on Civil Disorders was headed by Otto Kerner, former governor of Illinois. The report was cited for its candor, as it placed the blame for black frustration on white racism.

26 Nathan Hare, "How White Power Whitewashes Black Power," in *The Black Power Revolt*, ed. Floyd B. Barbour (Boston: Porter Sargent, 1968), p. 188.

27 Malcolm X, "The Ballot or the Bullet."

28 Speech given by Maulana Karenga at Purdue University, December 12, 1968.

29 *The Plot Against Black America*, New York, Harlem Progressive Labor Party, 1966.

30 Malcolm X, "The Ballot or the Bullet."

31 *Ibid.*

32 Speech given by Walter Bremond at the University of Southern California, August, 1968.

33 Speech given by Adam Clayton Powell at the University of California, Los Angeles, October, 1967.

34 Malcolm X, "The Ballot or the Bullet."

35 *Ibid.*

Archie Epps

CHAPTER 17
The Theme of Exile
in the Harvard Speeches

Malcolm X saw himself and the Negro group as exiles in a sense
akin to that of the stranger and the criminal fugitive. The very
society was a jungle for him. He was lost there. Not only lost, but
threatened by a daily violence. Even as he became less sectarian
in religious views, his assessment of the Negroes' future in the
secular sphere remained narrow and reactionary. But Malcolm X's
racism, which was considerable, was pieced together helter-skelter,
very much the product of his public anger. As a solution, he urged
Negroes to seek a new world. This world was actually located in

several places during the course of his career. The Harvard speeches reflect these changes in his thought very nicely. The speeches had one thing in common. The locale of his exile was, by imagination and fact, the ghetto of Negro America.

Malcolm X behaved very much like a prophet in the Harvard speeches. His new world was described in apocalyptic language, which was, for him, the appropriate place to call a halt to the cruel mechanism of American society which held Negro history in its grasp. But each Harvard speech found Malcolm X describing a fantastic and unreal homeland for the Negro. It was first the orthodox Muslim world, then a devastated America, and finally Africa.

Malcolm X continued to call for revolution throughout his public career. But he also urged escape. Revolution was his public strategy. Escape was his private strategy. Malcolm X actually sought this latter strategy only for himself. In speaking before Negro audiences, he sometimes gave his private strategy away, however. That he did so while advocating revolution was a major paradox of his life and thought. Malcolm X's new world was, therefore, a very private hideaway. When he described it to others, with political strategy in mind, it was inevitably romantic in character, very like his notion of life in Africa before the Negro was forced under the yoke of slavery and brought to America.

The Harvard speeches contain both Malcolm X's public and private strategies. It is not easy to separate one from the other, especially since his notion of revolution was romantic and thus highly personal. Surely Malcolm X would have discovered that to make revolution in a modern society requires a thorough comprehension of that society; requires a revolutionary as modern as is the opponent. Of course, Malcolm X, like the black power advocates, did not mean revolution when he used the word. Malcolm X actually called for a "street rumble" of sorts; that is surely different from either revolution or guerrilla warfare. What Malcolm X urged was anomic behavior on the part of the Negro masses. In this regard, the paradox drawn earlier between his public strategy of revolution and his private strategy of escape very nearly disappeared. Upon closer analysis, history will show that a strategy of escape really informs mass outbursts such as the Negro riots of recent summers. Malcolm X actually betrayed his confusion over the actual worth of this strategy in the Harvard speeches.

The first Harvard speech was the most romantic. Here the prophetic style was very pronounced. Since this first speech occurred at the height of Malcolm X's orthodox Black Muslim period, the new world was thoroughly apocalyptic in nature. The call to violence in this context was, curiously enough, merely a side product of a strategy of escape. The call to violence really served a ridiculous logic: If the whites won't give us a separate black state in the United States (Malcolm argued), we will wreak havoc on the nation. Why didn't the Black Muslims simply leave? The counter argument was that American whites had to provide the separate state here as some kind of compensation for the free labor exacted from the Negroes over the years. But the Black Muslims and Malcolm X did not really press the point. An alternate solution, equally acceptable to them, was a mass Negro exodus to the orthodox Muslim world.

The theme of exile lay just at the surface of nearly all Malcolm X's formulations in this first Harvard speech. The Black Muslims did not really wish to engage white Americans in battle. The overriding argument of the first Harvard speech was first the destruction of America by apocalyptic means. The new world Malcolm X foresaw would be built atop the rubble of a devastated society. "I must remind you," Malcolm X said, ending the first Harvard speech, "that your own Christian Bible states that God's coming will bring about a great separation." "Then everyone," he concluded, "will be able to live . . . 'under his own vine and fig tree.' " "Otherwise," Malcolm X warned, ". . . all of you who are sitting here, your government, and your entire race will be destroyed and removed from this earth."[1]

The vantage point of the Black Muslims was indeed curious. But there was something of fancy and fact in their preoccupations.

The view of society that informed Malcolm X's first Harvard

speech was almost idyllic. His brand of prophecy also hid a barely visible element of the absurd. Was Malcolm X a prophet or a jester? Did he really believe that a small but motley band of men and women, the Black Muslims, represented such ultimate power?

Both the prophet and the jester were exiles living within a society. Each kept himself on an island in fact or in imagination. While the prophet was a religious leader, the jester played his role before the holders of power, before the throne. A jester's audience was a mirror image of his worst self. And his job was to change the frown of the crowd into a smile. There were, of course, sweet clowns and bitter clowns. Malcolm X was a bit of both, full of illusions and sometimes free of them. The bitter clown Thersites in *Troilus and Cressida* "regards the world as a grim grotesque place":[2]

. . . The parrot will not do more for an almond than he for a commodious drab. Lechery, lechery! still wars and lechery! Nothing else holds fashion. A burning devil take them! (V, 2)

The prophet and the jester both performed the role of judge. Jan Kott helps give perspective to the jester's philosophy: "When established values have been overthrown, and there is no appeal to God, Nature, or History, from the tortures inflicted by the cruel world, the clown becomes the central figure in the theatre. He accompanies the exiled trio—the king, the nobleman, and his son—on their cruel wanderings through the cold endless night which has fallen on the world; through the 'cold night' which, as in Shakespeare's *King Lear,* 'will turn us all to fools and madmen.' "[3] The jester was the realist and the pessimist. The prophet was the optimist of the two. Although the prophet forecast destruction, as Malcolm X did, he also held out a glimmer of hope. At the end of the first Harvard speech, Malcolm X admitted there was still hope for America. "Why don't you repent while there is yet time?" he asked.[4] Malcolm X as prophet seemed to peer into an abyss. As jester he often played the role of a madman. In some speeches, Malcolm X seemed to imagine a white man in the shape of Gloucester of *King Lear*. "After his eyes have been gouged out," Kott says of Lear, "Gloucester wants to throw himself over the cliffs of Dover into the sea. He is led by his own son [by Edgar] who feigns madness. Both have reached the depths of human suffering. . . . They walk together."[5] The scene here could be transferred to our time. This scene set in America would require a change in language. Malcolm X, as Edgar, would tell Gloucester of Negro men below on city streets who look like ants, dwarfed by a massive modern technology. Gloucester, played by an American white, would have an answer for Malcolm X, a comment on the little Negroes below. It is not Shakespeare's Gloucester who gives us the response relevant to our time, however. Kott found the most meaningful response for us in Slowacki's *Kordian*. This Edgar commanded Gloucester to look into an abyss filled with animals and men:

Come! Here, on the top stand still. Your head will whirl,
When you cast your eyes on the abyss below your feet.
Crows flying there halfway no bigger are than beetles.
And there, too, someone is toiling, gathering weed.
He looks no bigger than a human head.
And there on the beach the fishmen seem like ants . . .[6]

Malcolm X also saw animals and men living together in America. It was his way of describing a cruel society. He was not alone in this view. Recently, two white public officials of American cities saw a similar world below. In their view, Negroes were the animals. And animals could only be frightened into flight by fire. If not frightened, they would certainly be destroyed in the flames of Hell. Bugs and beetles were plotting to destroy the cities by riot. Gloucester must listen to these white men. He would then hear an explanation of what lay below him in our time and place. To Gloucester's question, 'What lay below?' they would answer:

The degenerate thugs who hide in darkened windows and shoot down police and firemen . . .[7]

* * *

One had a solution:

We must fight fire with fire. Fear and only fear will stay those hoodlums from injuring decent people. They must know that when they
go to war with the City of Philadelphia they will be fighting a terrible
enemy.[8]

Gloucester committed suicide in Kott's *King Lear*. "The blind
Gloucester falls over on [an] empty stage. . . . In an Elizabethan
production, the blind Gloucester would have climbed a non-
existent height and fallen over on flat boards,"[9] being a clown.
Gloucester as a jester is difficult to understand except in the theatre
and world of Beckett. In that world, animals and men are on the
stage together. Beckett's world is our world. It was Malcolm X's
world.

[A man] goes and sits down on a big cube. The big cube is pulled
from under him. He falls. The big cube is pulled up and disappears
in flies. He remains lying on his side, his face towards auditorium,
staring before him.

(*Beckett*, ACT WITHOUT WORDS, p. 60)[10]

Malcolm X as the clown would not stare ahead. He would smile,
and the prophet would appear to become the Uncle Tom. Malcolm
X often gave speeches with laughter in his voice. The first Harvard
speech was full of this. He predicted destruction, but then he took
his words back. "This evening since we are all here . . . together,"
Malcolm X said, saying it again as if to mock integration, "both
races face to face, we can question and examine ourselves the
wisdom or folly of what Mr. Muhammad is teaching."[11] Malcolm
X would have laughed here, the laughter evoking a hundred years
of cynicism among Negroes over white goodwill. He really wished
to say something else. "This evening since we are all here together," he would have begun again, "both races face to face,
'fear and only fear will stay these [white] hoodlums.' The evil
features of this wicked old world," he would rush to say, as he
did say elsewhere in that speech, "must be exposed, faced up to,
and removed in order to make way for the new world."[12] Malcolm
X, the clown, had become the judge and executioner. He became
like a little boy chasing flies.

The image of flies in *King Lear* was taken over from *Othello*. In *Lear* the image of little boys chasing flies, according to Kott, "contains one of man's ultimate experiences":[13]

As flies to wanton boys are we to th' gods.
They kill us for their sport.

(LEAR, IV, 1)

Desdemona: I hope my noble lord esteems me honest.
Othello: O, ay! as summer flies are in the shambles,
That quickens even with blowing. . . .

(OTHELLO, IV, 2)

Malcolm X assumed that every Negro would very rightly think himself a fly in the hands of white men, of the whites as judge. Malcolm X reversed these roles, of course. Elijah Muhammad was the judge, Malcolm X, the clown before Muhammad's seat of power. The whites were then as flies to a new black god. Left in the hands of the judge, the whites would perish.

White man . . .
    'You're a beast; you've got one-third animal blood.'
He is the devil.
        (*Sermon by a minister of the Black Muslim Chicago Temple*)[14]

In the face of this assessment of the whites in America, Elijah Muhammad and Malcolm X could only choose two alternatives. They could fight for survival among the whites or leave the society altogether. Elijah Muhammad urged escape, and Malcolm X, repeating after him, in the early period, also urged escape. Elijah Muhammad thought the cities were already filled with fire.

. . . You don't know yourself nor your enemies; or rather are lost in love for our enemies. I know you, who love your enemy don't like that I tell you this truth. But, I can't help it—come what may. God has put upon me this mission, and I must do His will or burn.
        (*Elijah Muhammad*, MESSAGE TO THE BLACK MAN, p. 22)

The rioters of Watts, California, put Elijah Muhammad's admonition into "street language." The rioters, however, did not wish to leave destruction of the society in "the hands of the judge or of

God." It was their self-appointed mission to set fire to the society. The very slogan of the Watts riot to burn the city became the password in Negro ghettos across the country. The slogan echoed Elijah Muhammad's imagery of fire. The Watts rioters meant to encourage each other with the call to riot. A bitter clown would have told them the slogan was ironic and indeed suggested self-immolation. The slogan called fire down on the rioters themselves and on the society. They shouted:

Burn, baby, burn!

Malcolm X tried to play the bitter clown during his second Harvard speech. The second speech was hesitant in a new way because he took on this different role. The date of the second speech was, of course, one reason Malcolm X was rather unsure of himself. Two weeks before, he had resigned from (indeed been forced out of) the Black Muslim movement. The dispute with Elijah Muhammad had been over Malcolm X's public indiscretion, his referring to President Kennedy's assassination as "chickens coming home to roost." The dispute had other overtones as well. One such element was the different way Elijah Muhammad and Malcolm X understood the role of leader and defined policy. Malcolm X viewed the chances of achieving the Black Muslim policy of racial separation as impractical for the moment. His private view of the matter seemed sarcastic and ambiguous. It was the view of an embittered leader. The sarcasm was directed at everyone around him; at his lieutenants; at the whites, of course; at the society; and very much at the incumbent Negro leaders. Elijah Muhammad came within this purview, if only by inference. Malcolm X saw himself at the bottom of the heap now, beside the poor Negro folk. He seemed to challenge white and Negro leaders who stood on the top. There was white exploitation and Negro exploitation:

The black people in this country are beginning to realize that what sounds reasonable to those who exploit us doesn't sound reasonable to us. There just has to be a new system of reason and logic devised by us who are at the bottom, if we want to get some results in this struggle that is called the Negro revolution.

(SECOND HARVARD SPEECH)

What did Malcolm X have in mind? "The only real solution to our problem," Malcolm X began, "just as the Honorable Elijah Muhammad has taught us, is to go back to our homeland and to live among our own people. . . . I still believe [in] this. But that is a long-range program. And while our people are getting set to go back home, we have to live here in the meantime. So in the Honorable Elijah Muhammad's long-range program, there's also a short-range program: the political philosophy which teaches us that the black man should control the politics of his own community."[15]

Malcolm X's short-range program was explicitly separatist in nature. Put simply, Malcolm X urged Negroes to gain control of their communities, reassert African culture and, in the process, prepare to use violence against the whites. Actually, the control of Negro communities, politically and economically, required a prior independence of the larger society and the presence in the community of the "stuff" of modern life. In actuality, the Negro communities were not off in Africa somewhere, as Malcolm X often imagined, but were, rather, small impotent parts of a vast modern-industrial complex. The African culture Malcolm X had in mind was not authentic in any way. If Negroes were to reassert the African soul, as he urged, it first had to be conceived and created, and then, probably, only out of the imagination. The utter romanticism of these policies was only outdone by the talk of violence. The call to violence, as was to be seen among the black power partisans, was really a call to madness, confusion, and more separatist policies. Malcolm X did not foresee the cost in Negro life and property these policies would require.

Malcolm X foresaw what it would cost him, however. The second Harvard speech contained a very curious set of disclaimers. The disclaimers marked the limits of Malcolm X's conception of what Negro leadership could accomplish. "I am not a politician," he said. "I'm not even a student of politics. I'm not a Democrat. I'm not a Republican. I don't even consider myself an American."[16] What was he then? Malcolm X, the Negro and the man, was all that remained of his previous career as a Black Muslim minister. His lowly status was akin to the status of a fugitive. Such a status cost Malcolm X his previous certainty about his public strategy. He seemed betwixt and between a new *rite de passage*. The direction of his movement, in thought at least, was toward a kind of primitive Marxism. The Negro masses were his true companions. The Negro masses had been betrayed by incumbent Negro leaders. Malcolm X had been betrayed by Elijah Muhammad. His public strategy finally began to convey something of his realism and pessimism over Negro life chances in contemporary America.

The substance of the public strategy in the second speech was, however, very pessimistic. Malcolm X's pessimism was revealed in the pivotal images of exile used at the beginning and at the end of this speech. . . . The black people," he said, "were . . . disenchanted, disillusioned."[17] The Negro did not wish to integrate with whites; in fact, he never thought of it. The thoughts most central to the contemporary Negro, according to Malcolm X, had to do with going back to Africa. Accordingly, Malcolm X always combined images of captivity with images of escape. The Negro wished to leave the "alley," "ghetto," "penitentiary," "bounds," "captivity." The images of captivity were dark in tonal color. They suggested a sinking motion. Malcolm X saw the Negro trapped, trapped in "dirt." The Negro had been "let down." His portrait of the Negro face in exile was strongly drawn, full of suffering and foreboding. Malcolm X argued that if his policy was followed, the face of the Negro exile would stop its bitter wailing. A sad and dark sky surrounded the landscape of Malcolm X's Negro captivity. The sun had set. This was not the promised land. Indeed time and again the white politicians had promised more. "This feeds the hopes of the people," Malcolm X said, ". . . and after the politicians have gotten what they are looking for, they turn their back on the people of our community."

"The black people today," Malcolm X admitted, "are beginning to realize that it is a nightmare to us. What is a dream to you is a nightmare to us. What is hope to you has long since become hopeless to our people . . . in the ghetto, in the alley where the masses of our people live. . . ."[18] The pivotal image of "going home" represented Malcolm X's solution to Negro captivity. It was a very intimate and personal image. The rhetoric associated with it, in one instance, was first of the Negro slang idiom and then romantic in a nineteenth-century manner. "Our people are getting set to go back home . . ."[19] Malcolm X said in one place. And then he combined the image of the family tree with a romantic view of the past and the present. "We will reach back and link ourselves to those roots, and this will make the feeling of dignity come into us; we will feel that as we lived in times gone by, we can in like manner today. If we had civilizations, culture, societies, and nations hundreds of years ago, before you came and kidnapped us and brought us here; so we can have the same today."[20] It is, is it not, a rather heroic view of the Negro past and a rather irrelevant remedy for the present and a mere dream for the future. Separate civilizations and societies were really only possible in the medieval world. Even in slavery, the relationship of the Negro to the larger American society, and thus to modernity, was more intimate than we have been willing to admit. And even if it was not intimate, modernity remains that requirement which the Negro group must meet if it is to cope in the modern world.

Martin Kilson, in an unpublished essay, has said very plainly what shape the pursuit of political modernity must take on if it is to succeed. Kilson had the black power advocates in mind here, but his prescriptions also serve as a critique of Malcolm X's policies. He argued, in one sense, that the leadership group which was capable of performing the task of modernization in Negro communities was, for want of a better term, the Negro tertiary elite. "As a problem," Kilson begins, "the phenomenon of Black Power is one of leadership: where, in what numbers, of what quality and skill, is leadership to be located, capable of meeting the black masses in the ghettoes at their own threshold of existence."[21] He continues: "Even a lower class as structurally incoherent as the Negro lower class has a stratum near it that performs basic leadership roles. We know very little about this group—compared, say, to what is known about the Negro middle and professional classes. . . . It includes such people as owners of flop houses, poolrooms, shoeshine stands, bars, dingy barber shops, grocery and eating places, and numbers writers and other quasi-underworld sorts. This leadership group is awfully small," Kilson concludes, "and, given the limited resources at hand, very restricted in the range of functions it can perform. Yet it is, in some sense, a viable group: it has patterned and predictable arrangements and especially a set of institutionalized interests that must be nurtured and advanced."[22] Most importantly, the tertiary elite has the "attitudes and outlook" basic to such a leadership role.

Malcolm X was of the tertiary elite, as was his father. He had tremendous organizing skills. The Black Muslim movement grew from a mere 400 under Elijah Muhammad to 40,000 under Malcolm X's initiative. But Malcolm X (for personal and ideological reasons) misread the modern world. His long dependence on the religious ideologies of the Black Muslim movement, and later on black nationalism, as sources of a coherent view of the world, left him ill-suited to lead a movement for the political modernization of the Negro group. At the same time, the perpetual sense of crisis and doom that pervaded the final months of his life certainly took a great toll of his energy and intellect.

If Malcolm X misread the modern world on questions of policy and political strategy, he certainly read its philosophy correctly. The chief characteristic of modern life was that "action develops under great stress."[23] Negro life has always developed in a crucible. The third, and final, Harvard speech was an intensely personal speech. Although it alternated between romanticism and realism, it conveyed an intense search by Malcolm X for a humane view toward whites. But Malcolm X played the sweet clown one moment and the bitter clown the very next.

A dispute was going on in Malcolm X's mind about "the existence of a moral order in a cruel and irrational world." The dispute went on in Shakespeare's *Troilus and Cressida*. As Kott suggested, "Hamlet, the Prince of Denmark, [had] faced the same trial."[24] Ironically, Malcolm X used the example of Hamlet in the third speech to symbolize the dispute within him and to justify his call for violence. For Malcolm X, Hamlet was a simple, violent fellow. Hamlet had a right to murder because he had been wronged. "There was another man back in history," Malcolm X began, obviously comparing himself, "whom I read about once, an old friend of mine whose name was Hamlet, who confronted, in a sense, the same thing our people are confronting in America."[25] Hamlet was debating whether he could be himself, Malcolm X argued. Locating himself in the medieval world, Malcolm X claimed that an obvious strategy lay before the Negro and before him. "As long as you sit around suffering the slings and arrows and are afraid to use some slings and arrows yourself, you'll continue to suffer."[26] Malcolm X's Hamlet was also Shakespeare's Prince, a man of high birth, someone betwixt and between things; a dramatic character who was the stuff of heroics and tragedy. Ossie Davis, in Malcolm X's eulogy, called Malcolm X the Negro people's Black Prince. So the world of Malcolm X and the world of Hamlet were similar to Davis at least. But, as Kott suggests, Hamlet can be interpreted in a number of ways. At first, we must not be bothered by the juxtaposition of the medieval and modern world by Ossie Davis—or by Malcolm X for that matter. It does not matter. It does not matter for Malcolm X. What matters was that a Negro man was trapped in exile in the ghetto. Hamlet said Denmark was a prison. He was in exile in his own country, in his own castle. Malcolm X said America was a prison. He was in exile in his own country, and was suffering because of it. What a fate for Malcolm X. He had nearly found his way through the jungle only to find himself trapped again. Besides, he was alone for the first time in his public career. When Malcolm X came to the second Harvard speech he was surrounded by six Negro guards. When he came to the third and final Harvard speech he came alone.

Malcolm X's Hamlet was a moralist and an intellectual and a philosopher, as he was. "The moralist," Kott contended, was "unable to draw a clear-cut line between good and evil. . . . The intellectual [was] unable to find sufficient reason for action: [and to] the philosopher, the world's existence was a matter of doubt. 'To be' means for [Hamlet] to revenge his father and to assassinate the King; while 'not to be' means—to give up the fight."[27] The Negro hustler was distinguished by his capacity to act; to steal or to murder. The Black Muslim minister was distinguished by his ability to find a sufficient reason for action, for giving the Negro folk an ethic, whether it was of hate or of pride. Malcolm X, the man, in the end was not distinguished by anything at all, except, perhaps, by "finding himself in a compulsory situation, a situation he [did] not want but which [had] been thrust upon him. He [was] looking for inner freedom, and did not want to commit himself."[28] But Malcolm X continued his round of speaking engagements after the third Harvard speech. He accepted the choice imposed on him, "but only in the sphere of action."[29] Kott sums up the last few days of Malcolm X's life: He was committed in what he did, not in what he thought. Malcolm X was inwardly starved. "We should take political action," Malcolm X said, "for the good of human beings; [and action] that will eliminate the injustices."[30] The formulation did not have the old bite to it. Malcolm X sounded here very like a bland liberal, perhaps for the first time in his public career. In the end, it had all overwhelmed Malcolm X. He now stood between life and death, where few men stand to tell of it, and spoke to the society out of a frightening abyss. Malcolm X could not help complain of the burdens he had borne. Other men had spoken similar words.

. . . Had it pleased heaven
To try me with affliction, had they rained
All kinds of sores and shames on my bare head,
Steeped me in poverty to the very lips,
Given to captivity me and my utmost hopes,
I should have found in some place of my soul
A drop of patience. But, alas, to make me

The fixed figure for the time of scorn
To point his slow unmoving finger at.
Yet could I bear that too; well, very well.
(OTHELLO, IV, 2)

* * *

. . . 'Tis not so now.
. . . When we shall meet at compt,
This look of thine will hurl my soul from heaven,
And friends will snatch at it. . . .
O cursed, cursed slave! whip me, ye devils
From the possession of this heavenly sight!
Blow me about in winds! roast me in sulfur!
Wash me in steep-down gulfs of liquid fire!
(OTHELLO, V, 2)

Malcolm X had also fixed his eyes on the slave period and identified, for the first time here, the cruelest kind of white man in
history. Again he was in the midst of powerful beasts. No region
of his mind seemed free of the memory of slavery.

. . . How could they make us slaves?
They had to do the same thing to us that
we do to a horse. When you take a horse out
of the wilds, you don't just jump on him
and ride him, or put a bit in his mouth
and use him to plow with. No, you've got
to break him in first. Once you break
him in, then you can ride him. Now the
man who rides him is not the man who breaks
him in. It takes a different type of man
to break him in than it takes to ride him.
It takes a cruel man to break him in, a
mean man, a heartless man, a man with
no feelings.

. . . If you find the role that that
slave maker played, I'm telling you, you'll
find it hard to forget and forgive, you'll
find it hard.[31]

Yet, Malcolm X bore it all reasonably well for all that, for all that. But most of what he drew from Negro history and American society were archaic and cruel ideas, useless things to calm a raging race war. The Negro did wish to be stirred up by a vigorous and courageous voice. But being a practical people, he also valued a good sense of direction. The Negro also wished desperately for a full racial pride. This was the only relevant legacy left by Malcolm X. But paradox appeared even here. Malcolm X left the Negro not only racial pride, but a certain arrogance that has now become the façade of an essentially rhetorical black nationalism.

NOTES

1 Malcolm X, *The Harvard Forum of March 24, 1961.*
2 Jan Kott, *Shakespeare Our Contemporary* (Anchor Books Edition, 1966), p. 82.
3 *Ibid.,* p. 141.
4 Malcolm X, *The Harvard Forum of March 24, 1961.*
5 Jan Kott, *Shakespeare Our Contemporary,* p. 142.
6 *Ibid.,* p. 143.
7 Ronald Sullivan, "Racism Linked to 'Spineless Leaders,'" Statement attributed to Mayor Thomas J. Whelan of Jersey City, New Jersey. A speech before the 71st annual convention of the New Jersey Patrolmen's Benevolent Association. Cf. text of speech, p. 7. The quotation is completed thus: ". . . The degenerate things who hide in darkened windows and shoot down police and firemen will be rewarded and encouraged to shoot and loot again." *The New York Times* (Early City Edition, September 27, 1967). Mr. Sullivan was kind enough to discuss this speech with me.
8 John P. Carr, "D'Ortona Urges Hiring of 1000 New Policemen." City Council President Paul D'Ortona commenting on the North Philadelphia Riot of August 28, 29, 1967. *The Philadelphia Inquirer* (September 1, 1964), pp. 1, 3.
9 Jan Kott, *Shakespeare Our Contemporary,* p. 146.
10 Samuel Beckett, "Act Without Words I," *Krapp's Last Tape and Other Dramatic Pieces* (First European Edition, 1960), p. 132.
11 Malcolm X, *The Harvard Forum of March 24, 1961.*
12 *Ibid.*
13 Jan Kott, *Shakespeare Our Contemporary,* p. 114.

14 Anna Bontemps and Jack Conroy, *Anyplace But Here* (New York, 1966), p. 242.
15 Malcolm X, *The Harvard Forum of March 18, 1964.*
16 *Ibid.*
17 *Ibid.*
18 *Ibid.*
19 *Ibid.*
20 *Ibid.*
21 Martin Kilson, "On Black Power," unpublished essay (fall, 1967), p. 8.
22 *Ibid.*, p. 9.
23 Jan Kott, *Shakespeare Our Contemporary*, p. 77.
24 *Ibid.*, p. 77.
25 Malcolm X, *The Harvard Forum of December 16, 1964.*
26 *Ibid.*
27 Jan Kott, *Shakespeare Our Contemporary*, p. 62.
28 *Ibid.*, p. 62.
29 *Ibid.*, p. 69.
30 Malcolm X, *The Harvard Forum of December 16, 1964.*
31 Malcolm X, "Malcolm X on Afro-American History," *International Socialist Review* (March–April, 1967), p. 33.

Parke G. Burgess

CHAPTER 18
The Rhetoric of Black Power:
A Moral Demand?

"Black Power" has displaced "Freedom Now" as the most significant symbol of the civil rights movement. "Freedom Now" was
a challenge directed primarily at the South; "Black Power" challenges the culture at large, more particularly in the North. The
rhetoric of Black Power is a response to a long history of communications between white and black in American culture—finally
putting Negro citizens unmistakably on the offensive, stating their
claims as citizens and human beings. This change of strategy,
however, may be shocking to a large number of Americans accus-

From *The Quarterly Journal of Speech*, Vol. LIV (April 1968), pp. 122–
133. Reprinted by permission of The Speech Communication Association
and the author.

tomed to seeing the Negro on the defensive. The nonviolent rhetoric of Freedom Now continued this trend while the rhetoric of Black Power clearly reverses it. Thus, many if not most Americans find this new rhetoric abhorrent. They do not like being told, especially by Negroes, that their culture is wrong. As the current retort has it: "This time, they've gone too far!"

Neither the culture at large nor its leadership takes pains to distinguish sharply between the violence of deeds and the violence of words. If the one is threatening and therefore to be discredited and ultimately suppressed, then so is the other. The growing tendency of the culture to respond in this way to the rhetoric of Black Power could spell tragedy for Negro and culture alike. For both now seem bent upon a collision course. If the collision course is to be altered or reversed, then the civic culture may have to alter its strategy so that both parties to the conflict may undertake a different level of talk and action. Essential to such a change, however, is an alternative interpretation of the rhetoric of Black Power.

The apparent necessity for the culture at large and its leadership to answer this rhetoric threat for threat and rejection for rejection, whether in word or deed, hardens responses to the rhetoric of Black Power. This necessity may, however, be only apparent. Perhaps Black Power advocates actually do intend to "burn the culture down," to employ the idiom of H. Rap Brown, or to persuade others to do so. The leadership of the culture need not respond in kind, when to do so serves to assign this extreme meaning to the rhetoric of Black Power. By the same token, the President of the United States need not have labeled extreme Black Power advocates "poisonous propagandists."[1] Norman Cousins need not have responded in kind with a harsh editorial entitled "Black Racism" in *Saturday Review* later in the same month; he took pains to call Black Power advocates "violence-prone extremists" and "dangerous fools."[2] If the culture and its leadership choose to respond as if illegitimately attacked, they thereby solidify this particular interpretation of the rhetoric of Black Power as the ground for a battle on the public stage.

The rhetoric of Black Power may be interpreted in another way, however. Perhaps these militant Negro advocates utter not a call to arms but a call for justice, a call uttered outside law and order because they see no recourse within the institutions that prescribe what law and order actually mean for many Negro citizens. The rhetoric of Black Power may be the only strategic choice they have. Nevertheless, behind all the sound and fury of this rhetoric may lie the intention merely to force upon the culture a moral decision.

When the culture does decide to respond one way rather than the other, it will choose the strategy most suitable to its character as a democratic culture. No one, least of all the opponents, will consider an alternative interpretation, however, until convinced that an undesirable collision is all but inevitable without a change of course. Nor will anyone be convinced of this grave risk unless he first understands the major forces comprising the culture situation from which the conflict emerges, nor until he also understands how the rhetoric of Black Power necessarily causes the conflict to reach crisis proportions the moment it enters upon the public stage. Without the Black Power advocate the clear and present danger would not exist, yet the central issue of the crisis exists whether he proclaims it or not. Examination of the trends of the conflict will reveal why he apparently *must* proclaim it; this is the first task. Examination of the crisis will reveal what happens when he *does* proclaim it; this is the second task. The final task is to offer a reinterpretation of the rhetoric of Black Power as the basis for a solution that may reverse the collision course and allow the democratic culture to be true to itself.

The three forces most directly responsible for the civil rights crisis are: the issue at the heart of the crisis, the traditional strategy of the culture as applied to this particular crisis, and the strategy of the Negro advocate. All of these forces emanate from the political context which accords each its respective nature and power. Riots, demonstrations, and volatile talk occur in all countries. In the United States, however, these indicators of crisis have a special meaning because of the democratic culture. The three major forces shaping the crisis can be understood only after a brief digression into the fundamental nature of the democratic civic culture, its traditional profession of faith, its institutional commitments, and its understandable preference for consensus rather than conflict.

In a brilliant study of comparative democratic politics, Almond and Verba point out that a democratic civic culture functions efficiently only when relatively free from divisive conflict and strife.[3] Intense and persisting dissension over substantive issues on a culture-wide scale can be mortal. Consequently, citizens of the democratic culture tend to remain uninvolved in the decision-making process during stable periods, and, although always potentially active, they tend to become actively involved only when their interests are threatened. The tension between involvement and noninvolvement underlying normal operations of the civic culture allows its institutions to work with relative efficiency in practice, while restrained from excesses by an ideal of potential activism and involvement.

When a crisis such as the present one arises, however, the balance of tension between activity and passivity is affected. Activism heightens the conflict and a breakdown of efficient operations may threaten the normal functioning of the civic culture. Under such circumstances, the leadership and the culture at large will seek to redress the balance as quickly as possible and at minimal cost to the healthy functioning of the culture. The normal balance will be restored by satisfying the demands of those most active or by compromise. When compromise is impossible, however, and demands are not satisfied, activity may become so intense and widespread that virtually no one remains passive. In this extreme, the crisis can provoke violence, even civil war, not an unknown occurrence in American experience.

While over-activity is a sign of crisis in a democratic culture, an abundant source of crisis is the necessary tension between freedom and order. The democratic civic culture professes a fundamental moral commitment to the freedom of self-determination (liberty, equality before the law, equality of opportunity) without which it is not democratic. Yet the culture is also committed to the processes, procedures, and institutions that protect this ideal and actually permit its realization in everyday life; it is committed to "business as usual." The civic culture must maintain a balance between these two commitments—freedom and order—since a marked imbalance toward one would threaten the other, as occurs in anarchy (freedom without order) and tyranny (order without freedom). Therefore, a threat to either commitment can induce a crisis, as an attempt to restore the customary balance.

A peculiar tendency apparent in American political tradition poses dangers when crises occur; for the culture may then pay a price for its enthusiasm for consensus and tranquility. The critical balance between freedom and order, between activity and passivity appears weighted clearly in the direction of order and passivity even in normal, stable times. The basic freedoms at the moral foundation of the culture are themselves actually realized for most citizens within the institutions and processes by which "business as usual" is conducted; they become submerged there, and they are unconsciously identified with the system itself. As Louis Hartz indicates, a nation "born free" has little need to make an issue of freedom;[4] consequently, citizens can afford to forget about freedom during daily operations of the culture. This imbalance of tensions is preferred also because most citizens have benefitted greatly from "business as usual": "They never had it so good!" As a result, they have an understandable commitment to order over freedom, and they may easily lose sight of the dependence of the system of order itself upon the democratic commitment to freedom as well as to order.

In normal times, any threat to individual freedom and activity is usually removed by traditional processes and procedures, and no crisis arises. Even in times of war, the external threat to the civic culture as a whole is believed to be so great that only extreme libertarians worry about the limits placed upon freedom, and again crises are normally avoided. "Business as usual" functions efficiently throughout the culture when the threat to freedom is relatively localized or when it is aimed at the survival of the culture itself. However, when the threat is no longer localized and does not yet endanger the survival of the culture as a whole, the potential for internal crisis arises. The civil rights conflict is a classic, if not historic, case. A minority suffers restriction of freedom and becomes excessively active in order to counteract the complacency, or even the aggressive opposition, of those citizens who may feel that freedom of other citizens is expendable. A crisis may be about to be born.

The movement of the culture in relation to such crisis should be clear and understandable. The strategy that is natural and traditional to the democratic civic culture emerges, by extension, when a widespread and intense crisis threatens to upset the preferred balance of tensions. The culture at large and its leadership, in particular, tend to insist upon an increased emphasis on order and passivity so as to restrict freedom and activity and consequently to return to the required state of equilibrium and tranquility. Having no other option in the face of what may be or may become a threat to its existence, the civic culture necessarily utilizes its traditional strategy to suppress the threat. Yet it may be unable to exercise this option against such a threat without also threatening its character as a democratic culture.

From the point of view of many Negro citizens, the character of the civic culture may be precisely what is at stake in the civil rights crisis. These citizens appear to seek what they have not been given, what they cannot actually take, and yet what the democratic culture, being democratic, cannot in good faith deny them: self-determination as citizens and human beings. Negroes do not ask that the basic system be altered or that something new be added to it: they cannot be identified, on this issue, with the far left or the far right. Negro citizens are in dead-center. Thus, the substantive issue dividing them from the culture at large is its denial of their right to self-determination. To resolve the issue, the culture need only reverse its denial. The issue remains unresolved, however, and worse, the crisis appears to intensify despite recent progress in civil rights reform.

How can this be? There is no controversy about the inconsistency in affirming the democratic commitment while denying its full application to Negroes, nor about the necessity to reverse this denial if the culture is to be true to itself. Why, then, does the culture not do in its many public acts what it has recently and repeatedly admitted in its public rhetoric that it must do? This is a question that long perplexed traditional civil rights advocates and framed the rationale for the rhetoric of Freedom Now, with its moral and legal emphasis upon the democratic commitment.

The inescapable conclusion is that the issue actually does not lie in the *fact* of the denial but in the *reason* for the denial. Since nearly everyone admits that the denial is morally illegitimate, then the continued denial appears to suggest that the culture does not wish to be true to itself. Yet, since the denial is not generally and systematically applied to any other group as it is to Negroes, then it is not a widespread denial of the democratic commitment itself, but only a denial of its application to Negro citizens.

Why the special treatment? The reason for the denial is revealed to be racist, and the true issue of the crisis becomes the racist moral issue. Both appear to posit the uniqueness of the Negro citizen as justification for denying him the right to self-determination. Is this justification legitimate? It is sometimes legitimate for the democratic culture to affirm its commitment to freedom and yet to deny freedom to individuals when the denial is justified, for example, with regard to aliens and some criminals; such individuals are not "citizens." However, since Negroes must certainly be considered "citizens," then the only ground on which the denial could be based is that these "citizens" are Negroes. The denial is racist and its justification is therefore illegitimate.

The core of the moral issue, then, is not the substantive and legalistic issue of self-determination for Negro citizens, nor even the moral fact of the culture's denial, but rather the racist issue that divides the culture at large from its Negro citizens. The expression of the issue in terms of self-determination and civil rights correctly denotes its substantive content in relation to the democratic tradition of civil culture, and thereby suggests steps to be taken to correct the denial once the culture decides to move fully in that direction. To express the issue in racist moral terms, however, denotes that the culture may not yet have decided to move fully in that direction, on racist grounds.

No other explanation of the conflict appears to reveal why the civic culture has moved so slowly to reverse its denial to Negro citizens, nor why the crisis harbors such intensity of feeling and divisiveness of purpose. Thus, the moral issue of race may be considered the engine that drives culture and Negro advocate alike to a choice of strategy that is likely to result in collision course.

During the earlier, civil rights stage of the conflict, the dominant leadership of the culture showed an awareness, as it still does, of the substantive moral contradiction and of the necessity to remove it. The leadership and many citizens consequently realized their responsibility to redress the imbalance of tension between order and freedom and to move in the direction of greater freedom and equality for Negroes. Seen as a civil rights crisis of relatively limited proportions, a proportionately limited application of traditional strategy appeared effectively to maintain the normal balance of tensions. It did so, however, at cost to some citizens and institutions (primarily in the South) and at the cost of limited gains for Negro citizens. These limited gains were consistent with the limited strategy and aims of traditional civil rights advocates and the limited willingness of citizens and institutions to respond to their strategy and to the strategy of the culture. One cannot deny, however, that the strategies of the Negro advocate and the civic culture worked more or less in harmony to achieve gains, however limited, under the aegis of the civil rights movement.

A shift in the issue can bring only a shift in the use and effectiveness of traditional strategy. Once Negro advocates move from the courts, the city halls, and other sanctioned centers of decision into the streets, or, with fiery words, upon the public platform, the response of the culture at large and of its leadership also shifts. The threat posed is perceived by the culture to be out of all proportion to the issue of the crisis, when the culture and its leadership are either unable or unwilling to recognize that the issue has shifted from civil rights to race. Thus, the culture may fail to realize that its traditional strategy, so recently effective, now becomes paradoxically ineffective.

The need to apply the strategy in a form less in harmony with Negro demands now increases and yet makes its application self-defeating, as more and more citizens and institutions become active. Citizens with racist inclinations who are especially threatened by the new turn of events will seek to employ the strategy to promote whatever policy or action is likely to minimize the threat to themselves. They will utilize any part of the system of order that tends, by tradition, to be racist in its structure or composition. They will press their denial of self-determination for Negro citizens on pragmatic rather than on moral grounds, unless they can find moral grounds having no obvious relationship to racism. They have nothing to lose and perhaps everything to gain by translating a personal threat to themselves into a crisis perceived by other citizens as a threat to the culture at large. The culture responds, in turn, with insistence upon order; it becomes overly acquiescent to "white backlash"; it moves forthrightly to resolve a crisis provoked by racism in the first place.

Greatly aggravated by the issue and, indirectly, by its effects upon incipiently racist citizens, the entire culture becomes more and more embroiled. Strong pressures within the culture to correct the denial of self-determination to Negro citizens give way to overriding pressure to redress the new imbalance of tensions. The national leadership in politics and other areas of decision hardens its attitude. This very result was most noticeable, for instance, after the riots of 1967. Even highly respected Negro civil rights leaders, to say nothing of nearly all other leaders, had to disown Black Power "extremists" and, of course, had to reject rioting in no uncertain terms, insisting with the rest of the leadership upon a return to law and order. Such reactions are not completely unjustified under the circumstances, but they can only postpone meeting the justified moral demands of Negro citizens. More important, however, the crisis appears more intense and widespread than ever, affected more positively by changes of season than by application of traditional strategy.

The racist, moral issue also creates a strategic paradox for the Negro advocate because of his peculiar relation to the culture as he advances his claim for self-determination. He does not advance it as worker, Democrat, intellectual, baseball player, or musician, but simply as a Negro. He cannot "pass" for anything else, being substantively a marked man. To the extent he is seen by others essentially as a Negro, he cannot be seen as are other citizens within the civic culture, as citizens "without respect to race, creed, or national origin."

It is quite normal for an advocate in the midst of crisis to be identified with his cause and to suffer the consequences, for good or ill. Yet he is rarely so completely identified with his cause that he cannot rise above it or leave it behind him and "return to private life." The situation of the Negro advocate is quite different and perhaps painfully abnormal. He does not suffer the consequences by reason of his identification wtih his cause but by reason of the fact that his cause is himself. He cannot simply leave his cause and "return to private life," since even when he returns he remains identified as a Negro.

The paradox he faces applies also to his relation to the claim he advances. The denial of the right to self-determination applies to him no matter what he attempts to *do* (it is the "door to other doors") and *because* of what he *is*. Unable to dodge the fact that he is essentially a Negro, he can hardly avoid the conclusion that must confront him regarding his advocacy: The right he demands is one he must be given in order to "belong" to the culture at all, and he can be given it *only as a Negro*.

When considered in the light of the issue of the crisis and of the strategy employed by the culture to resolve it, the strategic paradox of the Negro advocate becomes clear. His only available strategic alternative is to advance his claim in the way least likely to win acceptance in a culture apparently "designed" to suppress precisely the kind of conflict this crisis and his advocacy are designed to produce. Being unable to avoid the racist implications of his advocacy, he can neither withdraw nor succeed. Here may lie the tragic irony of the rhetoric of Black Power and its potential meaning to the culture at large. The unavoidable issue in the crisis demands unavoidably that the Negro advocate press that issue, even in the face of violence.

Analysis of the historical and cultural situation reveals that the stage is set for the rhetoric of Black Power to make its entrance and to tip the balance in the direction of a collision course. This rhetoric forces the issue and creates the strategic paradox for advocate and culture alike. No rhetoric could be more provocative in teasing out the inner logic of the moral crisis and the culture's strategy to resolve it. The reason is simple. The rhetoric of Black Power is framed as if it were aimed precisely at these ends; it is a direct response to the civic culture. Yet this particular way of responding is historically inconceivable without the movement that preceded it, for the rhetoric of Black Power is also an answer to the rhetoric of Freedom Now.

The civil rights movement has addressed the traditional rhetoric of the civic culture. Despite some progress before 1954 (in the armed forces, for example), and despite increasing interest and support by many white citizens since then, the culture at large has continued to say *No* to its Negro citizens in many systematic ways. The movement sought to change this response. In the early 1960's it scored some success under the banner of Freedom Now with its "non-violent" demonstrations and compelling moral tone. The culture's answer to this plea was complex and ambiguous. In the South it answered *Yes*, but perhaps only because to answer *No* to Martin Luther King would clearly have been to answer *Yes* to George Wallace and Paul Johnson. And who is to say that the violent reactions of some Southerners did not actually command stage-center? For example, President Johnson's "historic" Voting Rights Speech of 1965 came only after the tragedy of Selma. The rhetoric of Freedom Now was never persuasive in the North, where even Martin Luther King was stopped by "the white power structure," most notably in Chicago. Freedom Now appealed to the clear-cut legal issues in the South which were easily accommodated by "business as usual." Confronted by the more subtle machinations of the culture at large, this rhetoric seemed to get a response to which Negro citizens had long been accustomed: promises, delays, and piecemeal tokens could only be taken now as an actual denial.

King has said, with some pain, that the very success of the rhetoric of Freedom Now, the "positive gains" it in part produced, only made matters worse.[5] This rhetoric was most effective in raising the hopes and expectations of Negro citizens. When hopes and expectations were not realized, however, they seemed cynically to produce worse conditions, especially in Northern ghettos.

Tempers were thereby sensitized for a new level of talk that could not be dodged, talk that would demand rather than plead, that would insist that the civic culture honor its commitment to Negro citizens—or else. The ground was laid for the militant rhetoric of Black Power, a rhetoric that voiced its demand on a tonal scale somewhere between Martin Luther King and Malcolm X. It had learned its lessons from both men, in a school built by the culture itself.

The rhetoric of Black Power acknowledges what King's rhetoric did not. Unlike King's rhetoric, Black Power denies that a moral plea to the democratic conscience would gain a commensurate moral response. Except in the South, King was wrong. The rhetoric of Black Power reveals that King's strategy, although logically correct, was rhetorically inadequate. Logically speaking, a clearly moral issue demands a clearly moral strategy in keeping with the democratic traditions of the civic culture. Since discrimination is itself contrary to those traditions, the logical result of those traditions, the logical result of this strategy, its ultimate moral demand, would be integration as the true measure of equality and freedom. What Black Power advocates have realized (due in part to King's experience) are the rhetorical realities that made the strategy inadequate. King missed the gravity of the tension within the American tradition, exacerbated by his own efforts, between "business as usual" and the commitment to self-determination. By attempting to operate within that tradition, moreover, he necessarily underemphasized the uniqueness of the Negro, as a Negro, within the same tradition; he ignored the specifically racial conflict, the racist core of the moral crisis.

The rhetoric of Black Power is more perceptive and "corrects" both errors. It acknowledges, first, that America actually has no moral conscience in the face of a threat to its "traditions," which means that only power can meet entrenched power, racist or not. It acknowledges, secondly, that the culture now confronts the Negro not as a human being or citizen-minus-rights, but as a Negro who is not yet regarded by the culture as a citizen or a human being *because* he is a Negro. This rhetoric brings to the surface and loudly proclaims what heretofore had been fearfully hidden and yet silently worked its effects. It loudly confronts the racist moral conflict.

The answer to white power is Black Power—to white racism, black racism. But this usage of the term "black racism" must be clearly distinguished from its earlier usage by some American Negro citizens. The Black Power movement has its roots in a racist perception of cultural reality no less than the Black Muslim movement, for example. Yet "Black Power" is not merely a concept which reflects these realities nor a rallying symbol addressed to Negroes alone in order to unite them; if it were merely these, this movement would be indistinguishable from that of the Black Muslims. Unlike the idiom of the Black Muslims, however, the rhetoric of Black Power is significantly addressing the civic culture no less than Freedom Now did. It speaks directly to that culture, "courting" its acceptance; it does not withdraw into its own house, pulling down the blinds, absolutely refusing to communicate with the outside world, having "lost its suit." On the other hand, to continue the metaphor, it cannot in the nature of its case win acceptance by singing romantic songs and parading before the house of the beloved.

Black Power therefore signifies a rhetorical movement which seeks entrance into the hallowed and rich house of the American culture, *but on its own terms and by means which the culture understands and accepts*. It is ironic indeed that its terms are identical with those of the American promise (self-determination with no strings attached), and perhaps still more ironic that the means it employs, including the whole strategy of black racism, so precisely portray the means used against the Negro citizen, then and now. In these facts lie the tragic justice and sadness of the rhetoric of Black Power.

The powerful logic of this rhetoric originates from a white racist culture and is apparently forced upon black citizens against their deepest desires and better judgment by the naked and subtle power of that culture. Its adoption represents a last-ditch effort by these citizens to wrest final affirmation from generations of denial. The poignant irony of this rhetoric is revealed in the different ways it seems to stand the logic of the civic culture on its own head, taking its racist attitudes with deadly seriousness.

Contradicting its democratic, procedural ideal, the civic culture regards the Negro citizen not for what he can *do,* but for what he *is,* regardless of what he can do. He is regarded as substance. The rhetoric of Black Power begins from this historic fact and *responds* as substance. Regarding the Negro citizen essentially for his difference as substance, the culture segregates him on this basis, drawing procedural and organizational lines about him—lines he can seldom cross. The separatist rhetoric of Black Power accepts this language and *responds* as substance thus segregated. Having effectually prevented his access to the procedural pursuit of happiness on substantive grounds, America yet goads the Negro citizen in countless ways to get his, as everyone else gets theirs. Again taking America to mean what it says, Black Power demands for the Negro what he has been promised and threatens to get it by the only means America has left it—"by any means necessary." Especially trying to some Negroes, and clearly one of the tragedies of the ghetto riots, is this reduction of the American promise and the Negro answer to such crass, materialistic terms. It is as if Black Power advocates had once again captured and turned against itself one of the truisms of the civic culture—the democratic commitment to self-determination becomes an acquisitive and materialistic commitment to self-interest.

This is the ruthless but nevertheless valid logic of Black Power advocates. Its naked clarity and brutal honesty put the civic culture in an unenviable position. Like the honest parent caught stealing from his child's piggy bank, what does he do when the child calls him a liar and throws the bank through the nearest picture window out of disappointment and anger? The normal response is to focus upon the bad name and the broken glass and not upon the tragedy of the unjust act that may have caused both reactions. The normal response is to redress the balance by resorting to "business as usual" now clearly divorced from its moral foundation.

This response means to Negro advocates the use of traditional methods of establishing order and equilibrium, including force. It means "positive gains" only when there is token resistance against them, or, contrary to the rhetoric of the culture, when Negro demands for their achievement are violent in the extreme. Traditional strategy is interpreted as an essentially white racist response to Negro demands and thus provokes an increased hardening of a black racist response on the part of Negro citizens. The rhetoric of militant racism becomes more justified than ever.

Charging that the culture is racist and that it is moved by nothing but sheer power, the culture responds accordingly. As Norman Cousins observes, "When Negroes act like Ku Klux Klanners, they must be treated like Ku Klux Klanners."[6] Racism and power become the idiom of battle on both sides. Whatever the vocabulary of the culture may be, it is likely to be pregnant with the undertones and overtones of power, of force, of violence. And the intended target will be clear enough and often justifiable. As this response to the crisis intensifies, the full effect will be for the culture to consider Black Power advocacy in all its forms as violent, reprehensible, and un-American, and for Negroes to consider responses to it is but further evidence of the racist attitudes and rhetoric of the civic culture.

Such is the collision course predetermined by the paradoxical logic of both sides. By its own terms, this logic denies alternative interpretation and response. It would appear also to have inevitable and unavoidably harmful consequences for the civic culture: Citizens who fear increased violence and even incipient revolution may have good reason for their fears. To avoid these consequences would demand a change in course derived from a new strategy having a different logic. It would demand a reinterpretation of the rhetoric of Black Power and a commensurate response on the part of the culture at large and its Negro citizens.

The dialectic of racism and power can be transcended only by refusal to respond to the rhetoric of Black Power as if it were a call to battle. The civic culture can respond instead at a level more in keeping with the moral nature of the crisis. It can respond as if this rhetoric were a call for a just moral decision. Such a response appears neither artificial nor utopian; it may be more realistic than the present one and is certainly more just. The rapier-like logic of the rhetoric of Black Power and the elementary justice that beckons from beneath it leave no doubt that the men who talk this way mean what they say and that their appeal will probably convert an increasing number of Negro citizens in the future, for the appeal is largely to Negroes of the same mind who share the tragic lack of alternative. Beneath the call to arms may be a cry for justice and community, as beneath the anger may be disappointment and disillusion. The dominant leadership and particularly the mass media of the culture can respond to what lies beneath and cease to respond to what shouts on the surface.

This new response to the rhetoric of Black Power would require two admissions on the part of the culture and its leadership. Both would admit that the immoral racist denial constitutes the core of the present crisis. Both would admit that this denial offers adequate moral justification for the rhetoric of Black Power. These admissions would require, as a result, that the civic culture return unequivocally to its moral foundation as a democratic culture and meet there, at its own roots, the source of this crisis. In this way, the language of racism and power would be transcended through translation into the nonracist language of the democratic commitment. Such a shift in basic interpretation would call for a marked shift in strategy, and would portend different consequences for the civic culture and for its Negro citizens.

The civic culture would then repudiate traditional strategy in response to just Negro demands. The paradoxical effect of that strategy is that its movement toward order and away from freedom, as against Negro citizens, can only further exacerbate the crisis it seeks to forestall. Moreover, the trend of that strategy is typically to encourage greater and greater separation of institutional response from the democratic base of the civic culture. A strategy of moral commitment would reverse the trend; for the function of the new strategy would be to infuse institutional responses with the moral quality appropriate to them as institutions within the democratic culture.

By adopting the strategy of moral commitment the civic culture would acknowledge that racism of any kind is clearly immoral and therefore not to be recognized as grounds for behavior or policy. It can only do this if it accepts the black racist contention regarding the presence of, and absolute lack of moral justification for, white racism in the culture itself. The refusal to tolerate a racist justification would not be a refusal to admit its existence. On the contrary, the language of democratic morality could assert its power and its relevance exactly here: Standing firmly on moral grounds as the traditional strategy seldom can, it could be unequivocal in its demand of all citizens precisely at those points where its traditional form equivocates in the interest of "business as usual."

Further consequences would, of course, ensue. Application of the new strategy would initially intensify the crisis and not quickly resolve it. To admit and unequivocally to confront the presence of white racism within the culture would be to oppose a real force that cannot be ignored or averted. Citizens with this cultural malady will indeed have cause for alarm. They can be expected to continue to move for order and to intensify the crisis, but with a fervor magnified to meet what would be for the first time, an open assault upon them by the civic culture. Another consequence of repudiating traditional strategy in order to arrest tensions would result in the civic culture recalling that strategy, as it were, but in a significantly different way. The culture must maintain itself and it can do so only by pressing for order and passivity over freedom and activity. The significant difference of this re-application of old strategy would be its different target. The price to be exacted as a result of the application of institutional power and consequent loss of freedom would be paid by those who truly cause the racist crisis in the first place, and not by those whose civil rights and freedom have been unjustly withheld.

Yet even white racists might then expect better treatment under a strategy of moral commitment than Negro citizens often receive at present, especially with regard to violence. Under present strat-egy, the leadership of the culture often appears open to the charge that it considers violent acts of Negroes to be particularly repre-hensible and therefore demanding excessively punitive suppres-sion. Insofar as spokesmen of the new strategy sense the serious democratic commitment at stake in the racial crisis, however, any citizens continuing to respond violently in word or deed are more likely to be considered as misguided citizens, whatever their race, than as mere objects of ruthless "justice." The distinction is im-portant, for it entails a mood and a manner more suitable to the democratic tradition and certainly more conducive to minimal conflict at a time when punitive action may be required.

Fully implemented, the new strategy would unequivocally com-mit the culture at large to the democratic goals formerly sought by the civil rights movement and by black separatist citizens not widely represented within that movement. It would eliminate the need for the movement to advance minority claims against the balance of the civic culture. It also would eliminate the *raison d'être* of black separatists, including Black Power advocates. But the goal imposed upon the vast majority of citizens by the strategy of democratic commitment would be neither integration nor con-formity to white demands. The goal would be self-determination for Negro citizens, consistent with the cultural realities that actu-ally confront them.

A reinterpretation of the volatile rhetoric of Black Power may offer the democratic culture a strategic alternative to violent con-frontation and therefore a more desirable way to resolve the present crisis. If interpreted as calling America to its moral self, then this rhetoric forces upon America the acknowledgment that a racist moral conflict lies at the core of the crisis. The old rhetoric of "business as usual" loses its credibility. The new rhetoric of democratic commitment arises to meet the rhetoric of violence that must be repudiated and transcended so that the culture can be true to itself and to all of its citizens. From the irony of this tragedy, the culture may derive historic opportunity.

NOTES

1 *Time*, XC (September 22, 1967), 23.

2 Norman Cousins, "Black Racism," *Saturday Review* (September 27, 1967), 34.

3 Gabriel A. Almond and Sidney Verba, *The Civic Culture: Political Attitudes and Democracy in Five Countries* (Boston, 1965), Chapter XIII, especially pp. 344–356. Only the notion of balance between activity and passivity is taken directly from their study, which would consider the balance between freedom and order a function of several factors.

4 Louis Hartz, *The Liberal Tradition in America* (New York, 1955), Chapter II, *passim*.

5 Andrew Kopkind, "Soul Power," *The New York Review of Books*, Vol. IX, No. 3, 3. A review of King's book, *Where Do We Go From Here: Chaos* [*sic*] *or Community?*

6 Cousins, "Black Racism," p. 34.

Richard B. Gregg

A. Jackson McCormack

Douglas J. Pedersen

CHAPTER 19
The Rhetoric of Black Power:
A Street-Level Interpretation

"Black Power" is one of the most potent rhetorical phrases of our time. It implies more than it clarifies, and it gathers meaning from a social scene that discourages neutrality in thought and language. In the context of black demands, ghetto disorders, and numerous acts of passion and violence, the phrase easily assumes a variety of menacing connotations. It is what Kenneth Boulding calls a

From *The Quarterly Journal of Speech*, Vol. LV, No. 2 (April 1969), pp. 151–160. Reprinted by permission of The Speech Communication Association and the authors. Richard B. Gregg is Associate Professor, A. Jackson McCormack Lecturer, and Douglas J. Pedersen Instructor, all in the Department of Speech, Pennsylvania State University.

"powerful symbol," because it "condenses an enormous mass of information and experience in a single bit—there or not there, for me or against me, right or wrong."[1]

"Black Power" is a phrase ready-made for the mass media to conjure with, and a good deal of conjuring has been done.[2] The dramatic, sometimes inflammatory words of Eldridge Cleaver, Stokely Carmichael, Rap Brown, and other so-called militant black leaders are lifted from context to become dramatic headlines. The majority of American citizens must rely on second- or third-hand impressions conveyed by the media for their interpretation of the rhetoric of black power. White society generally feels threatened by the implications of the slogan, disappointed by the apparent reverse racism, and puzzled by the black man's sudden spurning of help from white society. Above all, white society is uncertain about how to respond to this latest thrust of black rhetoric. Effective response to the people of the hard-core black ghetto depends on an adequate understanding of the rhetoric of black power. The rhetoric reflects the contemporary situation as the black man perceives it, and the black man's actions, like the behaviors of us all, are decisively influenced by his perceptions.

An abundance of literature written or edited by blacks presents and elucidates the black power thesis and rationale.[3] The purpose of this paper is to provide some examples and interpretations of the rhetoric of black power based on observations made while conducting a class in oral communication in the Harrisburg ghetto.[4] The rhetorical statements and behaviors we shall discuss were not solicited by us but occurred within four contexts, not always mutually exclusive: (1) as a part of the communicative interaction between black students and white teachers during class time; (2) as part of the lectures on black history delivered by a local black leader, selected by the class to conduct the history sessions; (3) as part of the communicative interaction among the students; and (4) as part of an extended interview granted to a local radio reporter and later broadcast by a number of Pennsylvania radio stations during the spring of 1968.

1

The rhetoric of black power is essentially a call for the black man to rediscover himself as a substantial human being. Its primary themes center around black pride, black cohesiveness, and the need for political and economic power. These three themes illustrate the exhortative appeals of the rhetoric of black power. One strong element of appeal has to do with the development of a black mystique, a faith in the transcendent virtue and power of black identification, and a reordering of the black man's perceptual world so that "black" is a positive value to be sought after rather than spurned. A second element of appeal focuses on the more practical business of organizing the black community for the purposes of electing blacks to political office, boycotting businesses that practice segregation, and supporting black-owned and black-operated establishments of all kinds.

In the Harrisburg ghetto black leaders emphasized that practical power was dependent on and subordinate to self-discovery and identification. Self-identification necessarily involved participation in the new black mystique, and initiation into the black mystique required an understanding of the black man's historical and cultural roots. Therefore our students talked constantly about the need to "know" themselves in order to be men and escape from white subjugation. As one of the young men in the class phrased it, "For a man to be a man, he must make an effort hisself to find hisself and be hisself and not keep on being a nigger with his hand out, dependent on somebody else all the time."[5]

The students talked with an Office of Economic Opportunity employee who agreed to teach black history during regular class sessions. He was tall, muscular, very black, always composed, and was eulogized by various class members as "having himself all together." The class gave him their attention and respect, and he proved to be the most charismatic black leader we encountered. His history lectures were representative of all he said throughout the ten-week term.

The history teacher typically reminded his listeners of the significance of the movement awakening in black neighborhoods all across the country: "What we're witnessing today is the resurrection of the dead. Black people have been dead for four hundred years. They haven't known themselves; have hated themselves. They thought the only road to freedom was through assimilation into the white culture. But black people today are saying what your pioneers said—we'll build our own—create our own."[6] He introduced the subject of history by emphasizing that self-knowledge and an understanding of one's cultural heritage would result in freedom and power. His proof was historical example:

Ethiopia lasted for five thousand years. It is the oldest civilization known to man. It was only conquered once. Ethiopia was only conquered once and this was by the Italians in 1936 by using poison gas. . . . How did she retain her culture for over five thousand years? . . . It's because she had the knowledge of herself. Because she knew her history and she knew her heritage and because they were free people. They were free people mentally and you couldn't enslave them. The only thing you could do was kill them and then you freed them even more by doing that. So what I'm trying to say is, we're talking in terms of revolution, of black revolution in this country. It must first be a thing where black people begin to know who they are.

Each history session was prefaced with remarks of this nature which served to focus the listener's attention on the main theme to be developed: "Self-discovery and knowledge is the essential ingredient for psychological emancipation and freedom." The idea is simply stated but springs from a complicated and sophisticated understanding of human nature in general and the specific perceptual world of the black man in particular. A person cannot be self-reliant unless he knows what his strengths and weaknesses are and has the confidence to initiate action and withstand the inevitable trials and tensions that are a part of all human activity. The black man's long historical subjugation in the role of second-class citizen has taken heavy toll.[7] Black leaders clearly realize that ghetto conditions are not conducive to self-awareness and pride, particularly for the young male, and they are pressing hard to overcome negative self-concepts formed by years of deprivation. Black history provides a logical starting point for self-discovery and a new identity. Consequently, local black leaders operated on a premise stated by Ernst Cassirer: "What we seek in history is not the knowledge of an external thing but a knowledge of ourselves."[8]

The "resurrection of the dead," as the teacher of black history phrased it, begins with an understanding of the way history is written: "All history is slanted according to the culture which produces it." For examples of cultural bias the teacher referred to the religious paintings by Da Vinci and Michelangelo that pictured the Christ figure as a white man. Only one person in those paintings was portrayed as a black man, he said, "And that was Judas!" The class enjoyed the example and snickered. The black teacher turned quickly to the white man's understanding of Africa, " 'Darkest Africa,' 'Black Africa,' like black as a cat, or black Monday. They see black as bad," he reiterated, "because they are white and want to see it that way."

Introductory remarks such as these focused the students' perception both affectively and intellectually. To be free, the black man had to turn to introspection, find his individual self in the roots of ancient black cultures, exorcise the white man's degrading history, gain a black perspective on the world from which he came, and redefine his contemporary situation. The black teacher was now ready to "run it down."

"Those who teach you to hate yourself," he said, "they are your enemy. But remember now, we're not talking about hate, we're talking about loving black." Next the teacher turned to a swift kaleidoscopic discussion of ancient black cultures: "Ancient Egypt, black Egypt, the cradle of civilization," "Ethiopia—land of the burnt faces, ruler for years over Egypt," "The Zulu warriors, most feared by all the tribes." Remarks about the ancient cultures were not extensive. Complete historical explication was not the order of the day, but the students must understand that black people could not be relegated to the status of savages, that black cultures were sometimes superior to white cultures, and that black cultural achievements in all categories had equalled those of whites.

Next the black teacher shifted from black culture to black historical figures: "Moses was a black man—that's right, brother, a black man who led the black Jews out of Egypt." "The original concept of God was introduced by Nefertiti." "In Carthage, in North Africa, Hannibal was a black man, black as the brother's jacket there, and he took a fleet of elephants over the Alps and defeated the Romans." "Did you know that Washington, D.C., our nation's capital, was planned and laid out by Benjamin Banneker, a black man? ['I didn't learn that in school!'] They won't teach it to you in school, brother—we got to learn it on our own and pass it on."

The data introduced by the black history teacher to this point served as specific pieces in the building of a new black self-image. He did not imply that black students should try to emulate the cultural patterns of the past, but recognize the quality of the heritage that *is* a part of contemporary black society. The necessary elements of a viable black culture had been suppressed by colonial domination, and the black man was led to believe that they never existed. He was expected to accept the role allocated him by white society: "That's what integration is all about, brother. That's what integration as the white liberal uses the term is all about. We haven't been 'emasculated' yet [the vocal emphasis implied that 'emasculated' was white terminology and inappropriate], but if we keep shufflin' up, saying 'yassuh, boss' to the white man, allowing him to divide us, to buy off our leaders, we won't have anything to be proud of. We're talking about survival, about the need for revolution, a revolution in your mind." The words are words of exhortation, but the delivery was low-keyed and reasoned in tone. Audience response was equally low-keyed and serious.

The mood shifted, the time for fun was at hand, and it came at the expense of white mythology. The black teacher indicated the shift by a suddenly relaxed bearing, a twinkle in his eye, and a grin at the corners of his mouth. The Tarzan epic became the first vehicle for debunking the white man's perceptions:

Let's take Tarzan. Tarzan [chuckle]. Dropped out of an airplane when he was a baby and landed on his head in the jungle. Can you imagine that, brothers? [Laughter.] The only people living in the jungle, of course, are black savages. Black savages and animals. But the savages are so bad, so wild, so inferior, that Tarzan is raised by the apes! Hear that. The apes! [More Laughter.] Tarzan grows up and is so strong that when he says "oom gawa" the lions run, the elephants dance away, snakes climb the highest magnolia bush, trees shiver, and black men scatter like flies.

Now I want you to know, I have searched, I have read many books, I have looked through *Encyclopedia Afrikaner*, I have met many brothers from all over Africa, met scholars, and I'm here to tell you there is no such word as "oom gawa"!

The conclusion of the narrative brought gales of laughter, hand-clapping, and foot-pounding; the tension that had accumulated during the early part of the lecture dissipated completely. The Tarzan episode was an effective piece of rhetoric, presented so that language, tone, and gesture combined to emphasize the improbable and ludicrous nature of the story. The episode served as a metaphorical instrument, at once unmasking false pretensions to white superiority and by implication erasing the stereotype of the savage black African. One student exclaimed, "Just think. I used to go to those movies and cheer for Tarzan! Brother, I just didn't know!"

The El Cid narrative was also done with great relish and humor. It was as metaphorical as the Tarzan episode and served the same purpose, except that it emphasized the awesomeness of blackness:

We've all heard about El Cid, better known as Charlton Heston [the black teacher chuckled]. El Cid, a real together cat from Europe who decided he would drive the Moors back to Africa. He got himself 100,000 warriors to do the job—the Moors had 15,000 men.

Get the picture now. The valley. El Cid and his 100,000 warriors on top looking down. The Moors in the valley, dressed in African clothing, in white, with large swords which whistled as they whirled them over their heads. Swords so strong that when they came down they went through man, shield, and horse [class laughter]. Contrary to what you may have heard, El Cid took a look at those Moors and died of a heart attack [more laughter].

The El Cid narrative was pregnant with symbolism. The scene is permeated with the violence of military clash and racial conflict. El Cid made the initial decision to press the conflict. The Moors were trapped in a valley, with El Cid's superior force enjoying the military advantage of controlling the heights. Yet El Cid is vanquished quickly, without armed conflict, and his demise augers the symbolic downfall of all he stands for.

One can, without great imagination replace the Moors and El Cid with the generic concepts "Black Men" and "White Men." White society with its wealth and authority commands the heights. White society, afraid of black power and black freedom, presses the engagement and thinks of suppression, by force if necessary. "Law and order" becomes a convenient rhetorical cover for the impulse to put the black man down and keep him down. The situation, laced with the threat of violent confrontation, forces the black man to think of violent means of self-defense.[9]

The denouement of the El Cid narrative, however, revealed the black teacher's idealized hope for the eventual outcome of the struggle. With proper spirit, strength in cohesiveness, and the correct weapons, the black man could claim a psychological victory that would improve the black condition. What was the "weapon" to be? Did the notion of weaponry imply inevitable armed revolution in the streets?

Anybody that's going to jeopardize your life and the life of your babies and your mothers and your daughters and your wives by running out there with a little Molotov cocktail against the 82nd Airborne Infantry division is crazy and a fool. . . .
  We're talking about black people getting together and creating themselves a real program for survival. . . . When you start talking to the brothers about a real program, you know, when you start talking to the brothers about opening up cultural centers, man, where we can sell our disekis [African shirt-like garments], when you talk about delivering black history to the masses, then they say, "Aw, man, like, you know, that's not where it's at." But that is where it's at.

After you burn it down, brother, where are you going? If you don't have anything to replace it?

What is the answer? What will the weapon be? The black teacher indicated that it would be the practical business of organizing communities, voting for black interest, controlling black affairs. The practical theme of the rhetoric of black power came to the fore:

Now, will you look at your community? Who controls the economy of that community? Do you? You don't control the economy of that community. So you got to develop a program to put the economy of that community under your hands by developing and buying from your own. Who controls the politics of our community? Who are our ward leaders? And if our ward leader is one of us, who controls him? You don't control him. You got to control the politics of your community. Who tells you what type of entertainment to have in your community? Who sets up the criteria, the financial criteria?

The black teacher felt the need for proof when he turned to the matter of practicality. He built his argument by recalling the deeds and words of black leaders, both past and present:

Years ago, in the Southland, which was an agricultural land, the economy was dying. Then a man, small in stature, but large in intellect, took a little peanut and saved the south.

Booker T., in his Atlanta Compromise speech, said we could be one nation but separate. He said, "Don't ask the white men for anything, get a trade and go back to the farms and get your own thing together." For many years I said, "Oh, this cat is a Tom." But he wasn't a Tom. What he was talking about, brother, was building your own.

In 1918, Marcus Garvey had a movement. He created his own business, had his own church, his movement swept across this country. He had a unified program. We haven't got a unified program now, brothers.

Malcolm X, one of the greatest black men who has ever lived, he brought a program of freedom to the black man. The same program Martin Luther King brings.

Several times the black teacher juxtaposed the program and teaching of Martin Luther King with someone generally believed to be more militant, such as Malcolm X or Stokely Carmichael.

Whenever he did so, his words were accompanied by the dramatic gesture of holding up one hand to signify King, the other hand to signify the more militant party, then bringing the two hands together, clasping them in symbolic unification. Authoritative argument served two purposes. The black teacher called upon the rhetorical words and postures of recognized black leaders to bolster his assertion that a program of black power meant black initiative in the black community. At the same time, concerned about divisiveness in the black community, he brought leaders of varying outlooks together under the same tent: "All of our leaders have a program for helping black people. Why should we fight each other? We need to drop such labels as 'militant,' 'revolutionary,' 'Uncle Tom.' Those are white man's terms, the terms of the mass media. We must not let the mass media label us. We must pull together to build a new nation."

At the end of every history lesson, the black teacher would issue the call for black fellowship, black self-identification, black identification through group unity, black control of black communities, and black initiative for community improvement. The themes of black mystique and practical community effort came together in peroration to present the essence of black power.

2

How is one to interpret the nature and function of the local rhetoric of the black man?

Well, you come up to my street and I'll show you all how the garbage piles up and everything. Our neighborhood is the last one to get garbage pick-up and they only get around here when they feel like it. Let a little snow fall, or a little rain develop, and the trucks will go to the white community, but they may not get here for weeks.

. . . and when we ask them to tear down all them rat-infested, condemned houses, what did they tell us? They tell us, "Don't try to rush us into anything . . . we got to get a bid on it." The mayor's been promising and promising month after month and year after year and if we go back and tell him the same damn thing they put a article in the paper saying, "We gonna do this here and we gonna do that there."

They put it back in the obituary columns, like they did when three colored boys got stabbed up at MacDonalds, you didn't hear much about that. But when the white boy got stabbed up at the place they put it on the front page . . . opened it up that he was such a good little boy. Like a young priest. A regular Eagle Scout. Belonged to this and that, officer in this here and that there. A perfect angel. But come to find out, he drinks wine. He runs around with wine-heads. He was a gang leader. In fact, he got in trouble that night for some of his friends. That's what it's like. I'm through with it.[10]

Conversations such as these indicate that substandard conditions demanding a change were clear to all. Nearly all the students contributed grievances from personal experiences and observations. Furthermore, the grievances were always specific when the discussion turned to a serious consideration of community problems.

Much frustration in the black community required justification and direction. The need to erase the black man's perception of himself as an inferior being, an image perpetrated and sustained by the white community, was particularly urgent. Equally important, those initiated into the black movement had to understand that they could not build self-pride by prolonging the kind of paternalistic relationship encouraged by the white liberal community. Continuing to ask for and accepting the white man's favors would keep the black man in psychological, if not actual, subjugation, for the black man would never discover his own capabilities or those of his community. The new image had to promote confidence and independence; it was of necessity a "non-white" image.

The rhetorical message contained in the history lessons was not developed as an argument, but more closely resembled exhortation as Edwin Black describes the genre.[11] The rhetorical function was not one of leading to judgment, but was concerned with creating a new frame of reference and imposing a new set of perceptions and values. The data *per se* of the historical accounting were not of ultimate importance, but the symbolic interpretation was crucial. The heart of the message was not, "Here is the way you can be." Rather it was, "Here is the way you are. You have accepted white perception for so long that you believe you are incapable. But your heritage asserts the opposite. Once you discover what you are, you can, as black men, achieve what you want." By the fifth week of the term, the students gave every evidence of having assimilated the message: "Well, the particular problems in this city is, number one, inferior education; number two, unemployment; number three, depleted housing—which are the main problems that exist in this city. Now in order for you to get these things I think the most important thing that should be brought out is in the field of history. Because once a child, a black child, has an identity and can associate himself with someone and something of the past then this child can become beneficial to mankind."[12]

The manner in which the young men and women in the class internalized and repeated black power themes leads us to conclude that the rhetoric of the current black movement is a kind of parareligious catechism, to be believed because "it is so." The rhetoric attacking and condemning white society was redundant, and encomiums to blackness were often delivered as a litany. At times, students turned directly to us with accusations of deceit and evil intentions. But shortly after such diatribes someone in the class would admonish us to "cool it, man; we weren't talking about you." At first we were puzzled by the apparent contradictions in the situation. Then we began to understand what was happening. The student's rhetorical exercises were "proofs" to each other that they were worthy of participation in the black fellowship. Demonstrated belief in the positive qualities of blackness was essential to membership in the fellowship. For students in the Harrisburg class symbolic identification with black was made easier by the presence of white teachers because they had something specific to polarize against. But, except for those occasions when our white responses or intentions were being tested, the primary audience was perceived to be black peers. We were white and not eligible for baptism into the black movement. Any attempt on our part to join with or respond to the black catechism was irrelevant.

Implications of our local experience may apply to the current societal black confrontation. White society will influence the behavior of blacks partly through the way it chooses to respond to the rhetoric of black power. The major problem now facing white society appears to be knowing when and how to respond. At this moment, the society at large chooses to believe that it is being addressed directly by black power spokesmen and responses are shaped accordingly. Apparent elements of threat in the rhetoric of black power leads to the reactionary arming and training of troops to quell expected riots. Such response, like the international arms race, will inevitably increase tensions as blacks reciprocate in kind in the face of what appears to them to be a threat to their very existence.

A second category of response, suggested by Parke Burgess, is certainly more sensible and humane. Burgess recommends that white society interpret the confrontation within the framework of morality, admitting racism to be the primary issue involved. This painful admission would lead to a new rhetoric of democratic commitment which would permeate the basic institutions of American culture and so transcend the need for violence.[13] Without denigrating the notion that white society ought to examine its moral stance carefully, our experience leads us to question Burgess' assumption that the rhetoric of black power is significantly addressing white culture in the same way that "Freedom Now" did. The rhetoric we heard in the ghetto, in the streets, in the midst of a predominantly black environment, leads us to believe that the black power message is intended for black people; the new black sorioreligious movement is restricted to black people; black power rhetoric is aimed primarily at the salvation of black souls and the creation of a black kingdom. The white audience is irrelevant to the primary intent of black power advocates. Even when black power spokesmen may be overheard by white audiences, their message is intended for black people. The idea that the rhetoric of black power addresses white society is a perception founded, not unreasonably, on a strong belief in white responsibility for the plight of the black man. Burgess' suggestion has appeal because white society is morally involved and because we consider ourselves capable of acting on the basis of moral judgments. History indicates, however, that our culture's moral character, so far as the self-determination of nonwhite minority groups is concerned, is an unfulfilled potential. Black power advocates who now represent the leadership factions most influential with black youth, significantly, no longer believe in the essential morality of the culture at large: "The civil rights bill was passed back in 1870 or something, and they say 'laws take time.' Well, how long does the white population in this country need? I mean they say 'equality' and 'democracy.' They preach democracy and the black man practices it. Example: Anyone can come live in the black ghetto—anyone—Puerto Rican, Jew, Italian, anyone. But can't anyone go live in the white community."[14]

None of this means that black power adherents refuse to talk to the culture at large. The black youth we met were willing, even eager, to "tell it like it is" in very specific terms. They talked to white authorities about the necessity for teaching black history in the schools, putting a halt to police brutality in the ghetto, obtaining better garbage pick-up, improving housing and employment opportunities, and the like. But their inherent pessimism concerning the attitudes and behavior of white culture did not dissipate. Whitey would throw a sop from time to time, particularly when he felt threatened by imminent disorder, but when he could safely ignore black people he would do so. In the long run, the rebuilding of black communities would have to be undertaken by black people. As members of the Harrisburg class would say, "Whitey is irredeemable. Don't waste time trying to talk to him. Let's get our own scene going and do our own thing. Let civil rights leaders [a pejorative expression when used by members of this group] talk to the man like they've been doing without success for 410 years; let's us talk to our brothers and sisters."[15]

Regardless of white society's ability to respond morally, those committed to the efficacy of black power do not believe in the possibility of such response. The black man sees the creation of job opportunities in the summer as an attempt to reduce the possibility of riot. When the season changes the black brothers will be the first men laid off. Whitey preaches equal opportunity but carefully controls promotion policies so that black people do not achieve positions of prominence. Those blacks fortunate enough to move into middle-class society either sell their souls and leave their brothers behind or have been duped by Whitey and carefully removed from influential positions in the black community.

Most integration policy is perceived to be, intentionally or unintentionally, part of the larger scheme to maintain white supremacy. Integration schemes are perceived to be harmful in their very conception for they are based on the spirit of "what we can, or ought to, do for them." Thus white culture dispenses what favors it wishes, black culture is placed in the position of receiving gratefully, and the essential relationship of black man to white man remains unchanged. For the black man who believes in the tenets of black power, the premise that a meaningful black-white relationship can be constructed on a foundation of morality is a myth to be discarded. "We view this as a myth because we believe that political relations are based on self-interest; benefits to be gained and losses to be avoided."[16] Consequently a white rhetoric of reconciliation will face very hard going indeed. But the idea of self-interest contained in the above statement opens a new possibility for response to black rhetoric.

3

One of the troublesome connotations of black power rhetoric is its apparent reverse racism which exalts blackness and seems to call for some kind of separation of the races. Apartheid is not a concept easily accepted by a democratic society. Although some black spokesmen have called for the creation of a separate black nation, white society has probably once again overreacted to black rhetoric. In many ways, black power spokesmen are being extremely realistic when they call for black control of school boards, housing projects, political leaders, and private enterprise ventures in black neighborhoods. Black identity and acceptance will ultimately depend on the efforts of black men who will create their own culture, their own reason for being, and their own contributions to humanity. Their hope is that white society, acting from a selfish instinct for self-preservation and personal gain, will allow black men to run their own affairs, refrain from meddling in black affairs, and ultimately accept black contributions because they benefit all of human existence. In many cases white society, with its wealth, channels of power, and technological and managerial know-how will be able to play a helpful role, though not as the Great Emancipator some people might envision. What the black power advocate calls for is the creation of a black culture within the larger white culture.

Therefore, the most useful rhetoric in the years ahead will be a rhetoric of coexistence: "Coexistence primarily calls for maximum feasible participation by blacktown, minimum participation by whitetown. Let blacks do it themselves. Let them choose their own leaders. Don't try to run things. Stay away until you are invited, and go away when you have provided whatever it is that you can offer blacktown. Don't offer advice unless you are asked for it. Push neither strings nor friendship at blacktown: it is suspicious of both. Trust young people, for the rising generation is blacktown's saving remnant."[17]

Coexistence calls for a new beginning in black-white relations. It will demand that white society refrain from reacting in kind to the rhetoric of the black man, who is intent on calling his brothers to rally to the objectives of black culture. A new rhetoric must be initiated based on the kind of self-interest that leads to mutual welfare ending ultimately in mutual respect.

NOTES

1 Kenneth Boulding, *Conflict and Defense* (New York, 1962), p. 281.
2 For a general discussion of media coverage, see *Report of the National Advisory Commission on Civil Disorders* (New York, 1968), pp. 362–386. For more specific discussion, see Robert L. Scott and Wayne Brockriede, "Hubert Humphrey Faces the 'Black Power' Issue," *Speaker and Gavel*, IV (November 1966), 11–17 and Wayne E. Brockriede and Robert L. Scott, "Stokely Carmichael: Two Speeches on Black Power," *Central States Speech Journal*, XIX (Spring 1968), 3–13.
3 See, for example, *The Black Power Revolt*, ed. Floyd B. Barbour (Boston,

1968) ; *Malcolm X. Speaks*, ed. George Breitman (New York, 1965) ; Stokely Carmichael and Charles V. Hamilton, *Black Power* (New York, 1967) ; *Is Anybody Listening to Black America?* ed. C. Eric Lincoln (New York, 1968) ; and Nathan Wright, Jr., *Black Power and Urban Unrest* (New York, 1967).

4 The class was composed of some forty black youths, ages 17 to 24. The background, nature, and development of the course is described in Richard B. Gregg and A. Jackson McCormack, " 'Whitey' Goes to the Ghetto: A Personal Chronicle of a Communication Experience with Black Youth," *Today's Speech*, XVI, No. 3, 25–30. A more comprehensive interpretation is provided in A. Jackson McCormack, "Some Aspects of Communicative Behaviors Toward White Persons of a Group of Young Leaders in a Black Ghetto: A Case Study" (unpublished M.A. thesis, Pennsylvania State University, 1968).

5 Most of the statements that appear in the paper are taken from tapes gathered for the radio interviewer, or from tapes of class activity recorded by one of the students.

6 Remarks from class lecture taped by one of the students. The quotations that follow, unless otherwise noted, are taken from the same tape.

7 For a listing of studies reporting the black man's negative self-evaluations as a result of his perceptions of white estimations of him, see Thomas F. Pettigrew, *A Profile of the Negro American* (Princeton, N.J., 1964), pp. 5 and 8, and Kenneth B. Clark, *Dark Ghetto* (New York, 1965), pp. 63ff.

8 Ernst Cassirer, *An Essay on Man* (New Haven, 1962, paperback edition), p. 203.

9 Robert L. Scott explores this aspect of the rhetoric of black power in "Justifying Violence—the Rhetoric of Militant Black Power," *Central States Speech Journal*, XIX (Summer 1968), 96–104. Our experience corroborates Scott's conclusions.

10 Conversation taken from taped radio show aired in April 1968.

11 The authors are indebted to Edwin Black's discussion of the nature of exhortation for their understanding of this aspect of black rhetoric. See his *Rhetorical Criticism* (New York, 1965), pp. 138–147.

12 Remarks taped for radio show.

13 Parke G. Burgess, "The Rhetoric of Black Power: A Moral Demand?" *QJS*, LIV (April 1968), 122–133.

14 Remarks taped for radio show.

15 Remarks made during a class session, tape-recorded by one of the students.

16 Carmichael and Hamilton, p. 75.

17 W. H. Ferry, "Blacktown and Whitetown: The Case for a New Federalism," *Saturday Review*, LI (June 15, 1968), 15.

Arthur L. Smith

CHAPTER 20
The Frames
of Black Protest Speaking

A few years ago Erwin Bettinghaus perceptively wrote that "when audiences of particular ethnic characteristics are exposed to messages, their responses will be determined in part by the characteristic experiences which they share with other members of the group and for which they have developed particular frames of references."[1] Just as ethnic audiences are victims of a certain determinism produced by their common experiences, the black protest speaker is also ruled by the circumstances of his environ-

This paper was originally presented at the Western Speech Association Convention, Portland, Oregon, November 1970. Printed by permission of the author.

ment. He shares the same rhetorical constellation as black audiences, because he must fashion his arguments from materials within a given context in order to be persuasive to them. When faced with white audiences, the context becomes even more limited, as there are rhetorical materials—linguistic, argumentative, and persuasive—that cannot be used for white audiences.

The position taken in this paper is that the black protest speaker, or writer, is in the employ of a determinism defined by the possibilities and complexities of social protest within a larger society, and further constricted by the peculiarity of the black experience. As a protest speaker he is met with limitations placed upon all protest speakers, but because he is black, a further constraint, based upon sociohistorical factors, exists. What he chooses as a speaker—in fact, what is available—is limited, and making do or creating with the strategies and alternatives prescribed by the American social condition is the real challenge to the black protest speaker. This, then, is fundamentally a question of rhetorical invention, because it deals with the coming to be of the novel. And too, the frame of reference for the new, the innovative, as it is created or discovered, comes from black life-styles. Invention must proceed from the available, and the black protester seeking to secure warrantable assent displays his creativity within the limitation of the possible resources. For the speaker, human creature that he is, creation is dependent upon the available, and the resourceful speaker first gathers materials that are close to him.[2] At this point, if we are to make more sense out of this problem, what we need to discuss is the relationship of the available resources to the proposed *invented thing*. That the *invented thing* comes to be because of the resources, and the resources determine what kinds of things will come into being, should be self-evident. While avoiding a detailed classificatory scheme (and, it is hoped, fragmentation), it is possible to speak of general bodies of materials that are indispensable to the speaker: uses and usages of words, prevailing behaviors, and hearerships. Theoretically all the words in the world are available for the speaker who can choose among them as they are needed; in reality, however, no speaker has actual access to all the uses and usages of all the possible words. An American speaker, black or white, will certainly not choose to speak to his American audiences in Yoruba or German unless there are special demands for the occasion; and even so, he might be limited by his knowledge of the language. Therefore the speaker will make use of those words that are accessible to him and to the majority of his audiences.

Prevailing behaviors refer to those characteristic rhetor actions (physical and verbal) of a certain culture, perhaps even defined by the rhetoricians of that cultural era. Some gestures, mannerisms, and language usages are satisfactorily employed, and are in vogue at one time and place and not at another. Mass media has made the prevailing behaviors culturally available to most rhetors. While attempts have been made by theorists and critics to explain and define an acceptable behavior for contemporary society, it has been universalized by the instruments of dissemination. Thus all speakers have theoretical if not actual access to the prevailing behaviors of the culture. Even so, accessibility, theoretical or actual, has not meant acceptability for those who choose not to employ the prevailing behavior.

A final general category of resources are hearerships: collections or gatherings of persons who maintain, if only for the duration of the speech occasion, a special relationship with each other, if only the hearing of a speaker. This paper is not the place to explore the advantages of this concept over that of audience; suffice it to say that the concept *hearership* includes a horizontal as well as vertical relationship between hearer and speaker. Hearerships are available materials for the speaker because he chooses which audiences he will address. By addressing some at the expense of others he may significantly alter the outcome of the speech on himself as well as on others. Thus, choosing audiences is as creative a task as choosing what to say; and in persuasive cases the one is assisted by the other.[3]

What has been outlined above are categories not unique to black protest speakers, but common to all speakers, inasmuch as the use of words, prevailing behaviors, and hearerships are available to all speakers. However, *how* the speaker chooses and what he chooses are matters of *what* is possible for him to choose. Consequently there are some positions, tactics, and usages considered off limits by a black protest speaker that are not restrictive for other speakers, black or white. This is rather clear in terms of word usages. If we accept the fact that there is a limited amount of words in the American language, possible coinages and combinations notwithstanding, then the notion of a relatively fixed system is conceived. Within such a system the black protest speaker uses only a portion of the word resources available to all; he coins expressions, appeals to his environment for others, and creates combinations as he moves back and forth across code boundaries. His rhetorical actions are determined by situations both within and without his control. Some he can do something about; in others he is helpless. Insofar as political behavior is usually determined by the individual, the black protest speaker possesses power to change his politics; but insofar as race and color are beyond his control, he can do nothing. However, if he chooses to alter those situations that are within his power, he ceases to be effective as a spokesman.[4] The black protest speaker may be the Ethiopian who cannot change his color, but he can change the political behavior that limits the resources for speech-making. But in discontinuing agitation against the established social and political systems, he jeopardizes his own existence as a spokesman, and in some cases as an individual. The latter case is particularly true if the person sees commitment to a principle as his reason to agitate, and when to do otherwise would be a denial of his individuality.

While the black protest speaker is situated within the same time and space dimensions as other speakers and can make use of the available resources of words, behaviors, and hearerships, he is constrained in a unique manner by circumstances, audiences, and personal attributes. The distinctiveness of this restriction is the frame of black protest. It is clear that the speaker's conception of what his mission is and what materials are available for the accomplishment of that mission has a temporal and spatial orientation. In some senses the black protest speaker's manifestation of this distinctiveness is dependent upon his choice or creation of audiences. This takes into account the fact that some audiences are found and others are created. When a black protest speaker addresses white audiences, he is restricted by his audiences' sophistication (what they know about black language), his personal attributes, and the aims of the speech. This has nothing to do with the unavailability of words; they are available in theory but may be unknown to the speaker (part of his personal knowledge), or if known, incompatible with the aims of the speech, and for all functional reasons, off limits. Thus, the effect is the same, and the speaker remains confined to a limited context. It should be emphasized that the choice of protest limits the number of usable words, arguments, and strategies. Many aspects of this contextual limitation are related only to white audiences; others are more universally true and observable. The black protest speaker must make sure that all the entrances and exits are covered as he speaks to white audiences; there can be no reckless abandon in language behavior that will allow misinterpretations or misunderstandings. The black protest speaker holds his cards close to his chest when faced with white audiences.

Speaking before white audiences the rhetor is not prepared to use ethnic humor that is permitted with black audiences. The fact that comedians such as Flip Wilson and Dick Gregory use ethnic humor on the entertainment stage is acceptable because the stage is not considered in the context of protest. This is true despite the social commentary frequently present on the stage. But when separated from the nightclub stage, these acts become much more political and the black comedian assumes the assets and liabilities of the black protest speaker. Among black speakers and audiences there exists a fraternity of perspective making it easy for ethnic humor to flow uninhibited. The black comedian who dabbles too much in protest ceases to be humorous to his white audiences—witty perhaps, but not funny.

Another aspect of black protest before white audiences is that the speaker does not employ all of the characteristic tonal behavior observable when blacks speak with blacks, but rather adopts what might be considered his most white-oriented speech behavior.[5] Certainly, Martin Luther King's "Been to the Mountain Top" speech in a Memphis church was not his speech to the Harvard University Law School; the speeches were different in tone because the speaker invented them differently. Intonation and tonal styling are substantive parts of the black speaker's invention. Furthermore, to the extent the black protest speaker employs these characteristic linguistic behaviors, he is comfortable with his audience. This is not to say that he cannot be at ease with "straight lectures" before white audiences, but that he is more likely to use nuances and idiosyncrasies that are comfortably black only with black audiences. Therefore the black protest speaker trying to persuade white audiences of the need for a social transformation is simultaneously exhibiting a distrust of whites by refusing them access into the inner linguistic secrets. Even in the most intense debate over social change the black protest speaker does not share all of his characteristic tonal patterns with white audiences; in fact, his speech further suggests what is, of course, true—that blacks and whites have different patterns of experiences. Black protest, then, is framed by characteristic rhetorical and linguistic practices that are products of a special experience, environment, and heritage.

Among the more universal manifestations of the idea that black protest speakers consult unique contexts are the arguments invented to assault segregation, discrimination, and injustice in American society. What blacks argued a hundred years ago is still argued today. In 1843 Henry Highland Garnet noticed "The gross inconsistency of a people holding slaves, who had themselves 'ferried o'er the wave' for freedom's sake, was too apparent to be entirely overlooked."[6] Frederick Douglass emphasized the same theme in his famous Fourth of July speech in 1852, "Whether we turn to the declarations of the past, or to the professions of the present, the conduct of the nation seems equally hideous and revolting. America is false to the past, false to the present, and solemnly binds herself to be false to the future."[7] Such language is not foreign to the arguments of Stokely Carmichael, Eldridge Cleaver, or Bobby Seale. While there may have been a proprioceptive change as one aspect of the problem activated a new discussion, the intent and structure have remained constant. Attempts to provide rhetorical solutions to political problems have produced many duplications from one era to the next, and the operating space seems more confining than ever.

The black protest speaker can only define two fundamental alternatives, *integration* or *separation,* and every argument is ultimately made for one or the other of these ends. When a speaker has only two alternatives, his speeches usually exhibit dullness or imagination. The better speakers have shown good imaginations as they have organized and structured speeches from the available materials with an end toward either integration or separation.

In relation to the two political goals of black protest, one can suggest that the politics has alternated between *provincial* and *mass phenomenon;* the tactics of protest from *verbal* to *activist;* and the ideology from *religious* to *political.* What the speaker decides is his direction, and that choice determines the restrictions upon his invention. It is not always that a protest speaker is free to choose, but if he chooses the provincial phenomenon, then certain limitations are placed upon him. For instance, if he chooses provincial over mass political phenomena as a channel for his aims, the instruments of mass dissemination are not essential to his rhetorical effort. In addition, there are technical limitations on him because of his choice. In a mass situation he would need to make some general appeals in order to save the movement from collapsing of a narrow focus. On a specific neighborhood problem he could concentrate on some narrow goals and make some particular appeals.

It is further true that the black protest speaker chooses between governing principles—that is, whether his protest will ultimately rest on religious or political bases. After choosing a position, arguments are created or discovered that are compatible with his rhetorical purpose. H. Rap Brown could never use the language of Martin Luther King or vice versa, yet each could use similar rhetorical strategies against segregation and discrimination. Their specific differences were inherent in the choices of governing principles, not in the nature of the problem.

For the black protest speaker certain relations are predetermined by social, linguistic, and ideational factors; these adhere in particular to subject matters and/or situations. Some speech actions linguistically possible might prove nonsensical for the black speaker in a given context. The rhetor speaking against racial prejudice in housing in a mass situation with television cameras present *could* recite Robert Frost, but such action could also be considered nonsense. Certain values are indeed implicit in the circumstances.

The black protest speaker, given his "arena of assumptions," invents speeches from the present social reality—the black man's experience in America and the other possible resources. He must consider what uses can be made of the available words, what facts can be drawn from the prevailing behaviors and employed successfully, and how true are the relationships between his language and reality. The frame of black protest, then, is not an artificial structure but one that exists as a living entity, just as the conditions that provoke the coming to be of the novel are powerful realities.

NOTES

[1] Erwin Bettinghaus, *Persuasive Communication* (New York: Holt, Rinehart and Winston, 1968), p. 37.

[2] For traditional views on the speaker's method of gathering ideas and arguments, see Carl H. Weaver, *Speaking in Public* (New York: American Book Company, 1966); Virgil Baker and Ralph Eubanks, *Speech in Personal and Public Affairs* (New York: David McKay, 1965); Charles Lomas and Ralph Richardson, *Speech: Idea and Delivery* (Boston: Houghton Mifflin, 1963); and Donald Bryant and Karl Wallace, *The Fundamentals of Public Speaking* (New York: Appleton-Century-Crofts, 1960).

[3] The Wingspread and Pheasant Run rhetoricians attempted to deal with this idea in the Committee on Rhetorical Invention. Taking much of their

thought from Chaim Perlman and Richard McKeon they outlined the concept in their report which is be published in a forthcoming book to be edited by Edwin Black.

4 It could be argued that James Farmer, the former director of the Congress of Racial Equality, lost much of his leadership role in the black community when he assumed office in the Nixon Administration.

5 Henry Mitchell, *Black Preaching* (New York: J. B. Lippincott, 1970), pp. 162–164.

6 Floyd Barbour, ed., *The Black Power Revolt* (Boston: Sargent, 1968), p. 35.

7 Herbert J. Storing, ed., *What Country Have I?* (New York: Macmillan, 1970), p. 32.

PART 5
Social and Historical Dimensions

There can be no meaningful interpretation of language and communication in black America without an eye to social and historical dimensions. Rhetoric emerges from a social milieu, and what is present in the voice and style of the black speaker is historically linked with the experiences of the people. Thus, Arthur L. Smith begins this section with a look at some sociohistorical perspectives on black oratory. In a provocative essay Ulf Hannerz explores the concept of soul. In the third article LeRoi Jones (Imamu Baraka) explains what he calls expressive language. Charles U. Larson perceptively sees the trust-establish-

ing function of black power. In a fifth article Robert D. Brooks presents the results of a study he made in "Black Power; the Dimensions of a Slogan." Next Larry S. Richardson considers Stokely Carmichael as a jazz artist. And Romeo B. Garrett, working with limited resources, sketches the outline of African survivals in American culture.

In some pioneering work a few years ago, Melville Herskovits suggested historical dimensions to black American language. Herskovits was roundly attacked by anthropologists and sociologists, including the eminent black sociologist E. Franklin Frazier, for arguing that certain Afro-American language behaviors could be traced to Africa. In this section the authors have been concerned with the social and historical dimensions present in black communication.

Arthur L. Smith

CHAPTER 21
Socio-Historical Perspectives
of Black Oratory

The study of black oratory is intricately interwoven with the study of black history; a central aspect of black history is the persistent public discussions related to the black man's American experience. Having to defend his humanity, to agitate for minimal rights, and to soothe the raw emotions of his mistreated brethren, the black speaker was often forced to develop articulate and effective speech behavior on the platform. That a principal dimension of black history is encompassed by platform activities in the form

From *The Quarterly Journal of Speech*, Vol. LVI, No. 3 (October 1970), pp. 264–269. Reprinted by permission of The Speech Communication Association.

of lectures, sermons, and agitations stands without question from the scholar familiar with the black past.

Unable to read or write English and forbidden by law in most states to learn, the African in America early cultivated his natural fascination with *Nommo*, the word, and demonstrated a singular appreciation for the subtleties, pleasures, and potentials of the spoken word which has continued to enrich and embolden his history. Thus, in part because of strict antiliteracy laws during slavery, vocal communication became for a much greater proportion of blacks than whites the fundamental medium of communication.

The study of black speeches, then, emphatically imposes itself upon any true investigation into black history. Bringing with them to America a fertile oral tradition augmented by the pervasiveness of *Nommo*, the generating and sustaining powers of the spoken word, the Africans' use of the word permeated every department of life.[1] As in African society, so in early African communities in America, disorganized and frustrated by overlordships though they were, the word influenced all the activities of men, all movement in nature. Plantation slaves could look up at the firmament and reorder the stars or they could gather to sing (which is also encompassed in *Nommo*) away their "trials and tribulations."[2] Everything appears to have rested upon the life-giving power of the word, life, death, disease, health, and, as the career of Nat Turner demonstrates, even liberation. For the word could not be considered static; it was then and is now dynamic and generative. Actually this concept embodies the idea of incantation as transformation; vocal expression reigns supreme.

And it is within this context that the almost methodical pathos of Martin Luther King can be viewed alongside the mournful utterances of Ray Charles; the vocal expressions of both simply reflect different parts of the same fabric. Occasionally expression seems expertly planned to evoke responses much like a speaker might prepare certain persuasive arguments with an eye toward a special kind of reaction. At other times expression bursts forth as "hallelujah," "doing my thing," or the creation of a totally new sound.

The sound of words can often assume as much importance as presentation of arguments in this situation. Yet this phenomenon bears little if any relationship to the elocutionary emphases of some years ago. What is at play is far more significant than the proper or correct pronunciation of words or the right use of chirologia and chironomia; in most cases the speaker transforms his audience through the spontaneous exaggeration of sounds combined with the presentation of vital themes. This is in some ways analogous to the African view that the power of transformation can never be in things which depend on men to control them, but must reside in *Muntu*, human beings.[3] Argument, because it is formulated and arranged by men, has no power of itself except as it is expressed by men. As a fetish has no power of its own but can only be efficacious when the word is spoken, so the proper expression by the right man of an argument or song may bring results. In this sense, therefore, black gospel preachers and blues singers are sharing in the same experiential spontaneity when they rely on vocal creativity to transform the audience.

With an African heritage steeped in oral traditions and the acceptance of transforming vocal communication, the Afro-American developed a consummate skill in using language to produce alternate communication patterns to those employed in his American situation. These channels remained rhetorical, even as they consciously or subconsciously utilized linguistic changes for communicative effectiveness. During slavery communication between different ethnic and linguistic clans was difficult, but the almost universal African regard for the power of the spoken word contributed to the development of alternate communication patterns in the work songs, Black English, sermons, and the Spirituals with their dual meanings, one for the body and one for the soul. It is precisely the power of the word whether in music or in speeches in today's black society that authentically speaks of an African past.[4] Thus to omit black rhetoric as manifest in speeches and songs from any proper investigation of black history is to ignore the essential ingredient in the making of black drama.

Let us look at this more closely. To understand contemporary black rhetoric in America means that one must understand that *Nommo* continues to permeate black activities.[5] This is not to say that all black people or most blacks, given the situation, can immediately identify the transforming power of vocal expression. It is apparent when a black person says, "Man that cat can rap." Or one can identify it through the words of the sister leaving a black Baptist church, "I didn't understand all those words the preacher was using, but they sure sounded good." Inasmuch as the *Nommo* experience can be found in many aspects of black life, one can almost think of it as a way of life. Therefore, the scholar, be he rhetorician or historian, who undertakes an analysis of the black past without recognizing the significance of vocal expression as a transforming agent is treading on intellectual quicksand.

What is clear is that the black leaders who articulated and articulate the grievances felt by the masses have always understood the power of the word in the black community. Their emergence has always been predicated upon the power of the spoken word. Indeed it is extremely difficult to speak of black leaders without speaking of spokesmen in the elemental sense, who were vocally brilliant and could move audiences with sudden tears or quick smiles. It is no fluke of history that men of letters or organizational talents have seldom been acclaimed "black leaders," it is rather a fact intricately related to the eminence of the spoken word within the black community. The able historian Carter G. Woodson understood this most clearly as indicated in his 1925 work *Negro Orators and Their Orations.*[6] Other black historians have given more than passing attention to the influence of black orators on the black community. In books by Eppse, Quarles, Ferris, and many others, significant commentary is devoted to the oratorical gifts of many black leaders.[7] Discussing the history of black rhetoric becomes, therefore, for the serious scholar an attempt to interpret the preeminence of the spoken word in Afro-American life and thought.

The central fact of black history in America is slavery, which stands astride every meaningful rhetorical pathway like a giant

Colossus. That black speakers before and after the abolition of slavery are concerned with it is immensely important in the development of black eloquence. While the stated theme of a given speech may be white racism, black pride, freedom, crime, poverty, desegregation, poor housing conditions, and voting rights, the underlying issue to be dealt with is always the slavery experience. What shall be made of it? How shall we more adequately deal with the residual effects of slavery? And how can black people regain their preslavery, indeed, pre-American heritage? What is more demonstrative of a people's proud heritage than the pre-American values and attitudes of Africans? When the Yoruba, Fanti, Efik, Congo, Dahomeans, and Mandingo arrived in America they had no past of family instability, disrespect for elders, and juvenile delinquency. So when the contemporary warrior-orators express the belief that white racism has been the chief obstacle to black psychological and physical liberation they are speaking of the central position of slavery in the black man's history.

As slavery is the central fact of black history in America, so antislavery is the crucible of black rhetorical expression. Although there had been black protest, vocal and physical, to slavery, a steady stream of orators against slavery did not spring forth until the turn of the 19th century. The demand upon blacks to defend themselves as human beings while agitating for equal rights combined with the need to correct false and demeaning characterizations of Africans provided constant practice on the platform. Many of the leading speakers gravitated toward the seminaries, learning the rules of homiletics and exegesis.[8] Once out of school they often applied practical lessons in public speaking and analysis to their natural gifts and were soon on their way to becoming accomplished orators. Not a few black speakers learned the rudiments of the "proper rules" of rhetoric from seminary training; others learned from the Quaker abolitionists.

The first recorded black speeches in America dealt with the institution of slavery. Peter Williams, James Forten, Theodore Wright, and Prince Saunders used their rhetorical abilities to state black grievances and to chart future directions for the race.

In 1808 Peter Williams spoke on the "Abolition of the Slave Trade" and expressed hope that Africans would soon be free. But the slave trade continued beyond the constitutional deadline in many instances, like a runner past the designated finish line, and slavery draped its misery more completely over its African subjects. However, Williams' speech expressed the universal optimism of a people who knew that things had to get better because nothing was more horrible than slavery. Although black spokesmen have seldom been priests, they have often been prophets. Subsequent to Williams' 1808 address other black speakers spoke optimistically of deliverance in both a practical and a mystical sense. One might refer to this phenomenon as black messianism. Characterized by prophetic visions, it is often present in the rhetoric of oppressed people. The black orators voiced their opposition to the oppressing agent and simultaneously looked for some type of manifestation, either in person or process, capable of alleviating their suffering, thereby bringing in the millennium. In their speeches messianism was manifest on two levels: (1) black salvation and (2) world salvation. Many black orators saw the black "saints" liberating the world. The orators like the poets spoke of "strong men coming," but unlike the poets they were often the embodiment of their rhetoric, or at least they and others thought so.[9] When Marcus Garvey stormed out of the West Indies in the first quarter of the twentieth century with his doctrine of psychic and physical migration to Africa, he became the sum total of black salvation to millions.[10] In fact, the psychological implications of the cult orators are that they believe, and their votarists believe them to be, the fulfillment of the rhetoric. One thinks immediately of the language of Daddy Grace: "The Bible says you shall be saved by Grace, I'm Grace."

In such a psychological climate, the name "Moses" grew as important in Africans' minds as the person had been in Israel's eyes, and occupied the future of blacks as he had dominated the history of Jews. "Go down Moses, Way Down in Egypt's Land, Tell O' Pharaoh to Let My People Go," was symbolic of the Africans' hope. It was this kind of optimism that swept the blacks in the North on January 1, 1808, the day slave trading was to be abolished. While the Northern blacks leaped with joy, the Southern whites put sharper thorns under the feet of the slaves. Blacks who were not enslaved could see a new day dawning which had neither the blemish of the trade nor the spot of the institution in its horizon. And their speeches reflected this optimism, Williams says: "But let us no longer pursue a theme of boundless affliction. An enchanting sound now demands your attention. Hail! Hail! glorious day, whose resplendent rising disperseth the clouds which have hovered with destruction over the land of Africa, and illumines it by the most brilliant rays of future prosperity. Rejoice, oh! Africans! No longer shall tyranny, war and injustice, with irresistible sway, desolate your native country. Rejoice, my brethren, that the channels are obstructed through which slavery, and its direful concomitants, have entailed on the African race."[11] Such optimism is born of a people obsessed with the future, particularly when the past has been so terrible.

The antislavery speeches of blacks soon came to have a discernible structure. The rhetor spoke of slavery's history and horrors, eulogized white philanthropists, mostly Quakers, and appealed to God for deliverance. Every black orator knew the institution of slavery from beginning to end, this was necessary knowledge for his speeches. And many black speakers worked closely with white philanthropists and abolitionists and therefore could speak easily of white contributions. The radical Quakers who were often in the middle of public discussions on the issue of slavery endeared themselves to black orators. Their exploits became incentives for blacks reluctant to agitate for the liberation of their enslaved brethren. Actually tailored for the times, the speeches almost always ended with some method of *mythication*.[12] Invocations, poems, and religious expressions calling on God to intervene in one way or another were prevalent in the speeches of black antislavery orators. Thus the black antislavery speakers contributed to the heightening of contradictions within the pre-Civil War American society by their constant use of religious symbolism to express their position and their redefinition of cultural heroes by honoring white abolitionists.

After the Civil War, vocal expression did even more to mold the ideas of Afro-Americans who could now assemble with relative ease. Several capable speakers appeared between 1865 and 1920 with various proposals and programs for black salvation. But of the parade of "orators" who marched across the stage in full view of the destitute black masses, only Marcus Garvey possessed the necessary combination of force and form to electrify millions. His bombastic oratorical performances, played out with sensitive understanding of a cultural phenomenon, made him the most widely acclaimed black spokesman of any generation. From Garvey's time onward the texture of black oratory would simultaneously contain something of his political and social opinion as it possessed a portion of his cultural and ethnic responsiveness.

However, the extensive implications of *Nommo* are not clearly sensed in a concentration on the political and social rhetoric of Afro-Americans. Probably only within the religious experience, when worshippers and leaders including preachers, deacons, and church mothers interact, does the concept blossom into its full communicative significance. The complexities of the religious interactive event, which can involve from one person responding to a preacher to nearly the whole congregation caught up in continuous response, ranging from weeping to shouts of joy, are indicative of the several interlocking communication networks that may be set off when the preacher gives the word.

Such response configurations are not begun automatically; every speaker does not possess the assurance that he will be successful in provoking a total response. In fact, some preachers never succeed in moving an audience to the total interactive event necessary for them to consider their speeches successful. These preachers must be satisfied with the occasional feedback expressed by an "amen" or a "Lord, help" offered by several members as the sermon is presented. Other preachers, through a delicate combination of vocal manipulations characterized by rhythm and cadence, and vital thematic expression usually developed in narrative form, can easily produce a creative environment when messages are intensified by audience response.

Understanding the oral emphasis within the traditional Afro-American churches one becomes aware of the close relationship between speech and music. The antiphonal pattern where the speaker presents a theme which is answered by respondents pervades Afro-American speech as it permeates African music. Writing of the relationship of African music to Afro-American music in *Blues People*, LeRoi Jones says: "The most salient characteristics of African, or at least West African, music is a type of song in which there is a leader and a chorus; the leading lines are sung by a single voice, the leader's, alternating with a refrain sung by the chorus."[13] While this pattern in music may be African in origin it is not uncommon to Afro-American religious singing. The leader "lines" the song and the congregation responds, thus fulfilling the antiphony.

Speech and music, as manifestations of *Nommo*, relate in still another manner within black churches. As earlier mentioned a speaker is not assured of a totally interactive audience unless he blends the proper vocal rhythms and thematic interests. In addition to these elements the communicative situation can be made more productive by audience conditioning through singing. In this sense, singing sets the stage or mood by preparing the audience emotionally and physically for the preacher whose communication task is made easier because of audience receptivity. Singing, then, in the black religious audience although instructive is much more palliative; it soothes the emotions and coheres the congregation. Not having to concentrate on rhetorical means to encourage cohesiveness the preacher inherits an attentive audience by virtue of the choir's work. In mounting the platform to speak to a religious audience the black preacher does not challenge *Nommo* but uses it, becomes a part of it, and is consumed in the fire of speech and music.

The sermon, as the principal spoken discourse during the religious service, can reflect the preacher's awareness of the audience's responsiveness. His voice proves extremely significant as he alternates stressed and unstressed syllables, giving even the pauses rhythmic qualities. Witnessing the mixed outpouring of breathing and syllabic patterns, it is clear to the observer that the preacher initiates and sustains a tension between the audience and himself through vocal expression. The basic vocal pattern is established by the preacher and is accompanied by a secondary pattern emanating from the audience. Thus the spoken word as a sermon appears to maintain the essential unity of the interlocking communication networks in its role as the main event of the religious service.

The socio-historical perspectives of black oratory, whether African or American based, share certain common grounds. Central to the understanding of the role of vocal expressiveness within the black community are *Nommo*, the generative and dynamic quality of vocal expression, and slavery, the primary fact of black existence in America. *Nommo* has continued to manifest itself in the black community, notably within the church; and slavery's role in American history, while providing a common reference point, has made all black speeches relative. Historically black oratory, sacred and secular, has been collective in the same sense that most artistic productions are created for and meant to be shared by entire audiences.

NOTES

1 See Janheinz Jahn, *Muntu: The New African Culture* (New York, 1961), pp. 121–156 and W. E. B. Du Bois, *The Souls of Black Folk* (Greenwich, Conn., 1961), pp. 15–22.

2 Benjamin Brawley, *The Negro Genius* (New York, 1937), pp. 5–21.

3 Jahn, pp. 128–131.

4 See Melville J. Herskovits, "The Contribution of Afroamerican Studies to Africanist Research," *American Anthropologist,* L (January–March 1948), 1–10; Merle Eppse, *The Negro, Too, in American History* (New York, 1938), p. 70; LeRoi Jones, *Blues People* (New York, 1969), pp. 43–49; and Leroi Jones, *Black Music* (New York, 1968), pp. 182–183. Additional breadth can be had on this subject by reading Melville J.

Herskovits, "African Literature," in *Encyclopedia of Literature,* ed. Joseph T. Shipley (New York, 1946), I, 3–15, and Richard A. Waterman and William R. Bascom, "African and New World Negro Folklore," in *Funk & Wagnalls Standard Dictionary of Folklore, Mythology, and Legend,* ed. Maria Leach (New York, 1949), I, 18–24.

5 Jahn, p. 230. A much broader view is provided by Leopold Sedar Senghor, "The Spirit of Civilisation or the Laws of African Negro Culture," *Presence Africaine,* Nos. 8–10 (June–November 1956), 58.

6 (Washington, 1925).

7 See Eppse; William Ferris, *African Abroad* (New Haven, Conn., 1913); and C. Eric Lincoln, *Sounds of the Struggle: Persons and Perspectives in Civil Rights* (New York, 1967).

8 Such outstanding orators as Samuel Ringgold Ward, Reverdy Ransom, and Henry Highland Garnet were products of the religious schools and theological seminaries.

9 The work of poets such as Paul Laurence Dunbar, Fenton Johnson, Jean Toomer, and Langston Hughes can be found in Arna Bontemps, *American Negro Poetry* (New York, 1963).

10 Edmund David Cronon, *Black Moses* (Madison, Wis., 1968), pp. 209–219.

11 Quoted in Woodson, p. 37.

12 Arthur L. Smith, *Rhetoric of Black Revolution* (Boston, 1969), p. 34.

13 p. xi.

Ulf Hannerz

CHAPTER 22
The Rhetoric of Soul:
Identification in Negro Society

I

The last few years have witnessed the emergence of a concept of "soul" as signifying what is "essentially Negro" in the black ghettos of the large cities of the Northern United States. In this paper, I will attempt to place this concept of "soul" in its social and cultural matrix, in particular with respect to tendencies of social change as experienced by ghetto inhabitants. In doing so, I will emphasize what I believe to be the dominant purpose of a

From *Race*, Vol. IX, No. 4 (April 1968), published for the Institute of Race Relations, London, by the Oxford University Press © Institute of Race Relations, 1968.

"soul" vocabulary among its users. There will be clear points of convergence between my view of "soul" and that stated by Charles Keil in his book *Urban Blues*.[1] However, I believe that Keil's personal evaluation of some of the features of black ghetto culture tends to obscure the issue in some ways, and I also feel that a clearer picture of the essential social-structural and social-psychological features may be achieved.

This paper is based on field work in a lower class Negro neighborhood in Washington, D.C. The field site seems to be in many ways typical of Negro slums in Northern American cities. It is situated at the edge of a large, ethnically homogeneous area. Its inhabitants share the common characteristics of America's lower class urban Negroes: Poverty, a high rate of unemployment, a considerable amount of crime, including juvenile delinquency, and widely varying family role-structures according to which it is relatively common that the adult woman dominates the family while the male is either absent or only temporarily attached—even when he is a permanent member of the household his participation in household affairs may be quite limited. (It should be noted that this is not said to be true of all households—it is only pointed out that unstable family relationships and female dominance are much more common among lower class Negroes than among the American people in general.) Of the adults at the field site—a block-long street lined by two- or three-story row houses—a minority was born in Washington, D.C. The majority are immigrants from the South, particularly from Virginia, North Carolina, and South Carolina. Apart from conducting field work in this area by means of participant observation in the traditional sense, I have paid attention to those impersonal media which have a significant part in ghetto life; these are particularly important in the context of this study. I refer here to media which are specifically intended for a lower class Negro audience: radio (three stations in Washington, D.C., are clearly aimed at Negroes), the recording industry, and stage shows featuring Negro rock-and-roll artists and comedians. (The term "rhythm and blues" used by whites to denote Negro rock-and-roll is now only infrequently used by the

Negroes themselves.) These media have played a prominent part in promoting the vocabulary of "soul." (It may be added, on the other hand, that both the local Negro press, such as the Washington *Afro-American,* and the national Negro publications, for example the monthly *Ebony,* are largely middle class oriented and thus of limited value in the understanding of life in the ghetto where few read them.)

II

What then is "soul"? As the concept has come to be used in urban ghettos over the last number of years, it stands for what is "the essence of Negroness" and, it should be added, this "Negroness" refers to the kind of Negro with which the urban slum dweller is most familiar—people like himself. The question whether a middle class, white-collar suburban Negro also has "soul" is often met with consternation. In fact, "soul" seems to be a folk conception of the lower class urban Negro's own "national character." Modes of action, personal attributes, and certain artifacts are given the "soul" label. Typically, in conversations, one hears statements such as, "Man, he got a lot of soul." This appreciative opinion may be given concerning anybody in the ghetto, but more often by younger adults or adolescents about others of their own categories. In particular, speaking in terms of "soul" is common among younger men. This sex differentiation of the use of "soul" conceptions, I will suggest below, may be quite important in the understanding of the basis of the use of the "soul" concept.

The choice of the term "soul" for this "Negroness" is in itself noteworthy. First of all, it shows the influence of religion on lower class Negroes, even those who are not themselves active church members—expressions of religious derivation, such as "God, have mercy!" are frequent in everyday speech among lower class Negroes of all age and sex categories, and in all contexts. A very great number of people, of course, have been regular churchgoers at some point or other, at least at the time when they attended Sunday school, and many are actively involved in church activities, perhaps in one of the large Baptist churches but at least as often in small spiritualist storefront churches. Although the people who use the "soul" vocabulary in which we are interested here are seldom themselves regular churchgoers, they have certainly been fully (although sometimes indirectly) exposed to the religious idiom; including such phrases as "a soul-stirring revival meeting."

Furthermore, the choice of a term which in church usage has a connotation of the "the essentially human" to refer to "the essentially Negro," as the new concept of "soul" does, certainly has strong implications of ethnocentrism. If "soul" is Negro, the non-Negro is "non-soul" and, it appears, somewhat less human. Although I have never heard such a point of view spelled out, it would seem to me that it is implicitly accepted as part of an incipient "soul" ideology. It is very clear that what is "soul" is not only different from what is not "soul" (particularly what is mainstream middle class American); it is also superior. "Soul" is an appraisive as well as designative concept.[2] If one asks a young man what a "soul brother" is, the answer is usually something like "someone who's hip, someone who knows what he's doing." It may be added here that although both "soul brother" and "soul sister" are used for "soul" personified, the former is more common. Like "soul," "soul brother" and "soul sister" are terms used particularly by younger males.

Let us now note a few fields that are particularly "soul." One area is that of music (where the concept may have originated—see the article on the "soul" movement among jazz musicians by Szwed),[3] particularly the field of progressive jazz and rock-and-roll. This has been seized upon by those actively engaged in these fields. James Brown, a leading rock-and-roll singer, is often referred to as "Soul Brother Number One"; two of the largest record stores in Washington, D.C., with practically only Negro customers, are the "Soul Shack" and the "Soul City." Recently a new magazine named "Soul" appeared; its main outlet seems to be these *de facto* segregated record stores. It contains stories on rock-and-roll artists, disc jockeys, and the like. Excellence in musical expression is indeed a part of the lower class Negro self-conception, and white rock-and-roll is often viewed with scorn as a poor imitation of the Negro genius. Resentment is frequently aimed at the Beatles who stand as typical of white intrusion into a Negro field. (Occasionally, a Beatle melody has become a hit in the Negro ghetto as well, but only when performed in a local version by a Negro group, such as the recordings of "Day Tripper" by the Vontastics. In such a case, there is little or no mention of its Beatles origin.)

The commercial side of Negro entertainment is, of course, directly tied to "soul" music. With counterparts in other large Negro ghettos in the United States, the Howard Theater in Washington stages shows of touring rock-and-roll groups and individual performers—each show usually runs a week, with four or five performances every day. Larger shows also make one-night-only appearances at the Washington Coliseum. Occasionally, a comedian also takes part; Moms Mabley, Pigmeat Markham, or Redd Foxx are among those who draw large Negro audiences but few whites.

The "emcees" of these shows are often celebrities in their own right—some, such as "King" Coleman and "Georgeous George" tour regularly with the shows, others are local disc jockeys from the Negro radio stations. In Washington such disc jockeys as "The Nighthawk" (Bob Terry) and "Soulfinger" (Fred Correy) make highly appreciated appearances at the Howard. Their station is WOL "Soul Radio": it is clear that the commercial establishments with a vested interest in a separate Negro audience have seized upon the "soul" vocabulary, using it to further their own interests as well as supporting its use among the audience. Thus there is also for instance a WWRL "soul brother radio" in New York. However, one should not view the "soul" vocabulary solely as a commercial creation. It existed before it was commercialized, and the fact that it seems so profitable for commercial establishments to fly the banner of "soul" also indicates that whatever part these establishments have in promoting it, it has fallen into fertile ground.

A second area of widespread "soul" symbolism is that of food. The dishes that are now "soul food" were once—and still are to some extent—referred to simply as "Southern cooking"; but in the Northern ghettos they increasingly come to stand for race rather than region. In the center of the Washington Negro area, for instance, there is a "Little Harlem Restaurant" advertising "soul food." There are a number of such foods; some of those which are most frequently mentioned as "soul foods" are chitterlings (a part of the intestine of the pig), hog maw (pig tripe), black-eyed peas, collard greens, corn bread and grits (a kind of porridge). Typically, they were the poor man's food in the rural South—in the urban North, they may still be so to some extent, but in the face of the diversity of the urban environment, they also come to stand as signs of ethnicity. (Thus in some Northern cities there are "soul food" restaurants catering to curious whites, much in the same way as any exotic cuisine.) One may note that references to "soul food" occur frequently in "soul music"; two of the hits of the winter 1966–67 were "Grits and Cornbread" by the Soul Runners and the Joe Cuba Sextet's "Bang Bang" with the refrain "corn bread, hog maw and chitterling." Sometimes, the names of "soul foods" may themselves be used as more or less synonymous with "soul." Negro entertainers on stage, talking of their experiences while journeying between ghetto shows around the country, sometimes refer to it as "the chitterling circuit," and this figure of speech usually draws much favorable audience reaction.

What, then, is "soul" about "soul music" and "soul food"? It may be wise to be cautious here, since there is little intellectualizing and analyzing on the part of the ghetto's inhabitants on this subject. I believe that this comparative absence of defining activity may itself be significant, and I will return to this possibility below. Here, I will only point to a few basic characteristics of what is "soul" which I feel make it particularly essentially Negro, referring again, of course, to urban lower class Negroes rather than to any other category of people.

There is, of course, the Southern origin. The "Down Country" connotations are particularly attached to "soul food"; however, although Negro music has changed more and the contemporary commercial rock-and-roll is an urban phenomenon, it is certainly seen as the latest stage of an unfolding musical heritage. Thus the things that are "soul," while taking on new significance in the urban environment, provide some common historical tradition for ghetto inhabitants. One might also speculate on the possibility that the early and from then on constant and intimate exposure to these foods and to this music—for radios and record players seem to belong to practically every poor ghetto home—may make them appear particularly basic to a "Negro way of life."

When it comes to "soul" music, there are a couple of themes in style and content which I would suggest are pervasive in ghetto life and which probably make them appear very close to the everyday experience of ghetto inhabitants.

One of these is the lack of control over the social environment. There is a very frequent attitude among "soul brothers"—that is, the ghetto's younger males—that one's environment is somewhat like a jungle where tough, smart people may survive and where a lot happens to make it worthwhile and enjoyable just to "watch the scene" if one does not have too high hopes of controlling it. Many of the reactions in listening to "progressive jazz" seem to connect to this view; "Oooh, man, there just ain't nothing you can do about it but sit there and feel it goin' all the way into you." Without being able to do much about proving it, I feel that exposure to experiences desirable or undesirable in which one can only passively perceive events without influencing them is an essential fact of ghetto life, for better or for worse; thus it is "soul."

Related to this is the experience of unstable personal relationships, in particular between the sexes. It is a well-known fact that among lower class urban Negroes there are many "broken" families (households without a husband or father), many temporary common-law unions, and in general relatively little consensus on sex roles. Thus, it is not much of an exaggeration to speak of a constant "battle of the sexes," and the achievement of success with the opposite sex is a focal concern in lower class Negro life. From this area come most of the lyrics of contemporary rock-and-roll music. It may be objected that this is true of white rock-and-roll as well; to this it may be answered that this is very much to the point. For white rock-and-roll is predominantly adolescent music, thus reaching people with similar problems of unstable personal relationships. In the case of lower class urban Negroes, such relationships are characteristic of a much wider age-range, and music on this theme also reaches this wider range. Some titles of recent rock-and-roll hits may show this theme: "I'm Losing You" (Temptations), "Are You Lonely" (Freddie Scott), "Yours Until Tomorrow" (Dee Dee Warwick), "Keep Me Hangin' On" (Supremes). "Soul" stands for a bitter-sweet experience; this often arises from contacts with the other sex, although there are certainly also other sources. This bitter-sweetness, of course, was typical already of the blues.

Turning to style, a common element in everyday social interaction as well as among storefront church preachers, Negro comedians, and rock-and-roll singers is an alternation between aggressive, somewhat boasting behavior, and plaintive behavior from an implicit underdog position.

This may not be the place to give a more detailed account of this style of behavior. However, as I said, it occurs in many situations and may itself be related to the unstable personal relationships, and the concomitant unstable self-conception, which was mentioned above. In any case, it seems that this style is seen as having "soul"; without describing its elements, "soul brothers" tend to describe its occurrences in a variety of contexts.

As I noted above, I have hesitated to try to analyze and define "soul," because what seems to be important in the emergence of the present "soul" concept is the fact that there is felt to be *something* which is "soul" rather than *what* that something is. There is, of course, some logic to this; if "soul" is what is "essentially Negro," it should not be necessary for "soul brothers" to spend too much time analyzing it. Asking about "soul" one often receives answers such as "you know, we don't talk much about it, but we've all been through it, so we know what it is anyway." Probably, this is to some extent true. What the lack of pronounced definition points to, in that case, is that "soul" vocabulary is predominantly for in-group consumption. It is a symbol of solidarity among the people of the ghetto, but not in more than a weak and implicit sense of solidarity *against* anybody else. "Soul" is turned inward; and so everybody who is touched by it is supposed to know what it means. So far there has been little interference with the "soul" vocabulary by outsiders, at least in any way noticeable to the ghetto dwellers. There have been none of the fierce arguments about its meaning which have developed around "black power," a concept which did not really evolve in the ghetto but is largely the creation of white mass media. "Black power" is controversial, and so white people insist on a definition. (And many black people, also depending on white media for news, tend to accept the interpretations of these media.) "Soul" is not equally threatening, and so ghetto dwellers can keep its mystique to themselves.

We may note in this context that the few interpreters of "soul" to the outside world are, in fact, outsiders; a kind of cultural brokers who give interested members of the larger society the "inside stuff" on the ghetto. But serving as such brokers, they hardly affect the uses of "soul" within the ghetto community. LeRoi Jones, the author, a convert to ghetto life who like so many converts seems to have become more militantly partisan than the more authentic ghetto inhabitants, has moved from a position where he rather impartially noted the ethnocentric bias of "soul"[4] to one where he preaches for the complete destruction of the present American society,[5] an activist program which I am sure is far out of step with the immediate concerns of the average "soul brother." Bennett, an editor of the middle class *Ebony* magazine, is not particularly interested in the "folk myth of soul" but explains what he feels that "soul" really is.[6] I am not convinced that his conception is entirely correct; it is certainly not expressed in the idiom of the ghetto. Keil, an ethnomusicologist, probably comes closer to the folk conception than anyone else, by giving what amounts to a catalogue of those ghetto values and experiences which its inhabitants recognize as their own.[7] In doing so, of course, one does not get a short and comprehensive definition of "soul" that is acceptable to all and in every situation—one merely lists the fields in which a vocabulary of "soul" is particularly likely to be expressed. This, of course, is what has been done in a partial and parsimonious way above.

Here we end the exposition of the "soul" concept. Summing up what has been said so far, the vocabulary of "soul," which is a relatively recent phenomenon, is used among younger Negro ghetto dwellers, and particularly young men, to designate in a highly approving manner the experiences and characteristics which are "essentially Negro." As such it is not an activist vocabulary for us in inter-group relations but a vocabulary which is employed within the group, although it is clear that by discussing what is "typically Negro" one makes an implicit reference to the non-Negro society. We turn now to an interpretation of the emergence of such a vocabulary in this group at this point of Negro history.

III

For a long time, the social boundaries which have constituted barriers to educational, economic, and other achievement by Negro Americans have been highly impermeable. Although lower class Negroes have to a considerable degree accepted the values of mainstream American culture in those areas, the very obviousness of the impermeability of social boundaries has probably prevented a more complete commitment to the achievement of those goals which have been out of reach. Instead, there has been an adjustment to the lower class situation in which goals and values more appropriate to the ascribed position of the group have been added to, and to some extent substituted for, the mainstream norms. Whether these lower class concerns, experiences, and values are direct responses to the situation or historically based patterns for which the lower class niche provides space is not really important here. What is important is that the style of life of the lower class, in this case the Negro lower class, is different from that of the upper classes, and that the impermeability of group boundaries and the unequal distribution of re-

sources between groups have long kept the behavioral characteristics of the groups relatively stable and distinct from one another,
although to a great extent, one of the groups—the lower class
Negroes—would have preferred the style of life of the other group
—the middle class whites—had it been available to them. As it has
been, they have only been able to do the best with what they have
had. In a way, then, they have had two cultures, the mainstream
culture with which they are relatively familiar, which has in many
ways appeared superior and preferable, and which has been closed
to them, and the ghetto culture which is a second choice and based
on the circumstances of the ascribed social position. (I will not
dwell here on the typical features of the two cultures and the relationship between them; articles by Miller[8] and Rodman[9] are en-
lightening discussions of these topics.)

This, of course, sounds to some extent like the position of what
has often been called "the marginal man." Such a position may
cause psychological problems. However, when the position is very
clearly defined and where the same situation is shared by many,
the situation is perhaps reasonably acceptable—there is a perfectly
understandable reason for one's failure to reach one's goal. Nobody of one's own kind is allowed to reach that goal, and the basis
of the condition is a social rule rather than a personal failure.
There are indications that marginality is more severely felt if the
barrier is not absolute but boundary permeability is possible although uncertain. According to Kerckhoff and McCormick,

An absolute barrier between the two groups is less conducive to personality problems than "grudging, uncertain and unpredictable acceptance." The impact of the rejection on an individual's personality
organization will depend to some extent upon the usual treatment
accorded members of his group by the dominant group. If his group
as a whole faces a rather permeable barrier and he meets with more
serious rejection, the effect on him is likely to be more severe than
the same treatment received by a more thoroughly rejected group
(one facing an impermeable barrier).[10]

My thesis here is that recent changes in race relations in the
United States have indeed made the social barriers to achievement

other, with similar problems of adjustment to a new situation. The use of "soul" rhetoric is a way of meeting their needs as long as it occurs in situations where they can mutually support each other. Here is, of course, a clue to the confinement of the rhetoric to in-group situations. If "soul" talk were directed toward outsiders, they might not accept the claims for its excellence—it is not their "folk myth." Viewing "soul" as such a device of rhetoric, it is also easier to understand why it is advantageous for its purposes not to have made it the topic of too much intellectualizing. As Geertz makes clear in his paper on "Ideology as a Cultural System,"[12] by analyzing and defining activity, one achieves maximum intellectual clarity at the expense of emotional commitment. It is doubtful that "soul" rhetoric would thrive on too much intellectual clarity; rather, by expressing "soul" ideals in a circumspect manner in terms of emotionally charged symbols such as "soul food" and "soul music," one can avoid the rather sordid realities underlying these emotions. As I pointed out above, the shared lower class Negro experiences which seem to be the bases of "soul" are hardly in themselves such as to bring out a surge of ethnic pride. That is a psychological reason for keeping the "soul" concept diffuse. There is also, I believe, a sociological basis for the diffuseness. The more exactly a "soul brother" would define "soul," the fewer others would probably agree upon the "essential Negroness" of his definition; and, as we have seen, a basic idea of the rhetoric of "soul" is to cast others into roles which satisfy them and at the same time support one's own position. If people are cast into a role of "soul brother" and then find that there has been a definition established for that role which they cannot accept, the result may be overt disagreement and denial of solidarity rather than mutual deference. As it is, "soul" can be an umbrella concept for a rather wide variety of definitions of one's situation, and the "soul brothers" who are most in need of the ethnocentric core conception can occasionally get at least fleeting allegiance to "soul" from others with whom in reality they share relatively little, for instance, individuals who are clearly upwardly mobile. On one occasion I listened to a long conversation about "soul music" in a rather heterogeneous group of young Negro men who all agreed on the "soulfulness" of the singers whose records they were playing, and afterwards I asked one of the men who is clearly upwardly mobile of his conception of "soul." He answered that "soul" is earthy, "there is nothing specifically Negro about it." Yet the very individuals with whom he had just agreed on matters of "soul" had earlier given me the opposite answer—only Negroes have "soul." Thus by avoiding definitions, they had found together an area of agreement and satisfaction in "soul" by merely assuming that there was a shared basis of opinion.

IV

Summing up what has been said, "soul" is a relatively recent concept used in the urban Negro ghetto, in particular by young men, to express what is "essential Negroness" and to convey appreciation for it. The point of view which has been expressed here is that the need for such a concept has arisen at this point because of increasingly ambivalent conceptions of the opportunity structure. While earlier, lack of achievement according to American mainstream ideals could easily be explained in terms of impermeable social barriers, the impression is gaining ground in the ghetto that there are now ways out of the situation. The young men who come under particularly great strain if such a belief is accepted must either achieve some success (which many of them are obviously still unable to do, for various reasons), explain that achievement is impossible (which is probably not as true as it has been), or explain that achievement according to mainstream ideals is not necessarily achievement according to their ideals. The emergence of "soul," it has been stated here, goes some way toward meeting the need of stating alternative ideals and also provides solidarity among those with such a need. In implying or stating explicitly that ghetto culture has a superiority of its own, the users of the "soul" vocabulary seem to take a step beyond devices of established usage which are terms of solidarity but lack or at least have less clear cultural references—for example the use of "brother" as a term of either reference or address for another

Negro. That is, it is more in the cultural than in the social dimension that "soul" is an innovation rather than just one more term of a kind. Of course, the two are closely connected. It is advantageous to maintain a diffuse conception of "soul," for if an intellectually clear definition were established, "soul" would probably be both less convincing and less uniting.

The view of "soul" taken here is one of a piecemeal rhetoric attempt to establish a satisfactory self-conception. For the great majority of "soul brothers" I am sure this is the major basis of "soul." It may be added that for instance LeRoi Jones[13] and Charles Keil[14] tend to give the impression of a more social-activist conception of "soul," although Keil tends to make it a prophecy rather than an interpretation. At least at present, I think that there is little basis for connecting the majority of "soul brothers" with militant black nationalism—there is hardly a "soul movement." "Soul" became publicly associated with black militancy as the term "soul brother" made its way to international prominence during recent ghetto uprisings—when Negro businessmen posted "soul brother" signs in their windows, it was noted by mass media all over the world. However, it is worth noting that this was an internal appeal to the ghetto moral community by black shopkeepers, not a sign of defiance of the outside world by the participants. It may be said that the outsiders merely caught a glimpse of an internal ghetto dialogue. Yet organized black nationalism may be able to recruit followers by using some kind of transformed "soul" vocabulary, and I think there are obviously attempts on its side to make more of "soul" than it is now. Certainly, there is seldom any hostility to black militants among the wider groups of self-defined "soul brothers," although the vocabulary of "soul" has not been extensively employed for political purposes. If it is so used, however, it could possibly increase the ghetto dwellers' identification with political nationalism. Thus, if at present it is not possible to speak of more than a "rhetoric of soul," it may be that in the future we will find a "soul movement." If that happens, of course, "soul" may become a more controversial concept, as "black power" is now.

NOTES

1 Charles Keil, *Urban Blues* (Chicago: University of Chicago Press, 1966).

2 Charles Morris, *Signification and Significance* (Cambridge, Mass.: The M.I.T. Press, 1964).

3 John F. Szwed, "Musical Style and Racial Conflict," *Phylon*, Vol. 27 (1966), pp. 358–66.

4 LeRoi Jones, *Blues People* (New York: William Morrow, 1963), p. 219.

5 LeRoi Jones, *Home: Social Essays* (New York: William Morrow, 1963).

6 Lerone Bennett, Jr., *The Negro Mood* (New York: Ballantine Books, 1965), p. 89.

7 Charles Keil, *op. cit.*, pp. 164 *et seq.*

8 Walter B. Miller, "Lower Class Culture as a Generating Mileu of Gang Delinquency," *Journal of Social Issues*, Vol. 14 (1958), pp. 5–19.

9 Hyman Rodman, "The Lower Class Value Stretch," *Social Forces*, Vol. 42 (1963), pp. 205–15.

10 Alan C. Kerckhoff and Thomas C. McCormick, "Marginal Status and Marginal Personality," *Social Forces*, Vol. 34 (1955), p. 51.

11 Kenneth Burke, *A Grammar of Motives and a Rhetoric of Motives* (Cleveland: Meridian Books, 1962), p. 562.

12 Clifford Geertz, "Ideology as a Cultural System," in David E. Apter (ed.), *Ideology and Discontent* (New York: The Free Press, 1964).

13 LeRoi Jones, *Home: Social Essays*.

14 Charles Keil, *op. cit.*

LeRoi Jones

CHAPTER 23
Expressive Language

Speech is the effective form of a culture. Any shape or cluster of human history still apparent in the conscious and unconscious habit of groups of people is what I mean by culture. All culture is necessarily profound. The very fact of its longevity, of its being what it is, *culture*, the epic memory of practical tradition, means that it is profound. But the inherent profundity of culture does not necessarily mean that its *uses* (and they are as various as the human condition) will be profound. German culture is profound.

From *Home: Social Essays* (New York: William Morrow & Company, 1963), pp. 166–172. Reprinted by permission of William Morrow & Company, Inc. Copyright © 1963, LeRoi Jones.

Generically. Its uses, however, are specific, as are all uses . . . of ideas, inventions, products of nature. And specificity, as a right and passion of human life, breeds what it breeds as a result of its context.

Context, in this instance, is most dramatically social. And the social, though it must be rooted, as are all evidences of existence, in culture, depends for its impetus for the most part on a multiplicity of influences. Other cultures, for instance. Perhaps, and this is a common occurrence, the reaction or interaction of one culture on another can produce a social context that will extend or influence any culture in many strange directions.

Social also means *economic*, as any reader of nineteenth-century European philosophy will understand. The economic is part of the social—and in our time much more so than what we have known as the spiritual or metaphysical, because the most valuable canons of power have either been reduced or traduced into stricter economic terms. That is, there has been a shift in the actual meaning of the world since Dante lived. As if Brooks Adams were right. Money does not mean the same thing to me it must mean to a rich man. I cannot, right now, think of one meaning to name. This is not so simple to understand. Even as a simple term of the English language, *money* does not possess the same meanings for the rich man as it does for me, a lower-middle-class American, albeit of laughably "aristocratic" pretensions. What possibly can "money" mean to a poor man? And I am not talking now about those courageous products of our permissive society who walk knowledgeably into "poverty" as they would into a public toilet. I mean, The Poor.

I look in my pocket; I have seventy cents. Possibly I can buy a beer. A quart of ale, specifically. Then I will have twenty cents with which to annoy and seduce my fingers when they wearily search for gainful employment. I have no idea at this moment what that seventy cents will mean to my neighbor around the corner, a poor Puerto Rican I have seen hopefully watching my plastic garbage can. But I am certain it cannot mean the same thing. Say to David Rockefeller, "I have money," and he will think you mean something entirely different. That is, if you also dress the part. He would not for a moment think, "Seventy cents." But then neither would many New York painters.

Speech, the way one describes the natural proposition of being alive, is much more crucial than even most artists realize. Semantic philosophers are certainly correct in their emphasis on the final dictation of words over their users. But they often neglect to point out that, after all, it is the actual importance, *power*, of the words that remain so finally crucial. Words have users, but as well, users have words. And it is the users that establish the world's realities. Realities being those fantasies that control your immediate span of life. Usually they are not your own fantasies, i.e., they belong to governments, traditions, etc., which, it must be clear by now, can make for conflict with the singular human life all ways. The fantasy of America might hurt you, but it is what should be meant when one talks of "reality." Not only the things you can touch or see, but the things that make such touching or seeing "normal." Then words, like their users, have a hegemony. Socially—which is final, right now. If you are some kind of artists, you naturally might think this is not so. There is the future. But *immortality* is a kind of drug, I think—one that leads to happiness at the thought of death. Myself, I would rather live forever . . . just to make sure.

The social hegemony, one's position in society, enforces more specifically one's terms (even the vulgar have "pull"). Even to the mode of speech. But also it makes these terms an available explanation of any social hierarchy, so that the words themselves become, even informally, laws. And of course they are usually very quickly stitched together to make formal statutes only fools or the faithfully intrepid would dare to question beyond immediate necessity.

The culture of the powerful is very infectious for the sophisticated, and strangely addictive. To be any kind of "success" one must be fluent in this culture. Know the words of the users, the semantic rituals of power. This is a way into wherever it is you are not now, but wish, very desperately, to get into.

Even speech then signals a fluency in this culture. A knowledge at least. "He's an educated man," is the barest acknowledgment of such fluency . . . in any time. "He's hip," my friends might say. They connote a similar entrance.

And it is certainly the meanings of words that are most important, even if they are no longer consciously acknowledged, but merely, by their use, trip a familiar lever of social accord. To recreate instantly the understood hierarchy of social, and by doing that, cultural, importance. And cultures are thought by most people in the world to do their business merely by being hierarchies. Certainly this is true in the West, in as simple a manifestation as Xenophobia, the naïve bridegroom of anti-human feelings, or in economic terms, Colonialism. For instance, when the first Africans were brought into the New World, it was thought that it was all right for them to be slaves because "they were heathens." It is a perfectly logical assumption.

And it follows, of course, that slavery would have been an even stranger phenomenon had the Africans spoken English when they first got here. It would have complicated things. Very soon after the first generations of Afro-Americans mastered this language, they invented white people called Abolitionists.

Words' meanings, but also the rhythm and syntax that frame and propel their concatenation, seek their culture as the final reference for what they are describing of the world. An A flat played twice on the same saxophone by two different men does not have to sound the same. If these men have different ideas of what they want this note to do, the note will not sound the same. Culture is the form, the overall structure of organized thought (as well as emotion and spiritual pretension). There are many cultures. Many ways of organizing thought, or having thought organized. That is, the form of thought's passage through the world will take on as many diverse shapes as there are diverse groups of travelers. Environment is one organizer of *groups*, at any level of its meaning. People who live in Newark, New Jersey, are organized, for whatever purpose, as Newarkers. It begins that simply. Another manifestation, at a slightly more complex level, can be the fact that blues singers from the Midwest sing through their noses. There is an explanation past the geographical, but that's the idea in tabloid. And singing through the nose does propose that the definition of singing be altered . . . even if ever so slightly. (At this point where someone's definitions must be changed, we are flitting around at the outskirts of the old city of Aesthetics. A solemn ghost town. Though some of the bones of reason can still be gathered there.)

But we still need definitions, even if there already are many. The dullest men are always satisfied that a dictionary lists everything in the world. They don't care that you may find out something *extra*, which one day might even be valuable to them. Of course, by that time it might even be in the dictionary, or at least they'd hope so, if you asked them directly.

But for every item in the world, there are a multiplicity of definitions that fit. And every word we use *could* mean something else. And at the same itme. The culture fixes the use, and usage. And in "pluralistic" America, one should always listen very closely when he is being talked to. The speaker might mean something completely different from what we think we're hearing. "Where is your pot?"

I heard an old Negro street singer last week, Reverend Pearly Brown, singing, "God don't never change!" This is a precise thing he is singing. He does not mean "God does not ever change!" He means "God don't never change!" The difference, and I said it was crucial, is in the final human reference . . . the form of passage through the world. A man who is rich and famous who sings, "God don't never change," is confirming his hegemony and good fortune . . . or merely calling the bank. A blind hopeless black American is saying something very different. He is telling you about the extraordinary order of the world. But he is not telling you about his "fate." Fate is a luxury available only to those fortunate citizens with alternatives. The view from the top of the hill is not the same as that from the bottom of the hill. Nor are most viewers at either end of the hill, even certain that, in fact, there is any other place from which to look. Looking down usually eliminates the possibility of understanding what it must be like to look up. Or try to imagine yourself as not existing. It is difficult, but poets and politicians try every other day.

Being told to "speak proper," meaning that you become fluent with the jargon of power, is also a part of not "speaking proper." That is, the culture which desperately understands that it does not "speak proper," or is not fluent with the terms of social strength, also understands somewhere that its desire to gain such fluency is done at a terrifying risk. The bourgeois Negro accepts such risk as profit. But does *clos-ter* (in the context of "jes a close-ter, walk wi-thee") mean the same thing as *closer?* Close-ter, in the term of its user is, believe me, exact. It means a quality of existence, of actual physical disposition perhaps . . . in its manifestation as a *tone* and *rhythm* by which people live, most often in response to common modes of thought best enforced by some factor of environmental emotion that is exact and specific. Even the picture it summons is different, and certainly the "Thee" that is used to connect the implied "Me" with, is different. The God of the damned cannot know the God of the damner, that is, cannot know he is God. As no Blues person can really believe emotionally in Pascal's God, or Wittgenstein's question, "Can the concept of God exist in a perfectly logical language?" Answer: "God don't never change."

Communication is only important because it is the broadest root of education. And all cultures communicate exactly what they have, a powerful motley of experience.

Charles U. Larson

*Black Power is not anti-white people; but is anti
anything and everything that serves to oppress. If
Whites align themselves on the side of oppression, then
Black Power must be anti-white. That, however, is not
the decision of Black Power.*[1]

CHAPTER 24
The Trust Establishing Function
of the Rhetoric of Black Power

The term *Black Power* is clearly one which encourages a variety
of interpretations as does the rhetoric surrounding the term; an
examination of professional journals in the Speech field alone
demonstrates that fact. Scott, for example, has called the rhetoric
"justificatory"[2] at one time, and has offered it in conjunction with
Smith as an example of "The Rhetoric of Confrontation" at another time.[3] Gregg, McCormack, and Pedersen interpret it as a
"parareligious catechism" which offers the Black Man a cathartic

From *Central States Speech Journal*, Vol. XXI, No. 1 (Spring 1970), pp.
52–56. Reprinted by permission of the author and the Central States Speech
Association. Charles U. Larson (Ph.D., University of Minnesota, 1968) is
Assistant Professor of Speech, Northern Illinois University.

device for the discovery of self.[4] That these interpretations are all correct, or at least partially correct, testifies to the ambiguity of the term and its rhetoric as well as to its richness. This paper attempts to explore further the richness inherent in the rhetoric of Black Power from a somewhat behavioral point of view by discussing Black Power persuasion in terms of the behavioral concept of trust and trust establishment. The rhetoric of Black Power is clearly directed towards various audiences at different times. Sometimes the messages seem specifically designed for Black people; at other times they seem directed to the White Power structure in particular; and in yet other cases the rhetoric seems aimed at Blacks but is meant to be overheard by Whites.[5] This examination focuses on Black Power rhetoric which is aimed at White auditors either directly or via "eavesdropping." Generally these are the messages delivered before White audiences. Underlying such an examination is a belief that the behavioral definition of trust is more applicable to ambiguous rhetorics like the one surrounding the Black Power movement than are the more traditional definitions. This notion is discussed below by comparing traditional and behavioral definitions of trust and by applying pertinent parts of the behavioral definition of the term to particular persuasive attempts made on behalf of Black Power. The thesis of this paper, then, is that the rhetoric of Black Power, particularly that which is directed to White auditors, is a trust establishing rhetoric when viewed from the behavioral conceptualization of the term.

Trust can be defined in many ways. A dictionary definition stresses things like "faith in someone," and "reliance in the character, ability, strength, or truth of someone or something."[6] Kim Giffin, in his discussion of "Interpersonal Trust in Small Group Communication," notes that traditional definitions of trust have been linked to factors which are "somewhat mystical and intangible."[7] The dictionary's "faith in someone" seems to be such an intangible factor; feeling that another will not harm us to help himself is another. Speech texts, though they do not directly discuss trust, usually include trust and trustworthiness under the term Ethos and discuss Ethos and its elements in terms of factors which are somewhat intangible and which relate to an internal sensing of good will or "high" Ethos. Words like *sincerity, honesty, truthfulness,* and *character* are used to describe the speaker who has high or good Ethos and who can therefore be trusted, but aside from the Aristotelean notion of reputation, most of our judgments of trust and Ethos are based on the "mystical and intangible" factors mentioned by Giffin. There are disadvantages to judgments like these, for it is difficult to identify why we trust another or what it is that he says or does that justifies our placement of trust. We usually end by saying something like, "I don't exactly know why I trust him; I only know that I do." In short, when trust is defined traditionally, whether separately or as an element in Ethos, one is forced to look at hypothetical rather than identifiable factors, and the term remains vague and obscure.

Behaviorists define trust quite differently; to them it is related to predictability, expectation, risk, reward and punishment as well as the interaction of these factors. Deutsch, for example, defines trust in this way: "An individual may be said to have trust in the occurrence of an event if he expects its occurrence and his expectation leads to behavior which he perceives to have greater negative motivational consequences if the expectation is not confirmed."[8] Giffin defines trust in the communication act as, "reliance upon the communication behavior of another person in order to achieve a desired but uncertain objective in a risky situation."[9] Operating from such a point of view and relying on prediction based on known factors of risk instead of internal sensing, changes the Trust-Distrust continuum to a continuum which might be labeled Predictable-Unpredictable; thus, one can trust someone if he can predict with some accuracy that individual's future behavior while he distrusts him if he cannot. The degree of trust held by the parties in any relationship is related then to the ability on the part of trustee and trustor to foresee behavior in terms of the risks involved and the rewards or punishments likely to accrue from accuracy in the prediction. An enemy could be trusted under this definition, even with your life, if the risks involved for the enemy should he take your life were great enough to deter him from murdering you or if the rewards for preserving his charge were great enough to motivate him to defend you. Operating from this point of view, the individual does not say, "I don't know why I trust him; I just do." Rather he says, "I trust him because in the past when risks like these were involved and when reward potential was similar, he behaved in a predictable manner." One needn't rely on intuition or feelings to determine trust if he uses this definition; instead, he relies on known quantities of risk, reward, punishment as well as the history of past behavior on the part of the trustee.

Shifting the emphasis of the trust relationship from intuition to economics inevitably affects the rhetoric by which the shift is articulated. This shift is particularly evident in Black Power rhetoric. Instead of bargaining for Civil Rights through the use of demands, sham issues, and compromise as the nonviolent movement did, Black Power rhetoric seeks trust by escalating the risks for untrustworthy (i.e., unpredictable) behavior through a series of confrontations, contingency statements which sound like threats, and non-negotiable demands couched in moral language under the rubrics of this new rhetoric. Urban sharecropping will be met with an equal measure of "morally justifiable" physical injury; and educational or employment tokenism and prejudice will be met with boycott, walkout, and eventually total ruin. By escalating the risks of unpredictable behavior, Black Power hopes to increase the predictability of the "good white folk" who promised and never delivered. Black-White trust is thus no longer based on intuitive feelings of good will but on economic realities and on the profit system. It will be profitable for White Power to stand and deliver full equality; it will be unprofitable for them to renege on the contract.

If the above analysis is accurate, then one should expect to observe trust establishing tactics in the rhetoric of Black Power. Giffin notes several factors which encourage the establishment of trust. Though Giffin's factors refer to situations in which a person (called "p") establishes a trust relationship with another person (called "o"), some of Giffin's factors or tactics are applicable and relevant to the rhetoric of Black Power. Giffin lists the following as some of the factors which encourage the establishment of trust relationship:

1. Communication from o indicates to p an intention on the part of o to reciprocate trust when offered by p.
2. Communication from o which indicates o's plan of reaction to a violation by p of o's trust in p.
3. Communication from o perceived by p as:
   a. descriptive rather than evaluative
   b. problem-oriented rather than oriented toward social control
   c. provisional rather than certain.[10]

These factors, as well as the general behavioral definition of trust as predictability offer an alternative perspective for interpretation when one looks at specific instances of Black Power persuasion. The typical Black Power oration defines a problem in descriptive and usually emotional terms. The cause of the problem is generally associated with the control of goods, services, and, as a result, of people by the White Power establishment. A solution to the problem is then usually suggested, and it generally includes a veiled threat, whose consequences can be avoided by those in power if they are willing to abandon the control of the goods and services directly involving Black People. If this condition is fulfilled, Blacks and Whites can exist in peace; if it is not met, chaos will be the inevitable result according to the Black Power advocates. These characteristics of the Black Power oration are remarkably similar to Giffin's trust establishing tactics. Consider the following statement which might be included in a Black Power speech: "America is a racist country, and it will have to change if it wants to avoid rebellion." The terms "racist" and "rebellion" have value loadings to be certain. However, in the context of the entire sentence, the terms are descriptive—they define the nature of a country and a likely result of that condition (i.e., the racist nature of a country and a likely result of that condition). Further, the statement sets up a provisional condition where certain criteria are to be met before reward or punishment is meted. Also, there is a clear indication of the trustee's likely reaction to a trust violation. Though the terminology of the statement is rather absolute, it seeks to describe not to evaluate and thus fulfills Giffin's factor 3.a. An examination of particular persuasive attempts on behalf of Black Power reveals variations on this "trust establishing" function which Giffin describes. For example, when Stokely Carmichael says, "We've got to build a power base that will be our protection. That if they touch one Black man in California while he's taking his wife to the hospital, if they touch one black man in Mississippi while he's walking down the highway, if they touch a group of Black people riding their horses on their day off in Detroit, that we will move to disrupt this whole damned country,"[11] he is, under the present definition of trust, indicating a plan of reaction to a potential violation of the trust relationship. He talks in terms which describe the provisions under which trust will be maintained, and at least rhetorically, he is moving toward a predictable Black-White relationship. In another city Carmichael says, "When the Negro community is able to control local offices, and negotiate with other groups from a position of organized strength, the possibility of meaningful political alliances on specific issues will be increased. That is a rule of politics and there is no reason why it should not operate here. The only difference is that we will have the power to define the terms of these alliances."[12] Carmichael describes the political aims of Blacks here and states an intention to trust the White Power structure but only when predictability is assured through power.

The trust establishing tactics described by Giffin as well as the behavioral approach to the notion of trust are clear in two statements by Charles Hamilton. In one place he describes the Black-White dilemma in terms of predictability saying, "Black Power must not be naïve about the intentions of White decision makers to yield anything without a struggle and a confrontation by organized power. . . . And it must be clear that Whites will have to bargain with Blacks or continue to fight them in the streets of the Detroits and the Newarks."[13] This statement stresses the importance of risk as an element in solving racial discord and as a necessary factor in increasing the predictability of the white power structure. It also speaks in terms which indicate the intention of establishing a trust relationship as well as the probable consequences of trust violations. Hamilton speaks of the provisions necessary for the establishment of interracial trust when he points out that "Resolution probably lies in the realization by white America that it is in her best interest not to have a weak, dependent, alienated black community inhabiting the inner cities and blowing them up periodically."[14] Neither of these two statements refers to the possibility of an intuitive feeling of good will between the races, but rather, they focus on the necessity of using risk as the barometer to predictability and hence to trust. Both statements describe the conditions requisite for Black-White predictability, and both imply the reaction on the part of Blacks to unpredictable and untrustworthy behavior on the part of the White community. The only evaluative aspects of the statements are those which imply profit or loss for trustee or trustor. They seem to exhibit some of the trust establishing tactics described earlier and to look at trust from a point of view which relies on predictability and not intuition.

Carmichael and Hamilton use a trust building strategy in their book *Black Power: The Politics of Liberation in America* when they articulate the nature of slum housing and slum landlords in profit motive terms. For example, in referring to improvements in slum housing they state, "The absentee slumlord is perpetuating a socially detrimental condition, and he should not be allowed to hide behind the rubric of property rights. The Black community must insist that the goal of human rights take precedent over property rights, and back up that insistence in ways which will make it in the self-interest of the White society to act morally. . . . No one should be naïve enough to think that an owner will give up his property easily, but the Black community, properly organized and mobilized, could apply pressure that would make him choose between the alternatives of forfeiture or compliance."[15]

As in earlier examples this statement focuses on describing a situation in terms of risk and predictability. The commentary emphasizes the need for an organization which can respond to untrustworthy action on the part of the slumlord and which, at the same time, reciprocates trust if the slumlord should offer it.

Examining the rhetoric of Black Power from the behavioral point of view as a trust establishing rhetoric sheds new light on the most distinctive Black movement since Marcus Garvey's "Back to Africa" crusade. It focuses on a function heretofore overlooked or misinterpreted. Instead of viewing the threats of Black Power advocates as crude and blatant forms of blackmail, as many critics have, the behavioral position views them as trust establishing tactics which are perfectly compatible with American tradition and with the Capitalistic economic system. Furthermore these tactics, when viewed as attempts to establish a trust relationship, bear a striking similarity to the tactics which almost every individual employs in his interactions with other persons in the marketplace. The rhetoric of Black Power can be seen in light of these similarities not only as a revolutionary rhetoric but also as an evolutionary rhetoric which reflects movement on the part of Black peoples toward full acceptance by traditional power loci. Such a view coincides with Arthur L. Smith's description of the rhetoric of Black revolution as a unifying rhetoric which attempts to establish cultural freedom among Black peoples through self-respect and pride.[16]

In conclusion, the trust establishing function of the rhetoric of Black Power moves the Black-White controversy to the familiar grounds of the profit system where both Black and White are motivated to "T.C.B.—take care of business."[17] In the words of Julius Lester, "Those Whites who have a similar vision and want to be a part of this new world must cast down their bucket where they are."[18]

NOTES

[1] Julius Lester, *Look Out, Whitey! Black Power's Gon' Get Your Mama* (New York: Grove Press, 1968), p. 140.

2 Robert L. Scott, "Justifying Violence—The Rhetoric of Militant Black Power," *Central States Speech Journal*, XIX (Summer 1968), 96–104.

3 Robert L. Scott, and Donald K. Smith, "The Rhetoric of Confrontation," *The Quarterly Journal of Speech*, LV (February 1969), 1–9.

4 Richard B. Gregg, A. Jackson McCormack, and Douglas J. Pedersen, "The Rhetoric of Black Power: A Street-Level Interpretation," *The Quarterly Journal of Speech*, LV (April 1969), 151–160.

5 See Arthur L. Smith, *Rhetoric of Black Revolution* (Boston: Allyn & Bacon, 1969), pp. 5–10, and Wilmer Linkugel, "New Directions in American Public Address," a paper delivered at the Illinois-Missouri State Speech Association Convention, St. Louis, November 7, 1969.

6 *Webster's Seventh New Collegiate Dictionary*, (Springfield, Mass.: G. & C. Merriam, 1965).

7 Kim Giffin, "Interpersonal Trust in Small Group Communication," *The Quarterly Journal of Speech*, LIII (October, 1967), 224.

8 Morton Deutsch, "Trust and Suspicion," *Journal of Conflict Resolution*, II (December 1958), 266.

9 Giffin, 224.

10 *Ibid.*, 233–234.

11 Stokely Carmichael, Speech delivered in Detroit, July 20, 1966. Found in *The Rhetoric of Black Power*, eds. Robert L. Scott and Wayne Brockriede (New York: Harper & Row, 1969), p. 94.

12 Stokely Carmichael, Speech delivered at Whitewater, Wisconsin on February 6, 1965. Found in Scott and Brockriede, p. 110. Originally the speech was published in the *Massachusetts Review* (Autumn 1966), 639–651.

13 Charles V. Hamilton, "An Advocate of Black Power Defines It," *New York Times Magazine* (April 4, 1968), 22–23 and 79–83.

14 *Ibid.*, 187.

15 Stokely Carmichael and Charles V. Hamilton, *Black Power: The Politics of Liberation in America* (New York: Vintage Books, 1967), p. 172.

16 Smith, Introduction and Chapters 1–3.

17 *Ibid.*, 185.

18 Lester, 142.

Robert D. Brooks

CHAPTER 25
Black Power:
The Dimensions of a Slogan

Many definitions of *Black Power* have appeared since June, 1966, when this slogan was generally adopted as the call letters of the civil rights movement.[1] The definitions have come almost entirely from black spokesmen: Carmichael, Brown, McKissick, Powell, Young, King, Wilkins and Cleaver.[2] All indeed are leaders and all presumably are authorities on the question, "What does *Black Power* mean?" However, two problems emerge when we attempt to unpack the meanings which these men have assigned the slogan.

From *Western Speech Journal* (Spring 1970), pp. 108–114. Reprinted by permission of the publisher and the author. Robert D. Brooks is Associate Professor in Public Address and Group Communication, Northwestern University.

First, the spokesmen-definers are black, and we may question how adequately their definitions bespeak the meanings which whites attribute to *Black Power*. The omission of white sentiment is serious if we are concerned with the implications the slogan may have for social change. Second, for us to know much about the spokesman-definer's black constituency is often difficult. What is its size? What measure of agreement exists within it about the meanings of the slogan? These problems generated the present study. We offer here a limited investigation of an attack we made on two related questions: (1) What does *Black Power* mean to specific groups of blacks and whites? (2) Within those groups, what degree of consensus obtains?

THE GROUPS

The study involved the comparison of meanings which the slogan elicited from three groups: black students, white students, and white urban policemen.

The first group consisted of forty-two black college students (twenty-five male and seventeen female) at the University of Illinois, Urbana. Most of these students, of both sexes, had been directly involved in at least one campus demonstration. Many had participated in several protests. These students were part of "Project 500," a program designed to recruit students primarily from the ghetto areas. A few were from New York and Philadelphia, but the vast majority were from Chicago's Southside.

The second group consisted of eighty white undergraduates (fifty-eight male and twenty-two female) from the same institution. They were enrolled in a large humanities course with students from all sections of the campus except engineering and agriculture. While they had witnessed campus racial demonstrations, very few had been directly involved in protest actions. In most respects they seemed representative of a white undergraduate student body at a large midwestern university.

The third group consisted of forty white male policemen. Approximately three-fourths of the policemen were from Chicago; others were from the urban areas of Rockford and East St. Louis, Illinois. They were enrolled in a police science extension course at the University of Illinois.

PROCEDURE

Each group was asked, "Define what the concept *Black Power* means to you." The question was asked and the definitions collected by persons known to the individual groups. A male member of the Black Students' Association collected the responses of the black students. An instructor in police science (an ex-Los Angeles policeman) gathered the materials from the policemen. The writer, a white instructor, collected the data from the white students. All of the participants were assured anonymity; they were required to identify themselves by race and sex only. Their hand-written definitions were transcribed verbatim upon cards which were coded in such a way that race, sex, and group membership were known only to this writer.

Preliminary analysis of the definitions indicate three dominant dimensions to the meaning of *Black Power* for these groups. (1) The aggression dimension: many definitions stated that violence or racial domination (black over white) was inherent in the concept. (2) The goals dimension: for many subjects *Black Power* was associated with specific goals; for others, none. (3) The mystique dimension: many subjects endowed the slogan with non-material attributes, such as self-identity, pride, and awareness. The general question, "What does *Black Power* mean?" could thus be posed more specifically as "How do the three groups differ with respect to these dimensions of the slogan?"

Four white judges (three professors and a doctoral candidate in speech-communication) were each given copies of the transcribed definitions. They were asked to classify them according to the presence or absence of each of the three themes. The few definitions on which the judges could not completely agree (less than 5%) were discarded. In other words, the between-judge reliability for the judges' classifications and the statistics presented below is 100%. Regrettably black experts in language analysis were not available as judges. However, judge bias was hopefully minimized by the absence of racial identification on the transcribed definitions.

RESULTS AND DISCUSSION

Perceived aggressiveness

In analyzing the definitions of our subjects, we classified as "Perceived Aggressiveness" those responses which stated that violence or black supremacy over whites was part of the meaning of *Black Power*. We found this dimension occurred in each of the three groups. One black male defined the concept in two words: "Kill Whitey." White coeds expressed these views: "I associate the concept *Black Power* with those blacks who have given up working within our system and who will do anything to gain what they want"; "*Black Power* refers to a movement allegedly to establish equality—but in reality it means a take-over"; a third white coed confessed that she was ". . . fearful of what all the blacks will do to gain their rights." A white policeman phrased the opinions of many of his colleagues (perhaps uneloquently, but accurately) when he defined *Black Power* thus: ". . . *Black Power* can be compared to the guerrilla wing of the N.V.A. [North Vietnamese Army] called Viet Cong—deadly and ruthless."

Yet many subjects seemed to go out of their way to deny that *Black Power* implied aggressive behavior. A black coed: "It is not an attempt by the black race to conquer the white." A white male undergraduate: "It is not a concept which denotes violence. It does not mean anything destructive, but has to do with constructive motives." A white policeman, a rare response from his group: ". . . just a few black people use the term to mean rioting." Ironically, these denials seem to be evidence that even those subjects who did not perceive aggressiveness in *Black Power* suspected that many of their peers did.

Their suspicions seem well-founded: 24% of the black students perceived aggressiveness in *Black Power*; 43% of the white students; 78% of the white policemen.[3] The basic finding is this: whites, far more frequently than blacks, perceived aggressiveness in *Black Power*. Perhaps of greater social significance is the finding that white policemen represent this racial distinction most acutely. Among four *black* policemen who were available in the early stages of this study, none defined *Black Power* as embracing aggression. Almost 80% of their white colleagues attributed violence or racial supremacy to the slogan. Interestingly, among all the subjects, only white policemen attributed this aggressiveness to Communist inspiration: 12% of the policemen took a red conspiracy view of the term *Black Power*.

LEVELS OF SPECIFICITY

Our society has lived with the slogan for three years. One would expect that *Black Power* would now be associated with specific goals. That expectation proved faulty in many instances. For example, several subjects in each group defined the concept quite generally, often almost tautologically. A black male undergraduate: "*Black Power* is my power." A black coed: "*Black Power* is the getting and achieving of power for my people." A white policeman: "It's just their way of showing that the black man is finally doing something about the conditions in which they live." A white male student: "*Black Power* is a force among Negroes which represents the power of the combined masses of the Negro." A white coed, perhaps expressing her intolerance for ambiguity: "*So much* has been said about *Black Power*. All it really means is the influence the black people have in the world today." These and similar definitions seem to say not much more than *Black Power* is black power. Several additional definitions from each of the groups were also quite general, merely mentioning *equality* or *rights* without specifying what forms of equality or what areas of rights.

However, a large minority of the *student* subjects mentioned specific goals for *Black Power*. To some, *Black Power* included control of those institutions which have a direct impact on black neighborhoods: schools, housing, urban planning, and welfare programs. For others, the goal referent was political: control of an autonomous black government; elected black office holders in the white power structure. The most frequent referent was economic: money; black ownership of factories and stores; jobs in banks, shops, and the sanitation department. But let us stress that specific responses were not in the majority. In short, in no group did as many as 50% of the definitions contain sure goal referents. The pattern is this: black students, 45%; white students, 47%; white policemen, 18%.[4]

Again, our attention is called to the police. Within the context of these data, the police seem to represent the deviant condition. What might account for the distinct lack of specific goal referents in their definitions? Our reasoning is this: most of the policemen centered their definitions on violence or reverse racism. In the main, those definitions discussed the *means* of *Black Power* (how it operates) rather than the *goals* of *Black Power* (what the movement seeks as objectives). Several policemen volunteered the opinion in their definitions that blacks did not know what they really wanted; others opined that the movement had no genuine objective, that it was merely the work of "trouble-makers." In short, the police appeared almost blind to the goals. The absence of specific goal meanings in the police definitions probably signifies that *Black Power* has little positive substance for white urban peace officers.

THE BLACK MYSTIQUE

A slogan signifies more than means and goals. There is another dimension: the spirit of the movement. The *New Frontier* slogan of the Kennedy era, for example, evoked not merely images of programs and objectives. Among other things, *New Frontier* called forth America's feelings about such vague concepts as *progress, challenge,* and *enterprise.* The rhetoric of the term *New Frontier* was laced with "Let's get the country moving again," "Let us begin," and "One man *can* make a difference." Similarly, many of the definitions of *Black Power* contained themes which almost defy objectification: soul, awareness, identity, and pride. Collectively, these themes signify a mystique dimension. In more innocent times we might have labeled it "the spiritual factor."

This dimension was central to one-fourth of the definitions. A black coed brought many of the mystique-related topics together in her definition: "Black is more than a color, it is a state of mind, of having pride, and determination, and soul." From one of her soul brothers: "*Black Power*—an awareness, a consciousness that instills a sense of pride in our culture." A white coed revealed some measure of her ability to empathize: "*Black Power*—a way of thinking, acting, and expressing, all from the 'black' point of view." A white male undergraduate: "*Black Power,* the spirit of the black people in America; the return to their culture; in essence, Black Pride." A white policeman, one of only five who could operate in the mystique realm: "The desire of the black people to be proud, and the desire to instill in other blacks a pride in what and who they are." The once again popular Garveyite slogan, "Black Is Beautiful," did not occur in any of the definitions. However, the theme of pride which underlies that motto appeared in slightly more than one-half of the mystique responses.

A breakdown of this dimension by groups reveals much the same ordering observed earlier: black students, 38%; white students, 26%; white policemen, 12%.[5] Which finding should be emphasized? That less than half the subjects attributed a transcendent meaning to Black Power, or that the white policemen's responses are again at the unsympathetic end of the continuum?

THE MEANING GAP

The meanings surveyed here are not static. Continuing developments in the movement will generate changes in the responses canopied by the slogan. Indeed, an entirely new catch-phrase with a different thrust could emerge. But some conclusions about the slogan *Black Power* should be hazarded because the findings illuminate an important area of race relations—communication.

The data of this study argue that there is considerable distance between the meanings attributed to the concept *Black Power* by the police and those by the young blacks. The social consequences of this meaning gap may well be substantial. The white urban policemen saw very little spiritual meaning, very few legitimate objectives, inordinate aggressiveness, and some measure of Communist conspiracy underlying the slogan. In sharp contrast, the black students endowed *Black Power* with an ethnic mystique; they were much more likely to associate the slogan with concrete goals, much less likely to conceive of it as as symbol of violence or racial supremacy. Perceptions as polarized as these may in part explain a policeman's proclivity to use his club and the black's conviction that white society is spiritually bankrupt.

Ostensibly, the semantic distance between these groups could be explained by the realities of police work. Compared with many other Americans, the policeman frequently encounters violence that could sensitize him to see aggression where there is none. Further, there may be little in his job that would nourish abstract thoughts about identity, awareness, unity, and pride in race. However, could not a similar case be made for ghetto youth? Sociological literature makes frequent reference to the violence of the ghetto. Hustling, muggings, gang wars, robbery, and weapon caches are facts of life there. A less comforting explanation for this difference may reside in a study of such questions as these: What kinds of personalities are drawn to police work? What racial relations information is included in the training programs of police academies?

The responses of white students suggest a more optimistic analysis. Their meanings were either similar to the black students' or closer to them than to the white policemen's. This affinity suggests a semantic bridge between student populations, a connection that may augur, however slimly, better race relations for the future.

At least the congruence of meanings we have observed here correlates well with Eldridge Cleaver's prognosis for America: ". . . the future rests with those whites and blacks who have liberated themselves from the master/slave syndrome. And these are to be found mainly among the youth."[6]

NOTES

[1] For an account of the origin of the slogan, see Haig A. Bosmajian and Hamida Bosmajian, *The Rhetoric of the Civil Rights Movement* (New York, 1969), pp. 26–27.

[2] For a survey of definitions of "Black Power," see John Walter, "Big Ten Short Course on 'Black Power,'" *Big Ten*, II (May 1968), pp. 24–25.

[3] The data were also analyzed to test the significance of the difference between these statistics. Z scores were computed according to the method discussed in Alan Edwards, *Experimental Design for Psychological Research*, revised edition (New York, 1960), p. 53. For the "Perceived Aggressiveness" dimension, the differences between the police and the black students and between the police and the white students are significant at the .01 level of confidence. The difference between the black and white students is significant at the .05 level of confidence. No statistically significant differences were observed between males and females of either race. The analysis here and below is two tailed.

[4] For "Specific Goal Referents," the differences between the police and the black students and between the police and the white students are significant at the .01 level of confidence. The difference between the black and white students is not statistically significant. Again, no statistically significant differences were found between the sexes of either race.

[5] For the "Black Mystique," the difference between the police and the black students is significant at the .01 level of confidence. The difference between the police and white students approaches but does not meet the .05 level of confidence. The difference between the student groups is not statistically significant. The sex variable was again found to be insignificant within either race.

[6] Eldridge Cleaver, *Soul on Ice* (New York, 1968), p. 67.

Larry S. Richardson

CHAPTER 26
Stokely Carmichael:
Jazz Artist

Four tragic, bewildering years have passed since that June evening in Greenwood, Mississippi, when Stokely Carmichael unleashed the term *Black Power*. Surely, his oratory has now become the "Magna Charta" of a protest movement which has affected the destiny of America. The rhetorical significance and implications of Carmichael and *black power* are established.[1] However,

From *Western Speech Journal* (Summer 1970), pp. 212–218. Reprinted by permission of the publisher and the author. Larry S. Richardson is Course Coordinator for Negro History and Problems at Edmonds Community College and is Director of Forensics at Edmonds, Washington, Senior High School. This paper was first presented at the Cal State Conference on Rhetorical Criticism, Hayward, California, April 1969.

I know of no critic who has observed that Carmichael's oratory may be a natural outgrowth of Negro culture, especially its music. Carmichael's oratory, I think, contains the elements of content, organization, and style that are analogous to the unique Negro art of jazz.

The relationship seems natural. The arts of any culture, most authorities agree, function as nonverbal storehouses of familiar forms and materials which any speaker may adapt as solutions to the practical problems of persuasion. Carmichael, I believe, has drawn both form and content from the storehouse of jazz for his speeches to his "brothers." I shall posit certain stipulations which apply equally to jazz and to Carmichael's oratory.

Orvil Dankworth characterizes pure jazz as "a specific kind of music . . . with quite strict rules," "an improvisatory art," "a feeling, a style."[2] We can surely agree that jazz is a small group thing that requires interaction, both internally within the group and externally with the audience. Similarly, I think Carmichael's oratory is group oriented, for interaction seems vital to the desired effect. Obviously, we may also view jazz as an "in-group" activity that comes alive only with the initiated. And my study of Carmichael's oratory indicates that his speeches come fully alive only when designed for an audience of his "brothers." The Boston and Whitewater speeches, containing "dignified" and "tame" messages, I shall use to illustrate Carmichael's adaptation to white audiences.[3] The Berkeley and Detroit speeches, involving black or pro-black power audiences, I shall use for contrasting examples to develop the thesis of this study.[4] In terms of message, I believe that Stokely Carmichael's speeches are "singing the blues" in the jazz tradition that grew out of the Negro spiritual:

Oh, nobody knows de trouble I've seen,
Glory, hallelujah

Langston Hughes states: "The blues are almost always sad songs, songs about being out of work, broke, hungry, far away from home . . . behind the sadness, there is almost always laughter and strength."[5] With a further examination of lyrics of various blues, we would generally find that they organize sadness and strength around a statement of hardship, a wish to escape to the promised land, and a mood of irony or humor. These elements we also have in Carmichael's oratory that describes white exploitation of black people:

The missionaries came with the Bible, and we had the land; when they left, they had the land, and we still had the Bible.[6]

Black power becomes the promised land, attainable but vague, he goes on to say:

And in order to get out of that oppression one must wield the group power that one has, not the individual power which this country then sets as the criteria under which a man may come into it [sic].[7]

The same sadness-laughter approach to message he also voices in the Detroit speech:

It's only because we don't own and control our communities that they are the way they are.

You've got to tell them that if we've got the money, the same amount of money that they put into their suburban schools, that we put in our schools, that we could produce black people who are just as capable of taking care of business, as they're producing white people. They've been stealing our money (applause) that's where the problem exists.[8]

The "blues" message has been identified and discussed by more moderate Negro leaders who believe that black power rhetoric is counterproductive to the long-range goals of the black man and even harmful to the Negro psyche. Dr. King's last speech says: "I think the aura of paramilitarism among the black militant groups speaks much more of fear than it does of confidence."[9]

Dr. Kenneth Clark, noted Negro psychologist, characterizes the rhetoric as retrogressive, sour grapes thinking generated by the current status of the black man "at the threshold of a non-segregated society." Clark points to the frustration caused by tension between the legal right to pass through the door of racial equality and the absence of training and background prerequisite to passage. He concludes:

Black power is a bitter retreat from the possibility of the attainment of the goals of any serious integration in America.

It is an attempt to make a verbal virtue of involuntary racial segregation ... the sour grapes phenomenon of the American racial scene.[10]

The message of Stokely Carmichael, though often viewed by whites as new and different, we may better understand and appreciate if we think of it as an oratorical version of the message of Negro spirituals and jazz blues. Its acceptance by many blacks is indicative, I think, of the current state of the ghetto psyche.

In so many ways jazz seems to relate to music as oratory does to language. Interaction between performer or speaker and the audience obviously characterizes both media and produces a unification of style and organization through definable stylistic devices developed by jazz musicians: individualization, aggressive use of materials, improvisation, omission, repetition, and audience participation.

Even the initiate recognizes that the jazz man individualizes his style through combinations of "sound" and melodic and rhythmic tendencies recognizable as unique to an individual. A few seconds of Charlie Parker or Coleman Hawkins on a recording make each easily identifiable. And so can we also recognize stylistic uniqueness in Stokely Carmichael's oratory—a unique, identifiable and memorable gestalt that amounts to "doing his thing." The jazz man swings, and Stokely "tells it like it is," projecting his very personal image to those who dig.

As the jazz musician uses sound for his material in an aggressive manner, I find Carmichael is aggressive in his use of style and organization. Carmichael's use of language, which, we shall surely agree, is the major factor in explaining his considerable impact on white sensibilities, seems less extreme when viewed as a jazz performance. In jazz we observe that the musician regularly tests the norms of musical convention; he employs large skips, extreme ranges and registers, and shocking timbre as he improvises his melodic lines; he makes his instrument squeak, honk, and moan; his facility is considered a mark of excellence in technique and individuality. We find the extreme becomes the norm if we compare it to "legitimate" music.

That many of the sounds of jazz have figurative or literal sexual symbolism is accepted. The jazz musician seems willing to portray human experience considered taboo by "squares," and I think that willingness is probably one reason for the gap between the initiated and the masses that often prevents the latter group from appreciating jazz.

Similarly, in his speeches I find Mr. Carmichael uses his material aggressively, often exceeding the norms of verbal convention. *All* white Americans are "honkies." The liberal who employs a Negro maid and the youth who participate in the Mississippi Project stand condemned by him for their lack of sensitivity. He calls Negro integrationists "Whitey Young" and "Uncle Tom Wilkins."

Carmichael, I find, makes rhetorical use of four-letter words and sexual allusions. Illustrating how the press had distorted news of the Alabama Freedom Democratic Party by calling it the Black Panther Party because of its ballot symbol, he suggests that the white rooster of the regular party be subject to the same treatment: "Our question is, why don't they call the Alabama Democratic Party the White Cock Party?"[11]

Jazz *is* improvisation, and I think Stokely Carmichael's rhetoric is also "improvisation"—extemporaneous, adaptive, and innovative. In jazz, improvisation usually is thought to elevate the performer to the supreme position, superior to the tunesmith who first composed the basic material. While the basic sequence of chords and relative duration values are retained by the performer, he produces a melodic line that is his own creation. Similarly, Stokely Carmichael, I believe, is an improviser. His style, concepts, and combinations represent unique and interesting arrangement, and his improvisation on syllogistic reasoning illustrates his improvisation. In the Berkeley speech, he says:

So people have been telling you anything all black is bad. Let's make that our major premise. Major premise: Anything all black is bad. Minor premise or particular premise: I am all black. Therefore . . . (delayed applause and laughter) I'm never going to be put in that bag.[12]

Conventional material is here employed in a pattern of improvisation. We can also liken the chordal structure of the jazz tune to the structure of the syllogism, which is familiar material to the college-age audience as the tune is familiar to the jazz fan.

We find further illustration in the way that Carmichael adapts his syllogism to the all-black audience of Detroit:

There's a thing called a syllogism. And it says like, if you're born in Detroit, you're beautiful; that's the major premise. The minor premise is—I am born in Detroit. Therefore, I'm beautiful. Anything all black is bad—major premise. Minor premise—I'm all black. Therefore (pause) yeah, yeah, (laughter and applause) yeah. You're all out there, and the man telling you about yourself, and you don't know it.[13]

I should add, probably, that seldom does a jazz man play a tune the very same way twice, although it is often almost the same. That Stokely Carmichael operates similarly in these cited passages (and in others) is also apparent, both in terms of invention and subsequent idea adaptation.

Jazz musicians, we have observed, frequently omit notes from phrases; I find Carmichael omits expected content elements. In many of Charlie Parker's recorded solos we have melodic lines where he omits notes; that is, in the course of an improvised line, he establishes a harmonic direction and then omits sounds. I believe the tendency of the line probably leads the listener to fill in the missing sounds mentally, whether they occur during or at the ends of phrases. In jazz the effect is widely used.

Stokely Carmichael, I can report, also uses omission and I believe he also succeeds in mentally involving listeners as participants instead of as passive observers; he omits words, lines of argument, and answers to questions. In the Berkeley speech, Carmichael says:

We must now set a criteria [sic], and if there's going to be any integration it's going to be a two-way thing.
We must question the values of this society, and I maintain that black people are the best people to do that, because we have been excluded from that society, and the question is, we ought to think whether or not we want to become a part of that society.[14]

White Americans might have difficulty with this line of argument, but I am confident the initiate knows what Carmichael means; the initiate fills in the details from his own experience, as in the classic enthymeme. The "syllogism ploy" discussed earlier in the essay is another example that illustrates how Carmichael uses omission successfully.

Repetition is another device we know as common to jazz musicians and to Carmichael. While we frequently experience it in many art forms, we find its literal character is notable when we compare Carmichael and jazz musicians. The jazz riff is melodic repetition and is considered basic to jazz structure. Endings are frequently repeated in jazz. Often, we observe in jazz that when these materials are repeated, they are compressed. Carmichael, I find, makes considerable use of the latter form of jazz repetition, a literal or compressed replay of the last part of a sentence or of the final sentence of a paragraph. Here is an example from the Berkeley speech:

I don't want any of your blood money. I don't want it, don't want any part of that system. And the question is how do we raise those questions? How do we raise them . . . how do we begin to raise them?[15]

The rhythmic prose we have throughout Carmichael's oratory I think is notable and, like most artistic rhythm, Carmichael bases his rhythms on the repetition of patterns. Although we may find the comparison of jazz rhythm with rhetorical rhythm difficult, we can surely feel a sense of rhythmic comparability between Carmichael's oratory and jazz. Through both literal and compressed repetition, I find Carmichael makes maximum use of rhythm, and its effect seems the same as in jazz—Carmichael swings.

Finally, I conclude that the jazz man and Stokely Carmichael share a capacity to elicit and exploit audience participation. Although we think the modern jazz setting is more subdued than in earlier days, I argue that a strong link between performer and audience remains, finding its expression in more subtle ways. In intimate jazz spots we have all surely observed as acceptable behavior polite attention during performance, applause at ends of choruses, fraternization between numbers, and subtle rhythmic movement of audience members. And we have also seen at the large jazz festivals that audiences are more demonstrative—they use boisterous applause, cheering, and whistling as means to feed back their approval of the music. In either setting, I think jazz men perform better when interaction is strong; they will always go "one more time" when the crowd is "digging."

Stokely Carmichael, in my view, similarly elicits overt audience response in the form of applause, laughter, or audience comment, and then he reacts to the response, thereby generating more response. I know of times that each sentence was followed by applause of increased intensity—the speaker and audience interacting to generate a crescendo that continued long beyond the final words of the idea sequence. The Detroit speech seems typical:

You send a black man to Vietnam to fight for rights, and he doesn't have any rights in his homeland, he's a black mercenary. You send a black man to Vietnam and he gets shot and they won't bury him in his land—he's a black mercenary (applause). He's a black mercenary (continued applause). And if we going to be black mercenaries they ought to pay us twenty-five thousand dollars a year and let us come home every weekend (laughter and applause). Since they are not going to do that, we are going to have to develop in our communities enough internal strength to tell everyone in this country that we're not going to your damn war, period (shouts and applause). We've got to do that (continued applause).[16]

Too many white Americans, I think, perceive literally the rhetoric of Stokely Carmichael. The backlash component of recent political events seems an indication of the anxiety produced by this literal interpretation; LeRoi Jones—black poet, playwright, and jazz critic—comments:

Form and content are both mutually expressive of the whole. And they are both equally expressive . . . each has an identifying motif and function. We want different content and different forms because we have different feelings. We are different peoples.[17]

I suggest that white Americans may better adjust to the reality of black power if they view the message as a newer version of an old thought pattern, one growing out of the Negro's life experience. I have illustrated how this pattern is manifested in the form of jazz, and I know of many whites who have experienced and appreciated its message, style, and organization. Through the jazz idiom, we may agree, whites have gained insight and empathy about the world of the black man. If whites will strive to perceive black rhetoric at a more sophisticated level than mere literality, then we may find they will also take a first step toward resolving the conflict between the races in a manner acceptable both to Negroes and whites.

NOTES

1 See, e.g., Robert L. Scott, "Justifying Violence—The Rhetoric of Militant Black Power," *CSSJ*, XIX (1968), 96–104; Wayne Brockriede and Robert L. Scott, "Two Speeches on Black Power," *CSSJ*, XIX (1968), 130; Parke G. Burgess, "The Rhetoric of Black Power: A Moral Demand?" *QJS*, XLIV (1968), 122–123.

2 Orvil Dankworth, *Jazz: An Introduction to Its Musical Basis* (London, 1968), p. vii.

3 Leon Friedman, ed., *The Civil Rights Reader* (New York, 1967), pp. 139–148; Robert L. Scott and Wayne Brockriede, *The Rhetoric of Black Power* (New York, 1969), pp. 96–111.

4 Charles M. Lomas, *The Agitator in American Society* (Englewood Cliffs, N.J., 1968), pp. 135–151; Scott and Brockriede, *The Rhetoric of Black Power*, pp. 84–95.

5 Langston Hughes, *First Book of Jazz* (New York, 1954), p. 21.

6 Lomas, pp. 140–141.

7 Lomas, p. 141.

8 Scott and Brockriede, *Rhetoric*, pp. 87–88.

9 "King's Last Tape," *Newsweek*, December 16, 1968.

10 Kenneth B. Clark, "The Present Dilemma of the Negro," *Journal of Negro History*, LIII (1968), 8.

11 Lomas, p. 140.

12 *Ibid.*

13 Scott and Brockriede, *Rhetoric*, p. 88.

14 Lomas, p. 146.

15 *Ibid.*

16 Scott and Brockriede, *Rhetoric*, pp. 89–90.

17 LeRoi Jones, *Black Music* (New York, 1967), p. 185.

Romeo B. Garrett

CHAPTER 27
African Survivals
in American Culture

African survivals in American culture have diminished markedly over the past one hundred years, but some are still existent and are interwoven into the cultural pattern of America and the Western Hemisphere itself. These are reflected in the words we speak, the songs we sing, the dances we perform, the instruments we play, the stories we relate, and the foods we consume.

The most recent work on Negro speech in the United States is that of Dr. Lorenzo Dow Turner, professor of English at Roosevelt

From *The Journal of Negro History*, Vol. LI, No. 4, (October 1966), pp. 239–245. Copyright © by The Association for the Study of Negro Life and History, Inc. Published in said *Journal* October 1966. Reprinted by permission.

University, Chicago. His search uncovered astonishing survivals of African culture and more than 4,000 African words, names and numbers still spoken among Negroes on the Georgia-South Carolina offshore islands, known to anthropologists as the Gullah region. Many of these words are employed by Negroes and whites throughout the United States.[1]

They lay bare the probable explanation of some of the oldest and newest Americanisms, from "tote" to "juke box." They reveal the identity, civilization and relative influence of the people from which most of America's 20,000,000 Negroes descend.

The word *tote*, meaning carry, has been found in print within seventy years after the first settlement at Jamestown, Virginia. It has no known English origin.

A frequently used word among southern Negroes is *pinder* for peanut (called *guba* and *pinda* in Gullah from identical words used by tribes in Angola). Also, the word *tater* for potato has been found in several West African languages.

The list covers many animals like *cooter* for tortoise (*kuta* in Gullah from two French West African tongues); *biddy* for chick (it means a bird in Congolese); and *jigger* (bug known as *jiga* in six African tongues).

The name *yam* as applied to the sweet potato may be a corruption of the African word *nyam* that was brought to this country by the Negroes. *Nyam* was the word the Negroes used for true yam or other large edible roots or tubers found in Africa. Later, it was incorrectly applied to large American sweet potatoes.

Our latest *juke boxes* come from the word "juke," a Senegalese term implying a wild time.

African names, too, have survived among Negroes. Two common ones are *Bobo* and *Anyike*. Professor Turner has connected 2,000 names in the United States with African languages.

Other scholars of African languages, including Serjeantson, corroborate the findings of Professor Turner. *Voodoo*, first found in 1880, is probably from Dahomey "vodu." *Gumbo* (Angolan ki-nyombo) appears first in America (1859). The word *gorilla* is alleged to be an African word. This was adopted as the specific name of the ape ("Trogladytes gorilla") by Savage in 1847 (*Journal of the Boston Natural History Society*); it is found as an English word first in 1853. *Banana* comes to us through Spanish from the native name in Guinea in 1597; *okra* 1707, through the West Indies; it appears first in Slaone's Jamica; *chimpanzee* 1738: "A most surprising creature is brought over in the Speaker, just arrived from Carolina, that was taken in a wood at Guinea. She is the female creature which the Angolans call Chimpanzee"; *cola, kola*, the seed, used for chewing, etc., from a West African tree; *zebra* 1600 from the Congo dialect.[2]

Other African words interwoven in the American English linguistic fabric are: *buckra, pickaninny, jazz, elephant, ebony, turnip, parsnip, oasis, canopic*, and *sorcery*.[3]

Negro spirituals are traceable to Africa. H. E. Krehbiel, the nineteenth-century pioneer authority on the Afro-American folksongs, after analyzing 527 Negro spirituals, found their identical prototypes in African music, concluding that the essential "intervallic rhythmical and structural elements" of these songs came from the ancestral homelands.[4]

These vestiges of African music rose to a higher harmonic development when there was blown through or fused into them the spirit of Christianity as the Negro slaves knew Christianity. At the psychic moment there was at hand the precise religion for the adverse conditions in which they found themselves thrust. This religion implied the hope that in the next world there would be a reversal of conditions. All men—slave and free, black and white, rich and poor, high and low—would be equal. The result was a body of song voicing all the cardinal virtues of Christianity—patience, forbearance, love, faith, and hope—through a necessarily modified form of primitive African music. The Negro took complete refuge in Christianity and the spirituals were literally forged of sorrow in the heat of religious fervor. They brought hope and comfort to a burdened people.[5]

The contribution of the transplanted African to musical expression in America was summed up by Walter Damrosch in a speech at Hampton Institute in 1912: "Unique and inimitable, Negro music is the only music of this country, except that of the American Indians, which can claim to be folk music." It is the finest distinctive artistic contribution America has offered the world.

Jazz, too, has its roots in Africa. Negro slaves from Africa brought the roots of such and planted them in the soil of slavery. The word "jazz" in an African dialect means "hurry up." That is just about the tempo of jazz. The culture patterns that produced jazz are the result of the Afro-American's accommodation to a sociocultural setting established and controlled by Euro-Americans. Afro-American music is characterized by tonal and rhythmic elements of African origin transformed by disciplines of Euro-American music.[6]

Leonard Feather, one of the most important jazz scholars and critics, explaining Afro-American orientation of jazz said:

"Jazz was the product of a specific social environment in which a group of people, the American Negroes, largely shut off from the white world, developed cultural patterns of their own."[7]

M. E. Hall, Music Department Chairman at Michigan State University, presenting the case for academic jazz in America wrote:

"Popular music at all levels, movie background music, television background music, musical comedy, all are growths of the jazz idiom. Europeans consider jazz to be our one important contribution to the culture of the world."[8]

The noted French music critic André Hodier wrote:

"What contemporary observer would have guessed that the folk music of a small group would become the language of an entire people fifteen or twenty years later and in a few more years, a world-wide phenomenon, with jazz bands existing simultaneously in Melbourne, Tokyo, and Stockholm."[9]

The African group said to have contributed most to the basic nature of jazz was the Dahomeans of West Africa. Their musical traditions merged with those of the French and became the leading influence when the "roots" of jazz were still forming in the West Indies. The Dahomeans later became a powerful cultural force in New Orleans. The Creoles, a group of French Negroes, settled in

Louisiana and were wealthy and as well educated as Europeans. They became an intellectual force in jazz development. Stripped of their property and rights as American citizens, they were forced into the Negro community. Many well-trained Creole musicians found it impossible to work as concert musicians and had to earn money by either teaching or playing "race" music. The techniques they developed as musicians were used to develop the music now called jazz.[10]

The liveliest and most rhythmic dances of the New World are of African origin. African ritual dance patterns, when brought to the New World, interacted with the secular dances from Europe with notable results. In Latin America among the combinations springing from this fusion of African and European dance forms were the beguine, the rhumba, the conga, and the habanera. The first of these originated in Martinique; the last three are Afro-Spanish. The rhumba was first performed among Cuban Negroes as a rural dance depicting simple farm chores. The conga and the newer mambo originated among the Congo Negroes of Cuba. The music of the habanera, which takes its name from Cuba's leading city, has an African rhythmic foundation that soon came to dominate the dance melodies of Latin America, as it does today; from it came the tango (after an African word "rangana") of Argentina. The national dance of Brazil, the samba, is derived directly from the wedding dance of Angola, the quizomba. The significant role of Africanisms in the dance of the Hispanic countries has been richly documented in the monumental studies of the contemporary Cuban scholar, Fernando Ortiz.[11]

The research of Professor Turner also shows that such United States dances as have the Charleston and Black Bottom originated in Africa. So also did calypso singing and musical instruments like the drums, xylophone, marimba, and gourd.

Another African survival is the folk story. Wherever the Negro has gone, tales have gone too, and with only minor alterations in plot. Negroes from the bulge of Africa brought with them legends, myths, proverbs, and the remembered outlines of animal stories that for centuries had been current at their native hearths. The best known of the adaptations of this folklore from the Dark Continent are the Uncle Remus tales, the African ancestor of Br'er Rabbit being Shulo the Hare. The very titles, such as Br'er Wolf and Sis' Nanny Goat, were carried across the Atlantic.[12]

Anthropologists attest that many of our most popular plants have their roots in Africa. Black-eyed peas traveled from Africa to North America in the holds of slave ships as food for the pitiful cargo. Africa's greatest contribution to the joy of eating is watermelon. Cultivated thousands of years ago in the Valley of the Nile, it is still found wild in the interior of Africa where it originated. Sometimes in dry periods it forms the only water supply.[13]

In the conquest of Mexico, Cortez was accompanied by a Negro who, finding in his rations of rice some grains of wheat planted them as an experiment and thus made himself the pioneer in wheat raising in the Western Hemisphere.[14]

It is the consensus of geobotanists that coffee, America's most popular nonalcoholic beverage, has as its birthplace Africa. Our word "coffee" is derived from Kaffa, Ethiopia, its place of origin. Originally coffee was eaten, not drunk. Wandering Ethiopian tribesmen ate wild coffee berries from the trees, or mixed them with fat. The practice continues in many African villages. Ugandans make a savory drink from coffee and bananas. Coffee is today one of Ethiopia's chief exports.[15]

Okra apparently originated in what the geobotanists call the Abyssinian center or origin of cultivated plants, an area that includes present-day Ethiopia, the mountainous or plateau portion of Eritrea, and the eastern, higher part of Sudan. Africans brought their favorite *okura* (okra) to Louisiana. Soon they were teaching the settlers how to make African stew, *kingombo* (gumbo) thickened with okra. Gumbo is to this day a favorite of Americans throughout the United States. When pecans were discovered growing wild in Louisiana, the African cooks creatively turned them into delicious pecan pies and pralines. Pralines were named for the French Duc de Plessis-Praslin who invented a similar confection in France made of sugared almonds. The use of *kola* as a drink originated with the Africans. Today, the extract of kola nuts is the basic ingredient of popular carbonated "cola" drinks throughout the United States and the world.[16]

The late Professor Carter G. Woodson, one of the world's most eminent authorities on Negro culture and history, stated in a letter to the author (November 18, 1947): "All around me I can see Africa in almost every Negro whom I meet, and I do not refer to color. It is true that law and custom cause the Negro to be assimilated gradually to the standard of the Caucasian with whom he comes in contact. But the 'Caucasianization' of the Negro is not yet complete in the United States and very far from being so in Cuba and Brazil."

NOTES

[1] Lorenzo D. Turner, *Africanisms in the Gullah Dialect* (University of Chicago Press, 1949).

[2] Mary S. Serjeantson, *A History of Foreign Words in English* (New York, 1962), pp. 246–49.

[3] *Ibid.*

[4] Benjamin Quarles, *The Negro in the Making of America* (New York, 1964), p. 30.

[5] Dorothy L. Conley, "Origin of the Negro Spirituals," *The Negro History Bulletin* (May 1962), p. 179.

[6] Harold McKinney, "Negro Music," *The Negro History Bulletin*, XXVII, No. 5 (February 1964).

[7] *Ibid.*, p. 120.

[8] *Ibid.*

[9] *Ibid.*

[10] *Ibid.*, p. 126.

[11] Quarles, *op. cit.*, p. 31.

[12] *Ibid.*

[13] Victor Boswell, "Our Vegetable Travelers," *The National Geographic Magazine*, Vol. XCVI, No. 2 (August 1949), pp. 193–211.

[14] Carter G. Woodson, "The Negro a Factor in the History of the World," (Washington 1940), p. 5.

[15] *The Ethiopian Herald*, Vol. 1, No. 48 (1959), p. 1.

[16] Ruth Fox, *Food Wonders of the World* (Battle Creek, 1964), p. 28.

Arthur L. Smith

CHAPTER 28
Markings of
an African Concept of Rhetoric

Any interpretation of African rhetoric must begin at once to
dispense with the notion that in all things Europe is teacher and
Africa is pupil. To raise the question of an imperialism of the
rhetorical tradition is to ask a most meaningful question as we
pursue the basic concepts of African rhetoric, because Western
theorists have too often tended to generalize from an ethnocentric
base. Clearly, what will have to be argued in this paper is the
existence of an African concept of communication. Elsewhere I
have given attention to broad outlines in the traditional African
background.[1] In this paper I hope to discuss some concrete propositions that might conceivably be drawn from traditional African
philosophy. Obviously, such a task is not easy because of the

absence of systematic guidelines to follow, but it is not impossible, inasmuch as anthropologists and sociologists studying some of the basic phenomena have left their research notes for us to investigate.[2] And furthermore, the details of African philosophy are being placed in focus for Western minds by many African writers, popular and scholarly.[3] Conceivably, from these sources it can be established that rhetorical differences within cultures rest upon the different emphases of similar phenomena rather than on purely biological differences among peoples.

Admittedly, nothing of the stature of Aristotle's *Rhetoric* appears in African cultural history, but long before there was a system of rhetoric, men engaged in speechmaking. It is generally agreed that the practice of public speaking predates the development of systematic treatises. Furthermore, what is in essence the Western appreciation of the written word is not historically shared by Africans, and such a statement does not imply cultural superiority or inferiority but cultural difference. Perhaps the question to be raised in this connection is: What is the purpose of the written word? The answer to this question speaks of the complex problem of cultural evaluation. Put simply, writing is used for communication and historical preservation. In traditional African society those two ends were admirably satisfied by the drum. Communication was swift and the range was great; in the event the first drummer was unable to reach all of the persons he wanted to, another at the outer fringes would take up the message for further transmission. And too, the drummer along with the village sage became a repository of all the necessary historical data relating to the village. Thus, while African culture did not produce a written treatise on rhetoric, it is, nevertheless, perhaps more so than Western society, an expressive society.[4] In a discussion on the difference between physique and culture, Sidney Mintz attempted to explore behavioral patterns of Afro-Americans by noting that seemingly minor behavioral patterns are tied to the expressive media, such as music, dance, drama, voice, and the like.[5] Mintz further notes: "it is reasonable to view these expressions as continuities with the African past, and as some evidence of the success of Afro-Americans in conserving cultural materials that could not be conserved in other aspects of life."[6] What is of importance to us is that Africans maintained an expressive sense that manifested itself as life-force in dance, music, and speech. Expression, therefore, is not the captive of the written word; it is revealed in life.

What if there had been a major African treatise on rhetoric emanating from the university at Timbuktu? Rhetoric, in fact, was later taught by several Islamic scholars, among them, Uthman Dan Fodio of Nigeria. But be that as it may, we cannot seek to find in African society values that correspond exactly to European standards. On the other hand, we must not attempt to fit European values into African society. There exist no universal measures for rhetorical standards. In a short recommendation to the second conference of the National Developmental Project on Rhetoric, I contended that we must ask ourselves this question: "Is rhetorical theory concerned only with speaking in a democracy?" That question can be extended to include another dimension: Is rhetoric strictly Western?

Unquestionably, in some senses it is, and it would be foolish to argue any other way. But to contend that as conventionally perceived it is universal in theory, practice, and evaluation as measured in Western society would be to argue for cultural imperialism. *De Inventione*, the *Arte of Speaking, Select British Eloquence*, and our most contemporary works are, for the most part, products of the Western mind. We should not generalize for all audiences in all cultures. This is perhaps as it should be in our scholarship. Despite the state of research in the field, rhetoric as often defined can be found in African culture. Man interacting vocally with another man for the purpose of getting him to act cooperatively has existed in Ghana as long as it has in Greece.

Yet man interacting in African society proceeds from different bases than man interacting in European society. The reason is simple. People respond to the ideal that is concealed in every fact of their existence, and this ideal is determined for them according to different views of life. Whatever approach to the universe, values, neighbors, and other relationships, however complex, people come to accept comprise the philosophical base of their culture. Although anthropologists and Africanists have given few discussions of symbolic interaction among Africans (in reality, speech-communication scholars have argued that this is their purview), they have provided significant data on the nature of African society. Abstracted from this knowledge are possible suggestions for a system of African rhetoric.

First, let us establish the dimensions of public speaking in any society. To stimulate one's fellow to cooperative action through the use of language is no mean task; it requires skill, knowledge of human nature, and the necessary physical organs to utter sounds. Skill implies a certain technical proficiency, an ability to use one's knowledge effectively. Thus the interrelationship of skill and knowledge of human nature is clearly the basis of any meaningful venture in public speaking. What we argue, then, is what rhetoricians have argued before, that public discourse is an art. Thonssen and Baird made much ado about the foundations of the art of speaking.[7] But art is that which is produced by a systematic application of skill in effecting a given result; of course, we could extend that to include the craft, occupation, or activity requiring such skill. Suffice it to say, while it has been made plain by rhetoricians that rhetoric is concerned with the systematic observation and classification of facts and the establishment of verifiable general principles, no one has denied that public discourse is an art.

African art is never *l'art pour l'art*; it is always functional. This is true whether we are speaking of music, sculpture, or public speaking. There can be no art without a functional objective within the mind of the artist; his work must do something, perform something, or say something. Public discourse as an art form can only be complete when it is productive, and hence functional. Now it might be thought that this is neo-Aristotelianism with an African cast. However, the difference is most important. Where neo-Aristotelian rhetoricians placed emphasis on the observer as far as judgment of discourse was concerned, Africans highlight the creative process of the artist. To be an observer is to be primarily interested in the product, but to be an artist means that the creation and its function in society are uppermost. Thus, the African sees the discourse as the creative manifestation of what is *called to be*. That which is *called to be* because of the mores and values of the society becomes the created thing; and the artist, or speaker, satisfies the demands of the society by calling into being that which is functional. Functionality in this case refers to the object (scultpure, music, poem, speech, etc.) possessing a meaning within the speaker and audience's world view.

In such a view of art public discourse becomes a power, and the fundament of rhetoric is not the discourse object but the creative attitude of the speaker. To say that public discourse becomes a power is only to emphasize the activity aspect of the discourse in African thought. One cannot speak of a speech as an object but of speech as an attitude. The power of effective action is the force of the public discourse; and the speaker who makes a speech never completes a discourse as object because completeness is to be found in action.

Now that we have said African art is never *l'art pour l'art*, it is possible to say a few words about the relationship between society and the public discourse. What is the meaning of the speech in traditional African society? In what sense can the speech be said to fit into the tribal cosmogony? These are not easy questions to answer, and yet it seems that the answers lie somewhere in the realms of African personality theory and African culture. Several scholars have recently attempted exploration of conceptual systems, theories of personality, and culture related to Africa. They have found that it is as impossible to speak of an "African mind" as it is to speak of an "Oriental temperament," and for some of the same reasons. When we speak of Africans we are talking about a multitude of attitudes, peoples, and philosophies, and in this circumstance to speak of an African mind is to speak foolishly. Thus we speak broadly of traditional African society.

African society is essentially a society of harmonies, inasmuch as the coherence or compatibility of persons, things, and modalities is at the root of traditional African philosophy. Several scholars have commented on the nature of traditional African law as being concerned with the restoration of equilibrium.[8] In customary African law not establishment of guilt but rather the smooth and peaceful running of the community is the primary consideration.[9] In fact, Adesanya, a Nigerian writer, declares "this is not simply a coherence of fact or faith, nor of reason and traditional beliefs, nor of reason and contingent facts, but a coherence of compatibility among all disciplines."[10] The concatenation of everything exists so tightly that to subtract one item is to paralyze the system.

The public discourse, therefore, cannot exist apart from the mutual compatibility of the entire traditional world-view. In force, for force is active form and content operating harmoniously, the speech is logically linked to the society. Obviously, this type of society appears rigid and constricting to most Western peoples, but, on the other hand, in customary African society the possibilities are plentiful. Clearly the difference lies in two varied conceptions of the speech and the speaker. Merriam has written that "In Euro-American Society there is a tendency to compartmentalize the arts and to divorce them from aspects of everyday life; thus we have 'pure' as opposed to 'applied' art as well as the 'artist' and 'commercial artist' or 'craftsmen,' who are also differentiated both in role and in function."[11] The speech is a functioning and integral part of the society and cannot be separated from the entire world-view because the word power is indeed the generative power of the community.[12] Additionally, traditional African philosophy cannot make the distinction of "speaker" and "audience" to the degree found in rhetorical traditions of Euro-American society. Separateness of speaker or artist from audience in Euro-American society is based upon the degree of participation. But in African society the coherence among persons and things accord so that music, dance, or *Nommo* must be a collective activity.[13] Melville Herskovits observed that distinctions of artist and audience are foreign to traditional African culture,

"Art is a part of life, not separated from it."[14] This does not mean that there are no individual speakers or artists but rather that their performance becomes a collective experience. In Neo-African culture, particularly as expressed in North and South America, one gets the feel of this group performance in religious meetings and, indeed, in some secular gatherings. What are conventionally labeled reactions and responses of the audience might conceivably be better understood if we spoke of these phenomena as collective actions of participants. Afro-Americans viewing the movie *Cotton Comes to Harlem* are participating in the events of that movie not in the oral interpretation sense of "fulfilling the potential" but in creating the potential. The potential does not exist apart from the participants; thus when Godfrey Cambridge is "being seen" on the movie screen, the "audience" is being seen.

But African rhetoric is not only distinguished in its concern for coherence and participation but also in its relationship to the stability of the traditional society. Mutual compatibility of the several aspects of a philosophical perspective is only one benefit of coherence; another is the smooth operation of the village or tribe. In instances of conflict or disagreement among members of the society, public discourse must function to restore the stability that conflict creates. And too, within the speech the speaker is constantly restoring the internal harmony of the discourse through tone, volume, and rhythm. Delivery becomes, for the traditional African speaker, an opportunity to engage in a textual as well as a contextual search for harmony. The stability of the community is essential, and public speaking, when used in connection with conflict solution, must be directed toward maintaining community harmony. As a microcosmic example of the traditional African society's base in the harmony of all parts, the meaningful public discourse manifests rhetorical agreeableness in all its parts.

By the nature of traditional African philosophy, rhetoric in African society is an architectonic functioning art continuously fashioning the lives and attitudes of the people. The *word* is productive and imperative, calling forth and commanding. Its power derives from the traditional emphasis on the spoken word in

African society. Words as spoken by the chief or village physician may be effective because of the station, assigned or inherited, of the speaker, even though power inheres in vocal communication. The centrality of the word has existed for a long time in African communities. Jahn explains that ". . . the central significance of the word in African culture is not a phenomenon of one particular time."[15] Furthermore,

If there were no word, all forces would be frozen, there would be no procreation, no change, no life. "There is nothing that there is not; whatever we have a name for, that is," so speaks the wisdom of the Yoruba priests. The proverb signifies that the naming, the enunciation produces what it names. Naming is an incantation, a creative act. What we cannot conceive of is unreal; it does not exist. But every human thought, once expressed, becomes reality. For the world holds the course of things in train and changes and transform them. And since the word has this power, every word is an effective word, every word is binding.[16]

Thus because the word is imperative, it is the fundament as well as the fashioning instrument of traditional African society. All religion, music, medicine, and dance is produced by vocal expression, inasmuch as creativity is called into existence by man speaking. There is also a correlation between the effectiveness of the word and the power of the speaker as expressed by his personality and status. The more powerful the priest, the stronger his incantations and invocations. But no priest can exist apart from the word, indeed without the word, nothing can be, for the word creates reality.

The overwhelming importance of expression in African culture has been referred to by several scholars.[17] Expression possesses this place of significance in speech as well as in music in African society, and the interrelationship of the two expressive genres is well established. All study of African music requires verbal emphasis as well as demonstration because of the power of the expressive word.[18] Furthermore, the commonality of pitch, rate, volume, duration, and message content makes speech and music parts of the same expressive pattern. Wachsmann contends that

"In Africa a useful working hypothesis is that there is little music that does not have some affinity with words."[19] Since the word principle is behind all production and generation, it is possible to consider it as an architectonic system that gives existence to all things. Transformation is accomplished when a speaker employs words in any social situation in an attempt to bring about harmonious relationships within the traditional society. Whether the specific situation is an interpersonal conflict mediated by a chief or village elder, a natural disaster, or an attempt to persuade villagers to follow a certain course of action, transformation is sought through the expressive word. In this sense we can speak of an African architecton that influences communal behavior, in fact is the source and origin of that behavior.

I have discussed the place of the spoken word, the function of speaker, and the character of the audiences in an African concept of rhetoric. But one will ask: What is the substance of African public discourse? The questioner posing these queries would be exercising the contextual criteria provided by Western thought. To ask what is the *substance* is to see a dichotomy between form and substance, and this query does not plague African thought. Since form and content are *activity*, then *force* unifies what is called form and content in creative expression. The speech is meant to be alive and moving in all of its aspects so that separation of the members becomes impossible because the creative production is "an experience" or a happening occurring within and outside the speaker's soul. Thus, unlike the Euro-American, the African seeks the totality of an experience, concept, or system. Traditional African society looks for unity of the whole rather than specifics of the whole; such a concentration, which also emphasizes synthesis more than analysis, contributes to community stability because considerations in the whole are more productive than considerations in detail. Now it is clear that this has a very real bearing upon the making of a public discourse.

The public discourse convinces not through attention to logical substance but through the power to fascinate. Yet this does not preclude the materials of composition or the arrangement and structure of those materials; it simply expresses a belief that when images are arranged according to their power and chosen because of their power, the speaker's ability to convince is greater than if he attempted to employ syllogisms. The syllogism is a Western concept; *Nommo* is an African concept. When a speaker possesses visionary ecstasy, vivid but controlled, his audience's participation is more assured than if he exercised only syllogistic reasoning. Perhaps that is drawing the choices too clearly, inasmuch as few neo-Aristotelians would argue for a dichotomy of emotion and logic. However, it is necessary to state the polar positions to illustrate the emphasis of the traditional African speaker. What I am suggesting is that the African speaker means to be poet, not lecturer; indeed, the equipment of the two will always be different. So now it is possible to say that traditional African public discourse is given to concrete images capable of producing compulsive relationships and invoking the inner needs of audiences because of the inherent power of the images and not because of syllogistic reasoning. Additionally, the more powerful the speaker, the more fascinated the audiences will be.

We have discussed some concrete rhetorical ideas drawn from traditional African philosophy. Yet our work can only be heuristic until we can establish more explicitly the parameters of traditional African philosophy; this means that the universals within several systems must be identified, because one cannot speak of African philosophy with any real degree of accuracy. There are philosophies; but as a growing number of Africanists are discovering, there are concepts that transcend the boundaries of tribe or village. Furthermore, the implications for systems of African rhetoric might emerge once African philosophies are explored; but this will take a whole new school of scholars. Meanwhile the markings that I have discussed here should provide serious students of the field with a launching pad.

NOTES

[1] See Arthur L. Smith, "Socio-Historical Perspectives of Black Oratory," *The Quarterly Journal of Speech* (October 1970).

2 See Noel O. King, *Religions of Africa* (New York: Harper & Row, 1970); John Paden and Edward Soja, eds., *The African Experience* (Evanston: Northwestern Press, 1970); Robert LeVine, *Dream and Deeds: Achievement Motivaiton in Nigeria* (Chicago: University of Chicago Press, 1966); Jean Vansina, *Kingdoms of the Savanna* (Madison: University of Wisconsin Press, 1968); B. N. Colby, "Ethnographic Semantics," *Current Anthropology*, VII (1966), pp. 3–32; A. K. Romney and R. G. D'Andrade, eds., *Transcultural Studies in Cognition*, special issue of the *American Anthropologist*, LXVI (June 1964); Jack Berry and Joseph Greenberg, "Sociolinguistic Research in Africa," *African Studies Bulletin* IX (September 1966), pp. 1–9; and Arthur Tuden and Leonard Plotnicov, eds., *Social Stratification in Africa* (New York: Free Press, 1970).

3 Among the leading West African writers are Wole Soyinka, Sembene Ousmane, Chinua Achebe, Leopold Senghor, Sekou Toure, Amos Tutuola, and Cyprian Ekwensi. While all of these writers, with the exception of one or two, have concentrated on popular writing, there are strong signs of a serious investigation of African life and thought at both the African Studies Center at the University of Ibadan in Nigeria and the Institute of African Studies at the University of Ghana.

4 Joseph White, "Toward a Black Psychology," *Ebony* (September 1970), pp. 45–52.

5 Sidney Mintz, Foreword in Norman Whitten, Jr., and John F. Szwed, *Afro-American Anthropology* (New York: Free Press, 1970), p. 5.

6 *Ibid.*

7 Lester Thonssen and A. Craig Baird, *Speech Criticism* (New York: Ronald Press, 1948), Chapter 2.

8 See Hilda Kuper and Leo Kuper, eds., *African Law: Adaptation and Development* (Los Angeles: University of California Press, 1965).

9 Paul Bohannan, *Justice and Judgment Among the Tiv* (London: Oxford Press, 1957), p. 6.

10 Adebayo Adesanya, "Yoruba Metaphysical Thinking," *ODU,* 5 (Ibadan, 1958), p. 39.

11 Alan Merriam, "African Music," in William Bascom and Melville Herskovits, *Continuity and Change in African Culture* (Chicago: University of Chicago Press, 1958), p. 49.

12 Smith, "Socio-Historical Perspectives of Black Oratory."

13 I have used the term *Nommo* elsewhere in my writings. It is a term borrowed first from the Dogon tribe by Janheinz Jahn to express the complexities and dimensions of communication in African society.

14 Melville Herskovits, *Man and His Works* (New York: Knopf, 1948), p. 379.

15 Janheinz Jahn, *Muntu: The New African Culture* (New York: Grove Press, 1961), p. 134.

16 *Ibid.*, p. 133.

17 For instance, Leopold Senghor, "Der Geist der Negro Afrikanischen Kultur," *Schwarze Ballade*, Janheinz Jahn, ed. (Frankfurt: Verlag, 1965), pp. 203–227.

18 Klaus Wachsmann, "Ethnomusicology in Africa," *The African Experience*, John Paden and Edward Soja, eds. (Evanston: Northwestern Press, 1970), p. 135.

19 *Ibid.*

Arthur L. Smith

CHAPTER 29
The Rhetoric of Psychical
and Physical Emigration

In the continuing drama of black liberation protest, several distinct philosophies have been proposed as workable methods of resolving the American dilemma. The rhetorical complexities of this historic psychical and physical struggle must be viewed as the most enduring protest movement in the national life. With its spokesmen and masses, themes and programs, the black protest has reflected almost all possible political philosophies for oppressed people. At no time in Afro-American history, not even during the New Deal, when most blacks as well as whites were swept up by the charisma of Franklin Roosevelt, has the protest ceased. Black protest has utilized many techniques—legal, illegal, and legitimate—and has been fueled by the most exotic to the most American philosophy.

This paper primarily considers the Back to Africa movement to be a manifestation of a model rhetoric for the hopeless who feel compelled to emigrate both psychically and physically. It is a critique of a social movement whose existence italicizes the uses of persuasion by spokesmen who articulate the anxious wishes of hopeless people. Speech-communication scholars have not really begun to deal with the complexions of language, the scope of rhetoric and the uses of argument by the victims of oppression who seek to win assent to their views. Perhaps rhetoricians have been too much caught up in a cavalier fashion with the conception of rhetoric as a transaction (and one cannot have a transaction unless there is something with which to bargain) in the marketplace of ideas between people of similar perspectives. In fact, a new dimension in critical thinking might conceivably be introduced if we viewed the rhetoric of the oppressed as presenting us with nontraditional criticism problems. Persons who do not see themselves as sharers of the body politic or participants in the national destiny are quite susceptible to Back to Africa deliverance, spiritual or physical. Injustice and constant humiliation on the one hand make people interested in the politics of exclusivity on the other.

Back to Africa expresses, as a movement, a unique relationship to society. In this movement dialogue with the external society is only sought when such a relationship is absolutely necessary. Those times are few, but they do come. The central task seems to be enlisting blacks into the Back to Africa campaign, which means that persuasion becomes a primary function of the spokesmen who speak as the situation demands. Back to Africa advocates are products of social and political configurations that give them sanction. And to view Back to Africa as leader-centered or message-centered is to take sight of only one part of the social movement. Thus, while the variegated roles of leaders and messages will be discussed, the fundamental critique of the movement must consider its peculiar position vis-à-vis the total society. Messages and leaders have their functions only as emissaries of the distinct situational padishah that endows them with purpose. In this sense Back to Africa, both historically and contemporarily, is the classic example of a movement of those who have lost or never had political or social faith in America and, additionally, have no will to remain in this country. Furthermore, the spokesmen do not create the hopelessness; it already exists. Speakers may stir the mixture, but the ingredients have already been poured by observation and experience. Thus Back to Africa exists silhouetted against society, as most genuine social movements do, as an entity apart, creating and sustaining its themes. But at the same time, unlike most social movements in America, Back to Africa has sought to galvanize its followers for withdrawal from the society. As such it has occupied a significant position in black political thought, rejecting American society as other movements seek to alter it.

Two basic philosophies have tended to dominate the endless discussion of black liberation. Both begin at the same conditional reality and seek the same ultimate goal. While these philosophies —integration and separation—have often operated concurrently, each with its own constituency, one or the other has tended to take center stage in a given epoch. We may view them as *alternatives*, the principal choices isolated by blacks searching for answers to the race riddle in America.

Alternatives	*Rhetorical Manifestations*
Integration	Interdependence Equality in America
Separation	Back to Africa Separate States in America

What is clear is that all black protest can be included, more or less, within this design. In fact, the black spokesmen who have addressed themselves to black liberation have always chosen one or the other *alternative*. The reason is obvious. Blacks can only wish to be a part of the society or separate from it; this is true even in the rhetoric of revolutionaries who envision drastic change in the present societal structure that would permit blacks, chicanos, whites, and other groups to be integrated in the national life. What I have chosen to call *rhetorical manifestations* are the principal themes enunciated by the various spokesmen as they move toward one or the other *alternative*.

In other words, rhetorical manifestations answer the question: How have black spokesmen dealt thematically with the goals of integration and separation? In an analysis one would also want to examine the spokesman's use of other rhetorical measures in connection with this thematic expression. Investigation of the rhetoric of Booker T. Washington, W. E. B. Du Bois, Marcus Garvey, and Elijah Muhammad shows that these men were motivated by the themes relevant to their choice of *alternative*. While it would be interesting to explore what constraints exist in this design, the present focus is the alternative of separation as manifested in the rhetoric of Back to Africa. Persistently overshadowed by the themes designed to bring about integration, the Back to Africa movement, at one time the largest mass movement in American society, has always suffered from its failure to capture the minds of the opinion makers within the black community.

SOURCES

What circumstances and conditions produce a rhetoric of psychical and physical emigration? It should not be thought strange that a people unable to find acceptance in what to them has become an alien land should turn to the place of their origin. Rebuffed on every hand, discriminated against ever so subtly even when the laws were on the side of justice, many blacks, particularly during restoration of the South, longed to leave the country. Near the turn of the century a black sharecropper writing to the Colonization Society exclaimed after telling of the horrors perpetrated on blacks, "Oh my God help us to get out from here to Africa."[1]

Later Marcus Garvey underscored the problem:

It can plainly be seen that in the question of self-preservation and self-interest the whites nowhere, whether in America, England or France, are going to give way to the Negro to the detriment of their own. We need not look for constitutional protection, or even for philanthropic Christian sympathy, because if that is to be shown it will be to the race that is able to bestow it. Hence, the UNIA has but one solution for this great problem, and that is to work unceasingly for the bringing about of a National Homeland for Negroes in Africa.[2]

The rhetoric of Back to Africa has always sprung from social injustices, economic deprivations, physical abuses, and psychological intimidations. Wherever the movement has erupted in the United States, it has grown on the frustrations and discontents of blacks who were fed up with their miserable lot. They have manifested an intense unity and disillusionment in their desire to leave the country. And those men who rose to become spokesmen and leaders shared one fundamental fact: *They believed they were oppressed and perceived themselves as being in a disadvantageous position.* Indeed, this perception opened the door to many rooms of protest. They could acquiesce; they could engage in sporadic expressions of discontent; they could live in full-fledged revolutionary activity; or they could go to Africa. Those people in the Back to Africa movement chose to leave; others decided to remain in America. Garvey, while not the first certainly the greatest of the Back to Africa spokesmen, once said, "Some of our leaders in the Negro race flatter themselves into believing that the problem of black and white in America will work itself out, and that all the Negro has to do is to be humble, submissive and obedient and everything will work out well in the 'sweet by and bye.' "[3] And Bishop Henry Turner argued: "I would make Africa a place of refuge, because I see no other shelter from the stormy blast, from the red tide of persecution, from the horrors of American prejudice."[4]

Men like Garvey and Turner capitalized on the strong belief, created by the harsh realities of being black in white America, that there could never be harmonious relations among blacks and whites.

That Garvey, and Turner before him, could attract hundreds of thousands of blacks with the rhetoric of emigrationism can only be understood in the light of the ultimate political realization. Such people had come to believe and to argue that blacks could only find happiness in Africa; and they had begun to believe that integration was at worst impossible and at best impracticable. Thus, those who had listened intently to the rhetoric of Garvey, Turner, or Aaron Henry of the Republic of New Africa came to see new possibilities. When men have gloried at the university at Timbuktu, felt pride and awe at the mention of the stone city of Zimbabwe, ceased to dread the rain forests, they become exceptional missionaries convincing others that Africa is the place for the black man. The claim of Aaron Henry and Robert Williams among others, some with different political approaches, that America will never allow the black man peace in this society attests to the potency of the ultimate political realization in contemporary society.

LEADERS

As mentioned earlier, the role of the leaders, or spokesmen, which might be a better term, is only a part of the movement, and their rhetoric answers to one aspect of the movement. Herbert W. Simons' recently expressed leader-centered conception of persuasion in social movements is especially appropriate for considering the Back to Africa movement, which has always produced gifted persuaders.[5] Because the spokesmen for Back to Africa have more often than not embodied a mission-oriented complex, the movements have risen and, indeed, fallen with the leaders. Of course, this is not unique to the Back to Africa movement in black protest but rather is a pervasive phenomenon based upon the spokesman's ability to incorporate *Nommo*.[6] Even so the Back to Africa movements have usually experienced significant internal disintegration because of the vulnerability of the spokesmen or, as Herbert Simons explains, the incompatible demands upon them. Although the charismatic mission-oriented speaker might be excellent as an inspirer, he is often less than competent in the day-to-day operations of the organization. Thus, when finances are in shambles, competing imperatives of time and theme are impinging upon the organization, and ships fail to appear that would take the faithful to the promised land, the halo of mission seems all dull. Talk becomes empty, people complain of bombastic rhetoric, and votaries seek elsewhere to be fulfilled.

In most Back to Africa movements the leader assumes the role of prophet directing his people out of bondage and tyranny. The influence of Back to Africa in the nineteenth century is remarkable in view of the lack of information circulating about Africa in this country. This can be attributed to the prophets who were almost always exceptionally eloquent spokesmen, with rich imaginations and forceful deliveries. They made Africa the chosen land and swore to its place in world history. Perhaps no men spoke more fervently than Bishop Henry Turner and Marcus Garvey.

The most prominent and outspoken Back to Africa advocate between the Civil War and World War I was Bishop Turner. Turner possessed "a dominating personality, a biting tongue, and a pungent vocabulary which gained him high office and wide audiences, first in Georgia Reconstruction Politics and later in the African Methodist Episcopal Church."[7] It was as a traveling evangelist for the white Southern Methodist Church that he discovered the pervasiveness of prejudice in American society, even within the church. In New Orleans in 1858 his emerging black nationalism found something refreshing, a church operated and controlled by blacks, the A.M.E. Immediately he joined it and became one of the leading preachers, pastoring first in Baltimore and then in Washington. "After the general emancipation he became openly belligerent and urged the newly freed slaves to defend themselves vigorously when attacked or insulted."[8] As a freeborn person, he had never lived under the harsh bondage of slavery, but he had experienced enough racism and had seen enough cruelty to agitate for strong black organizations to combat prejudice. Devoting much of his energy to establishing the A.M.E. in Georgia, he argued that only in a church governed solely by blacks could the recently freed blacks find freedom to express themselves.[9]

When the national Republican Party was trying to organize the people in Georgia, Turner was their choice to organize the freedmen, because he was well known among party leadership. After he called the first Republican state convention in Georgia, he was elected to the 1867 Georgia Constitutional Convention and in 1868 was elected to the state legislature. As soon as he was elected and the legislature convened, his highest hopes were dashed when his white colleagues tried to disqualify blacks from holding elective office. On the house floor Turner gave a vehement speech denouncing the attempts of the house to dismiss the black representatives and demanding his rights as a free citizen. Turning to the blacks in the house he said, "White men are not to be trusted; they will betray you. . . . Black men, hold up your heads. . . . This thing means revolution."[10] The dismissal of the blacks made Turner's latent nationalism surface; he talked up black power in the state and encouraged blacks to vote the whites out of power. He applied for the office of U.S. minister to Haiti but was given the job of postmaster in Macon, Georgia. As the first black postmaster in the state, he became a rallying point for the masses looking for some assurance that blacks could make it in America. But two weeks after he was made postmaster the local whites succeeded in getting him dismissed, claiming theft and fraud. Disappointed, frustrated, and without an effective political power base, he returned to his church and started his campaign to get blacks to leave for Africa, arguing that the United States was a white man's nation and that blacks must leave.[11]

And like others before him and many to follow, Turner reasoned that if whites would not allow blacks to perform as part of this society, then blacks should establish their own nation in Africa. Depression, anxiety, and frustration—these were the marks of Turner's conversion; he was a victim of the white man's nationalism, and his response was a black man's nationalism. He urged members of the A.M.E. to follow the "urge of a mysterious providence," saying, "Return to the land of your Fathers. . . ."[12] Taking his own advice, the bishop toured West Africa to get on-the-spot information and returned to the United States more convinced then ever that if the black man is ever to acquire wealth or prestige, he will never do it by snubbing his native land. Turner's African trip made him much more effective as a nationalistic preacher and placed him in the forefront of black spokesmen in his day. And when he died in 1915, more than any other black person he had directed the Back to Africa movement and shaped its course for years to come. His relentless emigration rhetoric provided the arguments for other emissaries of the movement and gave Marcus Garvey a ready-made base.

Thus, when Garvey stepped ashore in America in 1916, he found a profound disillusionment among blacks, stemming directly from their humiliation in American society and stirred by the emigrationists before Garvey, but most notably Henry Turner. With Booker T. Washington dying in the same year as Turner, the black community was left without a popular leader. While no one rose to continue Washington's work, Garvey, inspired by Washington, followed in Turner's footsteps and called for emigration to Africa. Because blacks were frustrated with the slow pace of integration, discontent was exceedingly widespread. Blacks came to feel that more vigorous measures had to be taken to achieve political goals. The passions and needs of the time demanded a special brand of rhetoric to galvanize the downtrodden masses; Garvey was the rhetor.

But even in the attempt to emigrate to Africa Garvey felt the white man was placing obstacles. Indeed so much of black protest thought, whether integrationist or separationist, had dealt with overcoming the hurdles placed by the white man. This has been true whether the blacks are trying to be good capitalists, like the Muslims in Alabama, or are seeking to persuade Afro-Americans that they should leave for Africa. In fact, whites not only tried to prevent the Back to Africa campaign, Garvey saw them occupying the homeland itself. "The Negroes of the world say, 'We are striking homewards towards Africa to make her the big black republic.' And in the making of Africa a big black republic, what is the barrier? The barrier is the white man; and we say to the white man who now dominates Africa that it is to his interest to clear out of Africa now, because we are coming not as in the time of Father Abraham, 200,000 strong, but we are coming 400,-000,000. . . ."[13] Such language was sooner or later to bring him into conflict with whites who saw in such rhetoric signs of danger. In 1921 the FBI investigated the Universal Negro Improvement Association's attempt to purchase a ship, calling Garvey "a radical agitator who advocates the overthrow of the United States Government by force and violence."[14] Furthermore, the UNIA was said to be "the communist party which is affiliated with the Russian Soviet Government."[15] Troubles soon began to eat away at the fabric of Garvey's organization. Financial difficulties combined with the growing attempt of black intellectuals to dissociate themselves from Garvey made him more vulnerable to attacks by government officials. In 1923 he was convicted to five years in prison for fraud, and in 1927 he was deported to Jamaica after his sentence had been commuted by President Coolidge.[16]

More than any other black spokesmen, Turner and Garvey played upon the latent restlessness of the black masses in America. In appealing to the pride and dignity of their black listeners, they showed the far-reaching power of black nationalism for an oppressed people. Based upon the ultimate political awareness that blacks and whites cannot live together peaceably in the American society, the rhetoric of both men was tailored to speak the unspeakable for those who believed just as much.

MESSAGE

In the investigations of movements built and sustained by the spoken word, one must consider the spokesman's conception of existence, history, society, and value as expressed in his language. Such consideration, treating a special perspective about society and history, and examining a bitterness toward fate (not because of blackness but because of blackness in white America), identifies the overmastering metaphor that gives the movement its reason to exist.

Every black protest movement has its arching metaphor, and the Back to Africa movement, past and present, is no exception. It is the role of the leaders of these movements to provide the viewpoint that gives rise to the mission-oriented rhetoric of the secondary spokesmen. A principal spokesman, then, in the true sense of Back to Africa, must be capable of explaining the movement's special relationship to society and history. In Back to Africa the task is simple and complex. Its simplicity derives from the receptivity of the audience, made so by the decades of cruelty, of poverty, discrimination, and hopelessness (in an American context). The complexity of the task emerges in the gigantic rhetorical choices facing a Back to Africa spokesman. How will he deal with those questions of priority that constantly plague his time? And in what language? What response will be made to a given need? And in what manner? What should be the content of a certain structurization? And how much? Such questions help shape the metaphors of a social movement.

There seems to be little argument that the overmastering metaphor of the Back to Africa movement has dealt with psychical and physical activity. People are asked to go somewhere, either in mind or in body, but preferably both. The several manifestations of the metaphor respond to three foundation desires: unity, security, and black pride, which have been rhetorically expressed in terms of political, economic, and sociocultural goals. To study this movement, therefore, is to grasp the significance of this transaction between the larger and the encapsulated context and to see how the spokesman of the movement manipulates the minds and motives of his listeners to accomplish his end. The question "What role shall blacks play in the American society?" affords the creative spokesman of Back to Africa the opportunity to explore absurdity. "The more I remember the sufferings of my forefathers, the more I remember the lynchings in the Southern States of America, the more I will fight on even though the battle seems doubtful. Tell me that I must turn back, and I laugh you to scorn. Go on! Go on! Climb ye the heights of liberty and cease not in well-doing until you have planted the banner of the Red, the Black and the Green on the hilltops of Africa."[17] Emigration, as opposed to colonization (a white man's solution), was the only answer to an obvious dilemma. Bishop Henry Turner argued "there is no more doubt in my mind that we have ultimately to return ot Africa than there is of the existence of God."[18]

Standing above the minimetaphors of the movement's rhetoric is the metaphorical *Africa* encompassing and activating all the desires of the followers. Africa is both the underlying idea and the imagined nature; the principal subject and what it resembles; the idea and its reality. Thus when the Back to Africa spokesman appeals to his listeners to return home, he is using Africa as tenor and vehicle. Africa is the metaphor, in this sense, for unity, security, and black pride. And, in fact, the metaphor becomes the message.

But while Africa is both symbol and referent, it can only be experienced through psychical and physical activity. For the oppressed seeking an escape it becomes an exit from the anxieties of racial discrimination; it is the epitome of blackness. Occasionally, separationists have tried to convince blacks to settle in countries other than those in Africa; they have failed dismally. In Kansas, Colonel John M. Brown, a black politician, advocated Brazil as the Afro-Americans' new home. Although his plans for taking blacks to Brazil were elaborate, he had little success in raising money and even less in raising black passions. William Ellis, a black businessman in Texas, attempted to start a Mexican colony in 1889 to raise cotton and coffee, but despite support from the Mexican legislature, he gained almost no support among blacks.[19] From time to time blacks settled in the West Indies, but only Africa has had a magnetic effect upon the black community.

Despite the interest in Africa, indicated by the hundreds of thousands who joined the movements, an exceedingly small number of blacks actually made the trip back to Africa. Between the years 1816 and 1940, probably no more than 25,000 blacks migrated to the continent. Bishop Turner lamented in 1895, during the height of his Back to Africa agitation, that while 2,500 blacks had been lynched in the past ten years, only 361 had migrated to Africa.[20] Thus, counting the work of the American Colonization Society from 1816 to 1845 to colonize Liberia and Sierra Leone, in addition to the UNIA influence during the first quarter of the twentieth century, one could possibly get 25,000. For the many poor black men seeking passage to Africa, unable to raise the necessary money for their families, and harassed by their white neighbors for wanting to leave, the psychical avenue was the only way they could participate in Back to Africa.

Briefly then, this paper has concentrated on the Back to Africa movement as a manifestation, a classic revelation, of the rhetoric of people convinced that they have no hope in this society. The technical aspects of Back to Africa movements have been sketched only in broad outline. In fact, the focus of this paper has been on the movement as producer of rhetoric, showing that Back to Africa as a rhetorical manifestation emerges from a long standing disillusionment with American society.

NOTES

1 R. L. Davis to William Coppinger, August 31, 1891, American Colonization Society Papers, Manuscript Division, Library of Congress, Washington, D.C.

2 Amy Jacques-Garvey, ed., *The Philosophy and Opinions of Marcus Garvey* (New York: Atheneum, 1968), p. 49.

3 *Ibid.*, p. 57.

4 Edwin Redkey, *Black Exodus* (New Haven: Yale University Press, 1969), p. 33.

5 See Herbert Simons, "Requirements, Problems and Strategies: A Theory of Persuasion for Social Movements," *The Quarterly Journal of Speech*, LVI, (February 1970), pp. 1–11.

6 Arthur L. Smith, *Rhetoric of Black Revolution* (Boston: Allyn & Bacon, 1969), p. 34.

7 Redkey, p. 24.

8 *Ibid.*, p. 25.

9 Thaddeus E. Horton, "A Black Moses," in James T. Haley, ed. *Afro-American Encyclopedia*, (Nashville: Haley and Florida, 1895), pp. 35–38.

10 *Atlanta Constitution*, September 4, 1868.

11 Redkey, p. 27.

12 *Ibid.*, p. 29.

13 Edmund Cronon, *Black Moses* (Madison: University of Wisconsin Press, 1968), p. 66.

14 *Ibid.*, p. 99.

15 *Ibid.*

16 *Ibid.*, p. 142.

17 Garvey, p. 97.

18 Redkey, p. 29.

19 *Christian Recorder*, November 7, 1889; *Savannah Tribune*, October 19, 1889.

20 *Voice of Missions*, August 1895.